D1774099

HOUGHTON MIFFLIN HARCOURT

GO MATH!

HOUGHTON
MIFFLIN
HARCOURT

Curious George by Margret and H.A. Rey. Copyright © 2010 by Houghton Mifflin Harcourt Publishing Company. All rights reserved. The character Curious George®, including without limitation the character's name and the character's likenesses, are registered trademarks of Houghton Mifflin Harcourt Publishing Company.

Copyright © 2012 by Houghton Mifflin Harcourt Publishing Company.

All rights reserved. No part of this work may be reproduced or transmitted in any form or by any means, electronic or mechanical, including photocopying or recording, or by any information storage and retrieval system, without the prior written permission of the copyright owner unless such copying is expressly permitted by federal copyright law. Requests for permission to make copies of any part of the work should be addressed to Houghton Mifflin Harcourt Publishing Company, Attn: Contracts, Copyrights, and Licensing, 9400 South Park Center Loop, Orlando, Florida 32819.

Common Core State Standards © Copyright 2010. National Governors Association Center for Best Practices and Council of Chief State School Officers. All rights reserved.

This product is not sponsored or endorsed by the Common Core State Standards Initiative of the National Governors Association Center for Best Practices and the Council of Chief State School Officers.

Printed in the U.S.A.

ISBN 978-0-547-58790-5

19 0928 20

4500803101 C D E F G

If you have received these materials as examination copies free of charge, Houghton Mifflin Harcourt Publishing Company retains title to the materials and they may not be resold. Resale of examination copies is strictly prohibited.

Possession of this publication in print format does not entitle users to convert this publication, or any portion of it, into electronic format.

Dear Students and Families,

Welcome to **Go Math!**, Grade 2! In this exciting mathematics program, there are hands-on activities to do and real-world problems to solve. Best of all, you will write your ideas and answers right in your book. In **Go Math!**, writing and drawing on the pages helps you think deeply about what you are learning, and you will really understand math!

By the way, all of the pages in your **Go Math!** book are made using recycled paper. We wanted you to know that you can Go Green with **Go Math!**

Sincerely,

The Authors

Made in the United States
Text printed on 100% recycled paper
By using this paper in a typical print run, we achieved the following environmental benefits:*

- Trees Saved: 463
- Air Emissions Eliminated: 28,074 pounds
- Water Saved: 311,402 gallons
- Solid Waste Eliminated: 35,816 pounds

**Environmental impact estimates calculated using the Environmental Defense Fund Paper Calculator. For more information, visit www.papercalculator.org*

GO MATH!

Authors

Juli K. Dixon
Professor of Mathematics Education
University of Central Florida
Orlando, Florida

Miriam A. Leiva
Founding President, TODOS:
Mathematics for All
Distinguished Professor
of Mathematics Emerita
University of North Carolina Charlotte
Charlotte, North Carolina

Matt Larson
Curriculum Specialist for Mathematics
Lincoln Public Schools
Lincoln, Nebraska

Thomasenia Lott Adams
Professor of Mathematics Education
University of Florida
Gainesville, Florida

© Houghton Mifflin Harcourt Publishing Company

Number Sense and Place Value

COMMON CORE **Critical Area** Extending understanding of base-ten notation

1 Number Concepts 9

Domain Number and Operations in Base Ten

Common Core Standards CC.2.OA.3, CC.2.NBT.2, CC.2.NBT.3

CRITICAL AREA

DIGITAL PATH
Go online! Your math lessons are interactive. Use *i*Tools, Animated Math Models, the Multimedia eGlossary, and more.

Math Story
Whales
Social Studies

Look for these:
REAL WORLD
H.O.T. Higher Order Thinking

Use every day for Standards Practice.

© Houghton Mifflin Harcourt Publishing Company

2 Numbers to 1,000 53

Domain Number and Operations in Base Ten

Common Core Standards CC.2.NBT.1, CC.2.NBT.1a, CC.2.NBT.1b, CC.2.NBT.3, CC.2.NBT.4, CC.2.NBT.8

© Houghton Mifflin Harcourt Publishing Company

Addition and Subtraction

COMMON CORE

Critical Area Building fluency with addition and subtraction

CRITICAL AREA

3 Basic Facts and Relationships 117

Domain Operations and Algebraic Thinking

Common Core Standards CC.2.OA.1, CC.2.OA.2, CC.2.OA.4

DIGITAL PATH
Go online! Your math lessons are interactive. Use *i*Tools, Animated Math Models, the Multimedia eGlossary, and more.

Math Story

All About Animals

Science

Look for these:

REAL WORLD

H.O.T. Higher Order Thinking

Use every day for Standards Practice.

© Houghton Mifflin Harcourt Publishing Company

4 2-Digit Addition 169

Domain Number and Operations in Base Ten

Common Core Standards CC.2.OA.1, CC.2.NBT.5, CC.2.NBT.6, CC.2.NBT.9

© Houghton Mifflin Harcourt Publishing Company

5 2-Digit Subtraction 225

Domain Number and Operations in Base Ten
Common Core Standards CC.2.OA.1, CC.2.NBT.5, CC.2.NBT.9

6 3-Digit Addition and Subtraction 277

Domain Number and Operations in Base Ten
Common Core Standard CC.2.NBT.7

© Houghton Mifflin Harcourt Publishing Company

CRITICAL AREA

Measurement and Data

COMMON CORE **Critical Area** Using standard units of measure

7 Money and Time

Domain Measurement and Data

Common Core Standards CC.2.MD.7, CC.2.MD.8

8 Length in Customary Units

Domain Measurement and Data

Common Core Standards CC.2.MD.1, CC.2.MD.2, CC.2.MD.3, CC.2.MD.5, CC.2.MD.6, CC.2.MD.9

DIGITAL PATH
Go online! Your math lessons are interactive. Use *i*Tools, Animated Math Models, the Multimedia *e*Glossary, and more.

Math Story
Making a Kite

Look for these:

REAL WORLD

H.O.T. Higher Order Thinking

Use every day for Standards Practice.

© Houghton Mifflin Harcourt Publishing Company

© Houghton Mifflin Harcourt Publishing Company

CRITICAL AREA

DIGITAL PATH
Go online! Your math lessons are interactive. Use *i*Tools, Animated Math Models, the Multimedia *e*Glossary, and more.

Math Story

A Farmer's Job

Look for these:

REAL WORLD

H.O.T. Higher Order Thinking

Use every day for Standards Practice.

Geometry and Fractions

COMMON CORE **Critical Area** Describing and analyzing shapes

11 Geometry and Fraction Concepts 505

Domain Geometry

Common Core Standards CC.2.G.1, CC.2.G.2, CC.2.G.3

© Houghton Mifflin Harcourt Publishing Company

CRITICAL AREA

Whales

by John Hudson

© Houghton Mifflin Harcourt Publishing Company

COMMON CORE

CRITICAL AREA Extending understanding of base-ten notation

Some scientists study whales. Different kinds of whales swim along the west coast of the United States of America.

A scientist sees 8 blue whales.

Blue whales are the largest animals on Earth.

Social Studies

Where is the United States of America on the map?

© Houghton Mifflin Harcourt Publishing Company

The scientist also sees 13 humpback whales.
Humpback whales sing underwater.
Did the scientist see more humpback whales or more blue whales? more ______________ whales

Social Studies

Where is the Pacific Ocean on the map?

© Houghton Mifflin Harcourt Publishing Company

Whales also swim along the east coast of Canada and the United States of America. Pilot whales swim behind a leader, or a *pilot*. A scientist sees a group of 29 pilot whales.

Social Studies

Where is Canada on the map?

© Houghton Mifflin Harcourt Publishing Company

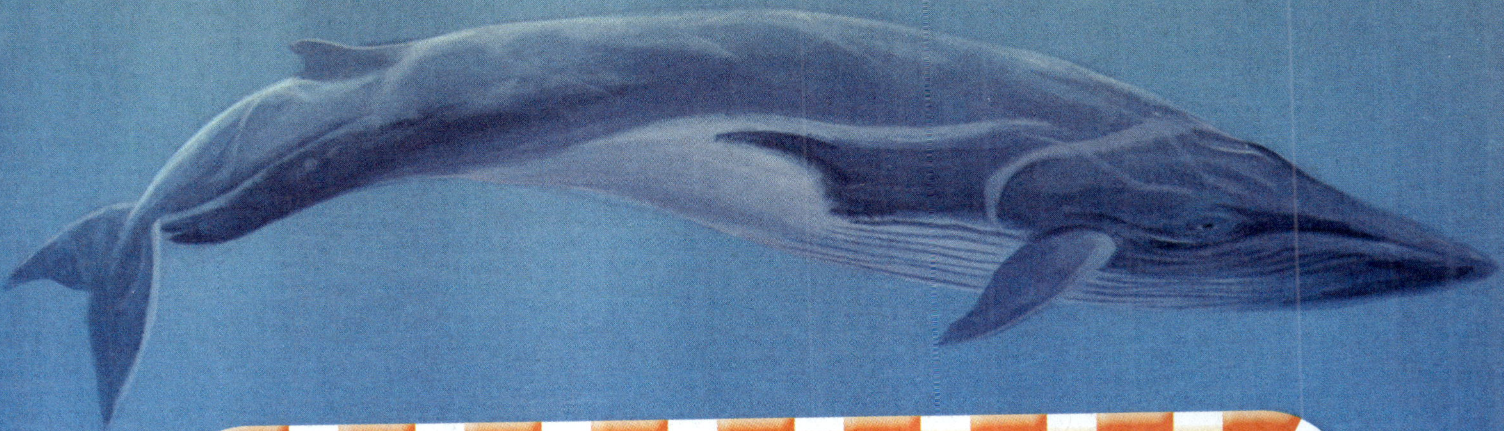

Fin whales are fast swimmers. They are the second-largest whales in the world. A scientist sees a group of 27 fin whales. How many tens are in the number 27?

_____ tens

Social Studies

Where is the Atlantic Ocean on the map?

© Houghton Mifflin Harcourt Publishing Company

Humpback whales swim to the warm water near Mexico for the winter. Humpback whales may have as many as 35 throat grooves. In the number 35, the _____ is in the ones place and the _____ is in the tens place.

Social Studies

Where is Mexico on the map?

© Houghton Mifflin Harcourt Publishing Company

Name ________________________________

Write About the Story

Look at the pictures. Draw and write your own story. Compare two numbers in your story.

Vocabulary Review

more	fewer
tens	greater than
ones	less than

Write Math

____

____

____

____

____

____

© Houghton Mifflin Harcourt Publishing Company

The Size of Numbers

The table shows how many young whales were seen by scientists.

Young Whales Seen	
Whale	**Number of Whales**
Humpback	34
Blue	13
Fin	27
Pilot	43

1. Which number of whales has a 4 in the tens place?

______

2. How many tens and ones describe the number of young blue whales seen?

_____ ten _____ ones

3. Compare the number of young humpback whales and the number of young pilot whales seen. Write > or <.

34 ◯ 43

4. Compare the number of young fin whales and the number of young blue whales seen. Write > or <.

27 ◯ 13

Math Board Write a story about a scientist watching sea animals. Use some 2-digit numbers in your story.

© Houghton Mifflin Harcourt Publishing Company

Chapter 1

Number Concepts

Curious About Math with Curious George

At a farmers' market, many different fruits and vegetables are sold.

If there are 2 groups of 10 watermelons on a table, how many watermelons are there?

© Houghton Mifflin Harcourt Publishing Company
Curious George by Margret and H.A. Rey. Copyright © 2010 by Houghton Mifflin Harcourt Publishing Company. All rights reserved. The character Curious George®, including without limitation the character's name and the character's likenesses, are registered trademarks of Houghton Mifflin Harcourt Publishing Company.

Name ______________________________

Show What You Know

Model Numbers to 20

Write the number that tells how many.

1. 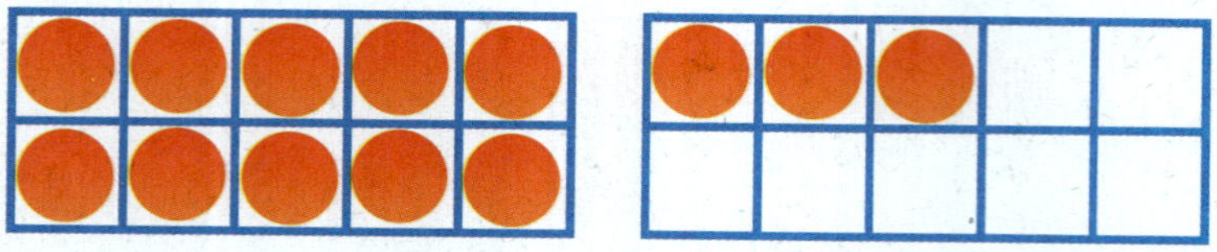

______

2. 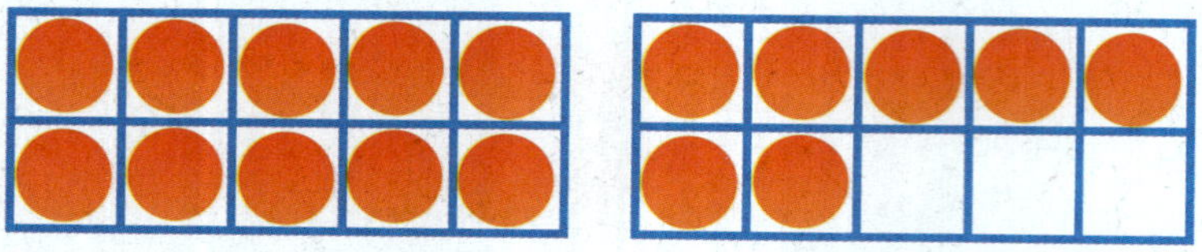

______

Use a Hundred Chart to Count

Use the hundred chart.

1	2	3	4	5	6	7	8	9	10
11	12	13	14	15	16	17	18	19	20
21	22	23	24	25	26	27	28	29	30
31	32	33	34	35	36	37	38	39	40
41	42	43	44	45	46	47	48	49	50
51	52	53	54	55	56	57	58	59	60
61	62	63	64	65	66	67	68	69	70
71	72	73	74	75	76	77	78	79	80
81	82	83	84	85	86	87	88	89	90
91	92	93	94	95	96	97	98	99	100

3. Count from 36 to 47. Which of the numbers below will you say? Circle them.

42 31 48 39 37

Tens

Write how many tens. Write the number.

4. 

______ tens

______

5. 

______ tens

______

Family note: This page checks your child's understanding of important skills needed for success in Chapter 1.

GO Online Assessment Options Soar to Success Math

© Houghton Mifflin Harcourt Publishing Company

Name ______________________________

Vocabulary Builder

Review Words
ones
tens
count on
count back

Visualize It

Fill in the boxes of the graphic organizer.
Write sentences about **ones** and **tens**.

ones → There are 10 ones in 1 ten.
ones → ______________________________

tens → ______________________________
tens → ______________________________

Understand Vocabulary

1. Start with 1. **Count on** by ones.

1, _____, _____, _____, _____, _____

2. Start with 8. **Count back** by ones.

8, _____, _____, _____, _____, _____

© Houghton Mifflin Harcourt Publishing Company

GO Online
- eStudent Edition
- Multimedia eGlossary

Chapter 1

Game Three in a Row

Materials • 15 • 15 •

Play with a partner.

1. Choose a leaf. Read the number on the leaf. Use to model the number.
2. Your partner checks your model. If your model is correct, put your on the leaf.
3. Take turns. Try to get 3 in a row.
4. The first player with 3 in a row wins.

5	21	13	19	20
25	15	7	8	12
11	9	14	16	24
22	23	17	18	10

© Houghton Mifflin Harcourt Publishing Company

Name ______________________________

Algebra • Even and Odd Numbers

Essential Question How are even numbers and odd numbers different?

HANDS ON
Lesson 1.1

COMMON CORE STANDARD CC.2.OA.3
Work with equal groups of objects to gain foundations for multiplication.

Listen REAL WORLD

Use [cube] to show each number.

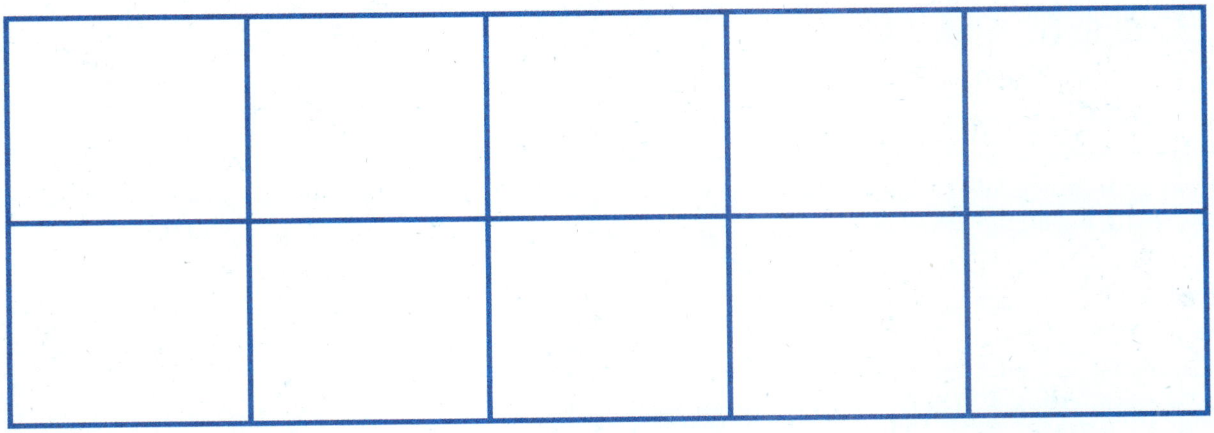

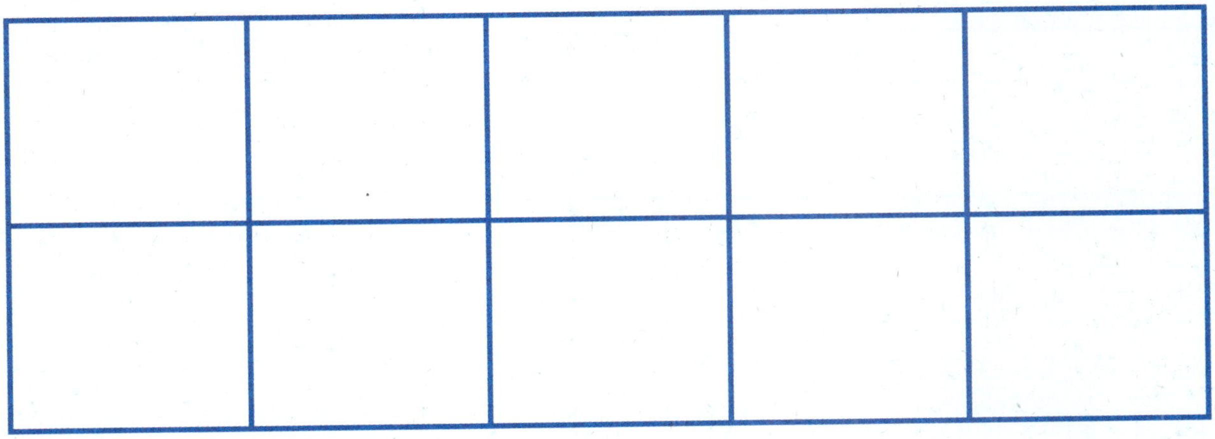

FOR THE TEACHER • Read the following problem. Beca has 8 toy cars. Can she arrange her cars in pairs on a shelf? Have children set pairs of cubes vertically on the ten frames. Continue the activity for the numbers 7 and 10.

Math Talk
When you make pairs for 7 and for 10, how are these models different? **Explain.**

MATHEMATICAL PRACTICES

© Houghton Mifflin Harcourt Publishing Company

Model and Draw

Count out cubes for each number. Make pairs.
Even numbers show pairs with no cubes left over.
Odd numbers show pairs with one cube left over.

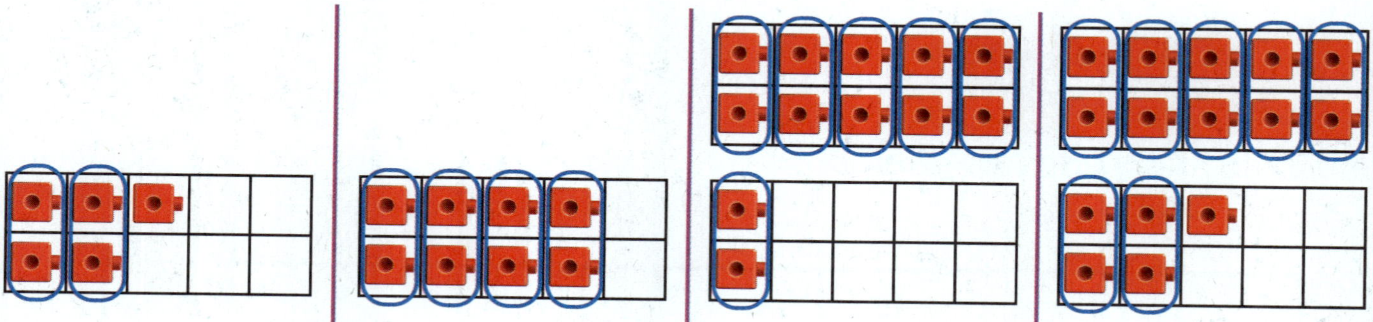

5 odd ____ 8 even ____ 12 ____ 15 ____

Share and Show

Math Board

Use cubes. Count out the number of cubes.
Make pairs. Then write **even** or **odd**.

1. 6 ____
2. 3 ____
3. 2 ____
4. 9 ____
5. 4 ____
6. 10 ____
7. 7 ____
8. 13 ____
9. 11 ____
10. 14 ____

© Houghton Mifflin Harcourt Publishing Company

Name ______________________

On Your Own

Shade in the ten frames to show the number.
Circle **even** or **odd**.

11. 17

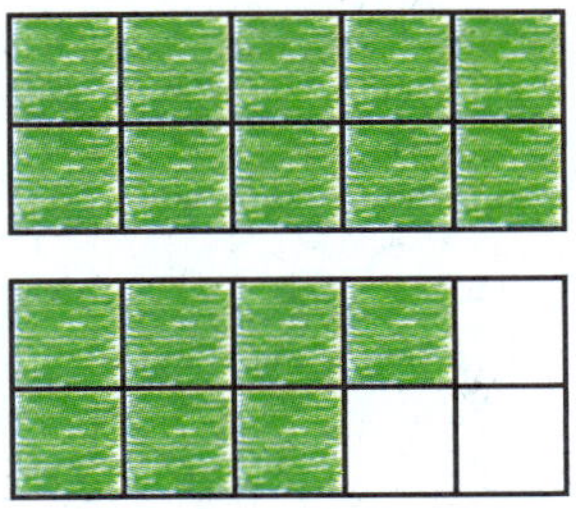

even odd

12. 16

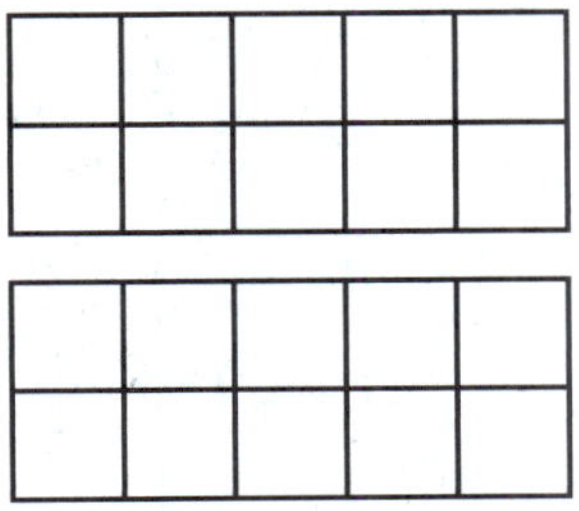

even odd

13. 19

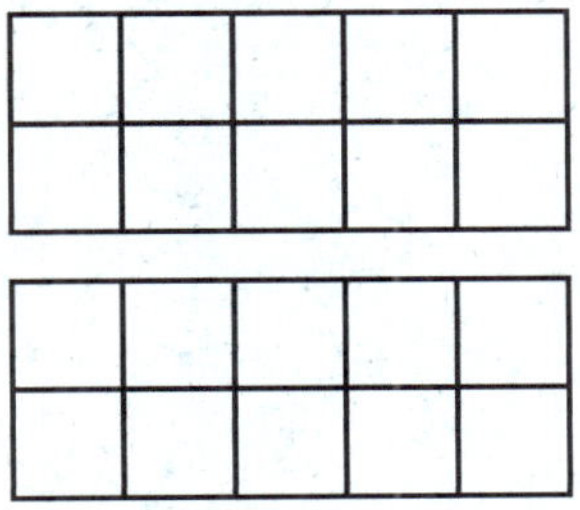

even odd

14. 15

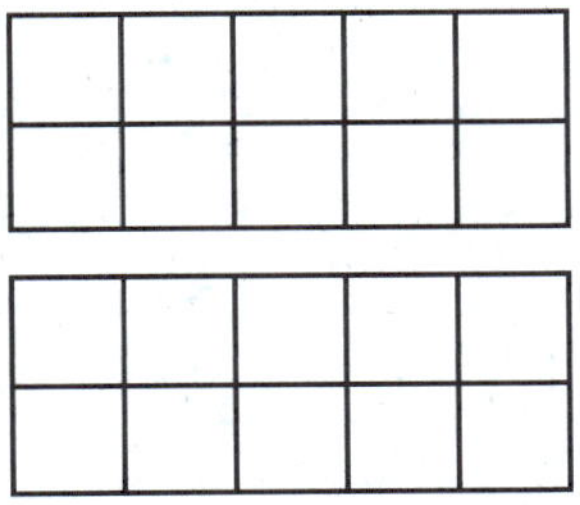

even odd

15. 20

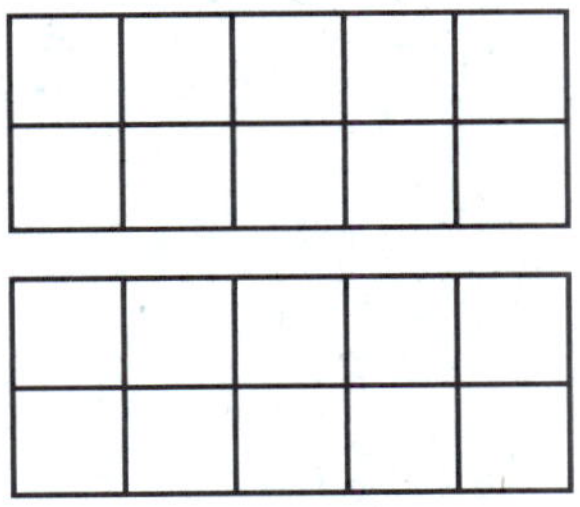

even odd

16. 18

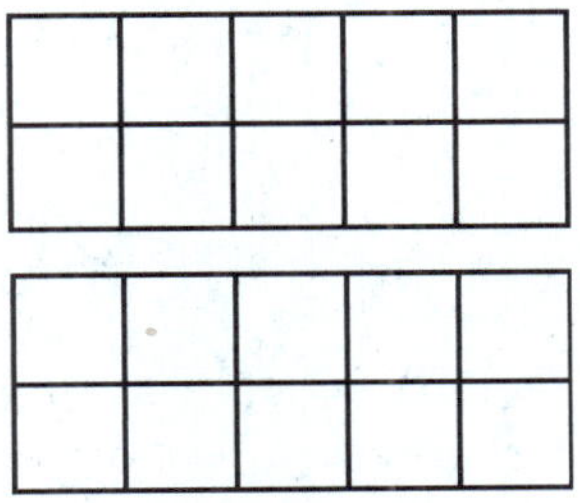

even odd

17. Which two numbers in the box are even numbers?

______ and ______

Explain how you know that they are even numbers.

____

____

____

© Houghton Mifflin Harcourt Publishing Company

PROBLEM SOLVING

Write Math

18. Fill in the blanks to describe the groups of numbers. Write **even** or **odd**.

________ **numbers**

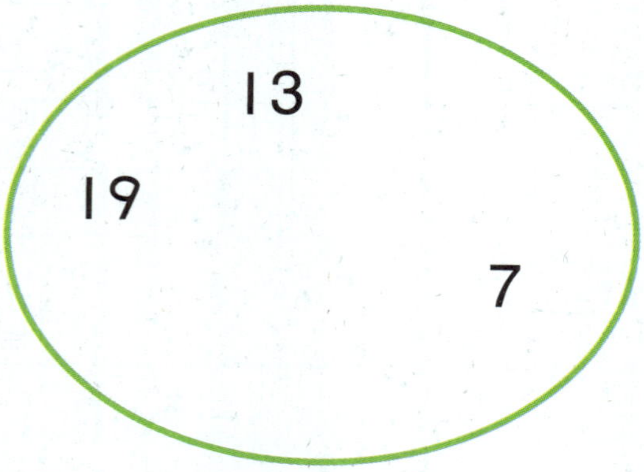

________ **numbers**

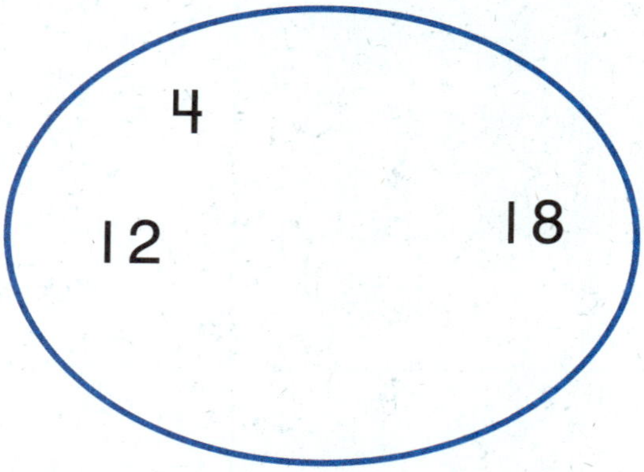

19. H.O.T. Write each of the following numbers inside the loop that it belongs in.

5 6 10 11 24 25

20. **Test Prep** There are an even number of girls and an odd number of boys in Gina's class. Which of these choices could tell about her class?

- ○ 8 girls and 12 boys
- ○ 9 girls and 8 boys
- ○ 10 girls and 7 boys
- ○ 11 girls and 9 boys

TAKE HOME ACTIVITY • Have your child show you a number, such as 9, using small objects and explain why the number is even or odd.

FOR MORE PRACTICE:
Standards Practice Book, pp. P3–P4

© Houghton Mifflin Harcourt Publishing Company

Name ____________________

Algebra • Represent Even Numbers

Essential Question Why can an even number be shown as the sum of two equal addends?

COMMON CORE STANDARD CC.2.OA.3

Work with equal groups of objects to gain foundations for multiplication.

Listen and Draw

Make pairs with your cubes. Draw to show the cubes. Then write the numbers you say as you count to find the number of cubes.

____________________ ______ cubes

FOR THE TEACHER • Give each small group of children a set of 10 to 15 connecting cubes. After children group their cubes into pairs, have them draw a picture of their cubes and write their counting sequence for finding the total number of cubes.

Math Talk

Do you have an odd number or even number of cubes? **Explain.**

© Houghton Mifflin Harcourt Publishing Company

Model and Draw

An even number of cubes can be shown as two equal groups.

You can match each cube in the first group with a cube in the second group.

$6 = 3 + 3$

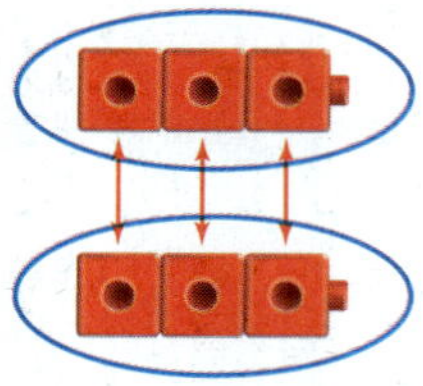

$10 = 5 + 5$

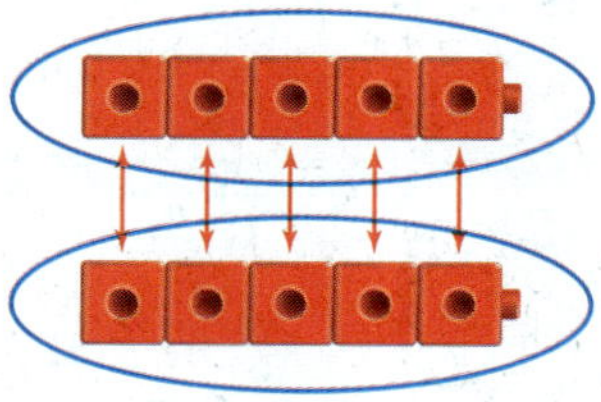

Share and Show

Math Board

How many cubes are there in all? Complete the addition sentence to show the equal groups.

1. ____ = ____ + ____

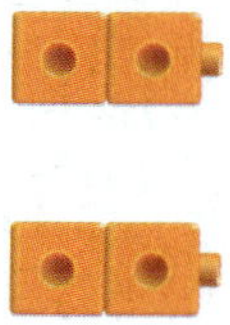

2. ____ = ____ + ____

3. ____ = ____ + ____

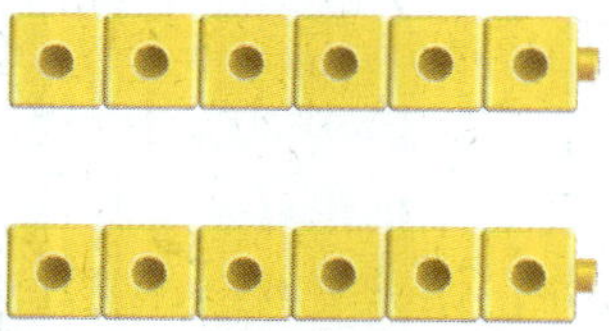

4. ____ = ____ + ____

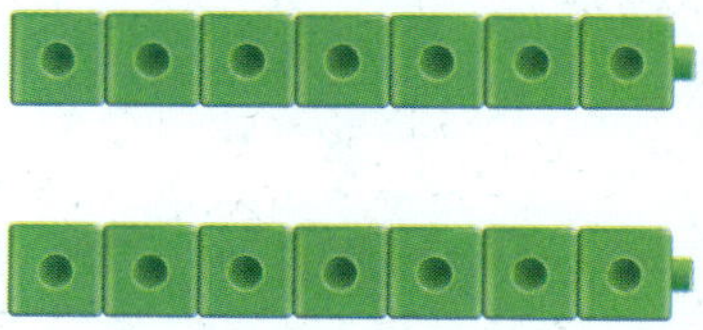

© Houghton Mifflin Harcourt Publishing Company

Name ______________________________

On Your Own

Shade in the frames to show two equal groups for each number. Complete the addition sentence to show the groups.

5. 10

____ = ____ + ____

6. 16

____ = ____ + ____

7. 20

____ = ____ + ____

8. 18

____ = ____ + ____

H.O.T. The number 7 is an odd number. Marc showed 7 with this addition sentence. Use Marc's way to show these odd numbers with addition sentences.

7 = 3 + 3 + 1

9. 5 = ____ + ____ + ____

10. 11 = ____ + ____ + ____

11. 9 = ____ + ____ + ____

12. 13 = ____ + ____ + ____

© Houghton Mifflin Harcourt Publishing Company

PROBLEM SOLVING REAL WORLD

Write Math

Solve. Write or draw to explain.

13. Jacob and Lucas each have the same number of shells. They have 16 shells altogether. How many shells do Jacob and Lucas each have?

Jacob: _____ shells

Lucas: _____ shells

14. H.O.T. Choose an even number between 10 and 19. Draw a picture and then write a sentence to explain why it is an even number.

____

____

____

15. **Test Prep** Which sum is an even number?

- ○ $1 + 2 = 3$
- ○ $3 + 2 = 5$
- ○ $5 + 5 = 10$
- ○ $5 + 6 = 11$

TAKE HOME ACTIVITY • Have your child explain what he or she learned in this lesson.

FOR MORE PRACTICE: Standards Practice Book, pp. P5–P6

© Houghton Mifflin Harcourt Publishing Company

Name ______________________________

Understand Place Value

Essential Question How do you know the value of a digit?

COMMON CORE STANDARD CC.2.NBT.3
Understand place value.

Listen and Draw REAL WORLD

Write the numbers. Then choose a way to show the numbers.

Tens	Ones

Tens	Ones

FOR THE TEACHER • Read the following problem. Have children write the numbers and describe how they chose to represent them. Tyler collects baseball cards. The number of cards that he has is written with a 2 and a 5. How many cards might he have?

Math Talk

Explain why the value of 5 is different in the two numbers.

MATHEMATICAL PRACTICES

© Houghton Mifflin Harcourt Publishing Company

Model and Draw

0, 1, 2, 3, 4, 5, 6, 7, 8, and 9 are **digits**.
In a 2-digit number, you know the value of a digit by its place.

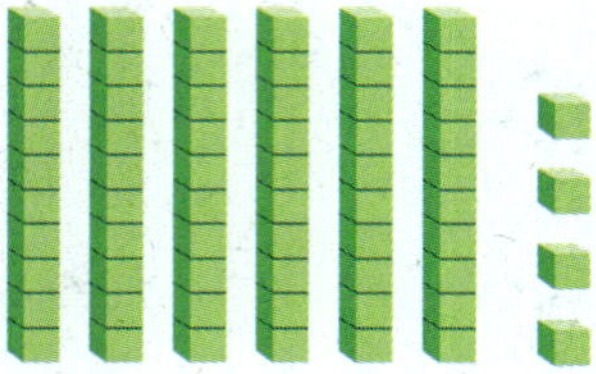

64

Tens	Ones
6	4

6 tens 4 ones

The digit **6** is in the tens place. It tells you there are 6 tens, or 60.

The digit **4** is in the ones place. It tells you there are 4 ones, or 4.

Share and Show

Math Board

Circle the value of the red digit.

1. 26

60 (6)

2. 58

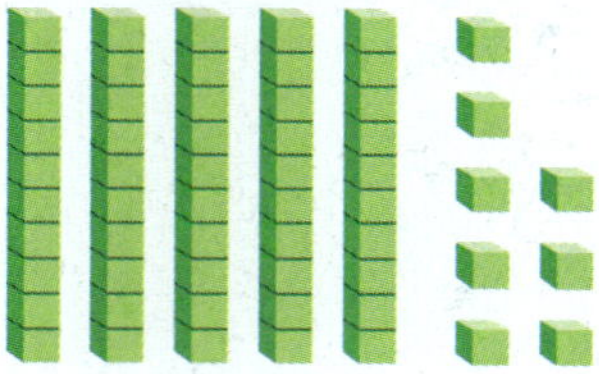

5 50

3. 40

40 4

4. 73

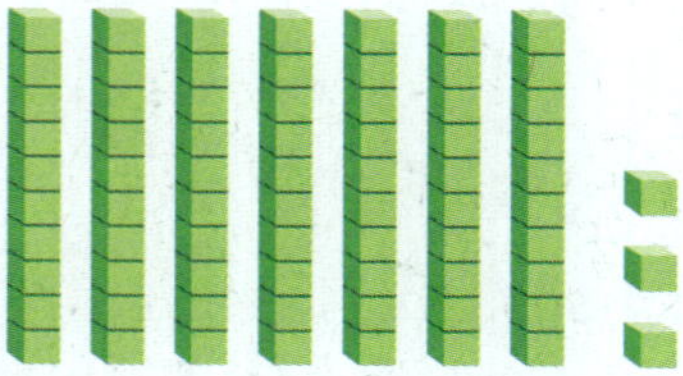

30 3

5. 24

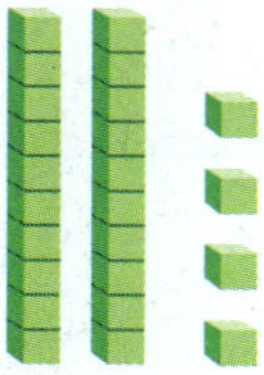

2 20

6. 61

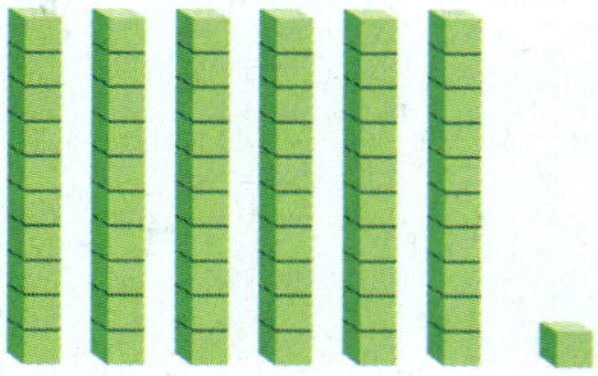

1 10

© Houghton Mifflin Harcourt Publishing Company

Name ____________________

On Your Own

Circle the value of the red digit.

7. 51

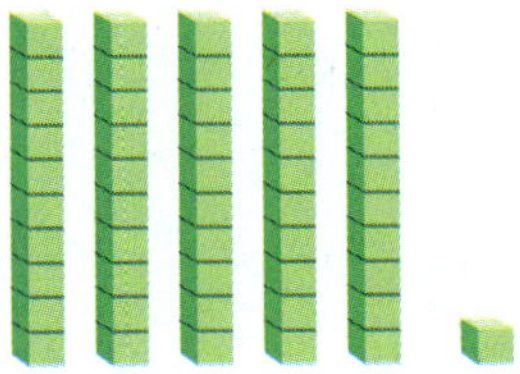

1 10

8. 49

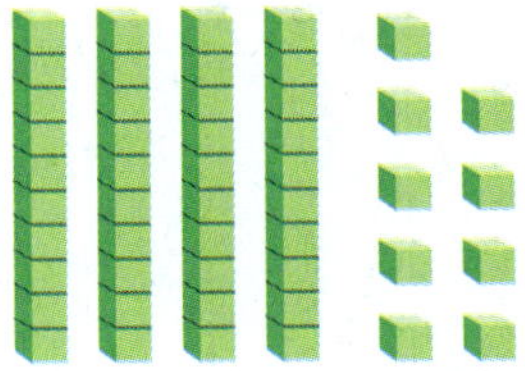

90 9

9. 70

7 70

10. 18

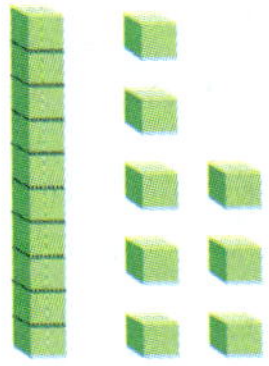

1 10

11. 65

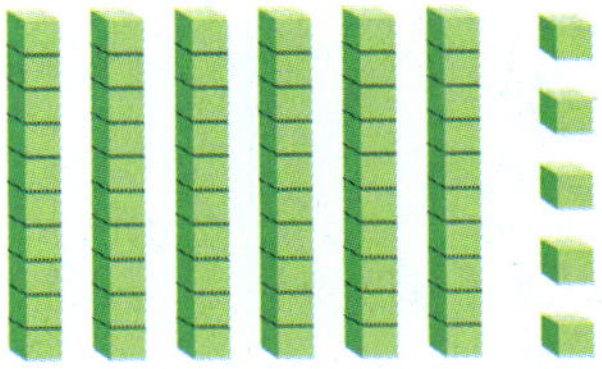

50 5

12. 33

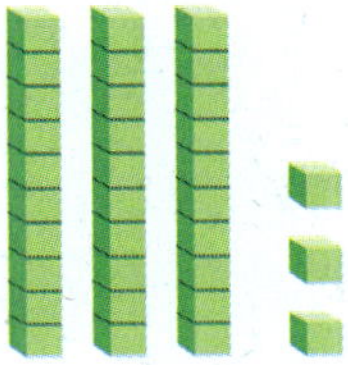

30 3

13. 30

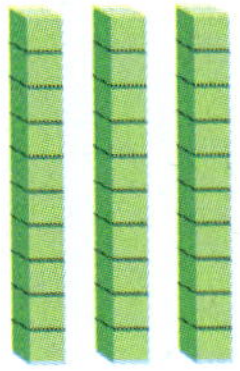

10 0

14. 46

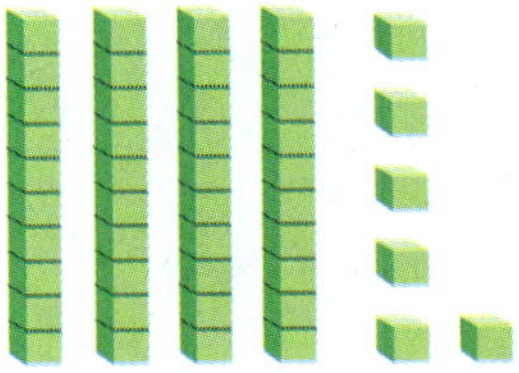

6 60

15. 54

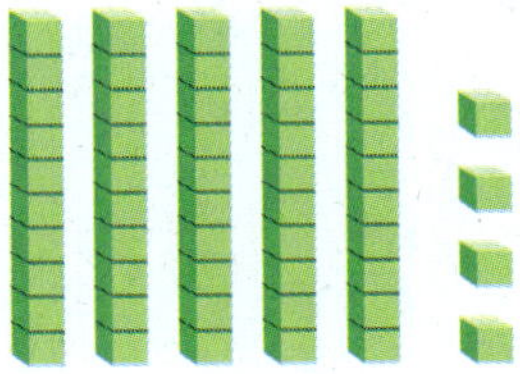

50 5

H.O.T. Look at the digits of the numbers. Draw quick pictures for the missing blocks.

16. 47

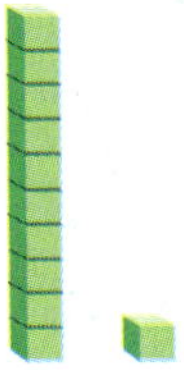

17. 52

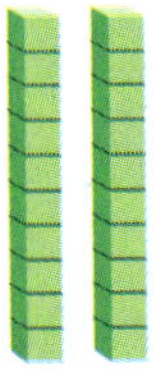

18. 63

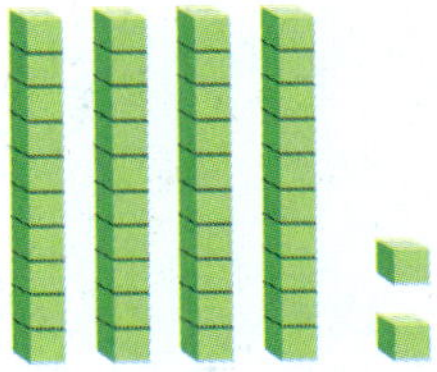

© Houghton Mifflin Harcourt Publishing Company

PROBLEM SOLVING

Write Math

Write the 2-digit number that matches the clues.

19. My number has 8 tens.

The digit in the ones place is greater than the digit in the tens place.

My number is ______.

20. In my number, the digit in the ones place is double the digit in the tens place.

The sum of the digits is 3.

My number is ______.

21. My number has the same digit in the ones place and in the tens place.

The digit is less than 6.

The digit is greater than 4.

My number is ______.

22. H.O.T. In my number, both digits are even numbers.

The digit in the tens place is less than the digit in the ones place.

The sum of the digits is 6.

My number is ______.

23. **Test Prep** Henry has 45 crayons. What is the value of the digit 5 in this number?

- ○ 4
- ○ 5
- ○ 9
- ○ 50

TAKE HOME ACTIVITY • Write the number 56. Have your child tell you which digit is in the tens place, which digit is in the ones place, and the value of each digit.

FOR MORE PRACTICE: Standards Practice Book, pp. P7–P8

© Houghton Mifflin Harcourt Publishing Company

Name ________________________________

Expanded Form

Essential Question How do you describe a 2-digit number as tens and ones?

COMMON CORE STANDARD **CC.2.NBT.3**
Understand place value.

Listen REAL WORLD

Use tens and ones blocks to model each number.

Tens	Ones

Math Talk
Explain how you know how many tens and ones are in the number 29.

MATHEMATICAL PRACTICES

FOR THE TEACHER • After you read the following problem, write 38 on the board. Have children model the number. Mac used 38 stickers to decorate a book of photos. How can you model 38 with blocks? Continue the activity for 83 and 77.

© Houghton Mifflin Harcourt Publishing Company

Model and Draw

What does 23 mean?

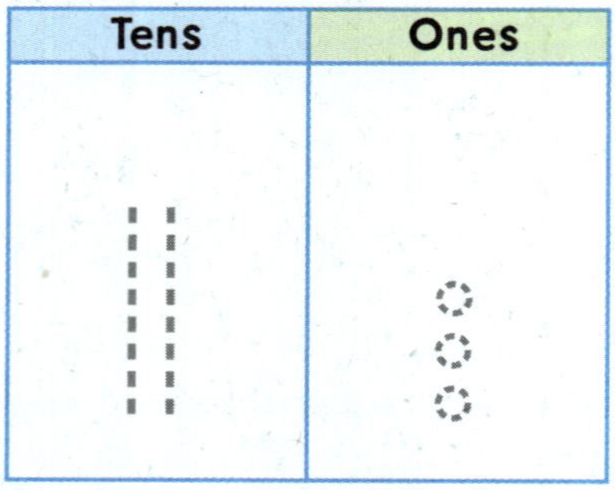

The 2 in 23 has a value of 2 tens, or 20.
The 3 in 23 has a value of 3 ones, or 3.

2 tens 3 ones

20 + 3

Share and Show

Math Board

Draw a quick picture to show the number.
Describe the number in two ways.

1. 37

_____ tens _____ ones

_____ + _____

2. 54

_____ tens _____ ones

_____ + _____

3. 16

_____ ten _____ ones

_____ + _____

4. 60

_____ tens _____ ones

_____ + _____

© Houghton Mifflin Harcourt Publishing Company

Name ______________________________

On Your Own

Draw a quick picture to show the number.
Describe the number in two ways.

5. 48

_____ tens _____ ones

_____ + _____

6. 31

_____ tens _____ one

_____ + _____

7. 59

_____ tens _____ ones

_____ + _____

8. 75

_____ tens _____ ones

_____ + _____

Write the number.

9. 8 tens 6 ones

_____

10. 40 + 2

_____

11. 70 + 3

_____

12. 9 tens 7 ones

_____

© Houghton Mifflin Harcourt Publishing Company

PROBLEM SOLVING

Write Math

H.O.T. Use crayons. Follow the steps.

13. Start at 51 and draw a green line to 43.
14. Draw a blue line from 43 to 34.
15. Draw a red line from 34 to 29.
16. Then draw a yellow line from 29 to 72.

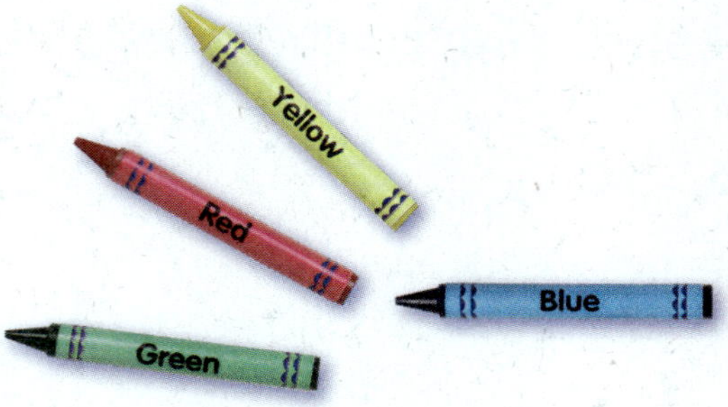

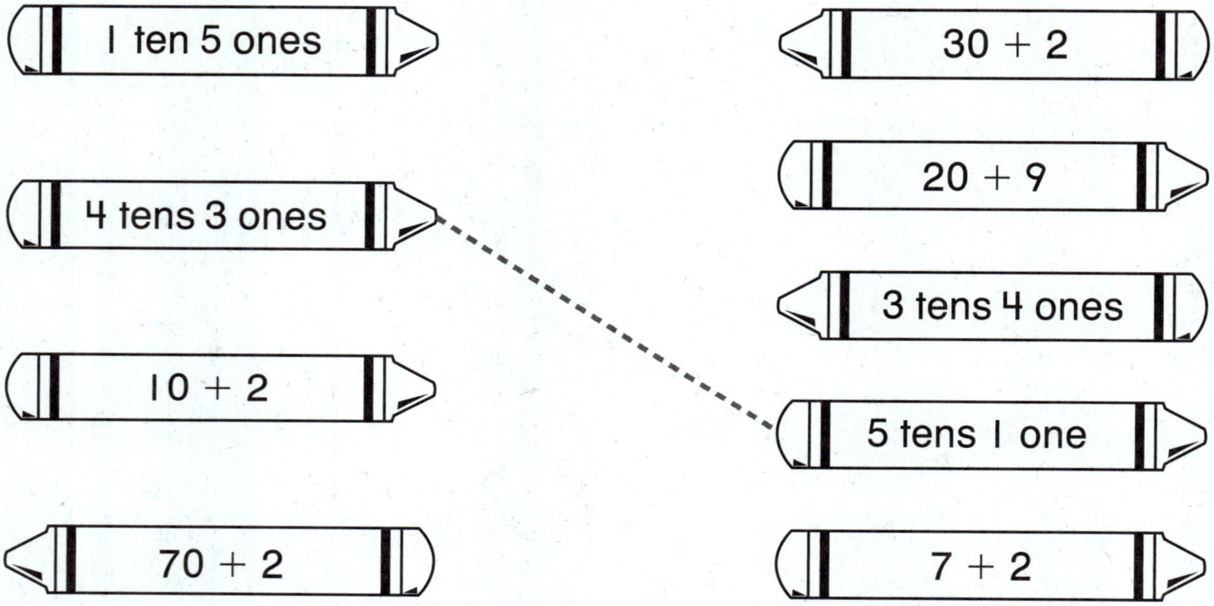

17. Test Prep Which of these is another way to describe 85?

- ○ 80 + 5
- ○ 50 + 8
- ○ 8 + 5
- ○ 50 + 80

TAKE HOME ACTIVITY • Ask your child to write 89 as tens plus ones. Then have him or her write 25 as tens plus ones.

FOR MORE PRACTICE:
Standards Practice Book, pp. P9–P10

© Houghton Mifflin Harcourt Publishing Company

Name ______________________

Different Ways to Write Numbers

COMMON CORE STANDARD CC.2.NBT.3
Understand place value.

Essential Question What are different ways to write a 2-digit number?

Listen and Draw REAL WORLD

Write the number. Then write it as tens and ones.

______ tens ______ ones

______ + ______

______ + ______

______ tens ______ ones

Math Talk
In 44, do both digits have the same value? **Explain.**

MATHEMATICAL PRACTICES

FOR THE TEACHER • Read the following problem. Taryn counted 53 books on the shelves. How many tens and ones are in 53? Continue the activity with the numbers 78, 35, and 40.

© Houghton Mifflin Harcourt Publishing Company

Model and Draw

A number can be written in different ways.

fifty-nine

5 tens 9 ones

50 + 9

59

ones	teen words	tens
0 zero	11 eleven	10 ten
1 one	12 twelve	20 twenty
2 two	13 thirteen	30 thirty
3 three	14 fourteen	40 forty
4 four	15 fifteen	50 fifty
5 five	16 sixteen	60 sixty
6 six	17 seventeen	70 seventy
7 seven	18 eighteen	80 eighty
8 eight	19 nineteen	90 ninety
9 nine		

Share and Show

Math Board

Look at the examples above.
Then write the number another way.

1. thirty-two

____

2. 20 + 7

____

3. 63

_____ tens _____ ones

4. ninety-five

_____ + _____

5. 5 tens 1 one

____

6. seventy-six

_____ + _____

7. twenty-eight

_____ tens _____ ones

8. 8 tens 0 ones

____

© Houghton Mifflin Harcourt Publishing Company

Name ______________________________

On Your Own

Write the number another way.

9. 2 tens 4 ones

____

10. thirty

_____ tens _____ ones

11. eighty-five

____

12. 54

_____ + _____

13. twelve

_____ + _____

14. 90 + 9

_____ tens _____ ones

15. 7 tens 8 ones

____

16. forty-one

_____ + _____

17. 39

____

18. 60 + 2

_____ tens _____ ones

H.O.T. Fill in the blanks to make the sentence true.

19. Sixty-seven is the same as _____ tens _____ ones.

20. 4 tens _____ ones is the same as _____ + _____.

21. 20 + _____ is the same as ______________.

TAKE HOME ACTIVITY • Write 20 + 6 on a sheet of paper. Have your child write the 2-digit number. Repeat for 4 tens 9 ones.

© Houghton Mifflin Harcourt Publishing Company

FOR MORE PRACTICE:
Standards Practice Book, pp. P11–P12

Name ______________________________

Mid-Chapter Checkpoint

Concepts and Skills

Shade in the ten frames to show the number.
Circle **even** or **odd**. (CC.2.OA.3)

1. 15

even odd

2. 18

even odd

Draw a quick picture to show the number.
Describe the number in two ways. (CC.2.NBT.3)

3. 35

_____ tens _____ ones

_____ + _____

4. 53

_____ tens _____ ones

_____ + _____

Test Prep

5. Which is another way to write 42? (CC.2.NBT.3)

- ○ 2 tens 4 ones
- ○ 40 + 2
- ○ twenty-four
- ○ 4 + 2

© Houghton Mifflin Harcourt Publishing Company

Name ______________________

Algebra • Different Names for Numbers

Essential Question How can you show the value of a number in different ways?

COMMON CORE STANDARD CC.2.NBT.3
Understand place value.

Listen and Draw REAL WORLD

Use   to show the number.
Make trades to show the number a different way.
Record the tens and ones.

_______ tens _______ ones

_______ tens _______ ones

_______ tens _______ ones

FOR THE TEACHER • Read the following problem. Drew has 26 pennies. What are some different ways he can show 26 with blocks? Have children start with 26 ones blocks. Then have them make trades and record the number of tens and ones in each of their models.

Math Talk
Describe the trades you made for different models.
MATHEMATICAL PRACTICES

© Houghton Mifflin Harcourt Publishing Company

Model and Draw

These are some different ways to show 32.

3 tens 2 ones

30 + 2

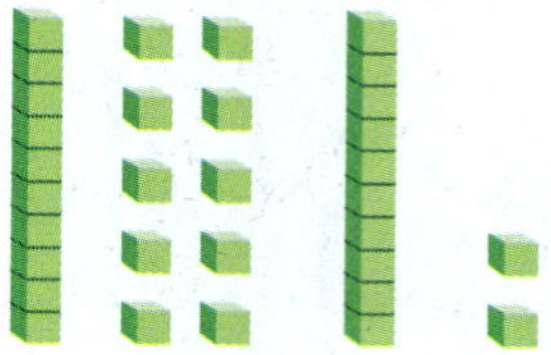

2 tens 12 ones

20 + 12

1 ten 22 ones

10 + 22

Share and Show

Math Board

The blocks show the numbers in different ways.
Describe the blocks in two ways.

1. 28

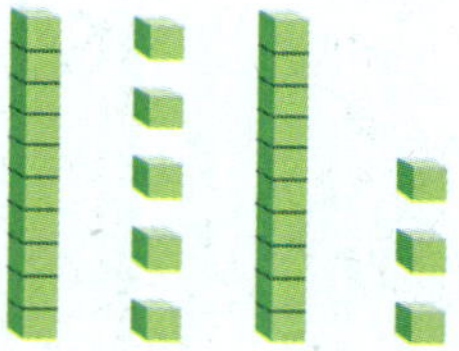

____ tens ____ ones

____ + ____

____ ten ____ ones

____ + ____

____ tens ____ ones

____ + ____

2. 35

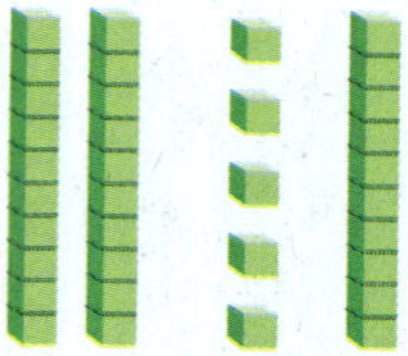

____ tens ____ ones

____ + ____

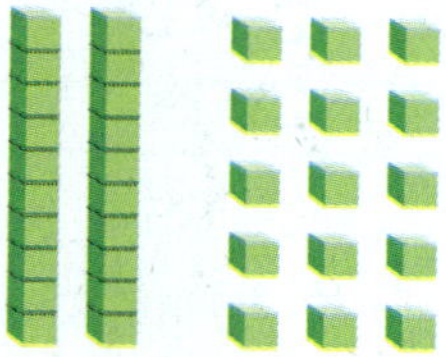

____ tens ____ ones

____ + ____

____ tens ____ ones

____ + ____

© Houghton Mifflin Harcourt Publishing Company

Name ____________________

On Your Own

The blocks show the numbers in different ways.
Describe the blocks in two ways.

3. 43

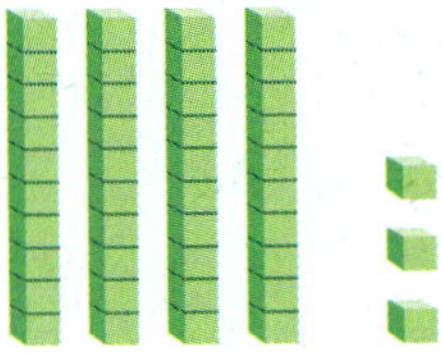

____ tens ____ ones

____ + ____

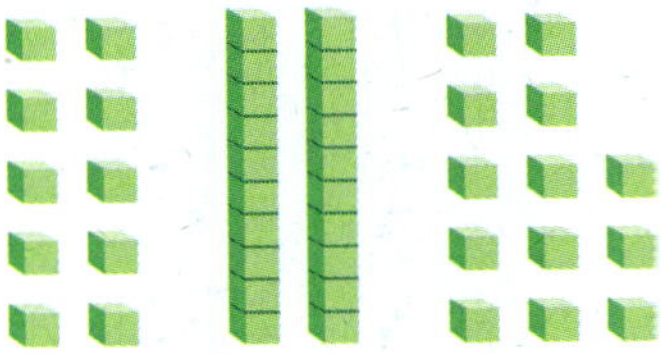

____ tens ____ ones

____ + ____

____ tens ____ ones

____ + ____

4. 30

____ tens ____ ones

____ + ____

____ tens ____ ones

____ + ____

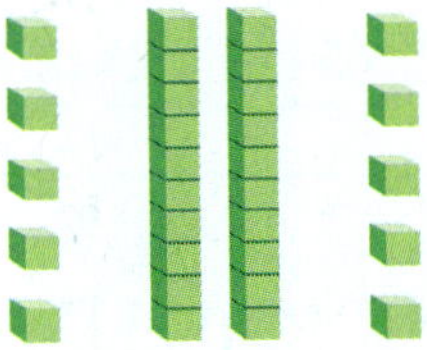

____ tens ____ ones

____ + ____

5. 41

____ tens ____ ones

____ + ____

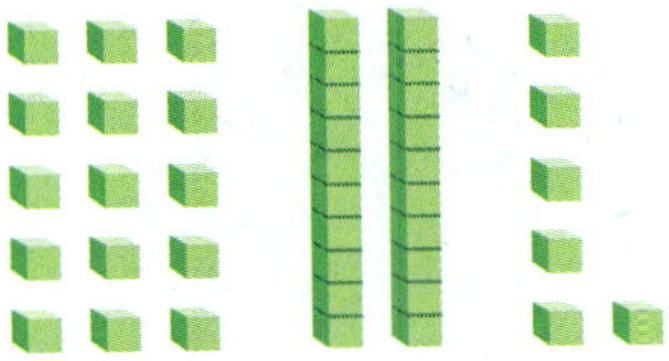

____ tens ____ ones

____ + ____

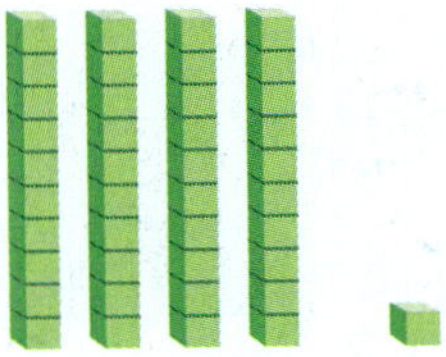

____ tens ____ one

____ + ____

6. H.O.T. Fill in the blanks to show 37 in two different ways.

____ tens ____ ones

____ tens ____ ones

© Houghton Mifflin Harcourt Publishing Company

PROBLEM SOLVING

Write Math

Circle the answer for each riddle.

7. A number has the digit 4 in the ones place and the digit 7 in the tens place. Which of these is another way to write this number?

$40 + 7$ $70 + 4$

$4 + 7$

8. H.O.T. A number is shown with 3 tens and 27 ones. Which of these is a way to write the number?

thirty

thirty-seven

fifty-seven

Fill in the blanks to make each sentence true.

9. ______ tens ______ ones is the same as $90 + 3$.

10. 2 tens 18 ones is the same as ______ + ______.

11. 5 tens ______ ones is the same as ______ + 17.

12. **Test Prep** Which of these is a way to show the number 42?

- ○ 1 ten 42 ones
- ○ 2 tens 4 ones
- ○ 3 tens 2 ones
- ○ 3 tens 12 ones

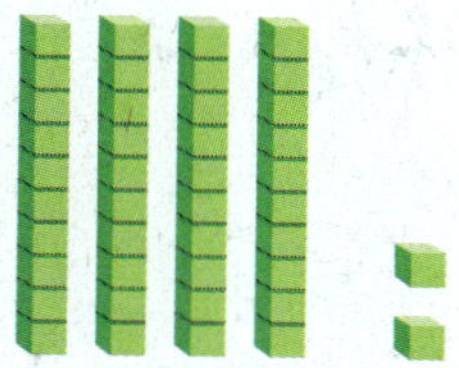

TAKE HOME ACTIVITY • Write the number 45. Have your child write or draw two ways to show this number.

FOR MORE PRACTICE: Standards Practice Book, pp. P13–P14

© Houghton Mifflin Harcourt Publishing Company

Name ______________________________

Problem Solving • Tens and Ones

Essential Question How does finding a pattern help you find all the ways to show a number with tens and ones?

COMMON CORE STANDARD CC.2.NBT.3
Understand place value.

Gail needs to buy 32 pencils. She can buy single pencils or boxes of 10 pencils. What are the different ways Gail can buy 32 pencils?

Unlock the Problem REAL WORLD

What do I need to find?

ways she can buy
32 pencils

What information do I need to use?

She can buy single pencils
or boxes of 10 pencils.

Show how to solve the problem.

Draw quick pictures for 32. Complete the chart.

Boxes of 10 pencils	Single pencils
3	2
2	12
1	
0	

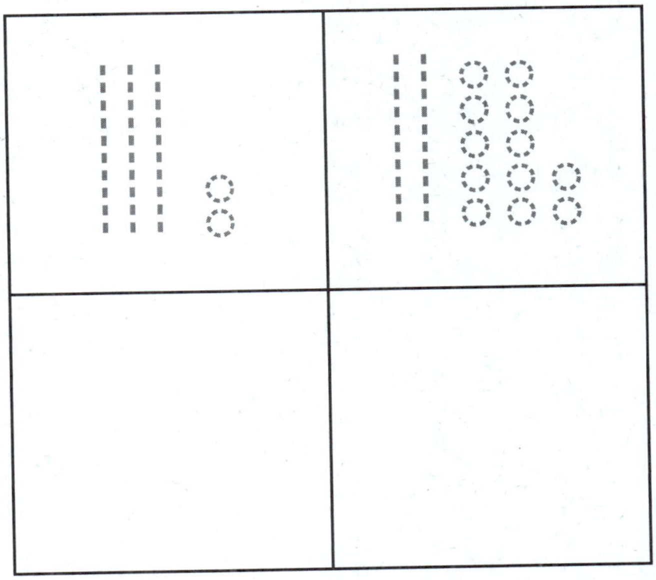

HOME CONNECTION • Your child found a pattern in the different combinations of tens and ones. Using a pattern helps to make an organized list.

© Houghton Mifflin Harcourt Publishing Company

Try Another Problem

Find a pattern to solve.

- What do I need to find?
- What information do I need to use?

1. Sara is putting away a pile of 36 crayons. She can pack them in boxes of 10 crayons or as single crayons. What are all of the different ways Sara can pack the crayons?

Boxes of 10 crayons	Single crayons

2. Mr. Winter is putting away 48 chairs. He can put away the chairs in stacks of 10 or as single chairs. What are all of the different ways Mr. Winter can put away the chairs?

Stacks of 10 chairs	Single chairs

Math Talk

Describe the pattern that helped you solve Exercise 2.

MATHEMATICAL PRACTICES

© Houghton Mifflin Harcourt Publishing Company

Name ______________________________

Share and Show

Math Board

Find a pattern to solve.

3. Philip is putting 25 markers into a bag. He can put the markers in the bag as bundles of 10 or as single markers. What are all of the different ways Philip can put the markers in the bag?

Bundles of 10 markers	Single markers

4. Stickers are sold in packs of 10 stickers or as single stickers. Miss Allen wants to buy 43 stickers. What are all of the different ways she can buy the stickers?

Packs of 10 stickers	Single stickers

5. Devin is sorting his 29 baseball cards. He can pack them in boxes of 10 cards or as single cards. What are all of the different ways Devin can sort the cards?

Boxes of 10 cards	Single cards

© Houghton Mifflin Harcourt Publishing Company

On Your Own

Solve. Write or draw to explain.

6. Mr. Link needs 30 cups. He can buy them in packs of 10 cups or as single cups. What are all of the different ways he can buy the cups?

Packs of 10 cups	Single cups

7. H.O.T. Zack has 6 marbles. Olivia gives him some more. Now he has 10 marbles. How many marbles did Olivia give him?

_____ marbles

8. Test Prep Lee can pack her toy cars in boxes of 10 cars or as single cars. Which of these is a way that she can pack her 24 toy cars?

- ○ 4 boxes of 10 cars and 2 single cars
- ○ 1 box of 10 cars and 24 single cars
- ○ 3 boxes of 10 cars and 14 single cars
- ○ 2 boxes of 10 cars and 4 single cars

TAKE HOME ACTIVITY • Have your child explain how he or she solved one problem on this page.

FOR MORE PRACTICE: Standards Practice Book, pp. P15–P16

© Houghton Mifflin Harcourt Publishing Company

Name ______________________________

Counting Patterns Within 100

Essential Question How do you count by 1s, 5s, and 10s with numbers less than 100?

COMMON CORE STANDARD CC.2.NBT.2
Understand place value.

Listen and Draw

Look at the hundred chart. Write the missing numbers.

1	2	3		5	6		8		10
11		13	14	15	16		18	19	20
	22	23	24		26	27	28	29	30
31	32		34	35	36		38	39	
41		43	44	45	46	47		49	50
51		53		55		57		59	60
	62		64	65	66	67	68		70
71	72	73	74		76		78	79	
81		83		85	86	87	88	89	90
	92		94	95	96		98		100

Math Talk

Describe some different ways to find the missing numbers in the chart.

MATHEMATICAL PRACTICES

HOME CONNECTION • Your child completed the hundred chart to review counting to 100.

© Houghton Mifflin Harcourt Publishing Company

Model and Draw

You can count on by different amounts.
You can start counting with different numbers.

Count by ones.

1, 2, 3, 4, ___5___, ___6___, ______, ______

29, 30, 31, 32, ___33___, ______, ______, ______

Count by fives.

5, 10, 15, 20, ______, ______, ______, ______

50, 55, 60, 65, ______, ______, ______, ______

Share and Show

Math Board

Count by ones.

1. 15, 16, 17, ______, ______, ______, ______, ______

Count by fives.

2. 15, 20, 25, ______, ______, ______, ______, ______

3. 60, 65, ______, ______, ______, ______, ______

Count by tens.

4. 10, 20, ______, ______, ______, ______, ______

5. 30, 40, ______, ______, ______, ______, ______

© Houghton Mifflin Harcourt Publishing Company

Name ____________________

On Your Own

Count by ones.

6. 23, 24, 25, ____, ____, ____, ____

7. 77, 78, ____, ____, ____, ____, ____

8. 52, ____, ____, ____, ____, ____, ____

Count by fives.

9. 30, 35, 40, ____, ____, ____, ____

10. 5, 10, ____, ____, ____, ____, ____

11. 70, ____, ____, ____, ____, ____, ____

Count by tens.

12. 20, 30, ____, ____, ____, ____, ____

Count back by ones.

13. 66, 65, 64, 63, ____, ____, ____

14. 18, 17, 16, 15, ____, ____, ____

© Houghton Mifflin Harcourt Publishing Company

PROBLEM SOLVING REAL WORLD

Write Math

Solve.

15. Andy counts by ones. He starts at 29 and stops at 45. Which of the following numbers will he say? Circle them.

31 20 47 35 46 40 39

16. Maya counts by fives. She starts at 5 and stops at 50. Which of the following numbers will she say? Circle them.

55 25 6 40 18 10 45

17. H.O.T. Tina wants to count backward by fives. If she starts at 40, what are the first six numbers she should say?

40, ______, ______, ______, ______, ______

18. Test Prep Which group of numbers shows counting by fives?

- ○ 5, 6, 7, 8, 9
- ○ 20, 25, 30, 35, 40
- ○ 10, 20, 30, 40, 50
- ○ 50, 49, 48, 47, 46

TAKE HOME ACTIVITY • With your child, practice counting by ones to 100, starting with numbers such as 58 or 62.

FOR MORE PRACTICE: Standards Practice Book, pp. P17–P18

© Houghton Mifflin Harcourt Publishing Company

Name ______________________________

Counting Patterns Within 1,000

Essential Question How do you count by 1s, 5s, 10s, and 100s with numbers less than 1,000?

COMMON CORE STANDARD CC.2.NBT.2
Understand place value.

Listen and Draw

Write the missing numbers in the chart.

401		403	404		406	407	408		410
411				415	416	417	418	419	
421	422	423	424	425		427	428	429	430
	432		434	435	436	437	438		
441	442	443	444		446	447		449	450
			454	455	456	457	458	459	460
461	462						468	469	470
	472	473	474	475	476	477		479	480
481	482		484	485	486				490
	492	493		495	496	497	498		

HOME CONNECTION • Your child completed the number chart to practice counting with 3-digit numbers.

Math Talk
What are the next three numbers that follow the counting in this chart? **Explain** how you know.

MATHEMATICAL PRACTICES

© Houghton Mifflin Harcourt Publishing Company

Model and Draw

Counting can be done in different ways.
Use patterns to count on.

Count by fives.

95, 100, 105, 110, 115, ______, ______

140, 145, 150, 155, ______, ______, ______

Count by tens.

300, 310, 320, ______, ______, ______, ______

470, 480, 490, ______, ______, ______, ______

Share and Show

Math Board

Count by fives.

1. 745, 750, 755, ______, ______, ______, ______

Count by tens.

2. 520, 530, 540, ______, ______, ______, ______

3. 600, 610, ______, ______, ______, ______, ______

Count by hundreds.

4. 100, 200, ______, ______, ______, ______, ______

5. 300, 400, ______, ______, ______, ______, ______

© Houghton Mifflin Harcourt Publishing Company

Name ______________________

On Your Own

Count by fives.

6. 215, 220, 225, ______, ______, ______, ______

7. 905, 910, ______, ______, ______, ______, ______

8. 485, ______, ______, ______, ______, ______

Count by tens.

9. 730, 740, 750, ______, ______, ______, ______

10. 160, 170, ______, ______, ______, ______, ______

11. 850, ______, ______, ______, ______, ______

Count by hundreds.

12. 200, 300, ______, ______, ______, ______, ______

Count back by ones.

13. 558, 557, ______, ______, ______, ______, ______

14. 311, 310, ______, ______, ______, ______, ______

© Houghton Mifflin Harcourt Publishing Company

PROBLEM SOLVING REAL WORLD

Write Math

Solve.

15. Lisa counts by fives. She starts at 120 and stops at 175. Which of the following numbers will she say? Circle them.

170 151 135

155 200 180

16. George counts by tens. He starts at 750 and stops at 830. Which of the following numbers will he say? Circle them.

755 690 780

760 795 810

17. H.O.T. Tony wants to count backward by tens. If he starts at 440, what are the first six numbers that he should say?

440, ________, ________, ________, ________, ________

18. Test Prep Which group of numbers shows counting by tens?

- ○ 360, 370, 380, 390, 400
- ○ 390, 391, 392, 393, 394
- ○ 395, 400, 405, 410, 415
- ○ 245, 240, 235, 230, 225

TAKE HOME ACTIVITY • With your child, count by fives from 150 to 200.

FOR MORE PRACTICE: Standards Practice Book, pp. P19–P20

© Houghton Mifflin Harcourt Publishing Company

Name ________________________________

Chapter 1 Review/Test

Vocabulary

Use a word in the box to complete each sentence.

even
odd
digits

1. The numbers 3 and 7 are __________ numbers. (p. 14)

2. 5 and 2 are __________ in the number 52. (p. 22)

Concepts and Skills

Draw a quick picture to show the number.
Describe the number in two ways. (CC.2.NBT.3)

3. 37

_____ tens _____ ones

_____ + _____

4. 73

_____ tens _____ ones

_____ + _____

Write the number another way. (CC.2.NBT.3)

5. forty-one

_____ + _____

6. 6 tens 3 ones

____

Shade in the frames to show two equal groups for each number. Complete the addition sentence to show the groups. (CC.2.OA.3)

7. 16

_____ = _____ + _____

8. 14

_____ = _____ + _____

© Houghton Mifflin Harcourt Publishing Company

Fill in the bubble for the correct answer choice.

TEST PREP

9. What is the value of the digit 7 in the number 75? (CC.2.NBT.3)

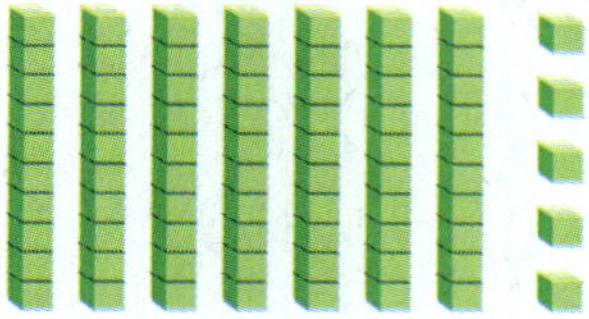

- ○ 7
- ○ 12
- ○ 17
- ○ 70

10. Which group of numbers shows counting by fives? (CC.2.NBT.2)

- ○ 76, 77, 78, 79, 80
- ○ 70, 75, 80, 85, 90
- ○ 20, 30, 40, 50, 60
- ○ 55, 54, 53, 52, 51

11. Which of the following is another way to describe the number 46? (CC.2.NBT.3)

- ○ 2 tens 16 ones
- ○ 3 tens 6 ones
- ○ 3 tens 16 ones
- ○ 4 tens 16 ones

© Houghton Mifflin Harcourt Publishing Company

Name ______________________

TEST PREP

Fill in the bubble for the correct answer choice.

12. Wesley has an odd number of red crayons and an even number of blue crayons. Which of these choices could be Wesley's crayons? (CC.2.OA.3)

- ○ 5 red crayons and 8 blue crayons
- ○ 6 red crayons and 7 blue crayons
- ○ 6 red crayons and 8 blue crayons
- ○ 7 red crayons and 9 blue crayons

13. Mrs. Shaw is buying 26 markers. She can buy them in packs of 10 markers or as single markers. Which of these is a way that she can buy the markers? (CC.2.NBT.3)

Packs of 10 markers	Single markers
2	6
0	26

- ○ 1 pack of 10 markers and 26 single markers
- ○ 6 packs of 10 markers and 2 single markers
- ○ 1 pack of 10 markers and 16 single markers
- ○ 3 packs of 10 markers and 6 single markers

14. Which group of numbers shows counting by tens? (CC.2.NBT.2)

- ○ 310, 311, 312, 313, 314
- ○ 230, 240, 250, 260, 270
- ○ 405, 410, 415, 420, 425
- ○ 195, 200, 205, 210, 215

© Houghton Mifflin Harcourt Publishing Company

Constructed Response

15. Shawna made a list of ways to write the number 26.

2 tens 6 ones
twenty-six
20 + 6

Draw a quick picture for 53. Then list three different ways to write the number 53. (CC.2.NBT.3)

____

____

____

Performance Task (CC.2.NBT.3)

16. Mrs. Payne is buying 32 pencils. She can buy them in packs of 10 pencils or as single pencils. What are all of the different ways Mrs. Payne can buy the pencils? Find a pattern to solve.

Packs of 10 pencils	Single pencils

Choose two of the ways from the chart. Explain how these two ways show the same number of pencils.

© Houghton Mifflin Harcourt Publishing Company

Chapter 2

Numbers to 1,000

Curious About Math with Curious George

The White House has 412 doors and 147 windows. Look at the digit 1 in each of these numbers. How do the values of these digits compare?

© Houghton Mifflin Harcourt Publishing Company
Curious George by Margret and H.A. Rey. Copyright © 2010 by Houghton Mifflin Harcourt Publishing Company. All rights reserved. The character Curious George®, including without limitation the character's name and the character's likenesses, are registered trademarks of Houghton Mifflin Harcourt Publishing Company.

Name ______________________________

Show What You Know

Identify Numbers to 30

Write how many.

1. 

____ leaves

2. 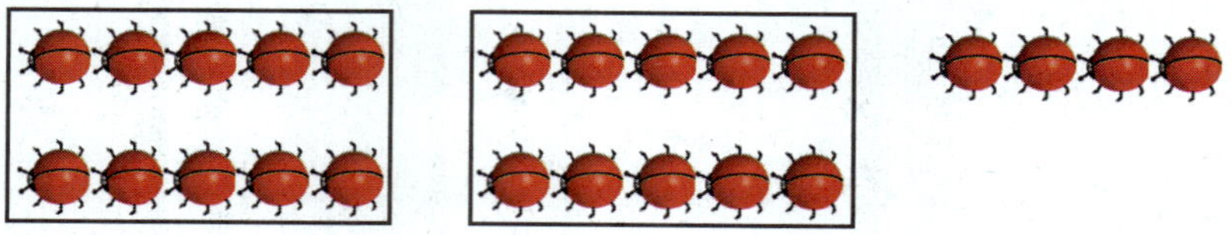

____ bugs

Place Value: 2-Digit Numbers

Circle the value of the red digit.

3. 47

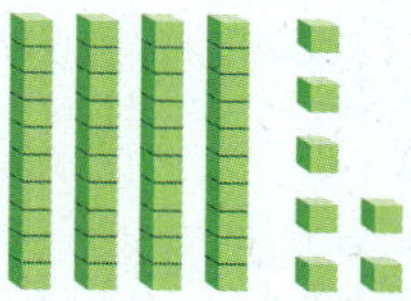

40 4

4. 84

4 40

5. 65

6 60

Compare 2-Digit Numbers Using Symbols

Compare. Write >, <, or =.

6. 

37 ◯ 42

7. 

40 ◯ 33

Family note: This page checks your child's understanding of important skills needed for success in Chapter 2.

GO Online Assessment Options Soar to Success Math

© Houghton Mifflin Harcourt Publishing Company

Name ____________________

Review Words
- more
- fewer
- digits
- tens
- ones

Vocabulary Builder

Visualize It

Fill in the boxes of the graphic organizer.
Write sentences using **fewer** and **more.**

fewer
- 9 pens is fewer than 11 pens.
- ____________________

more
- ____________________
- ____________________

Understand Vocabulary

Use the review words. Complete the sentences.

1. 3 and 9 are ____________________ in the number 39.
2. 7 is in the ____________________ place in the number 87.
3. 8 is in the ____________________ place in the number 87.

© Houghton Mifflin Harcourt Publishing Company

GO Online
- eStudent Edition
- Multimedia eGlossary

Chapter 2

Game: Fish for Digits

Materials

• 12 • 12 • 1

Play with a partner.

1. Name a place for a digit. You can say **tens place** or **ones place**. Toss the .
2. Match the number on the and the place that you named with a fish.
3. Put a on that fish. Take turns.
4. Match all the fish. The player with more on the board wins.

© Houghton Mifflin Harcourt Publishing Company

Name ______________________________

Group Tens as Hundreds

Essential Question How do you group tens as hundreds?

COMMON CORE STANDARDS **CC.2.NBT.1a, CC.2.NBT.1b**
Understand place value.

Listen and Draw REAL WORLD

Circle groups of ten. Count the groups of ten.

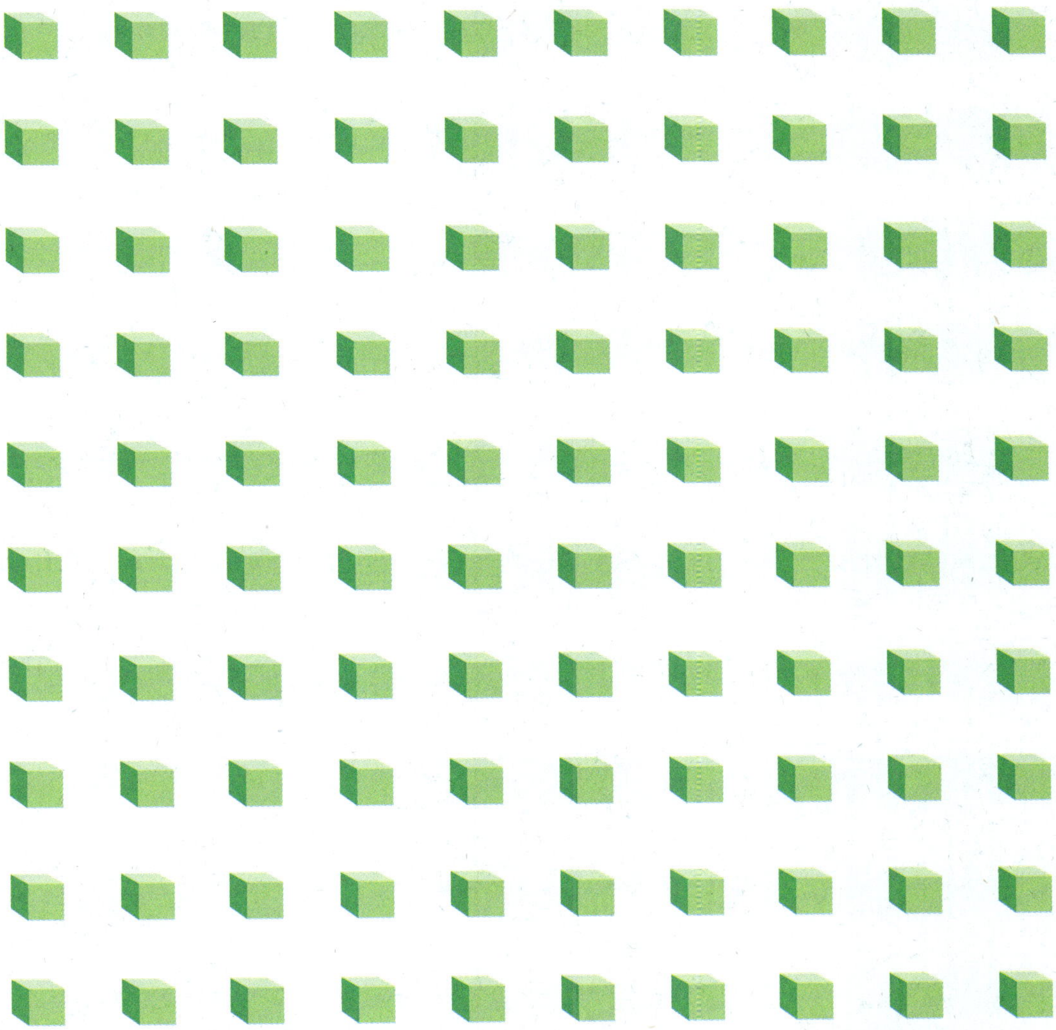

FOR THE TEACHER • Read the following problem and have children group ones blocks to solve. Bernie dropped 100 pennies. How many groups of 10 pennies can he make as he picks up the pennies?

Math Talk

How many ones are in 3 tens? How many ones are in 7 tens? **Explain.**

© Houghton Mifflin Harcourt Publishing Company

Model and Draw

10 tens is the same as 1 **hundred**.

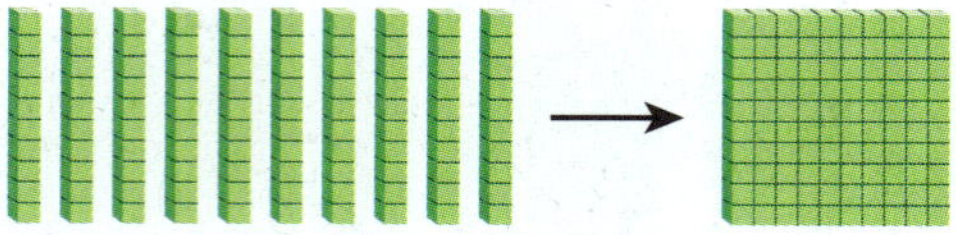

10 tens

1 hundred

100

Share and Show

Math Board

Write how many tens. Circle groups of 10 tens.
Write how many hundreds. Write the number.

1. 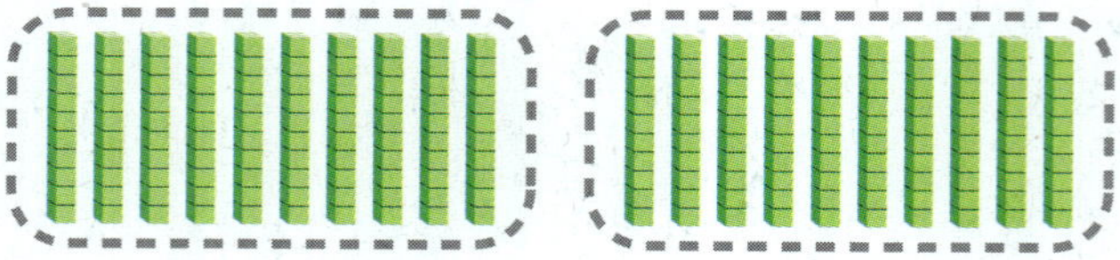

20 tens

_____ hundreds

_____

2. 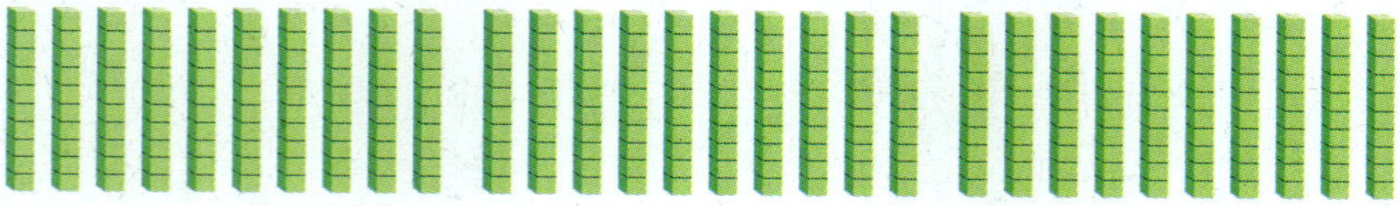

_____ tens

_____ hundreds

_____

3. 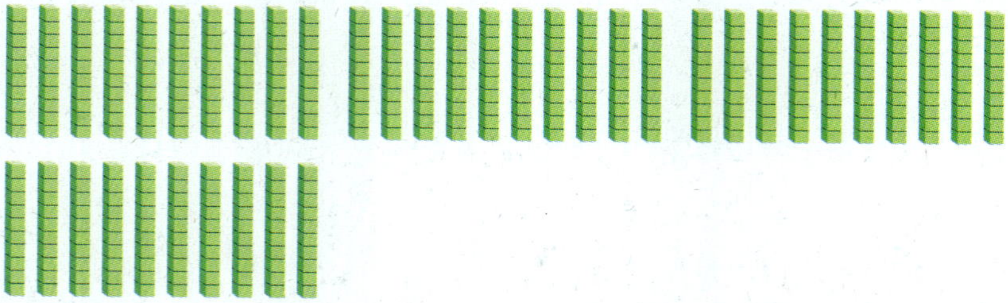

_____ tens

_____ hundreds

_____

4. 

_____ tens

_____ hundreds

_____

© Houghton Mifflin Harcourt Publishing Company

Name ____________________

On Your Own

Write how many tens. Circle groups of 10 tens.
Write how many hundreds. Write the number.

5.

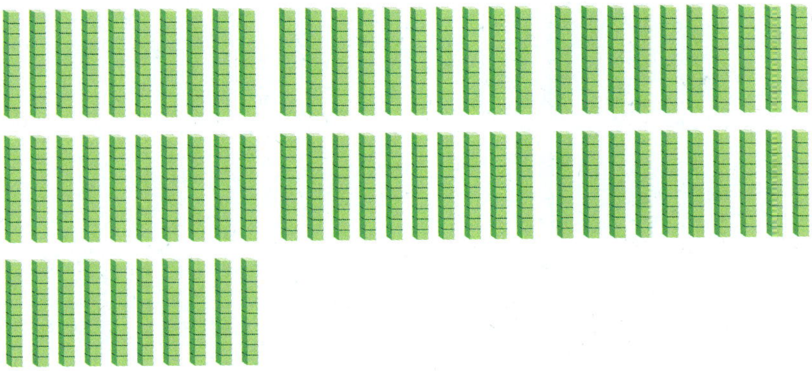

_____ tens

_____ hundreds

_____

6.

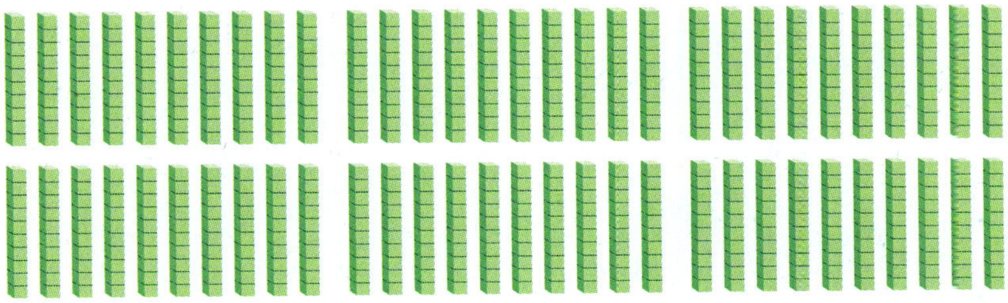

_____ tens

_____ hundreds

_____

7.

_____ tens

_____ hundreds

_____

8.

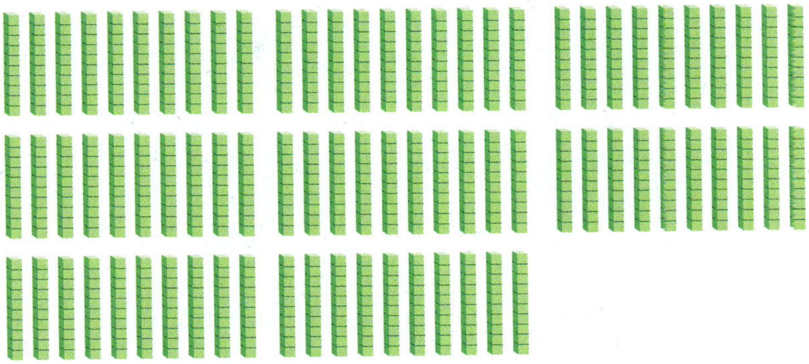

_____ tens

_____ hundreds

_____

© Houghton Mifflin Harcourt Publishing Company

PROBLEM SOLVING REAL WORLD

Write Math

Solve. Write or draw to explain.

9. Mrs. Martin has 20 boxes of paper clips. There are 10 paper clips in each box. How many paper clips does she have?

_______ paper clips

10. H.O.T. Wally has 400 cards. How many stacks of 10 cards can he make? Draw a quick picture to show your work.

_______ stacks of 10 cards

11. Test Prep Which number has the same value as 30 tens?

- ○ 310
- ○ 300
- ○ 30
- ○ 3

TAKE HOME ACTIVITY • Ask your child to draw a quick picture of 20 tens and then tell you how many hundreds there are.

FOR MORE PRACTICE: Standards Practice Book, pp. P25–P26

© Houghton Mifflin Harcourt Publishing Company

Lesson 2.2

Name ______________________________

Explore 3-Digit Numbers

Essential Question How do you write a 3-digit number for a group of tens?

COMMON CORE STANDARD CC.2.NBT.1
Understand place value.

Listen and Draw REAL WORLD

Circle groups of blocks to show hundreds. Count the hundreds.

________ hundreds

________ straws

FOR THE TEACHER • Read the following problem and have children circle groups of tens blocks to solve. Mrs. Rodriguez has 30 bundles of straws. There are 10 straws in each bundle. How many straws does Mrs. Rodriguez have?

Math Talk MATHEMATICAL PRACTICES

Describe how the number of hundreds would be different if there were 10 more bundles of straws.

© Houghton Mifflin Harcourt Publishing Company

Model and Draw

What number is shown with 11 tens?

11 tens

1 hundred 1 ten

110

In the number 110, there is a 1 in the hundreds place and a 1 in the tens place.

Share and Show

Math Board

Circle tens to make 1 hundred. Write the number in different ways.

1. 

____ tens

____ hundred ____ tens

____

2. 

____ tens

____ hundred ____ tens

____

3. 

____ tens

____ hundred ____ tens

____

© Houghton Mifflin Harcourt Publishing Company

Name ____________________

On Your Own

Circle tens to make 1 hundred. Write the number in different ways.

4.

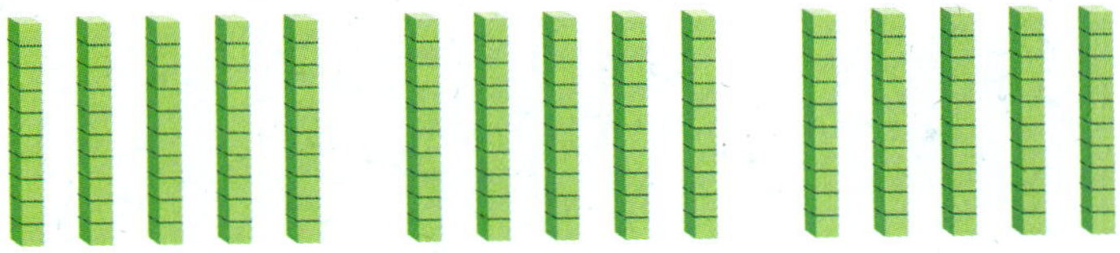

____ tens

____ hundred ____ tens

____

5.

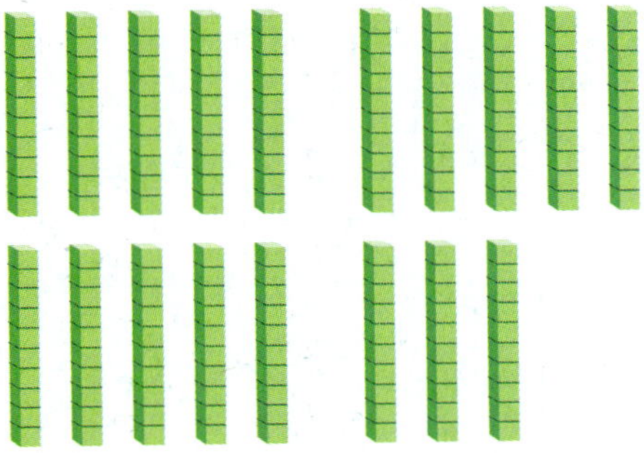

____ tens

____ hundred ____ tens

____

6.

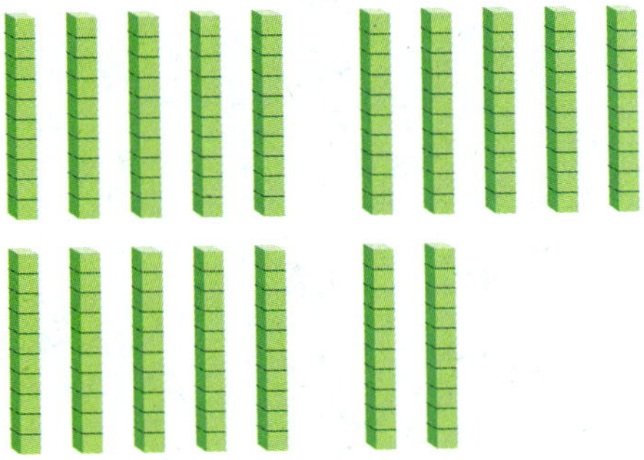

____ tens

____ hundred ____ tens

____

7.

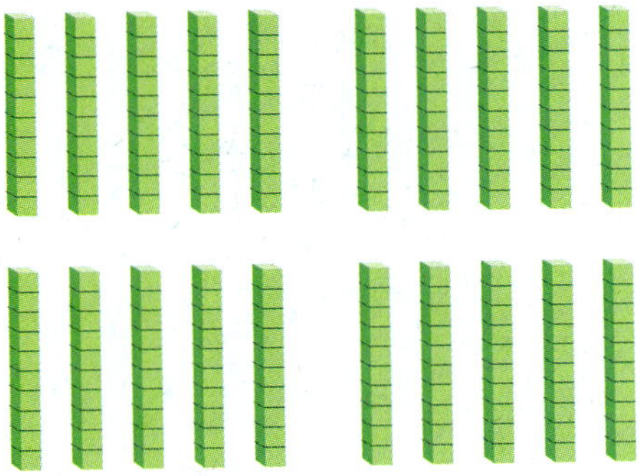

____ tens

____ hundreds ____ tens

____

© Houghton Mifflin Harcourt Publishing Company

PROBLEM SOLVING REAL WORLD

Write Math

Solve. Write or draw to explain.

8. Kendra has 120 stickers. 10 stickers fill a page. How many pages can she fill?

GO MATH!

_______ pages

9. There are 14 boxes of crackers. There are 10 crackers in each box. How many crackers are in the boxes?

_______ crackers

10. H.O.T. Ed has 150 marbles. How many bags of 10 marbles does he need to get so that he will have 200 marbles in all?

_______ bags of 10 marbles

11. Test Prep Which has the same value as 17 tens?

- ○ 17 ones
- ○ 17 hundreds
- ○ 1 ten 7 ones
- ○ 1 hundred 7 tens

TAKE HOME ACTIVITY • **Have your child draw 110 Xs by drawing 11 groups of 10 Xs.**

FOR MORE PRACTICE: Standards Practice Book, pp. P27–P28

© Houghton Mifflin Harcourt Publishing Company

Name ______________________________

Model 3-Digit Numbers

Essential Question How do you show a 3-digit number using blocks?

COMMON CORE STANDARD **CC.2.NBT.1**
Understand place value.

Listen and Draw REAL WORLD

Use . Draw to show what you did.

FOR THE TEACHER • Read the following problem. Jack has 12 tens blocks. How many hundreds and tens does Jack have? Have children show Jack's blocks and then draw quick pictures. Then have children circle 10 tens and solve the problem.

Math Talk

If Jack had 14 tens, how many hundreds and tens would he have? **Explain.**

MATHEMATICAL PRACTICES

© Houghton Mifflin Harcourt Publishing Company

Model and Draw

In the number 348, the 3 is in the hundreds place, the 4 is in the tens place, and the 8 is in the ones place.

Write the digits in the chart.

Hundreds	Tens	Ones
3	4	8

Show the number 348 using blocks.

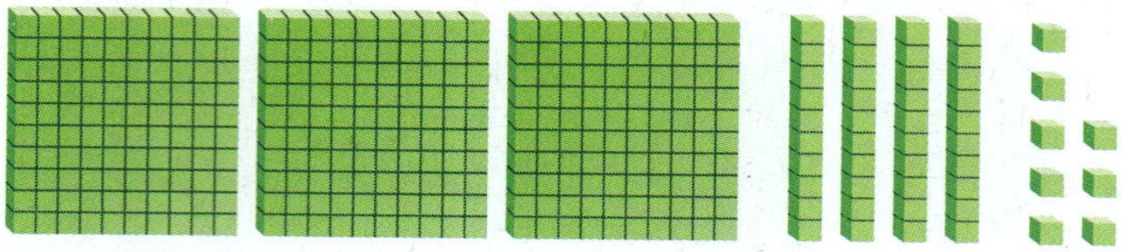

Draw a quick picture.

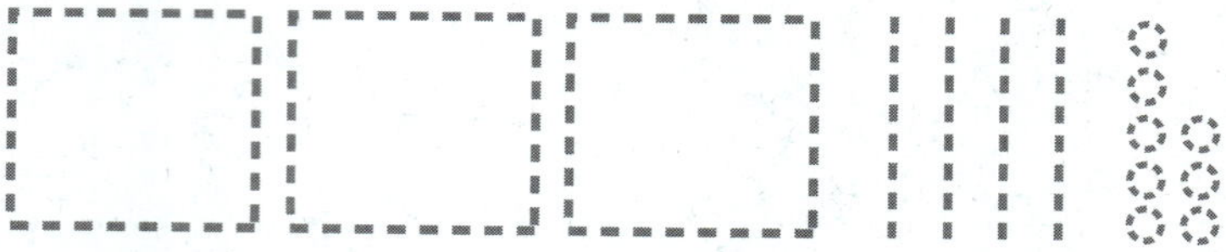

Share and Show

Math Board

Write how many hundreds, tens, and ones.

Show with 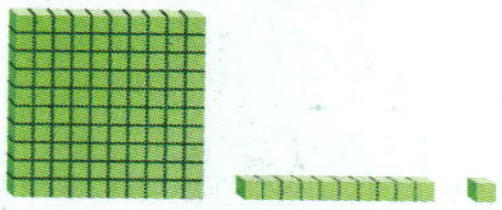. Then draw a quick picture.

1. 234

Hundreds	Tens	Ones

2. 156

Hundreds	Tens	Ones

© Houghton Mifflin Harcourt Publishing Company

Name ____________________

On Your Own

Write how many hundreds, tens, and ones.

Show with . Then draw a quick picture.

3. 125

Hundreds	Tens	Ones

4. 312

Hundreds	Tens	Ones

5. 245

Hundreds	Tens	Ones

6. 103

Hundreds	Tens	Ones

7. 419

Hundreds	Tens	Ones

8. 328

Hundreds	Tens	Ones

© Houghton Mifflin Harcourt Publishing Company

PROBLEM SOLVING

Write Math

Write the number that matches the clues.

9. A model for my number has 2 hundreds blocks, no tens blocks, and 3 ones blocks.

Hundreds	Tens	Ones

My number is ______.

10. A model for my number has 3 hundreds blocks, 5 tens blocks, and no ones blocks.

Hundreds	Tens	Ones

My number is ______.

11. H.O.T. How are the numbers 342 and 324 alike? How are they different?

____

____

____

12. **Test Prep** What number is shown with these blocks?

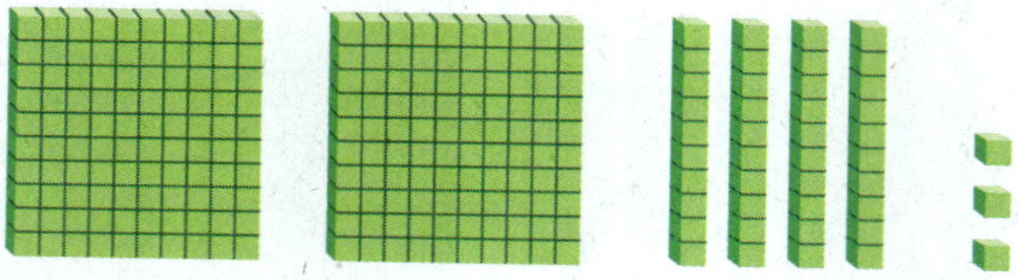

- ○ 432
- ○ 342
- ○ 243
- ○ 207

TAKE HOME ACTIVITY • Write the number 438. Have your child tell you the values of the digits in the number 438.

FOR MORE PRACTICE: Standards Practice Book, pp. P29–P30

© Houghton Mifflin Harcourt Publishing Company

Name ______________________________

Hundreds, Tens, and Ones

Essential Question How do you write the 3-digit number that is shown by a set of blocks?

COMMON CORE STANDARD **CC.2.NBT.1**
Understand place value.

Listen and Draw REAL WORLD

Write the number of hundreds, tens, and ones. Then draw a quick picture.

Hundreds	Tens	Ones

Hundreds	Tens	Ones

Math Talk MATHEMATICAL PRACTICES

Describe how the two numbers are alike. **Describe** how they are different.

FOR THE TEACHER • Read the following to children. Steven has 243 yellow blocks. How many hundreds, tens, and ones are in this number? Repeat for 423 red blocks.

© Houghton Mifflin Harcourt Publishing Company

Model and Draw

Write how many hundreds, tens, and ones there are in the model.
What are two ways to write this number?

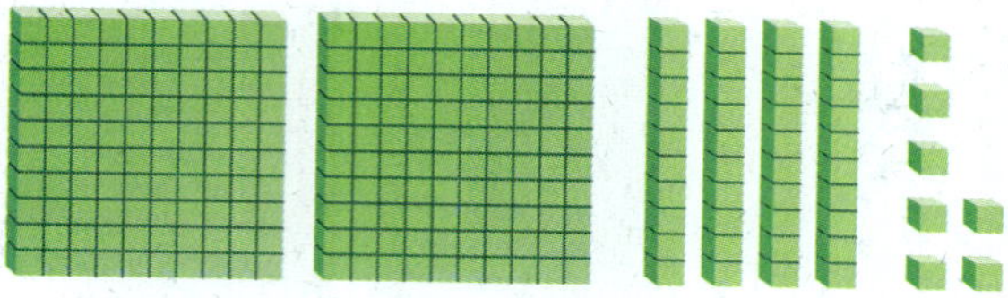

Hundreds	Tens	Ones
2	4	7

247

200 + 40 + 7

Share and Show

Math Board

Write how many hundreds, tens, and ones are in the model. Write the number in two ways.

1. 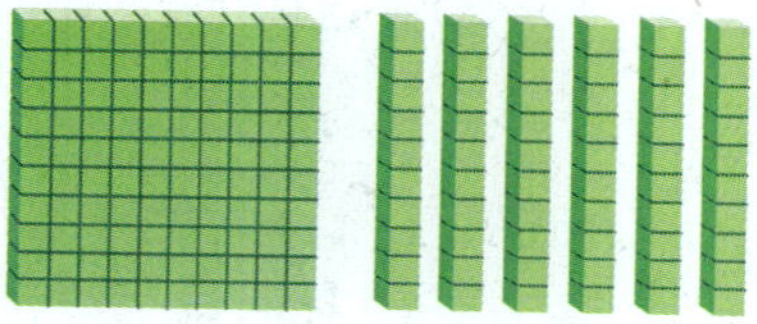

Hundreds	Tens	Ones

______

______ + ______ + ______

2. 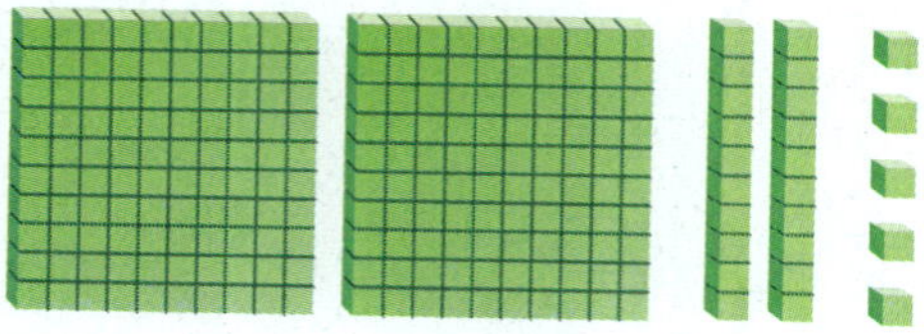

Hundreds	Tens	Ones

______

______ + ______ + ______

3. 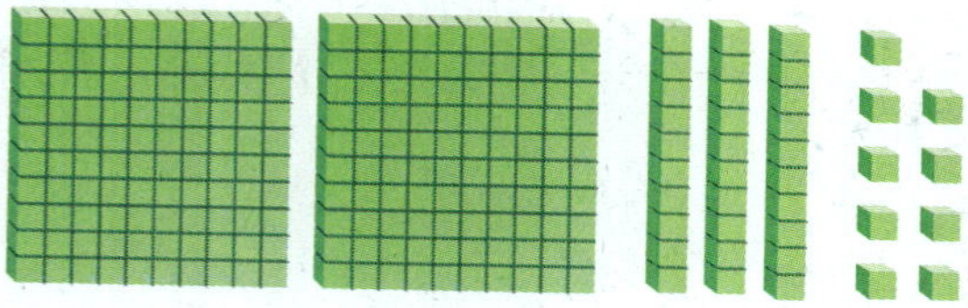

Hundreds	Tens	Ones

______

______ + ______ + ______

© Houghton Mifflin Harcourt Publishing Company

Name ______________________

On Your Own

Write how many hundreds, tens, and ones are in the model. Write the number in two ways.

4.

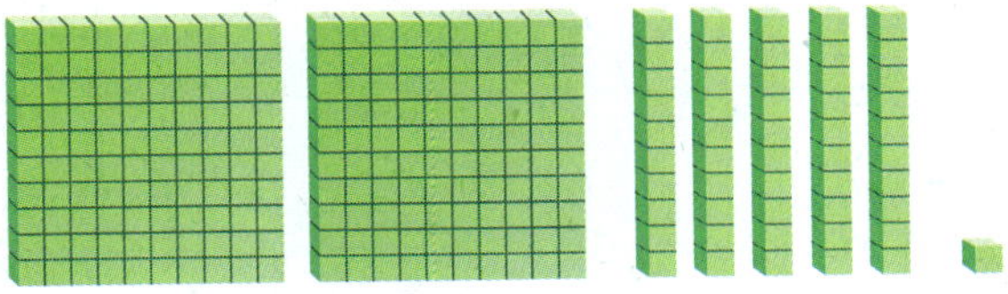

Hundreds	Tens	Ones

______

______ + ______ + ______

5.

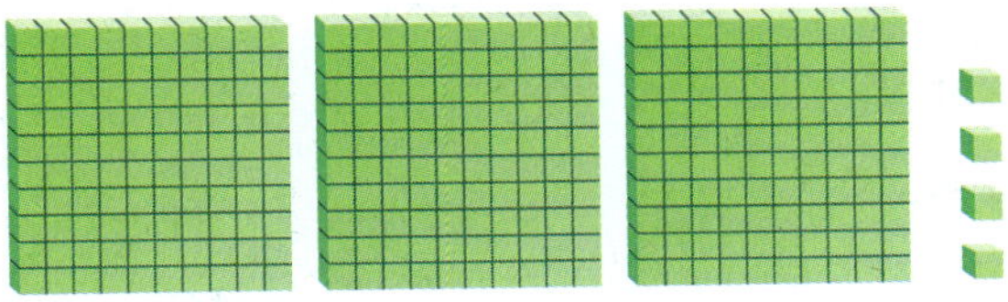

Hundreds	Tens	Ones

______

______ + ______ + ______

6.

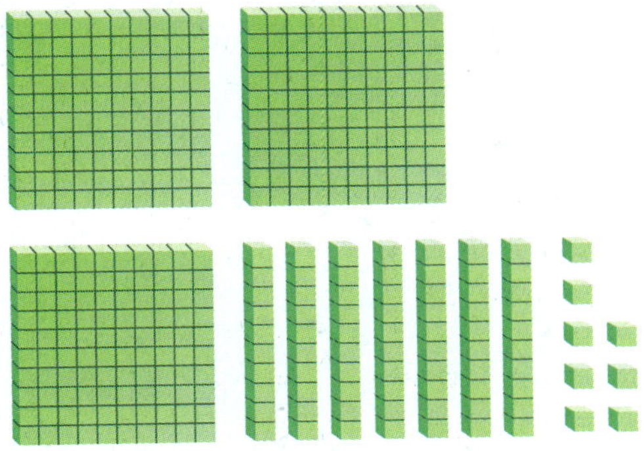

Hundreds	Tens	Ones

______

______ + ______ + ______

7.

Hundreds	Tens	Ones

______

______ + ______ + ______

© Houghton Mifflin Harcourt Publishing Company

PROBLEM SOLVING

Write Math

Write the number that answers the riddle. Use the chart.

8. A model for my number has 4 ones blocks, 5 tens blocks, and 1 hundreds block. What number am I?

Hundreds	Tens	Ones

_____

9. H.O.T. The hundreds digit of my number is greater than the tens digit. The ones digit is less than the tens digit. What could my number be? Write it in two ways.

_____ + _____ + _____

_____

10. Test Prep Karen has 279 pictures. How many hundreds are in this number?

○ 2 hundreds
○ 7 hundreds
○ 9 hundreds
○ 18 hundreds

© Houghton Mifflin Harcourt Publishing Company

TAKE HOME ACTIVITY • Say a 3-digit number, such as 546. Have your child draw a quick picture for that number.

FOR MORE PRACTICE: Standards Practice Book, pp. P31–P32

Name ______________________________

Place Value to 1,000

Essential Question How do you know the values of the digits in numbers?

COMMON CORE STANDARD CC.2.NBT.1
Understand place value.

Listen and Draw REAL WORLD

Write the numbers. Then draw quick pictures.

________ sheets of color paper

Hundreds	Tens	Ones

________ sheets of plain paper

Hundreds	Tens	Ones

FOR THE TEACHER • Read the following. There are 245 sheets of color paper in the supply closet. There are 458 sheets of plain paper by the computer table. Have children write each number and draw quick pictures to show the numbers.

Math Talk **Describe** how 5 tens is different from 5 hundreds.

MATHEMATICAL PRACTICES

© Houghton Mifflin Harcourt Publishing Company

Model and Draw

The place of a digit in a number tells its value.

327

The 3 in 327 has a value of 3 hundreds, or 300.
The 2 in 327 has a value of 2 tens, or 20.
The 7 in 327 has a value of 7 ones, or 7.

There are 10 hundreds in 1 **thousand**.

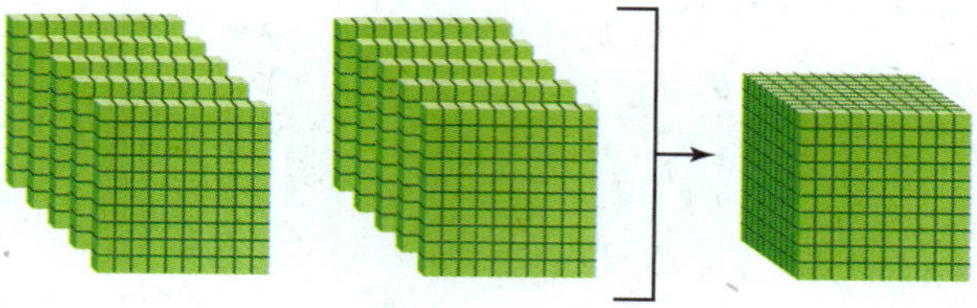

1,000

The 1 is in the thousands place and has a value of 1 thousand.

Share and Show

Math Board

Circle the value or the meaning of the red digit.

1. 702	2 ones	2 tens	2 hundreds
2. 459	500	50	5
3. 362	3 hundreds	3 tens	3 ones

© Houghton Mifflin Harcourt Publishing Company

Name ____________________

On Your Own

Circle the value or the meaning of the red digit.

4. 549	400	40	4
5. 607	7 ones	7 tens	7 hundreds
6. 1,000	1 one	1 hundred	1 thousand
7. 914	90	900	9,000
8. 380	800	80	8
9. 692	6 ones	6 tens	6 hundreds

H.O.T. Write the number that matches the clues.

10. Clues:

- The value of my hundreds digit is 300.
- The value of my tens digit is 0.
- The value of my ones digit is an even number greater than 7.

The number is ________.

© Houghton Mifflin Harcourt Publishing Company

PROBLEM SOLVING REAL WORLD

Write Math

11. Richard is making a Venn diagram. Where in the diagram should he write the other numbers?

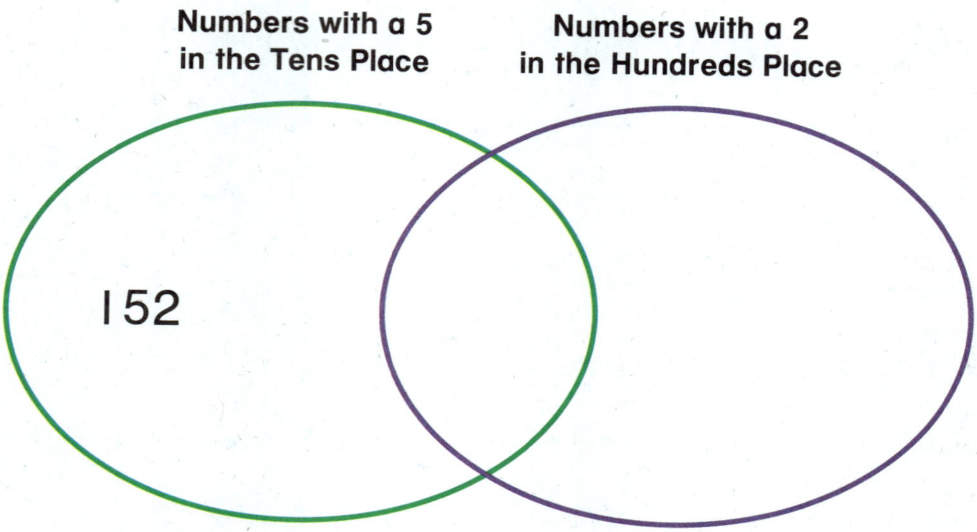

~~152~~
215
454
257
352
205
250

---

12. H.O.T. Describe where 752 should be written in the diagram. Explain your answer.

____

____

____

13. **Test Prep** Which of these numbers has the digit 4 in the tens place?

- ○ 64
- ○ 149
- ○ 437
- ○ 504

TAKE HOME ACTIVITY • Ask your child to write 3-digit numbers, such as "a number with 2 hundreds" and "a number with a 9 in the ones place."

FOR MORE PRACTICE:
Standards Practice Book, pp. P33–P34

© Houghton Mifflin Harcourt Publishing Company

Name ______________________________________

Number Names

Essential Question How do you write 3-digit numbers using words?

COMMON CORE STANDARD CC.2.NBT.3
Understand place value.

Listen and Draw

Write the missing numbers in the chart. Then find and circle the word form of these numbers below.

	12	13		15	16	17	18	19	20
21	22	23	24	25	26	27	28		30
31	32	33	34		36	37	38	39	40
41	42	43	44	45		47	48	49	50
51		53	54	55	56	57	58	59	60

forty-one　　ninety-two　　fourteen

eleven　　thirty-five　　forty-six

fifty-three　　twenty-nine　　fifty-two

Math Talk
Describe how to use words to write the number with a 5 in the tens place and a 7 in the ones place.

MATHEMATICAL PRACTICES

HOME CONNECTION • In this activity, your child reviewed the word form of numbers less than 100.

© Houghton Mifflin Harcourt Publishing Company

Model and Draw

You can use words to write 3-digit numbers.
First, look at the hundreds digit. Then, look at the tens digit and ones digit together.

245 → two hundred forty-five

713 → seven hundred thirteen

Share and Show

Math Board

Write the number using words.

1. 506

five hundred six

2. 189

3. 328

Write the number.

4. four hundred fifteen

5. two hundred ninety-one

6. six hundred three

7. eight hundred forty-seven

© Houghton Mifflin Harcourt Publishing Company

Name ________________

On Your Own

Write the number.

8. five hundred eighty

______

9. one hundred fifty-five

______

10. seven hundred seventeen

______

11. three hundred ninety

______

12. six hundred forty-three

______

13. nine hundred twelve

______

14. four hundred twenty-six

______

15. eight hundred seventy-one

______

Write the number using words.

16. 200

____

17. 632

____

18. 568

____

19. 321

____

© Houghton Mifflin Harcourt Publishing Company

PROBLEM SOLVING REAL WORLD

Write Math

Circle the answer for each problem.

20. Derek counts one hundred ninety cars. Which is another way to write this number?

119

190

910

21. Alma counted two hundred sixty-eight leaves. Which is another way to write this number?

$2 + 6 + 8$

$20 + 60 + 8$

$200 + 60 + 8$

22. H.O.T. My 3-digit number has a 4 in the hundreds place. It has a greater digit in the tens place than in the ones place. The sum of the digits is 6. What is my number? ________

Write the number using words.

____

23. Test Prep There are five hundred thirty-seven chairs at the school. Which shows this number?

○ 573
○ 537
○ 530
○ 357

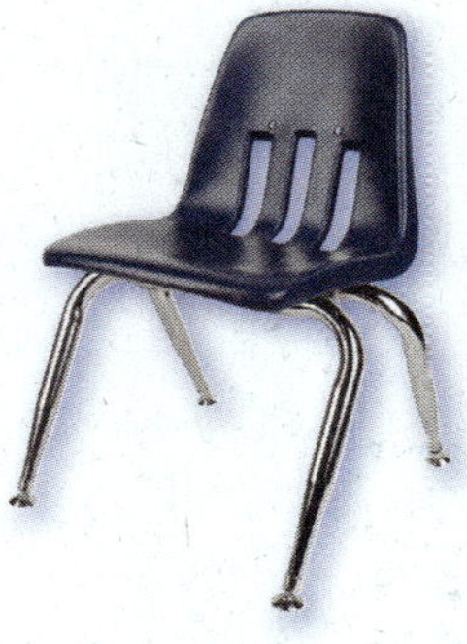

TAKE HOME ACTIVITY • Ask your child to write the number 940 using words.

FOR MORE PRACTICE:
Standards Practice Book, pp. P35–P36

© Houghton Mifflin Harcourt Publishing Company

Name ______________________________

Lesson 2.7

Different Forms of Numbers

Essential Question What are three ways to write a 3-digit number?

COMMON CORE STANDARD CC.2.NBT.3
Understand place value.

Listen and Draw REAL WORLD

Write the number. Use the digits to write how many hundreds, tens, and ones.

______

____ hundreds ____ tens ____ ones

______

____ hundreds ____ tens ____ ones

______

____ hundreds ____ tens ____ ones

FOR THE TEACHER • Read the following: Evan has 426 marbles. How many hundreds, tens, and ones are in 426? Continue the activity for 204 and 341.

Math Talk How many hundreds are in 368? **Explain.**

MATHEMATICAL PRACTICES

© Houghton Mifflin Harcourt Publishing Company

Model and Draw

You can use a quick picture to show a number.
You can write a number in different ways.

five hundred thirty-six

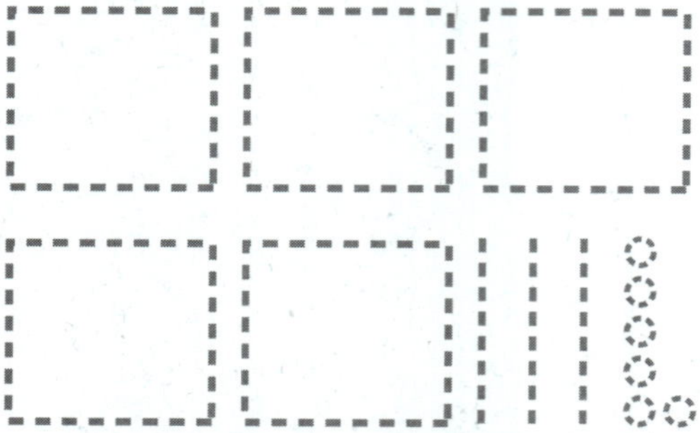

5 hundreds 3 tens 6 ones

500 + 30 + 6

536

Share and Show

Math Board

Read the number and draw a quick picture.
Then write the number in different ways.

1. four hundred seven

____ hundreds ____ tens ____ ones

______ + ______ + ______

______

2. three hundred twenty-five

____ hundreds ____ tens ____ ones

______ + ______ + ______

______

3. two hundred fifty-three

____ hundreds ____ tens ____ ones

______ + ______ + ______

______

© Houghton Mifflin Harcourt Publishing Company

Name ______________________________

On Your Own

Read the number and draw a quick picture.
Then write the number in different ways.

4. one hundred seventy-two

____ hundred ____ tens ____ ones

______ + ______ + ______

______

5. three hundred forty-six

____ hundreds ____ tens ____ ones

______ + ______ + ______

______

6. two hundred sixty-four

____ hundreds ____ tens ____ ones

______ + ______ + ______

______

Use words to write a number that matches the clue.

7. H.O.T. In this 3-digit number, there is a zero in the ones place.

____

TAKE HOME ACTIVITY • Ask your child to show the number 315 in three different ways.

© Houghton Mifflin Harcourt Publishing Company

FOR MORE PRACTICE:
Standards Practice Book, pp. F37–P38

Name ______________________________

Mid-Chapter Checkpoint

Concepts and Skills

Circle tens to make 1 hundred. Write the number in different ways. (CC.2.NBT.1)

1. 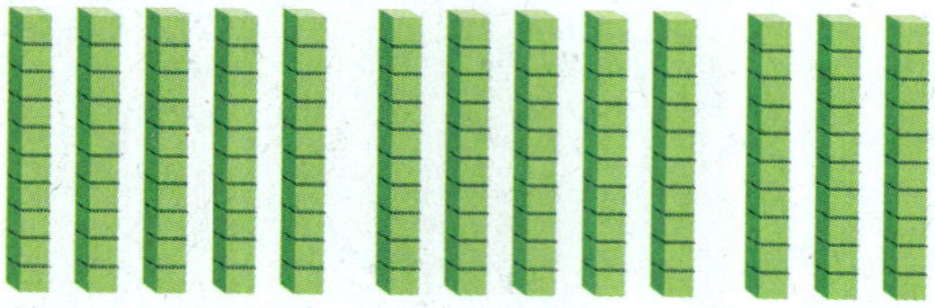

_____ tens

_____ hundred _____ tens

____

Write how many hundreds, tens, and ones are in the model. Write the number in two ways. (CC.2.NBT.1)

2. 

Hundreds	Tens	Ones

____

_______ + _______ + _______

Circle the value or the meaning of the red digit. (CC.2.NBT.1)

3. 528	5	50	500
4. 674	4 ones	4 tens	4 hundreds

Test Prep

5. Which is another way to write the number 645? (CC.2.NBT.3)

- ○ six hundred forty-five
- ○ 600 + 4 + 5
- ○ six hundred fourteen
- ○ 60 + 40 + 5

© Houghton Mifflin Harcourt Publishing Company

Name ____________________

Algebra • Different Ways to Show Numbers

COMMON CORE STANDARD CC.2.NBT.3
Understand place value.

Essential Question How can you use blocks or quick pictures to show the value of a number in different ways?

Listen and Draw REAL WORLD

Draw quick pictures to solve.
Write how many tens and ones.

_____ tens _____ ones

_____ tens _____ ones

Math Talk **Describe** how you found different ways to show 35 books.

MATHEMATICAL PRACTICES

FOR THE TEACHER • Read this problem to children. Mrs. Peabody has 35 books on a cart to take to classrooms. She can use boxes that each hold 10 books and she can also place single books on the cart. What are two different ways she can put the books on the cart?

© Houghton Mifflin Harcourt Publishing Company

Model and Draw

Here are two ways to show 148.

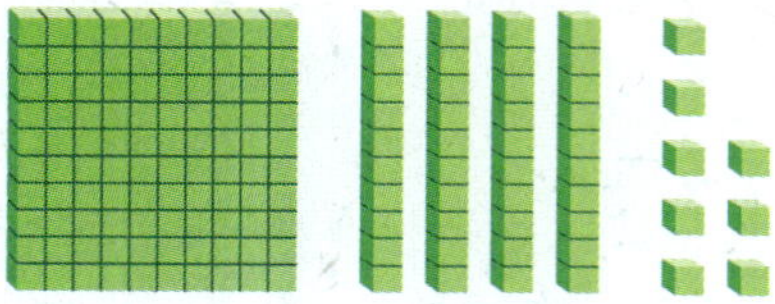

Hundreds	Tens	Ones
1	4	8

Hundreds	Tens	Ones
0	14	8

Share and Show

Math Board

Write how many hundreds, tens, and ones are in the model.

1. 213

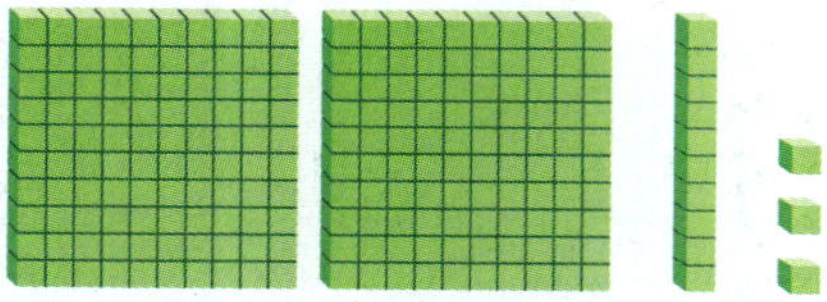

Hundreds	Tens	Ones

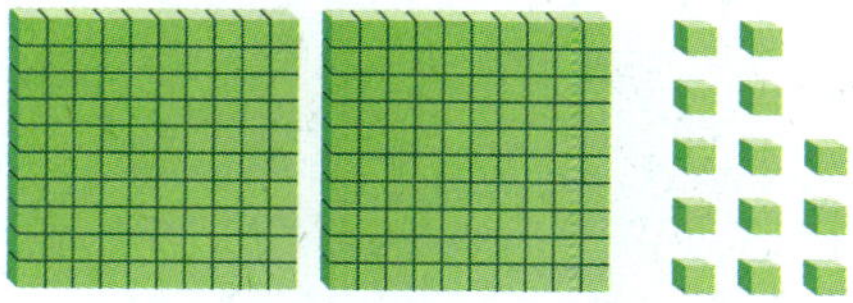

Hundreds	Tens	Ones

2. 132

Hundreds	Tens	Ones

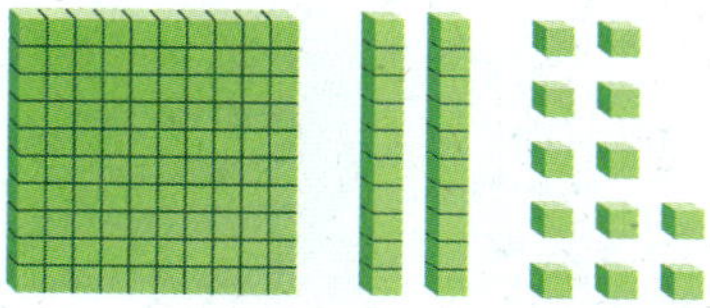

Hundreds	Tens	Ones

© Houghton Mifflin Harcourt Publishing Company

Name ______________________________

On Your Own

Write how many hundreds, tens, and ones are in the model.

3. 144

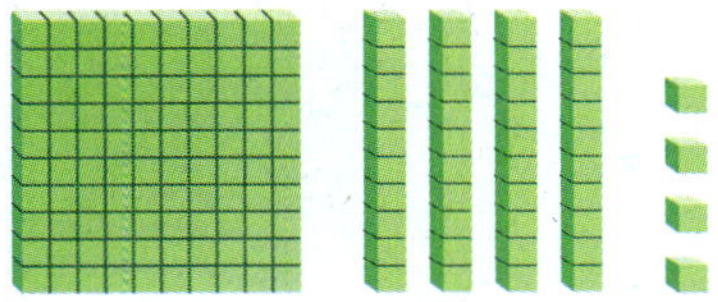

Hundreds	Tens	Ones

Hundreds	Tens	Ones

4. 204

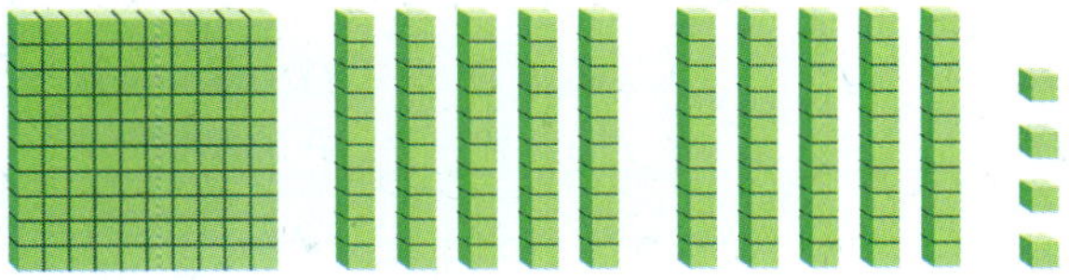

Hundreds	Tens	Ones

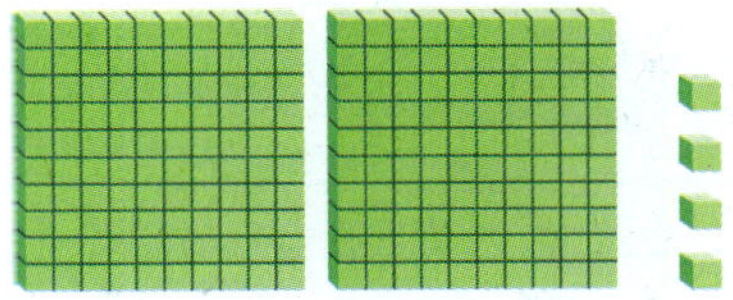

Hundreds	Tens	Ones

5. 157

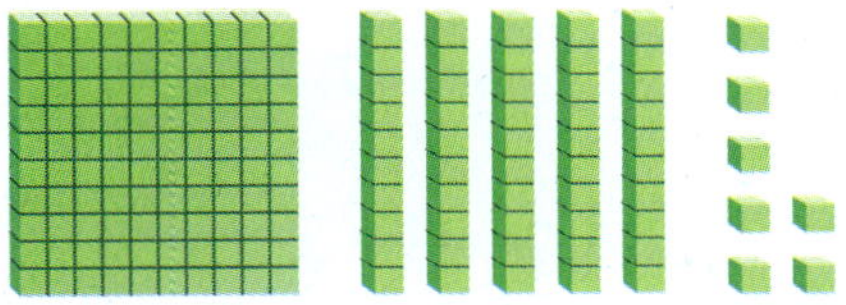

Hundreds	Tens	Ones

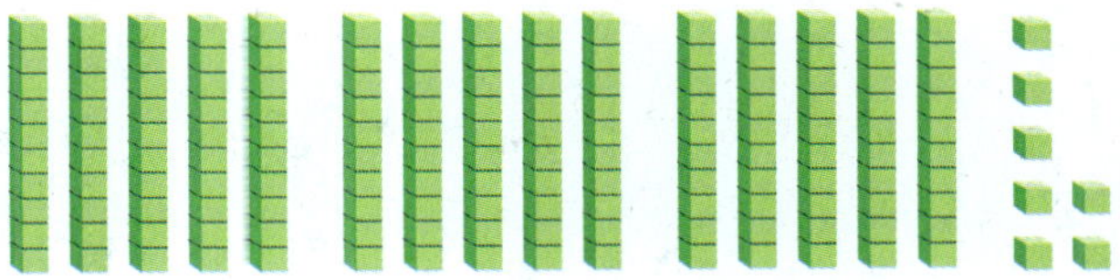

Hundreds	Tens	Ones

© Houghton Mifflin Harcourt Publishing Company

PROBLEM SOLVING REAL WORLD

Write Math

Marbles are sold in boxes, in bags, or as single marbles. Each box has 10 bags of marbles in it. Each bag has 10 marbles in it.

6. Draw pictures to show two ways to buy 324 marbles.

7. H.O.T. There is only one box of marbles in the store. There are many bags of marbles and single marbles. Draw a picture to show a way to buy 312 marbles.

8. ★ **Test Prep** What number is shown with these blocks?

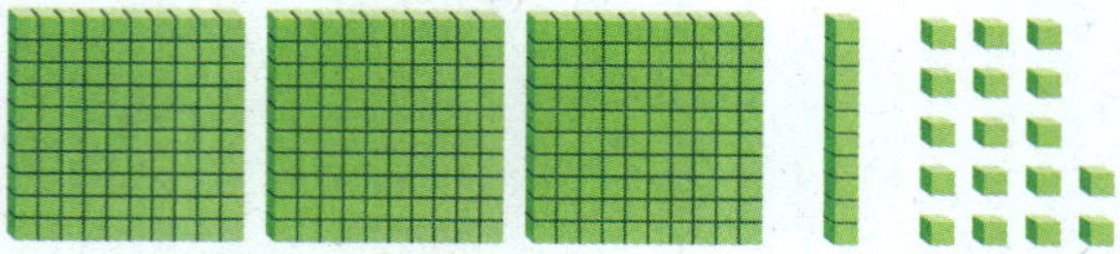

- ○ 173
- ○ 317
- ○ 318
- ○ 327

TAKE HOME ACTIVITY • Write the number 156. Have your child draw quick pictures of two ways to show this number.

FOR MORE PRACTICE: Standards Practice Book, pp. P39–P40

© Houghton Mifflin Harcourt Publishing Company

Name ______________________________

Count On and Count Back by 10 and 100

Essential Question How do you use place value to find 10 more, 10 less, 100 more, or 100 less than a 3-digit number?

COMMON CORE STANDARD CC.2.NBT.8
Use place value understanding and properties of operations to add and subtract.

Listen and Draw REAL WORLD

Draw quick pictures for the numbers.

Girls

Hundreds	Tens	Ones

Boys

Hundreds	Tens	Ones

Math Talk **Describe** how the two numbers are different.

MATHEMATICAL PRACTICES

FOR THE TEACHER • Tell children that there are 342 girls at Center School. Have children draw quick pictures for 342. Then tell them that there are 352 boys at the school. Have them draw quick pictures for 352.

© Houghton Mifflin Harcourt Publishing Company

Model and Draw

You can show 10 less or 10 more than a number by changing the digit in the tens place.

10 less than 264

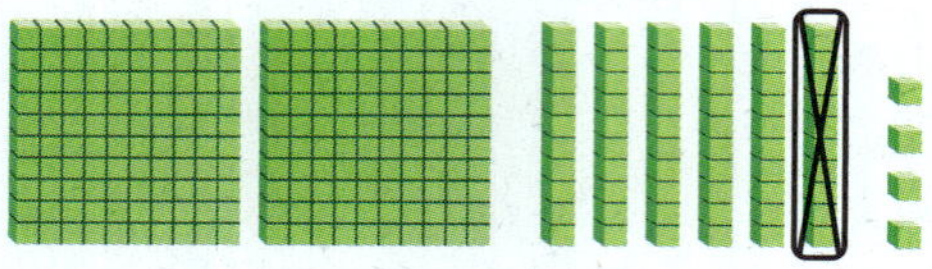

Hundreds	Tens	Ones
2	5	4

10 more than 264

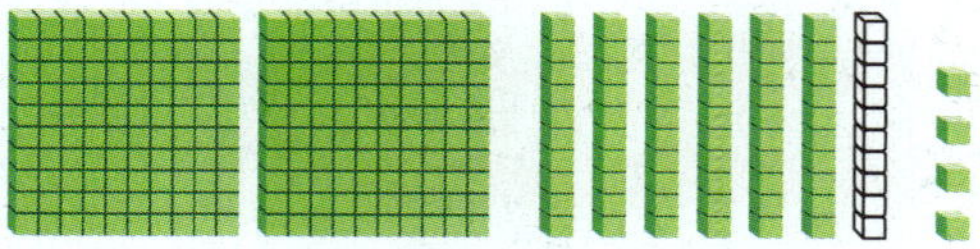

Hundreds	Tens	Ones
2	7	4

You can show 100 less or 100 more than a number by changing the digit in the hundreds place.

100 less than 264

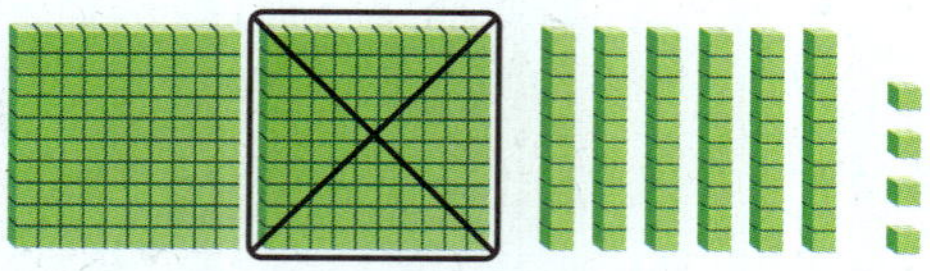

Hundreds	Tens	Ones
1	6	4

100 more than 264

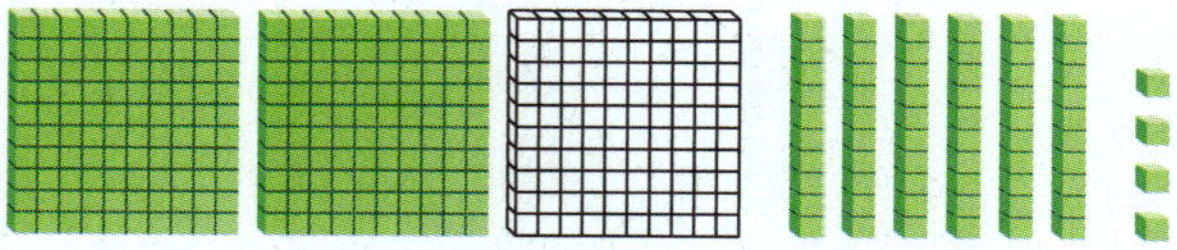

Hundreds	Tens	Ones
3	6	4

Share and Show

Math Board

Write the number.

1. 10 more than 648 ______

2. 100 less than 513 ______

3. 100 more than 329 ______

4. 10 less than 827 ______

© Houghton Mifflin Harcourt Publishing Company

Name ______________________________

On Your Own

Write the number.

5. 10 more than 471 ______	6. 10 less than 143 ______
7. 100 more than 555 ______	8. 100 less than 757 ______
9. 100 more than 900 ______	10. 10 less than 689 ______
11. 100 less than 712 ______	12. 10 less than 254 ______
13. 10 more than 986 ______	14. 100 less than 392 ______
15. 100 more than 485 ______	16. 10 more than 820 ______

H.O.T. Write numbers to make each sentence true.

17. 854 is ______ more than 844.

18. ______ is 100 less than 352 and 100 more than ______.

19. ______ is ______ more than 751.

© Houghton Mifflin Harcourt Publishing Company

PROBLEM SOLVING REAL WORLD

Write Math

Solve.

20. Juan's book has 248 pages. This is 10 more pages than there are in Kevin's book. How many pages are in Kevin's book?

_______ pages

21. There are 217 pictures in Tina's book. There are 100 fewer pictures in Mark's book. How many pictures are in Mark's book?

_______ pictures

22. H.O.T. Use the clues to answer the question.

Clues:

- Shawn reads 213 pages.
- Maria reads 100 more pages than Shawn.
- Gavin reads 10 fewer pages than Maria.

How many pages does Gavin read?

_______ pages

23. **Test Prep** Which number is 100 more than 786?

○ 686
○ 776
○ 796
○ 886

TAKE HOME ACTIVITY • Write the number 596. Have your child name the number that is 100 more than 596.

© Houghton Mifflin Harcourt Publishing Company

FOR MORE PRACTICE:
Standards Practice Book, pp. P41–P42

Name ______________________________

Algebra • Number Patterns

Essential Question How does place value help you identify and extend counting patterns?

COMMON CORE STANDARD CC.2.NBT.8
Use place value understanding and properties of operations to add and subtract.

Listen and Draw REAL WORLD

Shade the numbers in the counting pattern.

801	802	803	804	805	806	807	808	809	810
811	812	813	814	815	816	817	818	819	820
821	822	823	824	825	826	827	828	829	830
831	832	833	834	835	836	837	838	839	840
841	842	843	844	845	846	847	848	849	850
851	852	853	854	855	856	857	858	859	860
861	862	863	864	865	866	867	868	869	870
871	872	873	874	875	876	877	878	879	880
881	882	883	884	885	886	887	888	889	890
891	892	893	894	895	896	897	898	899	900

FOR THE TEACHER • Read the following problem and discuss how children can use a counting pattern to solve. At Blossom Bakery, 823 muffins were sold in the morning. In the afternoon, four packages of 10 muffins were sold. How many muffins were sold that day?

Math Talk
What number is next in the counting pattern you see? **Explain.**

MATHEMATICAL PRACTICES

Model and Draw

Look at the digits in the numbers. What two numbers are next in the counting pattern?

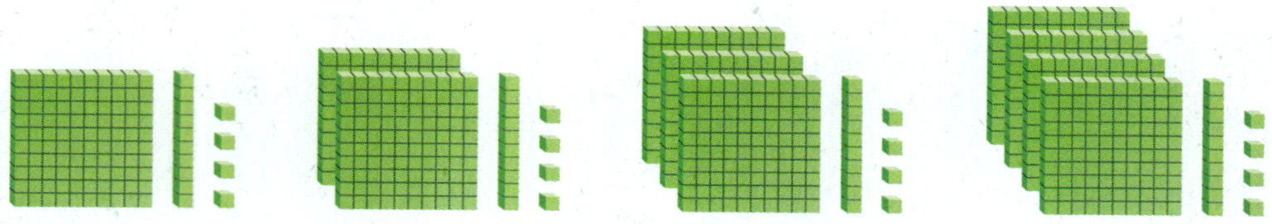

114, 214, 314, 414, ■, ■

The __________ digit changes by one each time.

The next two numbers are ______ and ______.

Share and Show

Math Board

Look at the digits to find the next two numbers.

1. 137, 147, 157, 167, ■, ■

The next two numbers are ______ and ______.

2. 245, 345, 445, 545, ■, ■

The next two numbers are ______ and ______.

3. 421, 431, 441, 451, ■, ■

The next two numbers are ______ and ______.

4. 389, 489, 589, 689, ■, ■

The next two numbers are ______ and ______.

© Houghton Mifflin Harcourt Publishing Company

Name ______________________

On Your Own

Look at the digits to find the next two numbers.

5. 193, 293, 393, 493, ■, ■

The next two numbers are ________ and ________.

6. 484, 494, 504, 514, ■, ■

The next two numbers are ________ and ________.

7. 500, 600, 700, 800, ■, ■

The next two numbers are ________ and ________.

8. 655, 665, 675, 685, ■, ■.

The next two numbers are ________ and ________.

H.O.T. Follow the directions. Write your own counting patterns.

9. Write a pattern in which the hundreds digit changes by one from number to number.

________, ________, ________, ________, ________

10. Write a pattern in which the tens digit changes by one from number to number.

________, ________, ________, ________, ________

© Houghton Mifflin Harcourt Publishing Company

PROBLEM SOLVING REAL WORLD

Write Math

Solve.

11. Luke wrote a number pattern starting with 237. He counted on by hundreds. Write the missing digits to show his pattern.

2 3 7, 3 __ __, __ 3 __, 5 __ __, __ __ 7

12. H.O.T. There were 135 pennies in a jar. After Robin put more pennies into the jar, there were 175 pennies in the jar. How many groups of 10 pennies did she put into the jar?

________ groups of 10 pennies

Explain how you solved the problem.

____

____

____

13. **Test Prep** Sandra wrote a number pattern starting with 806. She counted on by tens. Which of the following numbers could be in her pattern?

- ○ 706
- ○ 810
- ○ 826
- ○ 960

TAKE HOME ACTIVITY • With your child, take turns writing number patterns in which you count on by tens or by hundreds.

© Houghton Mifflin Harcourt Publishing Company

FOR MORE PRACTICE:
Standards Practice Book, pp. P43–P44

Name ____________________

Problem Solving • Compare Numbers

Essential Question How can you make a model to solve a problem about comparing numbers?

PROBLEM SOLVING
Lesson 2.11

COMMON CORE STANDARD CC.2.NBT.4
Understand place value.

Children bought 217 cartons of chocolate milk and 188 cartons of plain milk. Did they buy more cartons of chocolate milk or plain milk?

Unlock the Problem REAL WORLD

What do I need to find?

if the children bought more cartons of chocolate milk or plain milk

What information do I need to use?

_______ cartons of chocolate milk

_______ cartons of plain milk

Show how to solve the problem.

Model the numbers. Draw quick pictures of your models.

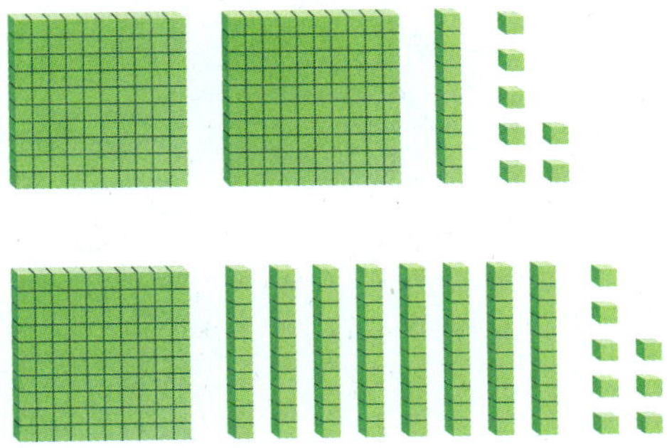

The children bought more cartons of ____________________ milk.

HOME CONNECTION • Your child used base-ten blocks to represent the numbers in the problem. These models were used as a tool for comparing numbers to solve the problem.

© Houghton Mifflin Harcourt Publishing Company

Try Another Problem

Model the numbers. Draw quick pictures to show how you solved the problem.

- What do I need to find?
- What information do I need to use?

1. At the zoo, there are 137 birds and 142 reptiles. Are there more birds or more reptiles at the zoo?

more ______________

2. Tom's book has 105 pages. Delia's book has 109 pages. Whose book has fewer pages?

______________ book

Math Talk

Explain what you did to solve the second problem.

MATHEMATICAL PRACTICES

© Houghton Mifflin Harcourt Publishing Company

Name ____________________

Share and Show

Math Board

Model the numbers. Draw quick pictures to show how you solved the problem.

3. Mary's puzzle has 164 pieces. Jake's puzzle has 180 pieces. Whose puzzle has more pieces?

____________ puzzle

4. There are 246 children at Dan's school. There are 251 children at Karen's school. At which school are there fewer children?

____________ school

5. There are 131 crayons in a box. There are 128 crayons in a bag. Are there more crayons in the box or in the bag?

in the ____________

6. There are 308 books in the first room. There are 273 books in the second room. In which room are there fewer books?

in the ____________ room

© Houghton Mifflin Harcourt Publishing Company

On Your Own

Choose a way to solve.
Write or draw to explain.

Write Math

7. Ms. Tyler sold 125 small cards and 118 large cards. Did she sell fewer small cards or fewer large cards?

fewer ____________ cards

8. A number has a 1 in the tens place. Which of these could be the number? Circle it.

three hundred fifty-one

one hundred fifty

three hundred fifteen

9. H.O.T. Which of these is another way to write the number 257? Circle it.

2 hundreds 57 tens

25 tens 7 ones

25 hundreds 7 ones

10. Test Prep Corey's book has 256 pages. Which of these numbers is greater than 256?

- ○ 157
- ○ 239
- ○ 281
- ○ 198

TAKE HOME ACTIVITY • Ask your child to explain how he or she solved one of the problems on this page.

FOR MORE PRACTICE:
Standards Practice Book, pp. P45–P46

© Houghton Mifflin Harcourt Publishing Company

Name ______________________________

Algebra • Compare Numbers

Essential Question How do you compare 3-digit numbers?

COMMON CORE STANDARD CC.2.NBT.4
Understand place value.

Listen and Draw REAL WORLD

Draw quick pictures to solve the problem.

More ______________ were at the park.

FOR THE TEACHER • Read the following problem and have children draw quick pictures to compare the numbers. There were 125 butterflies and 132 birds at the park. Were there more butterflies or more birds at the park?

Math Talk
Explain how you compared the numbers.

MATHEMATICAL PRACTICES

© Houghton Mifflin Harcourt Publishing Company

Model and Draw

Use place value to **compare** numbers. Start by looking at the digits in the greatest place value position first.

> is greater than
< is less than
= is equal to

Hundreds	Tens	Ones
4	8	3
5	7	0

4 hundreds < 5 hundreds

483 (<) 570

Hundreds	Tens	Ones
3	5	2
3	4	6

The hundreds are equal.

5 tens > 4 tens

352 (>) 346

Share and Show Math Board

Compare the numbers. Write >, <, or =.

1.

Hundreds	Tens	Ones
2	3	9
1	7	9

239 ◯ 179

2.

Hundreds	Tens	Ones
4	3	5
4	3	7

435 ◯ 437

3. 764
674

764 ◯ 674

4. 519
572

519 ◯ 572

© Houghton Mifflin Harcourt Publishing Company

Name ____________________

On Your Own

Compare the numbers. Write >, <, or =.

5. 378
504

378 ◯ 504

6. 821
821

821 ◯ 821

7. 560
439

560 ◯ 439

8. 934
943

934 ◯ 943

9. 475
475

475 ◯ 475

10. 736
687

736 ◯ 687

H.O.T. Write a 3-digit number in the box that makes the comparison true.

11. 526 < ☐

12. 319 > ☐

13. ☐ > 782

14. ☐ < 131

© Houghton Mifflin Harcourt Publishing Company

PROBLEM SOLVING REAL WORLD

Write Math

Solve. Write or draw to explain.

15. Mrs. York has 358 stickers.
Mr. Reed has 372 stickers.
Who has more stickers?

____

16. H.O.T. Seth has some number cards. Use the digits on these cards to make two 3-digit numbers. Use each card only once. Compare the numbers.

1	2	5
6	3	8

______ ◯ ______

17. ★ **Test Prep** Which of the following is true?

- ○ 453 > 354
- ○ 253 < 164
- ○ 391 > 417
- ○ 528 < 490

TAKE HOME ACTIVITY • Have your child explain how to compare the numbers 281 and 157.

FOR MORE PRACTICE:
Standards Practice Book, pp. P47–P48

© Houghton Mifflin Harcourt Publishing Company

Name ____________________

Chapter 2 Review/Test

Vocabulary

Use a word in the box to complete each sentence.

hundred
thousand
ten

1. 10 hundreds is the same as

   1 ____________________. (p. 74)

2. 10 tens is the same as 1 ____________________. (p. 58)

Concepts and Skills

Write how many tens. Circle groups of 10 tens.
Write how many hundreds. Write the number. (CC.2.NBT.1a, CC.2.NBT.1b)

3. 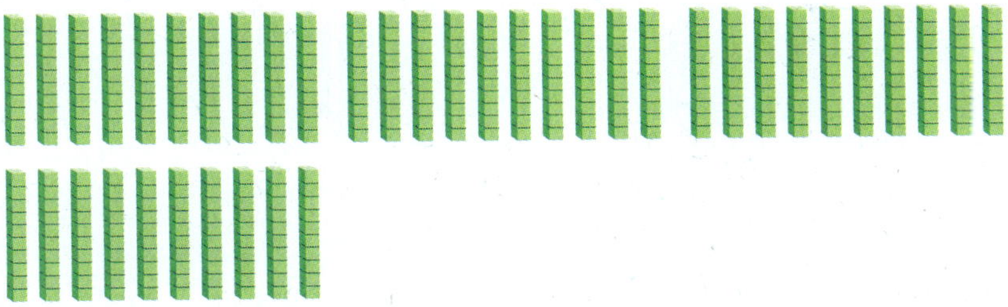

_____ tens

_____ hundreds

____

Read the number and draw a quick picture.
Then write the number in different ways. (CC.2.NBT.3)

4. two hundred thirty-five

_____ hundreds _____ tens _____ ones

________ + ________ + ________

____

Look at the digits to find the next two numbers. (CC.2.NBT.8)

5. 267, 367, 467, 567, ■, ■

The next two numbers are ________ and ________.

© Houghton Mifflin Harcourt Publishing Company

Fill in the bubble for the correct answer choice.

TEST PREP

6. Which is another way to name 14 tens? (CC.2.NBT.1)

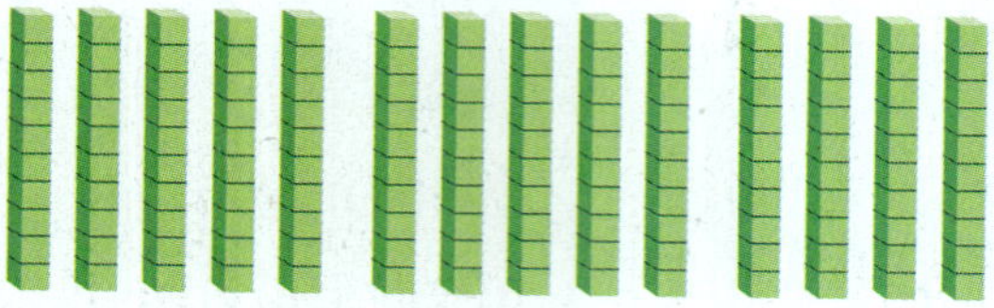

- ○ 1 ten 4 ones
- ○ 1 hundred 4 tens
- ○ 1 thousand 4 hundreds
- ○ 14 ones

---

7. There is a 3-digit number that has the digit 3 in the ones place, the digit 2 in the tens place, and the digit 4 in the hundreds place. What is the number? (CC.2.NBT.1)

- ○ 324
- ○ 342
- ○ 423
- ○ 432

---

8. Dylan has 324 baseball cards. Malia has 351 baseball cards.

Which of the following is true? (CC.2.NBT.4)

- ○ $324 > 351$
- ○ $324 < 351$
- ○ $324 > 432$
- ○ $351 < 243$

© Houghton Mifflin Harcourt Publishing Company

Name ______________________________

TEST PREP

Fill in the bubble for the correct answer choice.

9. What number is shown with these blocks? (CC.2.NBT.3)

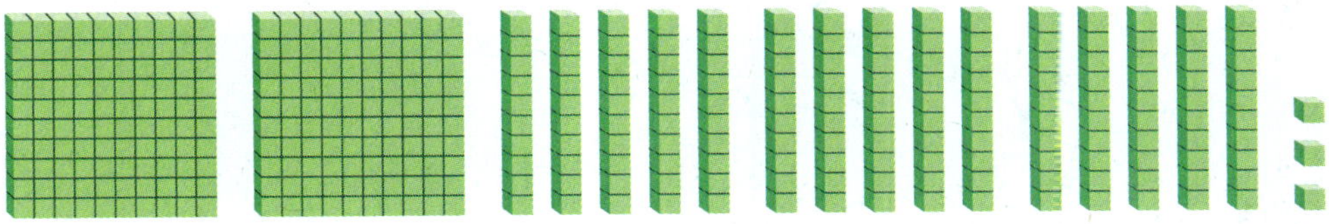

○ 173
○ 253
○ 353
○ 380

10. Mr. Grant has 437 sheets of paper. Ms. Kim has 100 fewer sheets of paper than Mr. Grant. How many sheets of paper does Ms. Kim have? (CC.2.NBT.8)

○ 337
○ 427
○ 447
○ 537

11. Which is another way to write the number 582? (CC.2.NBT.3)

○ five hundred eighteen
○ 500 + 8 + 2
○ five hundred twenty-eight
○ 500 + 80 + 2

© Houghton Mifflin Harcourt Publishing Company

Constructed Response

12. Write the number that is 10 less than 357 and the number that is 100 more than 357. (CC.2.NBT.8)

_______ 10 less   _______ 100 more

Explain how you found these numbers.

____

____

____

Performance Task (CC.2.NBT.1a, CC.2.NBT.3)

13. There are 100 books on the shelves. On the table, there are 15 stacks of books with 10 books in each stack. What 3-digit number tells how many books there are? _______

Draw a picture to explain your answer.

What are two other ways to write this number?

_______________________   _______________________

© Houghton Mifflin Harcourt Publishing Company

All About Animals

by John Hudson

© Houghton Mifflin Harcourt Publishing Company

COMMON CORE

CRITICAL AREA Building fluency with addition and subtraction

The giraffe is the tallest land animal in the world. Adult giraffes are 13 to 17 feet tall. Newborn giraffes are about 6 feet tall.

A group of 5 giraffes drinks water at a watering hole. A group of 5 giraffes eats leaves from trees. How many giraffes are there in all?

_____ giraffes

Science

How do giraffes care for their young?

© Houghton Mifflin Harcourt Publishing Company

The ostrich is the largest bird in the world. Ostriches cannot fly, but they can run fast. Ostrich eggs weigh about 3 pounds each! Several ostriches will lay eggs in a shared nest.

There are 6 eggs in a nest. Then 5 more eggs are put in that nest. How many eggs are in the nest now?

_____ eggs

How do ostriches care for their young?

© Houghton Mifflin Harcourt Publishing Company

Kangaroos can move quickly by jumping with their two back legs. When they are moving slowly, they use all four legs.

Western gray kangaroos live in groups called mobs. There are 8 kangaroos in a mob. 4 more kangaroos join the mob. How many kangaroos are in the mob in all?

_____ kangaroos

How do kangaroos care for their young?

© Houghton Mifflin Harcourt Publishing Company

Wild boars like to eat roots. They use their tough snouts to dig. Wild boars can be up to 6 feet long.

Wild boars live in groups called sounders. There is one sounder of 14 boars. If 7 of the boars are eating, how many boars are not eating?

_____ boars

© Houghton Mifflin Harcourt Publishing Company

How do wild boars care for their young?

Moose are the largest kind of deer. Male moose have antlers that may be 5 to 6 feet wide. Moose can trot and gallop. They are also good swimmers!

A ranger saw 7 moose in the morning and 6 moose in the afternoon. How many moose did the ranger see that day?

_____ moose

Science

How do moose care for their young?

© Houghton Mifflin Harcourt Publishing Company

Name ____________________

Write About the Story

Choose one kind of animal.
Draw a picture and write your own story about that kind of animal.
Use addition in your story.

Vocabulary Review

add   in all

giraffe

ostrich

kangaroo

Write Math

____

____

____

____

© Houghton Mifflin Harcourt Publishing Company

How many eggs are there?

Draw more ostrich eggs in each nest. Write an addition sentence below each nest to show how many eggs are in each nest now.

____

____

Choose a different animal from the story. Write another story that uses addition.

© Houghton Mifflin Harcourt Publishing Company

Chapter 3 Basic Facts and Relationships

Curious About Math with Curious George

Parrot fish live near coral reefs in tropical ocean waters. They use their sharp teeth to scrape food off of the coral.

Suppose 10 parrot fish are eating at a coral reef. 3 of the fish swim away. How many fish are still eating?

© Houghton Mifflin Harcourt Publishing Company
Curious George by Margret and H.A. Rey. Copyright © 2010 by Houghton Mifflin Harcourt Publishing Company. All rights reserved. The character Curious George®, including without limitation the character's name and the character's likenesses, are registered trademarks of Houghton Mifflin Harcourt Publishing Company.

Name ______________________________

Show What You Know

Use Symbols to Add

Use the picture. Use + and = to complete the addition sentence.

1.

3 ◯ 1 ◯ 4

2.

2 ◯ 3 ◯ 5

Sums to 10

Write the sum.

3. $\begin{array}{r} 4 \\ +\ 3 \\ \hline \end{array}$

4. $\begin{array}{r} 5 \\ +\ 0 \\ \hline \end{array}$

5. $\begin{array}{r} 2 \\ +\ 7 \\ \hline \end{array}$

6. $\begin{array}{r} 6 \\ +\ 2 \\ \hline \end{array}$

7. $\begin{array}{r} 9 \\ +\ 1 \\ \hline \end{array}$

Doubles and Doubles Plus One

Write the addition sentence.

8.

____ ◯ ____ ◯ ____

9.

____ ◯ ____ ◯ ____

Family note: This page checks your child's understanding of important skills needed for success in Chapter 3.

GO Online Assessment Options Soar to Success Math

© Houghton Mifflin Harcourt Publishing Company

Name ______________________________

Vocabulary Builder

Review Words
addition
subtraction
plus
minus
equals
count on
count back

Visualize It

Sort the review words in the graphic organizer.

Addition Words   **Subtraction** Words

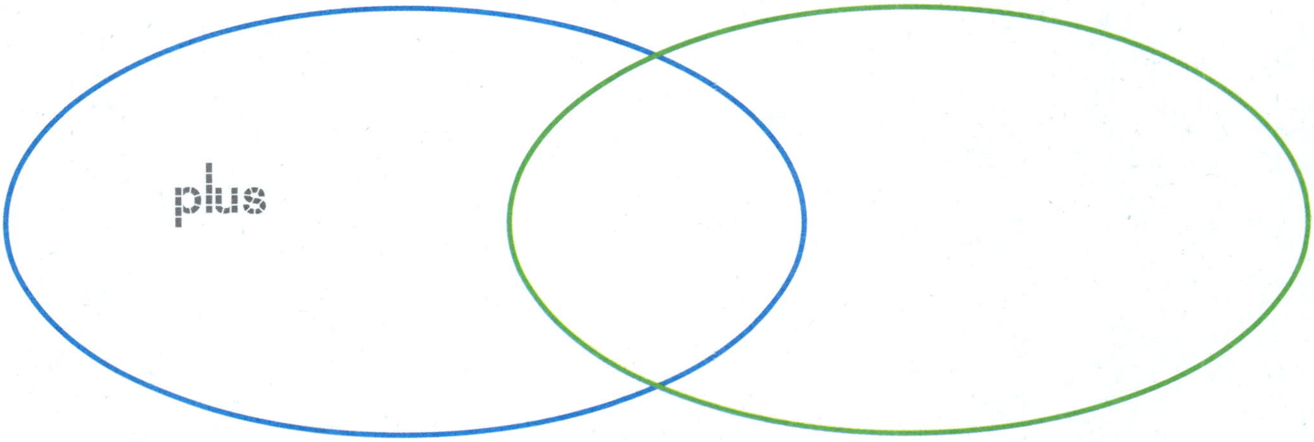

Understand Vocabulary

1. Circle the **addition** sentence.   3 + 6 = 9   9 − 6 = 3

2. Circle the **subtraction** sentence.   8 + 2 = 10   10 − 2 = 8

3. Circle the **count on** fact.   5 − 1 = 4   4 + 1 = 5

4. Circle the **count back** fact.   8 − 2 = 6   6 + 2 = 8

© Houghton Mifflin Harcourt Publishing Company

GO Online • eStudent Edition • Multimedia eGlossary

Game Caterpillar Chase

Materials

- 1 red cube
- 1 blue cube
- 1 number cube

Play with a partner.

1. Put your cube on START.
2. Toss the number cube, and move that many spaces.
3. Say the sum or difference. Your partner checks your answer.
4. Take turns. The first person to get to FINISH wins.

© Houghton Mifflin Harcourt Publishing Company

Name ______________________________

Use Doubles Facts

Essential Question How can you use doubles facts to find sums for near doubles facts?

COMMON CORE STANDARD **CC.2.OA.2**
Add and subtract within 20.

Listen and Draw REAL WORLD

Draw a picture to show the problem. Then write an addition sentence for the problem.

_____ ○ _____ ○ _____

_____ toy cars

FOR THE TEACHER • Read this problem and have children draw a picture for the problem. Nathan has 6 toy cars. Alisha gives him 6 more toy cars. How many toy cars does Nathan have now? After children write an addition sentence, have them name other doubles facts that they know.

Math Talk

Explain why $4 + 4 = 8$ is called a doubles fact.

MATHEMATICAL PRACTICES

© Houghton Mifflin Harcourt Publishing Company

Model and Draw

You can use doubles facts to find **sums** for other facts.

$3 + 4 = ?$	$7 + 6 = ?$
↓	↓
$3 + 3 + 1 = ?$	$7 + 7 - 1 = ?$
$3 + 3 = 6$	$7 + 7 = 14$
$6 + 1 = 7$	$14 - 1 = 13$
So, $3 + 4 =$ _____.	So, $7 + 6 =$ _____.

Share and Show

Math Board

Write a doubles fact you can use to find the sum. Write the sum.

1. $2 + 3 =$ _____

_____ + _____ = _____

2. $4 + 5 =$ _____

_____ + _____ = _____

3. $4 + 3 =$ _____

_____ + _____ = _____

4. $6 + 7 =$ _____

_____ + _____ = _____

5. $5 + 6 =$ _____

_____ + _____ = _____

6. $8 + 7 =$ _____

_____ + _____ = _____

© Houghton Mifflin Harcourt Publishing Company

Name ____________________

On Your Own

Write a doubles fact you can use to find the sum. Write the sum.

7. $3 + 2 =$ ____

____ + ____ = ____

8. $6 + 5 =$ ____

____ + ____ = ____

9. $5 + 4 =$ ____

____ + ____ = ____

10. $3 + 4 =$ ____

____ + ____ = ____

11. $6 + 7 =$ ____

____ + ____ = ____

12. $7 + 8 =$ ____

____ + ____ = ____

13. $8 + 9 =$ ____

____ + ____ = ____

14. $5 + 6 =$ ____

____ + ____ = ____

15. $7 + 6 =$ ____

____ + ____ = ____

16. $9 + 8 =$ ____

____ + ____ = ____

© Houghton Mifflin Harcourt Publishing Company

PROBLEM SOLVING REAL WORLD

Write Math

Solve. Write or draw to explain.

17. Andrea has 8 red buttons and 9 blue buttons. How many buttons does Andrea have?

_______ buttons

18. Henry sees 3 rabbits. Callie sees double that number of rabbits. How many rabbits does Callie see?

_______ rabbits

19. H.O.T. Mr. Norris wrote a doubles fact. It has a sum greater than 6. The numbers that he added are each less than 6. What fact might he have written?

____

20. Test Prep There are 7 blue hats and 6 red hats on a store shelf. How many hats are on the shelf?

- ○ 14
- ○ 13
- ○ 12
- ○ 10

TAKE HOME ACTIVITY • Ask your child to write three different doubles facts with sums less than 17.

© Houghton Mifflin Harcourt Publishing Company

FOR MORE PRACTICE: Standards Practice Book, pp. P53–P54

Name ______________________________

Practice Addition Facts

Essential Question What are some ways to remember sums?

COMMON CORE STANDARD **CC.2.OA.2**
Add and subtract within 20.

Listen and Draw REAL WORLD

Draw pictures to show the problems.

FOR THE TEACHER • Read the following two problems. Have children draw a picture and write a number sentence for each. On Monday, Tony recycled 3 cans and 6 bottles. How many containers did he recycle? On Tuesday, Tony recycled 6 cans and 3 bottles. How many containers did he recycle?

Math Talk
Explain how the two problems are alike. **Explain** how they are different. MATHEMATICAL PRACTICES

© Houghton Mifflin Harcourt Publishing Company

Model and Draw

These are some ways to remember facts.

You can count on 1, 2, or 3.

6 + 1 = 7

6 + 2 = 8

6 + 3 = 9

Changing the order of the **addends** does not change the sum.

8 = 2 + 6

8 = 6 + 2

Share and Show

Math Board

Write the sums.

1. 2 + 2 = ____ 2 + 3 = ____	2. 5 + 0 = ____ 2 + 0 = ____	3. 3 + 8 = ____ 8 + 3 = ____
4. ____ = 4 + 4 ____ = 4 + 3	5. 5 + 7 = ____ 7 + 5 = ____	6. ____ = 7 + 7 ____ = 7 + 8
7. ____ = 3 + 7 ____ = 7 + 3	8. 9 + 3 = ____ 3 + 9 = ____	9. ____ = 6 + 6 ____ = 6 + 5

© Houghton Mifflin Harcourt Publishing Company

Name ______________________________

On Your Own

Write the sums.

10. 7 + 1 = ____
    1 + 7 = ____

11. ____ = 4 + 0
    ____ = 9 + 0

12. 5 + 5 = ____
    5 + 4 = ____

13. 8 + 2 = ____
    2 + 8 = ____

14. 3 + 3 = ____
    3 + 4 = ____

15. 7 + 8 = ____
    8 + 7 = ____

16. ____ = 4 + 1
    ____ = 1 + 4

17. 0 + 7 = ____
    0 + 6 = ____

18. 8 + 8 = ____
    8 + 9 = ____

19. 5 + 3 = ____
    3 + 5 = ____

20. ____ = 9 + 9
    ____ = 9 + 8

21. 6 + 7 = ____
    7 + 6 = ____

Find the addends for each shaded box in the addition table. Write the facts for the shaded boxes.

+	0	1	2	3
0				
1				
2				
3				

22. ☐ + ☐ = ☐

23. ☐ + ☐ = ☐

24. ☐ + ☐ = ☐

25. ☐ + ☐ = ☐

© Houghton Mifflin Harcourt Publishing Company

PROBLEM SOLVING REAL WORLD

Write Math

Solve. Write or draw to explain.

26. Roger builds 4 toy airplanes. Then he builds 3 more toy airplanes. How many toy airplanes does he build?

_______ toy airplanes

27. Joanne made 9 clay bowls last week. She made the same number of clay bowls this week. How many clay bowls did she make in the two weeks?

_______ clay bowls

28. H.O.T. Sam painted 3 pictures. Ellie painted twice as many pictures as Sam. How many pictures did they paint?

_______ pictures

29. Test Prep Chloe draws 8 pictures. Reggie draws 1 more picture than Chloe. How many pictures do they draw?

- ○ 7
- ○ 9
- ○ 15
- ○ 17

TAKE HOME ACTIVITY • Ask your child to explain how he or she solved Exercise 28.

© Houghton Mifflin Harcourt Publishing Company

FOR MORE PRACTICE: Standards Practice Book, pp. P55–P56

Name ______________________________

Algebra • Make a Ten to Add

Essential Question How is the make a ten strategy used to find sums?

COMMON CORE STANDARD **CC.2.OA.2**
Add and subtract within 20.

Listen and Draw REAL WORLD

Write the fact below the ten frame when you hear the problem that matches the model.

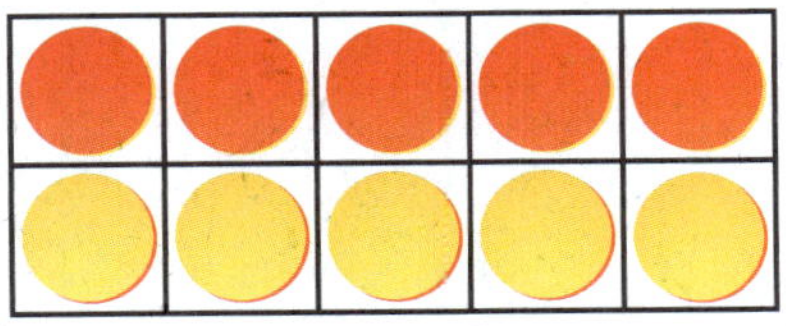

____

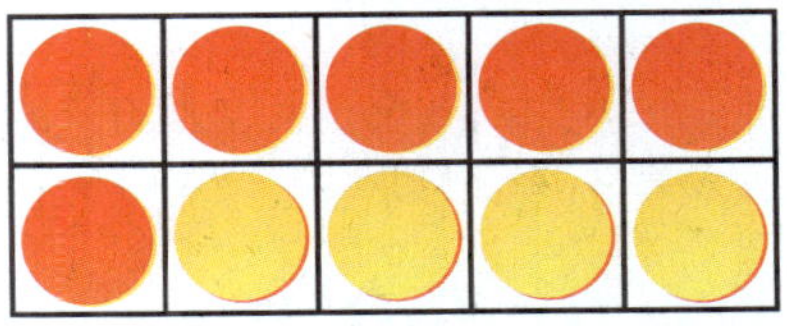

____

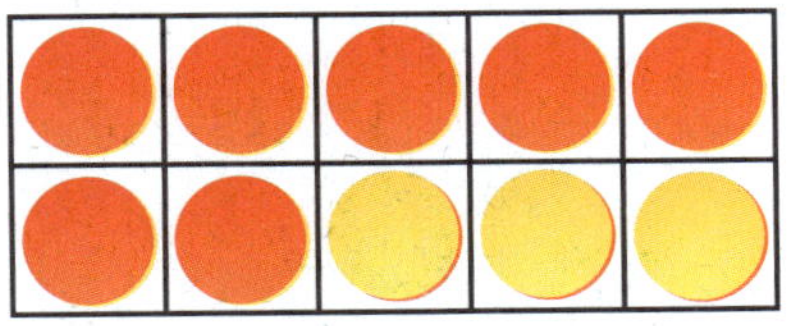

____

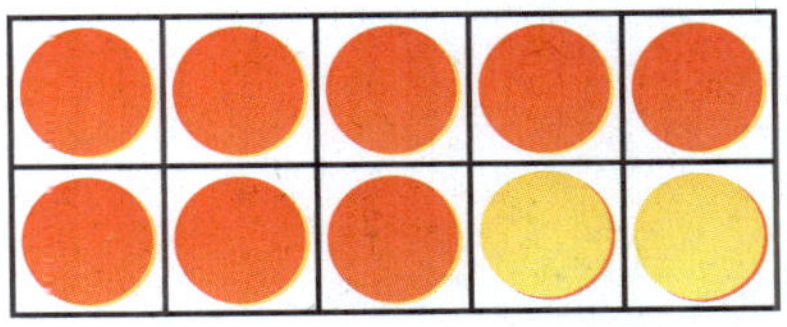

____

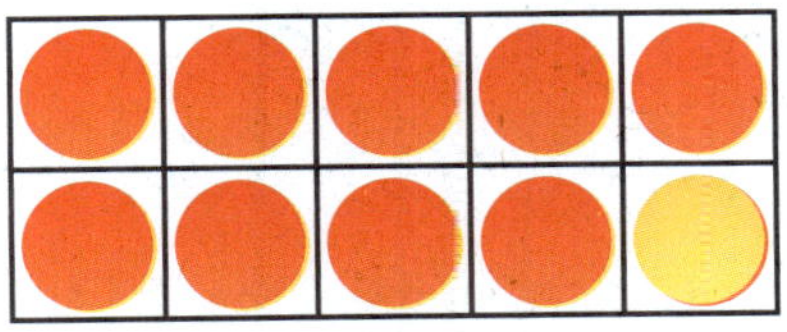

____

FOR THE TEACHER • Read the following problem. There are 6 dog bones and 4 dog biscuits. How many dog treats are there? Have children find the ten frame that models the problem and write the addition sentence. Repeat by revising the story for each addition fact represented by the other ten frames.

Math Talk **Describe** a pattern you see in these make a ten facts.

© Houghton Mifflin Harcourt Publishing Company

Model and Draw

7 + 5 = ?

You need to add 3 to 7 to make a ten.
Break apart 5 as 3 and 2.

7 + 5

7 + 3 + 2

10 + 2 = 12

So, 7 + 5 = ______.

Share and Show

Math Board

Show how you can make a ten to find the sum.
Write the sum.

1. 8 + 3 = ______

2 1

10 + ______ = ______

2. 2 + 9 = ______

1 1

10 + ______ = ______

3. 8 + 5 = ______

10 + ______ = ______

4. 4 + 7 = ______

10 + ______ = ______

5. 3 + 9 = ______

10 + ______ = ______

6. 7 + 6 = ______

10 + ______ = ______

© Houghton Mifflin Harcourt Publishing Company

Name ______________________

On Your Own

Show how you can make a ten to find the sum.
Write the sum.

7. $4 + 9 =$ ____
   3 1
   $10 +$ ____ $=$ ____

8. $9 + 8 =$ ____
   1 7
   $10 +$ ____ $=$ ____

9. $8 + 6 =$ ____
   $10 +$ ____ $=$ ____

10. $5 + 9 =$ ____
   $10 +$ ____ $=$ ____

11. $7 + 9 =$ ____
   $10 +$ ____ $=$ ____

12. $8 + 4 =$ ____
   $10 +$ ____ $=$ ____

13. $9 + 9 =$ ____
   $10 +$ ____ $=$ ____

14. $8 + 7 =$ ____
   $10 +$ ____ $=$ ____

H.O.T. Write the missing addend that makes the number sentence true.

15. $9 + 6 =$ ____ $+ 5$

16. $8 + 5 = 10 +$ ____

17. $7 +$ ____ $= 10 + 2$

18. ____ $+ 6 = 10 + 4$

© Houghton Mifflin Harcourt Publishing Company

MATHEMATICAL PRACTICES Model • Reason • Make Sense

PROBLEM SOLVING REAL WORLD

Write Math

Solve. Write or draw to explain.

19. There are 9 red bicycles at the store. There are 6 yellow bicycles at the store. How many bicycles are at the store?

_______ bicycles

20. There were 5 bees in a hive. Then 9 more bees go into that hive. How many bees are in the hive now?

_______ bees

21. H.O.T. Max is thinking of a doubles fact. It has a sum that is greater than the sum of $6 + 4$ but less than the sum of $8 + 5$. What fact is Max thinking of?

_____ + _____ = _____

22. **Test Prep** Natasha had 8 shells. Then she found 5 more shells. How many shells does she have now?

- ○ 3
- ○ 12
- ○ 13
- ○ 14

TAKE HOME ACTIVITY • Ask your child to name pairs of numbers that have a sum of 10. Then have him or her write the addition sentences.

FOR MORE PRACTICE:
Standards Practice Book, pp. P57–P58

© Houghton Mifflin Harcourt Publishing Company

Name ______________________________

Algebra • Add 3 Addends

Essential Question How do you add three numbers?

COMMON CORE STANDARD **CC.2.OA.2**
Add and subtract within 20.

Listen and Draw

Write the sum of each pair of addends.

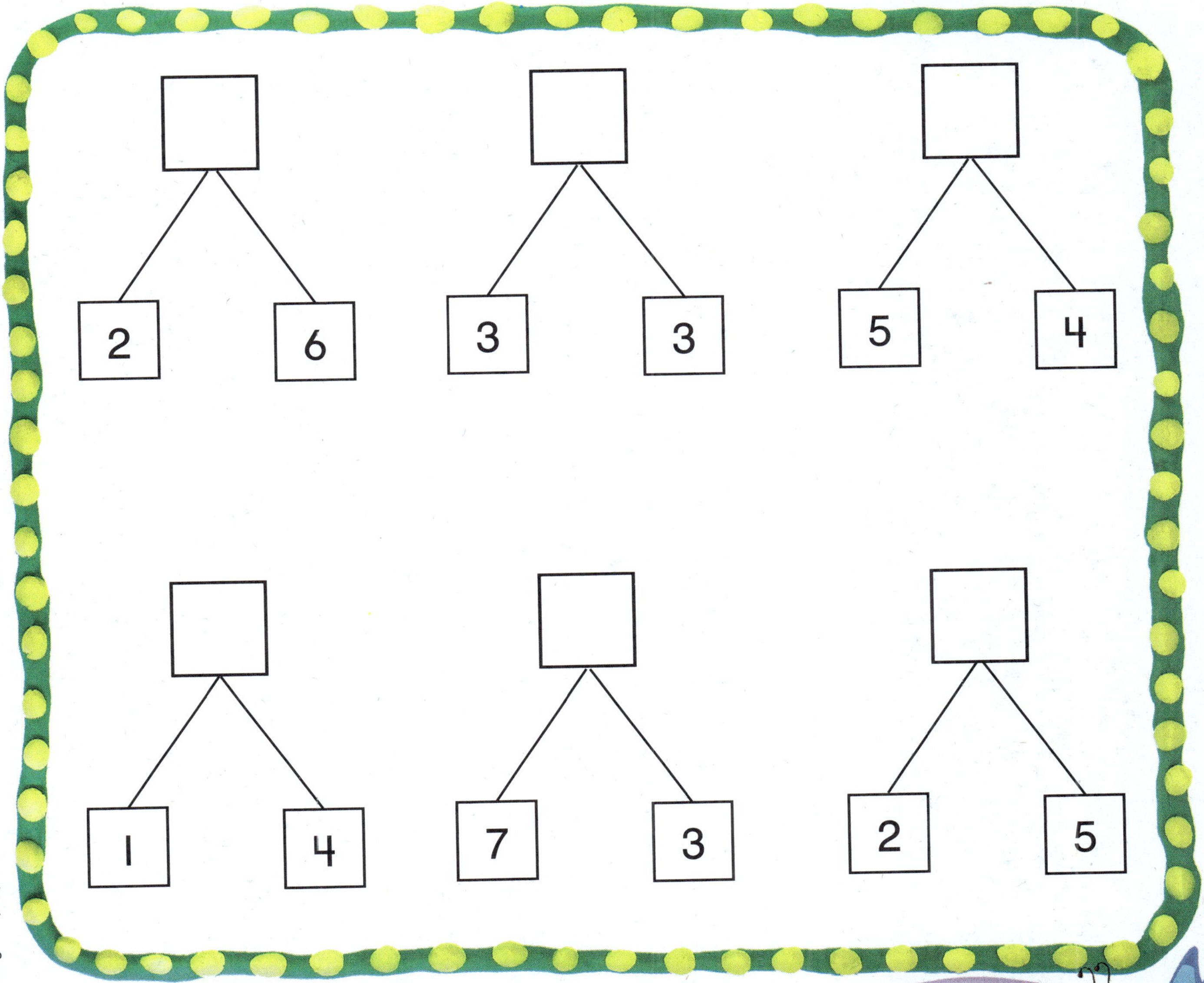

Math Talk
Describe how you found the sum of 5 and 4.
MATHEMATICAL PRACTICES

FOR THE TEACHER • After children have recorded the sum of each pair of addends, have them share their answers and discuss the strategies used.

© Houghton Mifflin Harcourt Publishing Company

Model and Draw

You can group numbers in different ways to add.

Choose two numbers.
Look for facts you know.

Changing the way the numbers are grouped does not change the sum.

3 + 2 + 7 = ?	3 + 2 + 7 = ?	3 + 2 + 7 = ?
5 + 7 = 12	3 + 9 = ____	10 + 2 = ____

Share and Show

Math Board

Solve two ways. Circle the two addends you add first.

1. 1 + 8 + 2 = ____ 1 + 8 + 2 = ____

2. 7 + 3 + 3 = ____ 7 + 3 + 3 = ____

3. 4 + 2 + 4 = ____ 4 + 2 + 4 = ____

4. 2 + 8 + 2 = ____ 2 + 8 + 2 = ____

5.
$$\begin{array}{r} 3 \\ 2 \\ +\ 6 \\ \hline \end{array} \qquad \begin{array}{r} 3 \\ 2 \\ +\ 6 \\ \hline \end{array}$$

6.
$$\begin{array}{r} 7 \\ 0 \\ +\ 2 \\ \hline \end{array} \qquad \begin{array}{r} 7 \\ 0 \\ +\ 2 \\ \hline \end{array}$$

© Houghton Mifflin Harcourt Publishing Company

Name ______________________

On Your Own

Solve two ways. Circle the two addends you add first.

7. $4 + 1 + 6 =$ ____ $4 + 1 + 6 =$ ____

8. $4 + 3 + 3 =$ ____ $4 + 3 + 3 =$ ____

9. $1 + 5 + 3 =$ ____ $1 + 5 + 3 =$ ____

10. $6 + 4 + 4 =$ ____ $6 + 4 + 4 =$ ____

11. $5 + 5 + 5 =$ ____ $5 + 5 + 5 =$ ____

12. $7 + 0 + 6 =$ ____ $7 + 0 + 6 =$ ____

13.
$$\begin{array}{r} 5 \\ 3 \\ +\ 4 \\ \hline \end{array} \qquad \begin{array}{r} 5 \\ 3 \\ +\ 4 \\ \hline \end{array}$$

14.
$$\begin{array}{r} 4 \\ 2 \\ +\ 5 \\ \hline \end{array} \qquad \begin{array}{r} 4 \\ 2 \\ +\ 5 \\ \hline \end{array}$$

H.O.T. Write the missing addend.

15.
$$\begin{array}{r} 5 \\ 5 \\ +\ \square \\ \hline 14 \end{array}$$

16.
$$\begin{array}{r} 4 \\ \square \\ +\ 4 \\ \hline 12 \end{array}$$

17.
$$\begin{array}{r} 3 \\ \square \\ +\ 7 \\ \hline 11 \end{array}$$

18.
$$\begin{array}{r} 5 \\ 3 \\ +\ \square \\ \hline 13 \end{array}$$

© Houghton Mifflin Harcourt Publishing Company

PROBLEM SOLVING REAL WORLD

Write Math

Choose a way to solve.
Write or draw to explain.

19. Beth eats 4 green grapes. Lin eats 3 red grapes and 6 purple grapes. How many grapes do they eat?

_______ grapes

20. There are 5 green grapes and 4 red grapes in a bowl. Eli puts 4 more red grapes in the bowl. How many grapes are in the bowl now?

_______ grapes

21. H.O.T. Nick, Alex, and Sophia eat 15 raisins in all. Nick and Alex each eat 4 raisins. How many raisins does Sophia eat?

_______ raisins

22. Test Prep Mrs. Morgan has 2 red apples, 7 yellow apples, and 2 green apples. How many apples does she have?

○ 4
○ 9
○ 10
○ 11

TAKE HOME ACTIVITY • Have your child describe two ways to add 3, 6, and 4.

FOR MORE PRACTICE:
Standards Practice Book, pp. P59–P60

© Houghton Mifflin Harcourt Publishing Company

Name ______________________________

Algebra • Relate Addition and Subtraction

COMMON CORE STANDARD CC.2.OA.2
Add and subtract within 20.

Essential Question How are addition and subtraction related?

Listen and Draw REAL WORLD

Complete the bar model to show the problem.

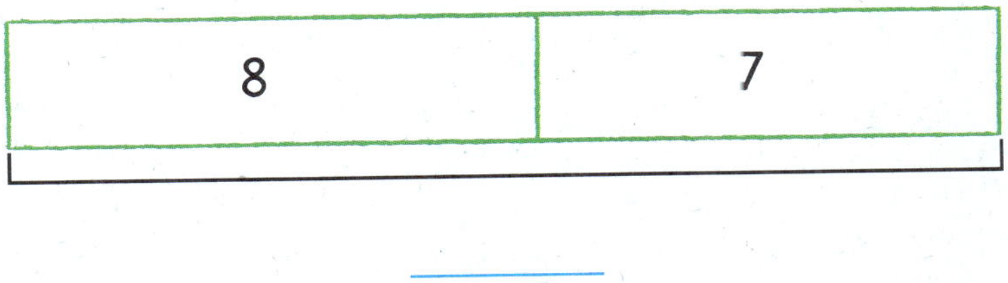

______ soccer balls

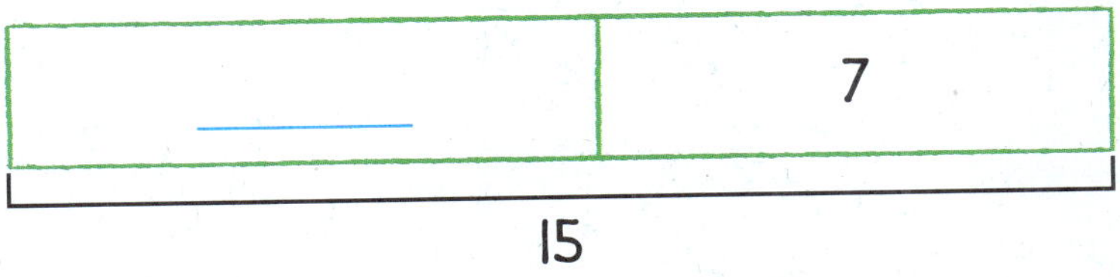

______ soccer balls

FOR THE TEACHER • Read the following problems. Have children complete the bar model for each. The soccer team has 8 red balls and 7 yellow balls. How many soccer balls does the team have? The soccer team has 15 balls inside the locker room. The children took the 7 yellow balls outside. How many soccer balls were inside?

Math Talk **Explain** how the bar models for the problems are alike and how they are different.

MATHEMATICAL PRACTICES

© Houghton Mifflin Harcourt Publishing Company

Model and Draw

You can use addition facts to remember **differences**. Related facts have the same whole and parts.

Think of the addends in an addition fact to find the difference for a related subtraction fact.

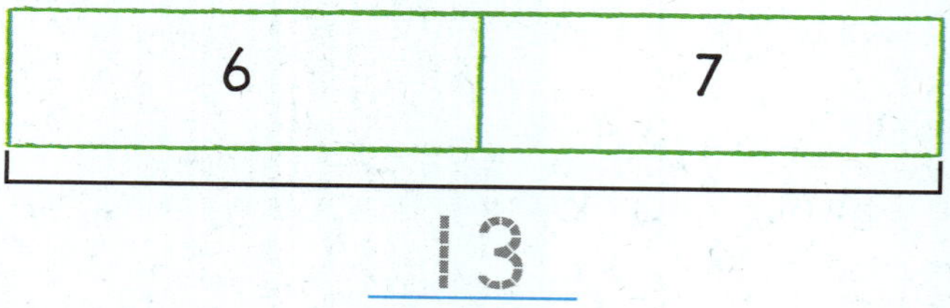

6 + 7 = 13

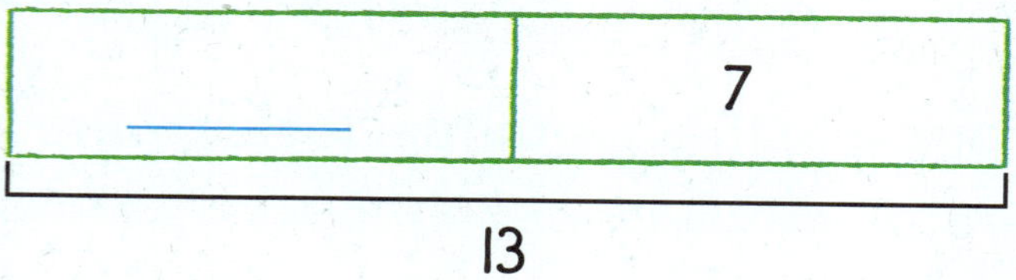

13 − 7 = ____

Share and Show

Math Board

Write the sum and the difference for the related facts.

1. 5 + 4 = ____ 9 − 4 = ____	2. 2 + 7 = ____ 9 − 2 = ____	3. 3 + 8 = ____ 11 − 8 = ____
4. 5 + 8 = ____ 13 − 5 = ____	5. 1 + 8 = ____ 9 − 1 = ____	6. 9 + 9 = ____ 18 − 9 = ____
7. 8 + 7 = ____ 15 − 8 = ____	✓8. 4 + 7 = ____ 11 − 7 = ____	✓9. 7 + 5 = ____ 12 − 7 = ____

© Houghton Mifflin Harcourt Publishing Company

Name ______________________________

On Your Own

Write the sum and the difference for the related facts.

10. $4 + 3 =$ ____ $7 - 3 =$ ____	11. $2 + 6 =$ ____ $8 - 6 =$ ____	12. $6 + 4 =$ ____ $10 - 6 =$ ____
13. $7 + 3 =$ ____ $10 - 7 =$ ____	14. $8 + 6 =$ ____ $14 - 6 =$ ____	15. $3 + 9 =$ ____ $12 - 9 =$ ____
16. $6 + 5 =$ ____ $11 - 5 =$ ____	17. $7 + 7 =$ ____ $14 - 7 =$ ____	18. $9 + 6 =$ ____ $15 - 9 =$ ____
19. $5 + 9 =$ ____ $14 - 9 =$ ____	20. $4 + 8 =$ ____ $12 - 4 =$ ____	21. $9 + 7 =$ ____ $16 - 7 =$ ____

H.O.T. Write a related subtraction fact for each addition fact.

22. $7 + 8 = 15$ ______________________	23. $5 + 7 = 12$ ______________________
24. $6 + 7 = 13$ ______________________	25. $9 + 8 = 17$ ______________________

© Houghton Mifflin Harcourt Publishing Company

PROBLEM SOLVING REAL WORLD

Write Math

Solve. Write or draw to explain.

26. Trevor has 7 kites. Pam has 4 kites. How many more kites does Trevor have than Pam?

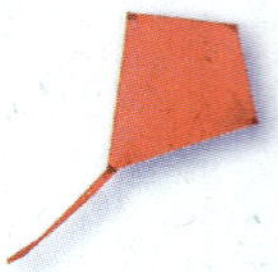

_____ more kites

27. H.O.T. Mr. Sims has a bag of 7 pears and a bag of 6 pears. His family eats 5 pears. How many pears does he have now?

_____ pears

28. Describe how you solved Exercise 27.

_____

_____

_____

29. Test Prep Carmen has 11 balloons. She gives 6 balloons to Mark. How many balloons does Carmen have now?

- ○ 5
- ○ 6
- ○ 7
- ○ 17

© Houghton Mifflin Harcourt Publishing Company

TAKE HOME ACTIVITY • Ask your child to name some subtraction facts that he or she knows well.

FOR MORE PRACTICE: Standards Practice Book, pp. P61–P62

Name ______________________

Practice Subtraction Facts

Essential Question What are some ways to remember differences?

COMMON CORE STANDARD CC.2.OA.2
Add and subtract within 20.

Listen and Draw REAL WORLD

Use Gina's model to answer the question.

Gina's Model

______________________ ______________________

______________________ ______________________

FOR THE TEACHER • Tell children that Gina put 4 color tiles inside the circle and then put 3 color tiles outside the circle. Then ask: What addition fact could be written for Gina's model? Repeat with stories for the three facts that are related to this addition fact.

Math Talk MATHEMATICAL PRACTICES
Explain how the different facts for Gina's model are related.

© Houghton Mifflin Harcourt Publishing Company

Model and Draw

These are some ways to find differences.

You can count back by 1, 2, or 3.

$7 - 3 = \_\_\_\_$

Start with 7.
Say: 6, 5, 4.

$9 - 3 = \_\_\_\_$

Start with 9.
Say: 8, 7, 6.

You can think about a missing addend to subtract.

$8 - 5 = \blacksquare$

$5 + 3 = 8$

So, $8 - 5 = \_\_\_\_$.

Share and Show

Math Board

Write the difference.

1. $6 - 4 = \_\_\_\_$	2. $10 - 7 = \_\_\_\_$	3. $\_\_\_\_ = 5 - 2$
4. $14 - 6 = \_\_\_\_$	5. $8 - 4 = \_\_\_\_$	6. $11 - 3 = \_\_\_\_$
7. $\_\_\_\_ = 7 - 5$	8. $6 - 5 = \_\_\_\_$	9. $5 - 0 = \_\_\_\_$
10. $13 - 9 = \_\_\_\_$	11. $9 - 3 = \_\_\_\_$	12. $\_\_\_\_ = 7 - 6$
13. $12 - 3 = \_\_\_\_$	14. $6 - 3 = \_\_\_\_$	15. $9 - 5 = \_\_\_\_$
16. $10 - 4 = \_\_\_\_$	✓17. $\_\_\_\_ = 8 - 3$	✓18. $13 - 5 = \_\_\_\_$

© Houghton Mifflin Harcourt Publishing Company

Name ______________________________

On Your Own

Write the difference.

19. 11 − 2 = ____	20. 9 − 7 = ____	21. ____ = 7 − 4
22. 12 − 5 = ____	23. 8 − 6 = ____	24. 7 − 0 = ____
25. ____ = 10 − 5	26. 15 − 8 = ____	27. 13 − 7 = ____
28. 10 − 8 = ____	29. 8 − 5 = ____	30. ____ = 9 − 6
31. ____ = 9 − 4	32. 11 − 8 = ____	33. 12 − 7 = ____

H.O.T. Write the differences. Then write the next fact in the pattern.

34. 10 − 1 = ____	35. 12 − 9 = ____	36. 18 − 9 = ____
8 − 1 = ____	13 − 9 = ____	17 − 8 = ____
6 − 1 = ____	14 − 9 = ____	16 − 7 = ____
4 − 1 = ____	15 − 9 = ____	15 − 6 = ____
____________	____________	____________

© Houghton Mifflin Harcourt Publishing Company

TAKE HOME ACTIVITY • With your child, practice saying subtraction facts from this lesson.

FOR MORE PRACTICE:
Standards Practice Book, pp. P63–P64

Name ______________________________

Mid-Chapter Checkpoint

Concepts and Skills

Write the sum. (CC.2.OA.2)

1. $3 + 6 =$ ____

2. $8 + 0 =$ ____

3. $7 + 7 =$ ____

4. $9 + 4 =$ ____

5. ____ $= 5 + 6$

6. $2 + 8 =$ ____

7. $3 + 7 + 2 =$ ____

8. $4 + 4 + 6 =$ ____

Show how you can make a ten to find the sum.
Write the sum. (CC.2.OA.2)

9. $9 + 7 =$ ____

$10 +$ ____ $=$ ____

10. $6 + 8 =$ ____

$10 +$ ____ $=$ ____

Write the sum and the difference for the related facts. (CC.2.OA.2)

11. $5 + 4 =$ ____

$9 - 4 =$ ____

12. $3 + 9 =$ ____

$12 - 9 =$ ____

13. $8 + 7 =$ ____

$15 - 8 =$ ____

Test Prep (CC.2.OA.2)

14. There are 9 flute players and 4 trumpet players in the band. How many flute players and trumpet players are there?

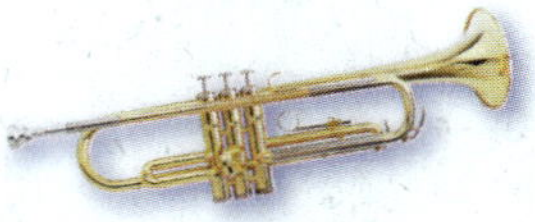

- ○ 14
- ○ 13
- ○ 11
- ○ 5

© Houghton Mifflin Harcourt Publishing Company

Name ______________________________

Use Ten to Subtract

Essential Question How does getting to 10 in subtraction help when finding differences?

COMMON CORE STANDARD CC.2.OA.2
Add and subtract within 20.

Listen and Draw REAL WORLD

Circle to show the amount you subtract for each problem.

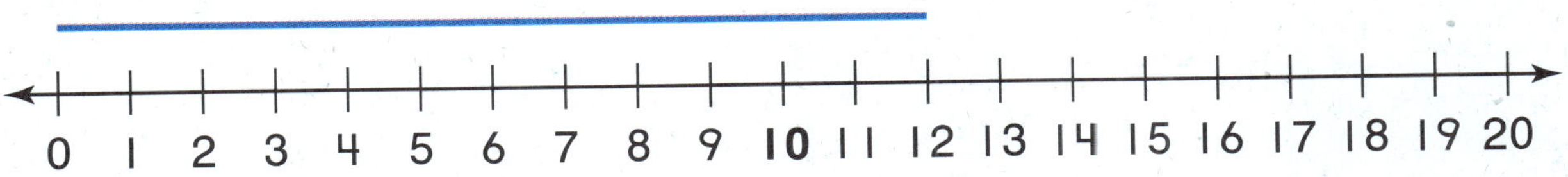

FOR THE TEACHER • Read the following problem. Scott has 13 crayons. He gives 3 crayons to Tyler. How many crayons does Scott have now? Have children circle the part of the blue line segment that shows what is subtracted from the total. Repeat for two more problems.

Math Talk
Describe a pattern in the three problems and answers.

MATHEMATICAL PRACTICES

© Houghton Mifflin Harcourt Publishing Company

Model and Draw

You can subtract in steps to use a tens fact.

14 − 6 = ?

4   2

Subtract in steps:
14 − 4 = 10
10 − 2 = 8

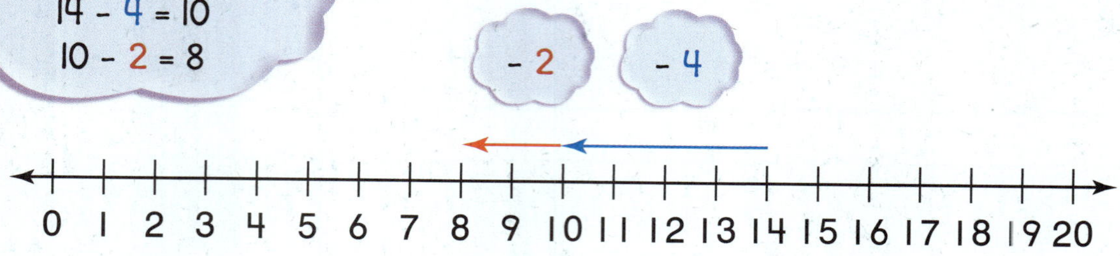

So, 14 − 6 = 8.

Share and Show

Math Board

Show the tens fact you used. Write the difference.

1. 12 − 5 = ____

2 3

10 − ____ = ____

2. 11 − 6 = ____

1 5

10 − ____ = ____

3. 15 − 7 = ____

10 − ____ = ____

4. 13 − 7 = ____

10 − ____ = ____

© Houghton Mifflin Harcourt Publishing Company

Name ______________________________

On Your Own

Show the tens fact you used. Write the difference.

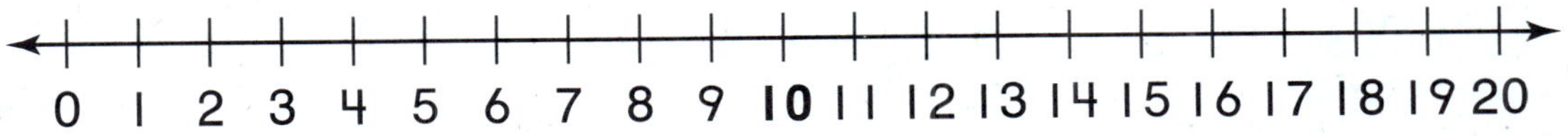

5. 13 − 5 = ____

10 − ____ = ____

6. 15 − 6 = ____

10 − ____ = ____

7. 12 − 8 = ____

10 − ____ = ____

8. 14 − 8 = ____

10 − ____ = ____

9. 12 − 6 = ____

10 − ____ = ____

10. 16 − 7 = ____

10 − ____ = ____

H.O.T. Write the missing number that makes the number sentence true.

11. 15 − 6 = 10 − ____

12. 11 − 7 = 10 − ____

13. 13 − 6 = 10 − ____

14. 16 − 8 = 10 − ____

© Houghton Mifflin Harcourt Publishing Company

PROBLEM SOLVING

Write Math

H.O.T. Write number sentences that use both addition and subtraction. Use each choice only once.

~~9 − 2~~
~~3 + 4~~
1 + 4
14 − 6
5 + 4
15 − 6
10 − 5
4 + 4

15. 9 − 2 = 3 + 4

7 = 7

16. ________ = ________

17. ________ = ________

18. ________ = ________

19. ★ **Test Prep** Andy scored 13 points in the first game and 7 points in the second game. How many more points did he score in the first game than in the second game?

- ○ 9
- ○ 6
- ○ 4
- ○ 3

TAKE HOME ACTIVITY • Ask your child to name pairs of numbers that have a difference of 10. Then have him or her write the number sentences.

FOR MORE PRACTICE: Standards Practice Book, pp. P65–P66

© Houghton Mifflin Harcourt Publishing Company

Name ______________________________

Algebra • Use Drawings to Represent Problems

Essential Question How are bar models used to show addition and subtraction problems?

Lesson 3.8

COMMON CORE STANDARD **CC.2.OA.1**

Represent and solve problems involving addition and subtraction.

Listen and Draw REAL WORLD

Complete the bar model to show the problem.
Complete the number sentence to solve.

______	______

______

______ + ______ = ______ ______ pennies

______	______

______

______ − ______ = ______ ______ pennies

FOR THE TEACHER • Read each problem and have children complete the bar models. Hailey has 5 pennies in her pocket and 7 pennies in her wallet. How many pennies does she have? Blake has 12 pennies in his bank. He gives 5 pennies to his sister. How many pennies does he have now?

Math Talk MATHEMATICAL PRACTICES

Explain how the problems are alike and how they are different.

© Houghton Mifflin Harcourt Publishing Company

Model and Draw

You can use bar models to show problems.

Ben eats 14 crackers. Ron eats 6 crackers. How many more crackers does Ben eat than Ron?

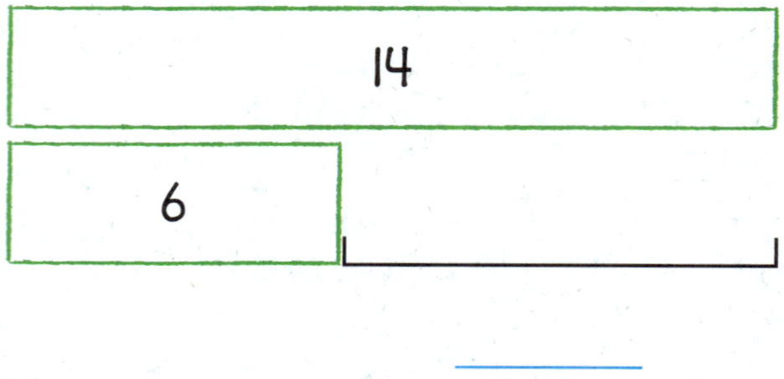

14 − 6 = 8
____

_____ more crackers

Suzy had 14 cookies. She gave 6 cookies to Grace. How many cookies does Suzy have now?

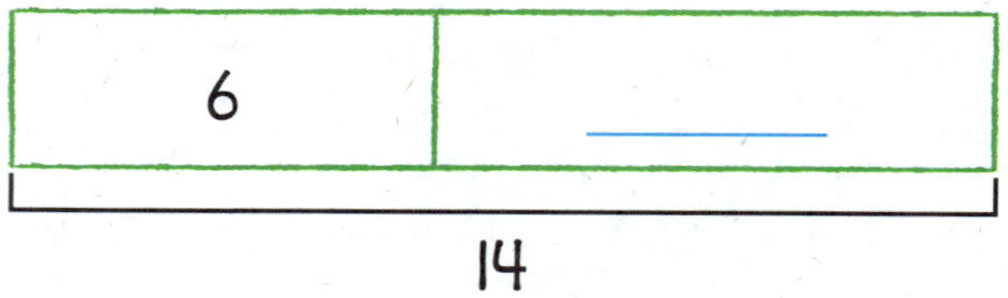

____

_____ cookies

Share and Show

Math Board

Complete the bar model. Then write a number sentence to solve.

1. Mr. James bought 15 plain bagels and 9 raisin bagels. How many more plain bagels than raisin bagels did he buy?

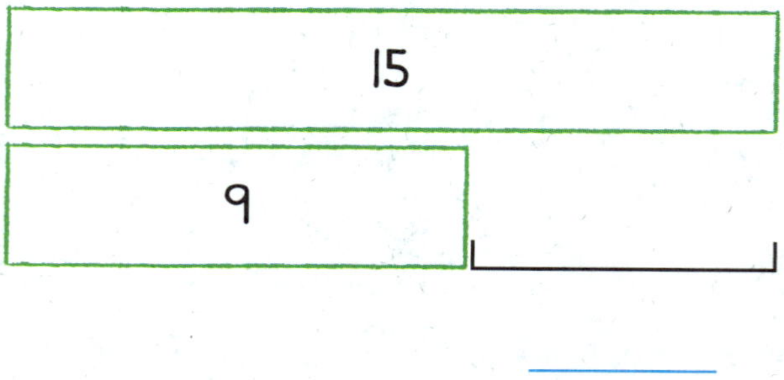

____

_______ more plain bagels

© Houghton Mifflin Harcourt Publishing Company

Name ______________________________

On Your Own

Complete the bar model. Then write a number sentence to solve.

2. Cole has 5 books about dogs and 6 books about cats. How many books does Cole have?

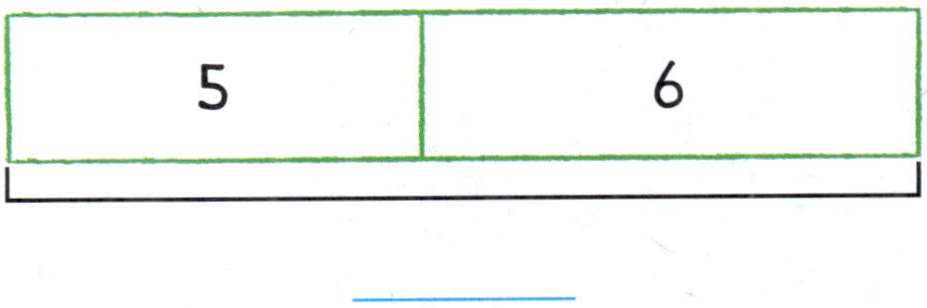

____

________ books

3. Miss Gore had 18 pencils. She gave 9 pencils to Erin. How many pencils does Miss Gore have now?

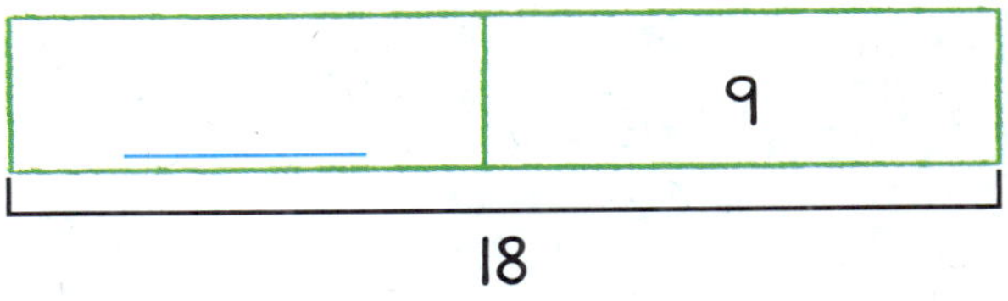

____

________ pencils

4. Anne has 16 blue clips and 9 red clips. How many more blue clips than red clips does she have?

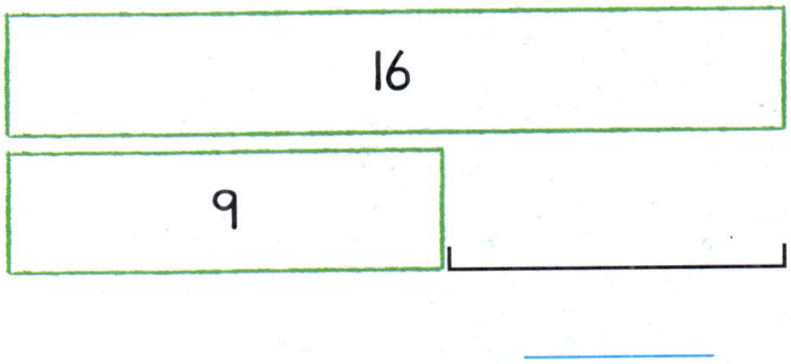

____

________ more blue clips

© Houghton Mifflin Harcourt Publishing Company

PROBLEM SOLVING REAL WORLD

Write Math

Use the information in the table to solve. Write or draw to explain.

Flowers Jenna Picked

Flowers	Number
roses	6
tulips	8
daisies	11

5. Jenna put all of the roses and all of the tulips into a vase. How many flowers did she put into the vase?

_______ flowers

6. H.O.T. Four of the daisies are white. The other daisies are yellow. How many daisies are yellow?

_______ yellow daisies

7. Test Prep Mrs. Johnson wants to put 18 flowers into a vase. She put 9 flowers into the vase. How many more flowers does she need to put into the vase?

- ○ 6
- ○ 8
- ○ 9
- ○ 15

TAKE HOME ACTIVITY • Ask your child to describe one way to solve this problem. There are 7 pennies in one pocket and 9 pennies in another pocket. How many pennies are there?

FOR MORE PRACTICE: Standards Practice Book, pp. P67–P68

© Houghton Mifflin Harcourt Publishing Company

Name ______________________

Algebra • Use Equations to Represent Problems

Essential Question How are number sentences used to show addition and subtraction situations?

COMMON CORE STANDARD CC.2.OA.1

Represent and solve problems involving addition and subtraction.

Listen and Draw REAL WORLD

Write a story problem that could be solved using this bar model.

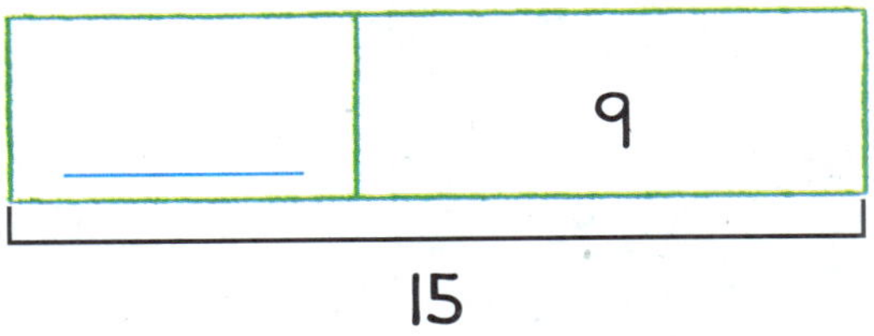

____

____

____

____

____

FOR THE TEACHER • Discuss with children how this bar model can be used to represent an addition or a subtraction situation.

Math Talk

Would you add or subtract to solve your story problem? **Explain.**

© Houghton Mifflin Harcourt Publishing Company

Model and Draw

A number sentence can be used to show a problem.

There were some girls and 4 boys at the playground. There were 9 children in all. How many girls were at the playground?

$$\blacksquare + 4 = 9$$

Think: $5 + 4 = 9$

So, there were 5 girls at the playground.

The ■ is a placeholder for the missing number.

Share and Show

Math Board

Write a number sentence for the problem.

Use a ■ for the missing number. Then solve.

1. There were 14 ants on the sidewalk. Then 6 ants went into the grass. How many ants were still on the sidewalk?

____

______ ants

2. There were 7 big dogs and 4 little dogs at the park. How many dogs were at the park?

____

______ dogs

© Houghton Mifflin Harcourt Publishing Company

Name ______________________________

On Your Own

Write a number sentence for the problem.

Use a ■ for the missing number. Then solve.

3. There were 13 girls flying kites. Some of the girls went home. Then there were 7 girls flying kites. How many girls went home?

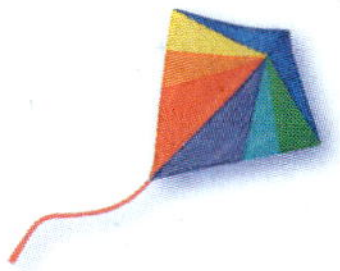

____

________ girls

4. There are 18 boys at the field. 9 of the boys are playing soccer. How many boys are not playing soccer?

____

________ boys

5. There were some ducks in a pond. Four more ducks joined them. Then there were 12 ducks in the pond. How many ducks were in the pond at first?

____

________ ducks

6. Matthew found 9 acorns. Greg found 6 acorns. How many acorns did the two boys find?

____

________ acorns

© Houghton Mifflin Harcourt Publishing Company

PROBLEM SOLVING REAL WORLD

Write Math

Read the story. Write or draw to show how you solved the problems.

At camp, 5 children are playing games
and 4 children are making crafts.
5 other children are having a snack.

7. How many children are at camp?

_____ children

8. H.O.T. Suppose 7 more children arrive at camp and join the children playing games. How many more children are playing games than children not playing games?

_____ more children

9. Test Prep Jon counted 12 butterflies and Tessa counted 7 butterflies. How many fewer butterflies did Tessa count than Jon?

○ 5
○ 7
○ 12
○ 19

TAKE HOME ACTIVITY • Ask your child to explain how he or she solved one of the problems on this page.

FOR MORE PRACTICE:
Standards Practice Book, pp. P69–P70

© Houghton Mifflin Harcourt Publishing Company

Name ________________

Problem Solving • Equal Groups

Essential Question How can acting it out help when solving a problem about equal groups?

COMMON CORE STANDARD CC.2.OA.4
Work with equal groups of objects to gain foundations for multiplication.

Theo puts his stickers in 5 rows.
There are 3 stickers in each row.
How many stickers does Theo have?

Unlock the Problem

What do I need to find?

how many stickers
Theo has

What information do I need to use?

5 rows of stickers
3 stickers in each row

Show how to solve the problem.

HOME CONNECTION • Your child used counters to act out the problem. Counters are a concrete tool that helps children act out the problem.

© Houghton Mifflin Harcourt Publishing Company

Try Another Problem

Act out the problem.
Draw to show what you did.

- What do I need to find?
- What information do I need to use?

1. Maria puts all of her postcards in 4 rows. There are 3 postcards in each row. How many postcards does Maria have?

_______ postcards

2. Jamal puts 4 toys in each box. How many toys will he put in 4 boxes?

_______ toys

Math Talk

Explain how acting it out and skip counting helped you solve the second problem.

MATHEMATICAL PRACTICES

© Houghton Mifflin Harcourt Publishing Company

Name ____________________

Share and Show

Math Board

Act out the problem.
Draw to show what you did.

Write Math

3. Mr. Fulton puts 3 bananas on each tray. How many bananas are on 4 trays?

_______ bananas

4. There are 3 rows of apples. There are 5 apples in each row. How many apples are there?

_______ apples

5. Dexter puts 5 grapes on each plate. How many grapes in all does he put on 4 plates?

_______ grapes

© Houghton Mifflin Harcourt Publishing Company

On Your Own

Choose a way to solve.
Write or draw to explain.

Write Math

6. Jon has 6 marbles. Amy gives him some more marbles. Now he has 13 marbles. How many marbles did Amy give to him?

_______ marbles

7. H.O.T. Angela used these counters to act out a problem.

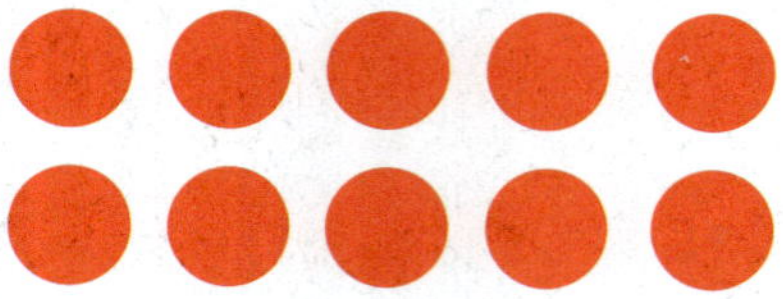

Write a problem about equal groups that Angela could have modeled with these counters.

____

____

____

8. **Test Prep** Brett has 3 rows of shells. There are 4 shells in each row. How many shells does he have?

- ○ 6
- ○ 7
- ○ 12
- ○ 15

TAKE HOME ACTIVITY • Ask your child to explain how he or she solved the problem in Exercise 8.

FOR MORE PRACTICE:
Standards Practice Book, pp. P71–P72

© Houghton Mifflin Harcourt Publishing Company

Name ______________________________

Algebra • Repeated Addition

Essential Question How can you write an addition sentence for problems with equal groups?

COMMON CORE STANDARD CC.2.OA.4
Work with equal groups of objects to gain foundations for multiplication.

Listen and Draw REAL WORLD

Use counters to model the problem.
Then draw a picture of your model.

FOR THE TEACHER • Read the following problem and have children first model the problem with counters and then draw a picture of their models. Clayton has 3 rows of trading cards. There are 5 cards in each row. How many trading cards does Clayton have?

Math Talk
Describe how you found the number of counters in your model.

© Houghton Mifflin Harcourt Publishing Company

Model and Draw

You can use addition to find the total amount when you have equal groups.

3 rows of 4

Write: 4 + 4 + 4 = ____

____ in all

Share and Show

Find the number of shapes in each row.
Complete the addition sentence to find the total.

1\.

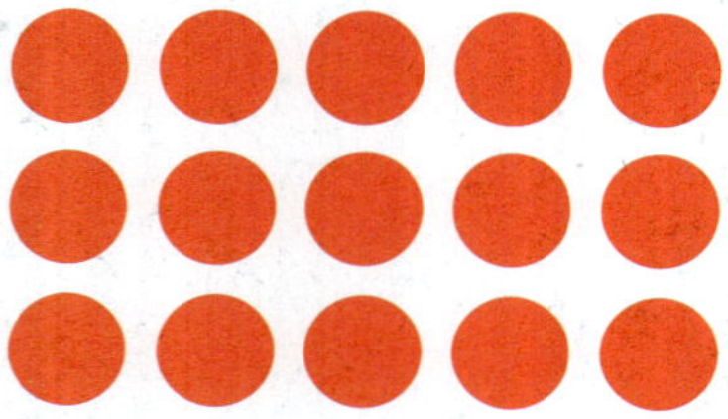

3 rows of ____

____ + ____ + ____ = ____

2\.

4 rows of ____

____ + ____ + ____ + ____ = ____

3\.

5 rows of ____

____ + ____ + ____ + ____ + ____ = ____

© Houghton Mifflin Harcourt Publishing Company

Name ______________________________

On Your Own

Find the number of shapes in each row.
Complete the addition sentence to find the total.

4.

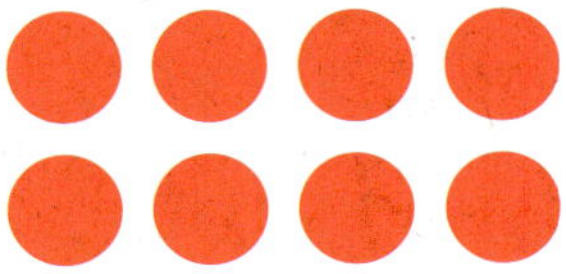

2 rows of ____

____ + ____ = ____

5.

3 rows of ____

____ + ____ + ____ = ____

6.

4 rows of ____

___ + ___ + ___ + ___ = ____

7.

4 rows of ____

___ + ___ + ___ + ___ = ____

8.

5 rows of ____

____ + ____ + ____ + ____ + ____ = ____

© Houghton Mifflin Harcourt Publishing Company

PROBLEM SOLVING REAL WORLD

Write Math

Solve. Write or draw to explain.

9. Mrs. Chen makes 5 rows of chairs. She puts 2 chairs in each row. How many chairs does Mrs. Chen use?

_______ chairs

10. Jorge has 3 fish bowls. There are 4 fish in each bowl. How many fish are in the bowls?

_______ fish

11. H.O.T. There are 6 photos on the wall. There are 2 photos in each row. How many rows of photos are there?

_______ rows

12. Test Prep Donna has 3 rows of toys. There are 5 toys in each row. How many toys does she have?

○ 15
○ 12
○ 8
○ 2

TAKE HOME ACTIVITY • Have your child use small objects to make 2 rows with 4 objects in each row. Then have your child find the total number of objects.

FOR MORE PRACTICE: Standards Practice Book, pp. P73–P74

© Houghton Mifflin Harcourt Publishing Company

Name ____________________

Chapter 3 Review/Test

Vocabulary

1. Circle the **sum**. (p. 122) 4 + 6 = 10

2. Circle the **difference**. (p. 138) 8 − 5 = 3

Concepts and Skills

Write the sum and the difference for the related facts. (CC.2.OA.2)

3. 8 + 4 = ____
   12 − 4 = ____

4. 5 + 9 = ____
   14 − 9 = ____

5. 6 + 5 = ____
   11 − 6 = ____

6. Complete the bar model. Then write a number sentence to solve. (CC.2.OA.1)

   Hudson had 13 grapes. He gave 5 grapes to his sister. How many grapes does Hudson have now?

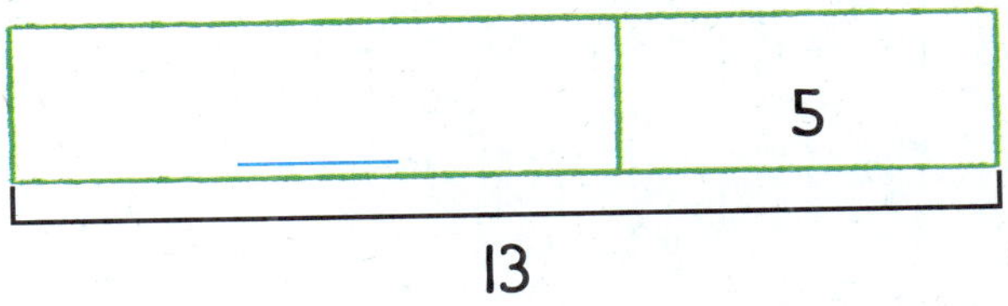

______________________ ____ grapes

Find the number of shapes in each row.
Complete the addition sentence to find the total. (CC.2.OA.4)

7. 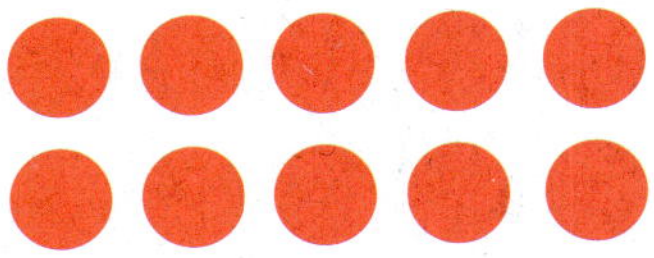

   2 rows of ____

   ____ + ____ = ____

8. 

   3 rows of ____

   ____ + ____ + ____ = ____

© Houghton Mifflin Harcourt Publishing Company

Fill in the bubble for the correct answer choice.

TEST PREP

9. There are 8 peaches in a basket. Mrs. Dalton puts 7 more peaches in the basket. How many peaches are in the basket now? (CC.2.OA.2)

- ○ 11
- ○ 13
- ○ 15
- ○ 16

10. Mr. Brown hiked 5 miles in the morning. He hiked 6 miles in the afternoon. How many miles did he hike? (CC.2.OA.2)

- ○ 9
- ○ 10
- ○ 11
- ○ 12

11. Erin put 3 apples, 4 bananas, and 5 oranges in a basket. How many pieces of fruit did she put in the basket? (CC.2.OA.2)

- ○ 7
- ○ 9
- ○ 11
- ○ 12

© Houghton Mifflin Harcourt Publishing Company

Name ______________________________

TEST PREP

Fill in the bubble for the correct answer choice.

12. It rained on 14 days in January. It rained on 8 days in February. On how many more days did it rain in January than in February? (CC.2.OA.2)

- ○ 6
- ○ 8
- ○ 14
- ○ 22

13. Chase saw 4 ladybugs and 9 ants on a rock. How many more ants than ladybugs did he see? (CC.2.OA.1)

- ○ 5
- ○ 6
- ○ 13
- ○ 15

14. Tina put some cups into 4 rows. There are 5 cups in each row. How many cups are there? (CC.2.OA.4)

- ○ 9
- ○ 10
- ○ 16
- ○ 20

© Houghton Mifflin Harcourt Publishing Company

Constructed Response

15. Kyle and Luis together have the same number of fish as Mary. How many fish does Luis have?

Kyle	Luis	Mary
5 fish	? fish	11 fish

Write a number sentence with a ■ for the missing number. Solve. Then explain how the number sentence shows the problem. (CC.2.OA.1, CC.2.OA.2)

____

____

____

Performance Task (CC.2.OA.1, CC.2.OA.2)

16. Morgan counts 6 ducks in a pond and some ducks on the grass. There are 14 ducks in all. How many ducks are on the grass? Draw or write to show how you found your answer.

How many more ducks are on the grass than in the pond? Draw or write to show how you found your answer.

© Houghton Mifflin Harcourt Publishing Company

Chapter 4

2-Digit Addition

Curious About Math with Curious George

The keys of a modern piano are made from wood or plastic. A modern piano has 36 black keys and 52 white keys. How many keys is this in all?

© Houghton Mifflin Harcourt Publishing Company
Curious George by Margret and H.A. Rey. Copyright © 2010 by Houghton Mifflin Harcourt Publishing Company. All rights reserved. The character Curious George®, including without limitation the character's name and the character's likenesses, are registered trademarks of Houghton Mifflin Harcourt Publishing Company.

Name ________________________________

Show What You Know

Addition Patterns

Add 2. Complete each addition sentence.

1. 1 + <u>2</u> = <u>3</u>	4. 4 + ____ = ____
2. 2 + ____ = ____	5. 5 + ____ = ____
3. 3 + ____ = ____	6. 6 + ____ = ____

Addition Facts

Write the sum.

7.	8.	9.	10.	11.	12.
7	8	6	4	9	8
+ 3	+ 8	+ 7	+ 4	+ 5	+ 7

Tens and Ones

Write how many tens and ones for each number.

13. 43

____ tens ____ ones

14. 68

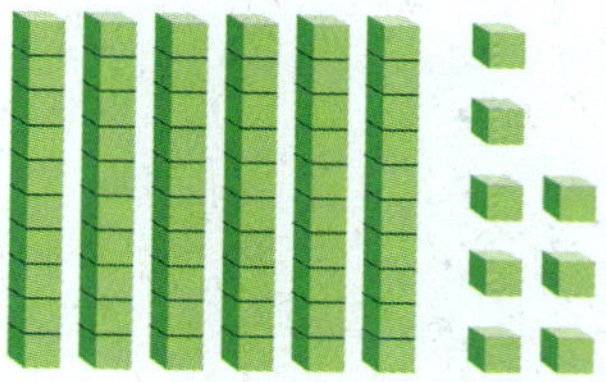

____ tens ____ ones

Family note: This page checks your child's understanding of important skills needed for success in Chapter 4.

GO Online Assessment Options Soar to Success Math

© Houghton Mifflin Harcourt Publishing Company

Name ______________________

Vocabulary Builder

Review Words
- sum
- addend
- digit
- tens
- ones

Visualize It

Use review words to fill in the graphic organizer.

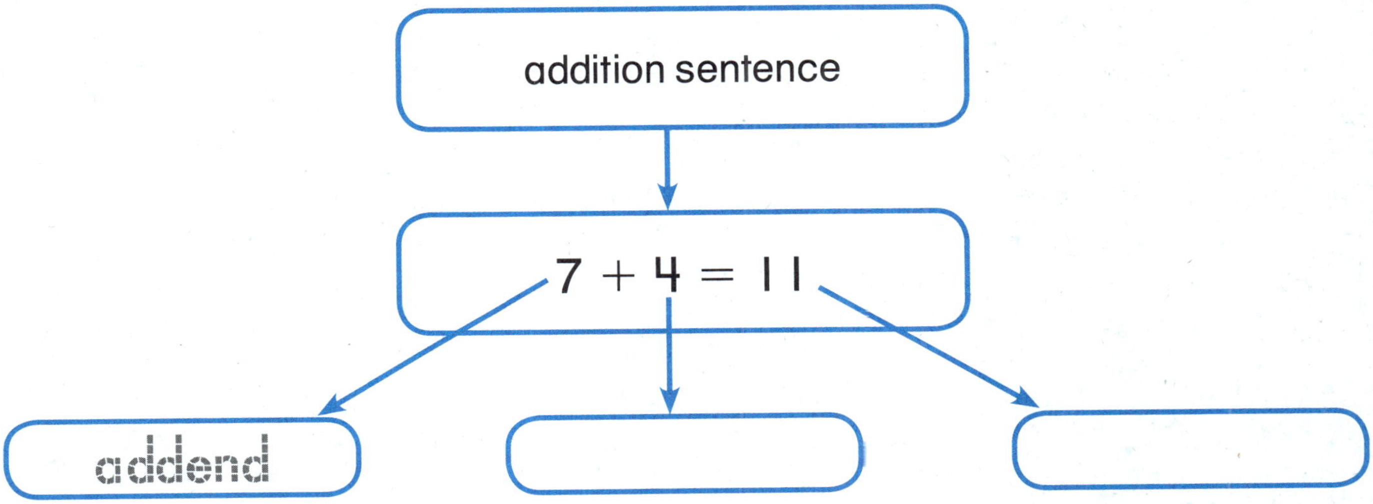

Understand Vocabulary

1. Write a number with the **digit** 3 in the **tens** place. ______

2. Write a number with the **digit** 5 in the **ones** place. ______

3. Write a number that has the same **digit** in the **tens** place and in the **ones** place. ______

4. Write a number with **digits** that have a **sum** of 8. ______

© Houghton Mifflin Harcourt Publishing Company

GO Online
- eStudent Edition
- Multimedia eGlossary

Game: What is the Sum?

Materials

- 12
- 12
- 1

Play with a partner.

1. Put your on START.
2. Toss the . Move that many spaces.
3. Say the sum. Your partner checks your answer.
4. If your answer is correct, find that number in the middle of the board. Put one of your on that number.
5. Take turns until both players reach FINISH. The player with more on the board wins.

START

$2 + 7$ | $6 + 5$ | $3 + 9$ | $0 + 7$ | $8 + 6$

FINISH

7	18	9	11	15
13	6	17	8	10
16	4	12	14	5

Left side: $9 + 8$ | $1 + 4$

Right side: $6 + 2$ | $8 + 7$

$5 + 8$ | $9 + 9$ | $7 + 9$ | $2 + 2$ | $4 + 6$ | $5 + 1$

© Houghton Mifflin Harcourt Publishing Company

Name ______________________

Break Apart Ones to Add

Essential Question How does breaking apart a number make it easier to add?

Lesson 4.1

COMMON CORE STANDARD CC.2.NBT.6

Use place value understanding and properties of operations to add and subtract.

Listen and Draw REAL WORLD

Use  . Draw to show what you did.

FOR THE TEACHER • Read the following problem. Have children use blocks to solve. Griffin read 27 books about animals and 6 books about space. How many books did he read?

Math Talk

Describe what you did with the blocks.

MATHEMATICAL PRACTICES

© Houghton Mifflin Harcourt Publishing Company

Model and Draw

Break apart ones to make a ten.
Use this as a way to add.

27 + 8 = ___?___

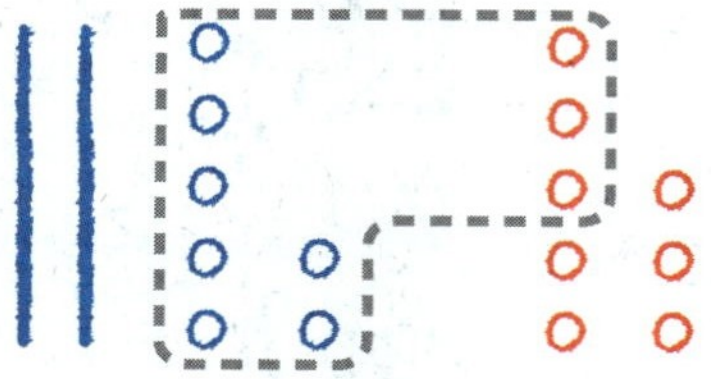

27 + 8 = ______

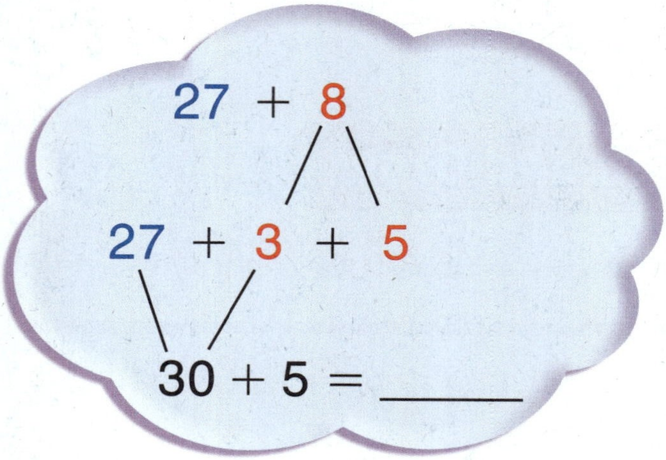

Share and Show

Draw quick pictures. Break apart ones to make a ten. Then add and write the sum.

1. 15 + 7 = ______

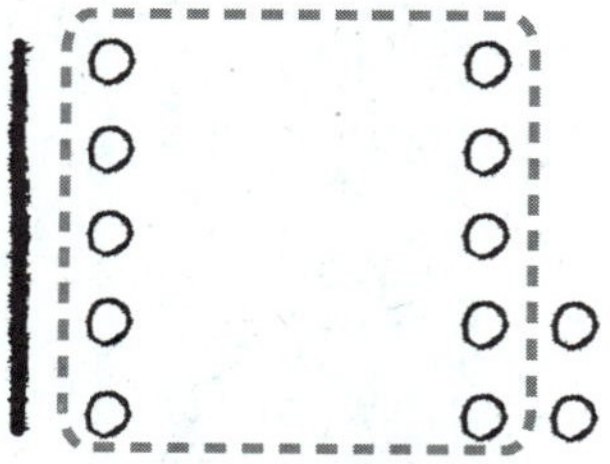

2. 26 + 5 = ______

3. 37 + 8 = ______

4. 28 + 6 = ______

© Houghton Mifflin Harcourt Publishing Company

Name ____________________

On Your Own

Break apart ones to make a ten.
Then add and write the sum.

5. 23 + 9 = ______

6. 48 + 5 = ______

7. 18 + 5 = ______

8. 33 + 9 = ______

9. 27 + 6 = ______

10. 49 + 4 = ______

11. 24 + 8 = ______

12. 58 + 7 = ______

13. 36 + 8 = ______

14. 47 + 9 = ______

H.O.T. Write the missing digit.

15. 49 + 7 = ☐6

16. 35 + ☐ = 44

17. ☐5 + 7 = 62

18. 2☐ + 8 = 35

19. 74 + 9 = 8☐

20. ☐6 + 5 = 81

© Houghton Mifflin Harcourt Publishing Company

MATHEMATICAL PRACTICES Model • Reason • Make Sense

PROBLEM SOLVING REAL WORLD

Write Math

Solve. Write or draw to explain.

21. Megan has 38 animal pictures and 8 people pictures. How many pictures does she have?

_______ pictures

22. Bruce counts 25 trees at the park and 7 trees on the way home. How many trees does he count?

_______ trees

23. H.O.T. Jamal has a box with some toy cars in it. He puts 3 more toy cars into the box. Now there are 22 toy cars in the box. How many toy cars were in the box before?

_______ toy cars

24. **Test Prep** Alicia puts 25 books on the shelf. Trenton puts 8 books on the shelf. How many books do they put on the shelf?

○ 17
○ 23
○ 33
○ 37

TAKE HOME ACTIVITY • Say a number from 0 to 9. Have your child name a number to add to yours to have a sum of 10.

FOR MORE PRACTICE:
Standards Practice Book, pp. P79–P80

© Houghton Mifflin Harcourt Publishing Company

Name ___________________________________

Use Compensation

Essential Question How can you make an addend a ten to help solve an addition problem?

COMMON CORE STANDARD CC.2.NBT.6

Use place value understanding and properties of operations to add and subtract.

Listen and Draw REAL WORLD

Draw quick pictures to show the problems.

FOR THE TEACHER • Have children draw quick pictures to solve this problem. Kara has 47 stickers. She buys 20 more stickers. How many stickers does she have now? Repeat for this problem. Tyrone has 30 stickers and buys 52 more stickers. How many stickers does he have now?

Math Talk

Describe how you found how many stickers Tyrone has.

© Houghton Mifflin Harcourt Publishing Company

Model and Draw

Take ones from an addend to make the other addend the next tens number.

Adding can be easier when one of the addends is a tens number.

25 + 48 = ?

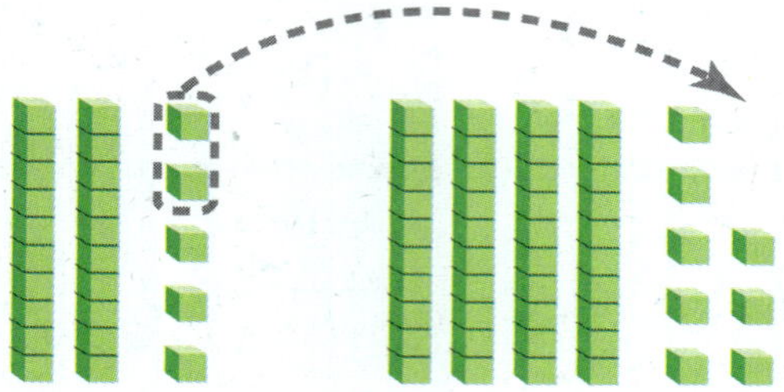

23 + 50 = ____

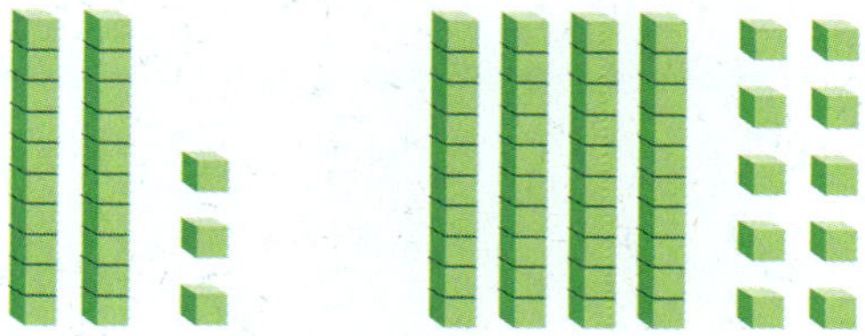

Share and Show

Math Board

Show how to make one addend the next tens number. Complete the new addition sentence.

1. 37 + 25 = ?

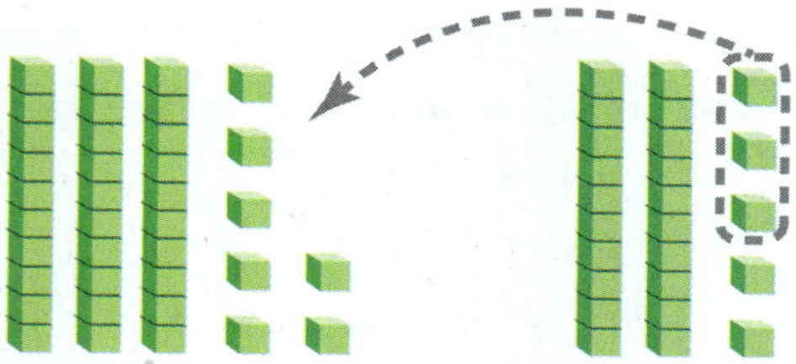

40 + ____ = ____

2. 27 + 46 = ?

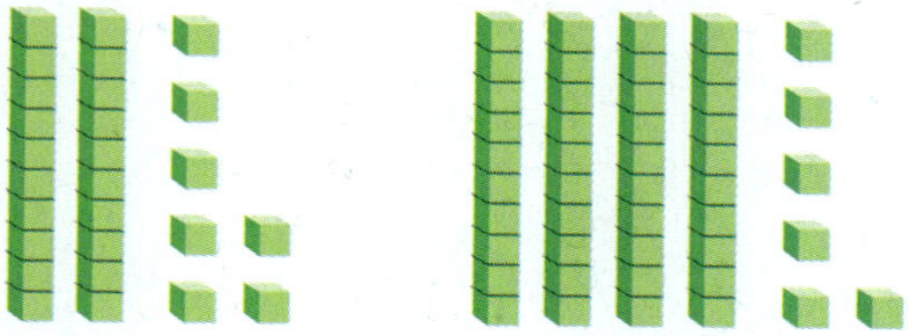

____ + ____ = ____

3. 14 + 29 = ?

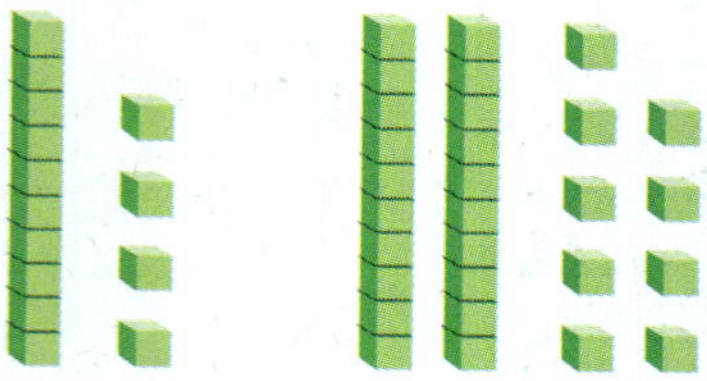

____ + ____ = ____

© Houghton Mifflin Harcourt Publishing Company

Name ______________________________

On Your Own

Show how to make one addend the next tens number.
Complete the new addition sentence.

4. 18 + 13 = ?

_____ + _____ = _____

5. 24 + 18 = ?

_____ + _____ = _____

6. 39 + 19 = ?

_____ + _____ = _____

7. 27 + 24 = ?

_____ + _____ = _____

8. 19 + 32 = ?

_____ + _____ = _____

© Houghton Mifflin Harcourt Publishing Company

PROBLEM SOLVING REAL WORLD

Write Math

Solve. Write or draw to explain.

9. Zach finds 38 twigs. Kelly finds 27 twigs. How many twigs do the two children find?

_______ twigs

10. H.O.T. The chart shows the leaves that Philip collected. He wants a collection of 52 leaves, using only two colors. Which two colors of leaves should he use?

_____________ and _____________

Leaves Collected

Color	Number
green	27
brown	29
yellow	25

11. **Test Prep** Keisha sees 28 small trees at the park. She sees 14 tall trees at the park. How many trees does she see at the park?

- ○ 52
- ○ 44
- ○ 42
- ○ 40

TAKE HOME ACTIVITY • Have your child choose one problem on this page and explain how to solve it in another way.

© Houghton Mifflin Harcourt Publishing Company

FOR MORE PRACTICE: Standards Practice Book, pp. P81–P82

Name ______________________________

Break Apart Addends as Tens and Ones

Essential Question How do you break apart addends to add tens and then add ones?

COMMON CORE STANDARD CC.2.NBT.6
Use place value understanding and properties of operations to add and subtract.

Listen and Draw

Write the number. Then write the number as tens plus ones.

☐ + ☐

☐ + ☐

☐ + ☐

Math Talk What is the value of the 6 in the number 63? **Explain** how you know.

MATHEMATICAL PRACTICES

FOR THE TEACHER • Direct children's attention to the orange box. Have children write 25 inside the large rectangle. Then ask children to write 25 as tens plus ones. Repeat the activity for 36 and 42.

© Houghton Mifflin Harcourt Publishing Company

Model and Draw

Break apart the addends into tens and ones.
Add the tens and add the ones.
Then find the total sum.

27	→	20 + 7
+48	→	40 + 8

60 + 15 = ____

60 + 15

10 5

70 + 5 = ____

Share and Show

Math Board

Break apart the addends to find the sum.

1. 35 → ____ + ____

+54 → ____ + ____

____ + ____ = ____

2. 43 → ____ + ____

+29 → ____ + ____

____ + ____ = ____

3. 56 → ____ + ____

+38 → ____ + ____

____ + ____ = ____

© Houghton Mifflin Harcourt Publishing Company

Name ________________________________

On Your Own

Break apart the addends to find the sum.

4. 14 → ____ + ____

+23 → ____ + ____

____ + ____ = ____

5. 37 → ____ + ____

+45 → ____ + ____

____ + ____ = ____

6. 54 → ____ + ____

+16 → ____ + ____

____ + ____ = ____

7. H.O.T. Write the missing numbers in the problem.

43 → ____ + ____

+ ____ → 30 + 7

____ + ____ = ____

© Houghton Mifflin Harcourt Publishing Company

PROBLEM SOLVING REAL WORLD

Write Math

Choose a way to solve.
Write or draw to explain.

8. Julie read 18 pages of her book in the morning. She read 17 more pages in the afternoon. How many pages did she read?

_______ pages

9. H.O.T. Christopher has 35 baseball cards. The rest of his cards are basketball cards. He has 58 cards in all. How many basketball cards does he have?

_______ basketball cards

10. ★ **Test Prep** Tomás has 17 art pencils. He buys 26 more art pencils. How many art pencils does Tomás have now?

○ 31
○ 33
○ 41
○ 43

© Houghton Mifflin Harcourt Publishing Company

TAKE HOME ACTIVITY • Write 32 + 48 on a sheet of paper. Have your child break apart the numbers and find the sum.

FOR MORE PRACTICE:
Standards Practice Book, pp. P83–P84

Name ____________________

Model Regrouping for Addition

Essential Question When do you regroup in addition?

COMMON CORE STANDARDS CC.2.NBT.6, CC.2.NBT.9

Use place value understanding and properties of operations to add and subtract.

Listen and Draw REAL WORLD

Use tens and ones blocks to model the problem.
Draw quick pictures to show what you did.

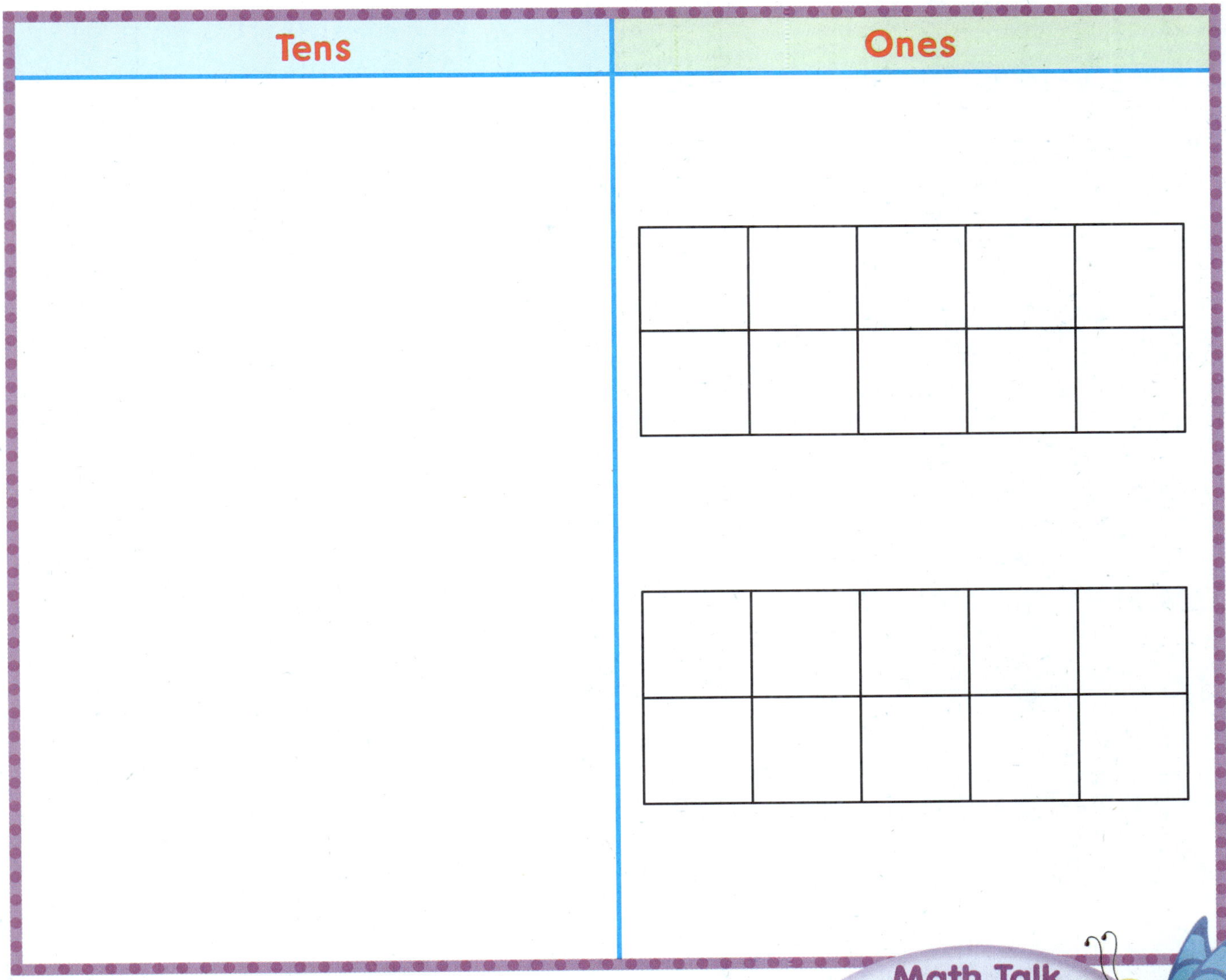

FOR THE TEACHER • Read the following problem. Brandon has 24 action figures. His friend Mario has 8 action figures. How many action figures do they have?

Math Talk

Describe how you made a ten in your model.

MATHEMATICAL PRACTICES

© Houghton Mifflin Harcourt Publishing Company

Model and Draw

Add 37 and 25.

Step 1 Look at the ones. Can you make a ten?

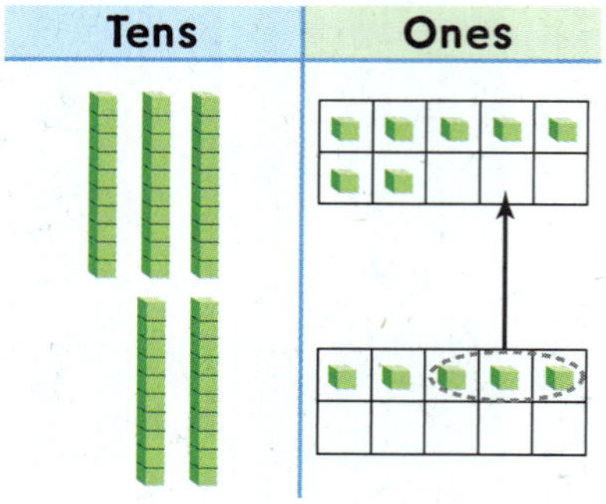

yes no

Step 2 If you can make a ten, **regroup**.

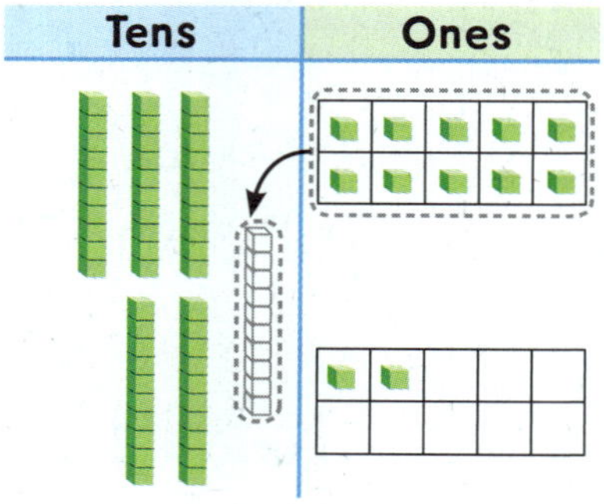

Trade 10 ones for 1 ten to regroup.

Step 3 Write how many tens and ones. Write the sum.

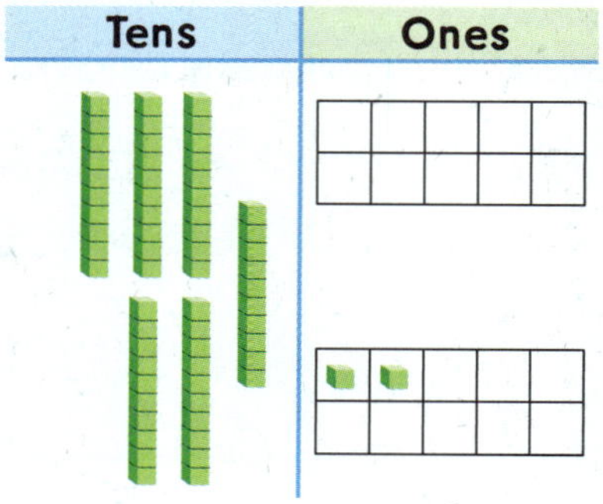

_____ tens _____ ones

____

Share and Show

Math Board

Draw to show the regrouping. Write how many tens and ones in the sum. Write the sum.

1. Add 47 and 15.

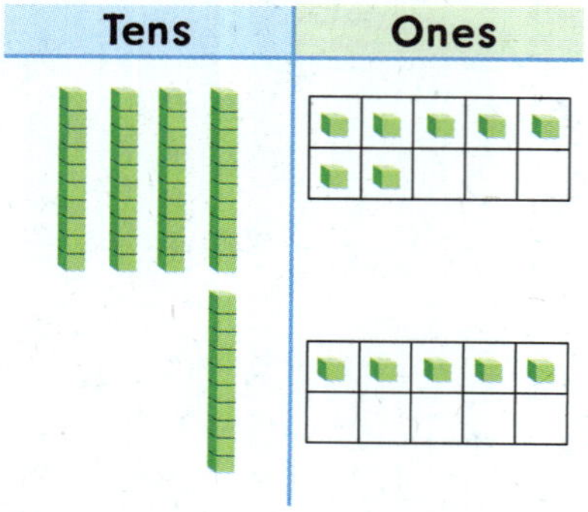

_____ tens _____ ones

____

2. Add 48 and 8.

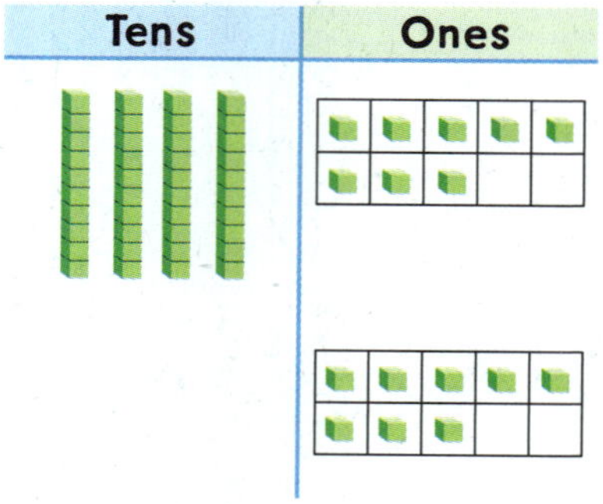

_____ tens _____ ones

____

3. Add 26 and 38.

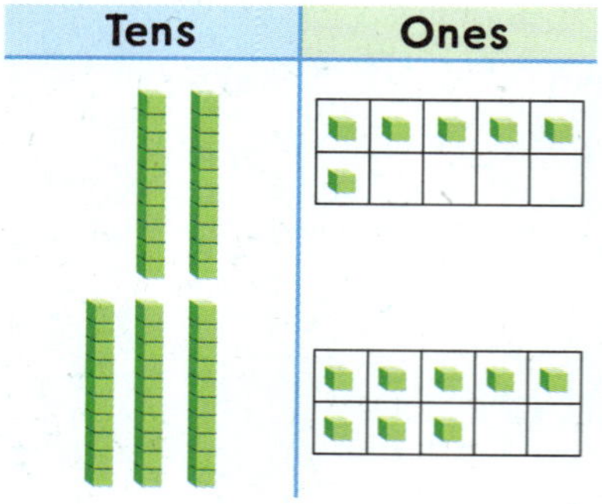

_____ tens _____ ones

____

© Houghton Mifflin Harcourt Publishing Company

Name ______________________________

On Your Own

Draw to show if you regroup. Write how many tens and ones in the sum. Write the sum.

4. Add 79 and 6.

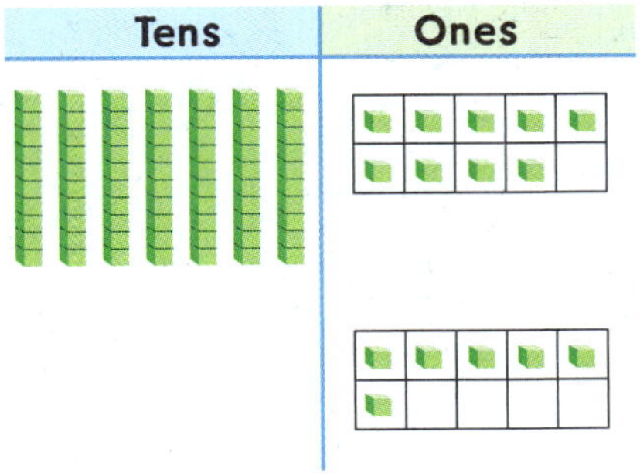

_____ tens _____ ones

____

5. Add 18 and 64.

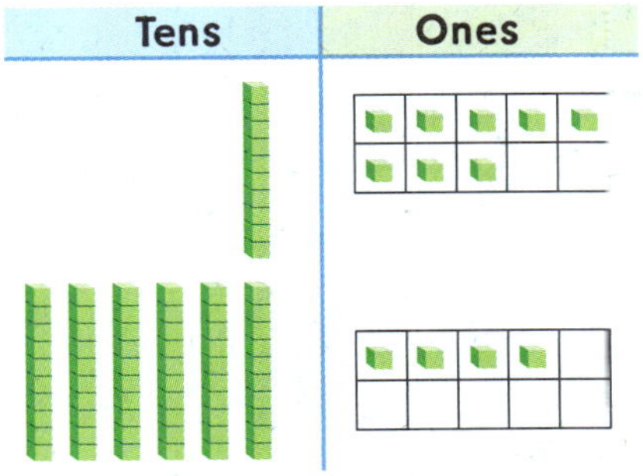

_____ tens _____ ones

____

6. Add 23 and 39.

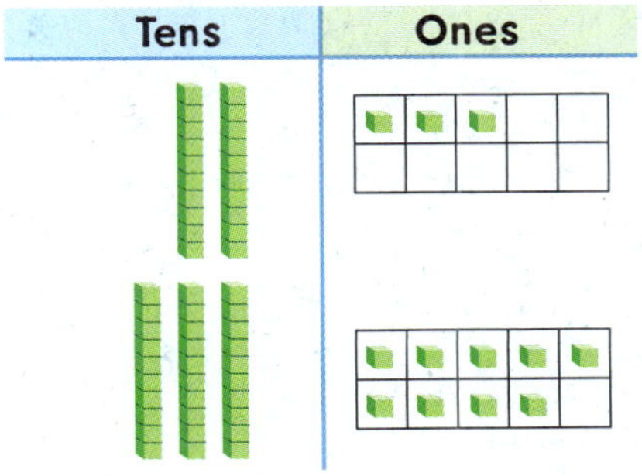

_____ tens _____ ones

____

7. Add 54 and 25.

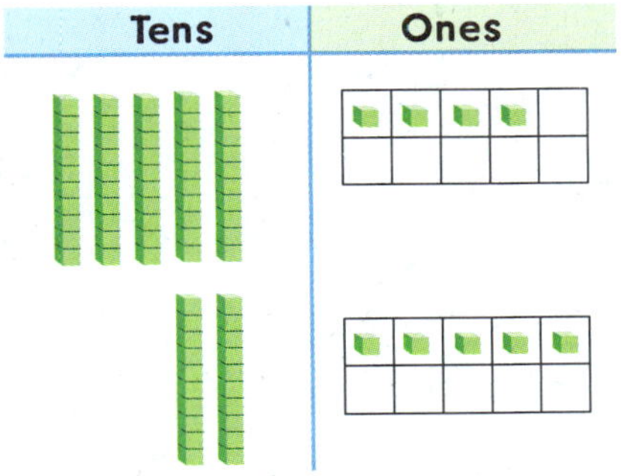

_____ tens _____ ones

____

8. Add 33 and 7.

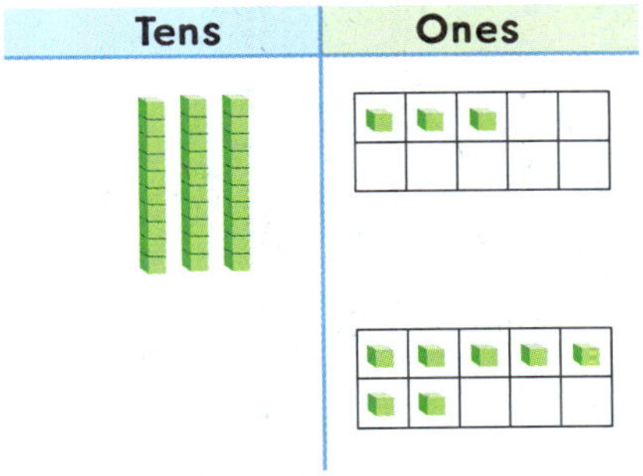

_____ tens _____ ones

____

9. Add 27 and 68.

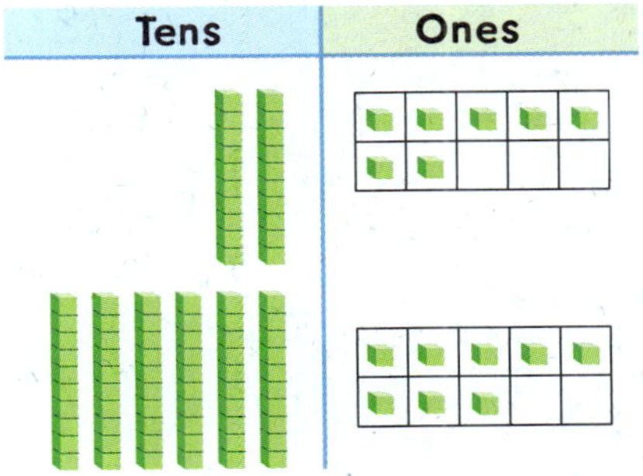

_____ tens _____ ones

____

10. H.O.T. Draw a quick picture for the missing addend.

8 tens 0 ones

80

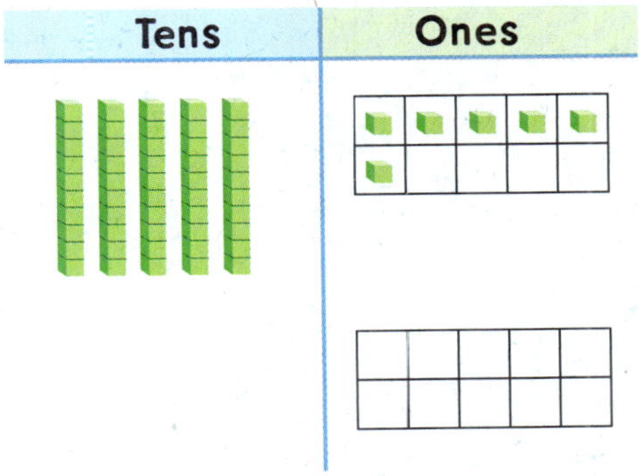

© Houghton Mifflin Harcourt Publishing Company

PROBLEM SOLVING REAL WORLD

Write Math

Choose a way to solve.
Write or draw to explain.

11. Kara has 25 toy animals and 12 books. Jorge has 8 more toy animals than Kara has. How many toy animals does Jorge have?

_________ toy animals

12. H.O.T. Tim has 36 stickers. Margo has 44 stickers. How many more stickers would they need to have 100 stickers altogether?

_________ more stickers

13. Test Prep Mrs. Sanders has two fish tanks. There are 14 fish in the small tank. There are 27 fish in the large tank. How many fish are in the two tanks?

- ○ 47
- ○ 41
- ○ 33
- ○ 31

© Houghton Mifflin Harcourt Publishing Company

TAKE HOME ACTIVITY • Ask your child to write a word problem with 2-digit numbers about adding two groups of stamps.

FOR MORE PRACTICE:
Standards Practice Book, pp. P85–P86

Name ______________________________

Model and Record 2-Digit Addition

Essential Question How do you record 2-digit addition?

COMMON CORE STANDARD **CC.2.NBT.6**
Use place value understanding and properties of operations to add and subtract.

Listen and Draw REAL WORLD

Use  to model the problem.
Draw quick pictures to show what you did.

Tens	Ones

Math Talk Did you trade blocks in your model? **Explain** why or why not.

MATHEMATICAL PRACTICES

FOR THE TEACHER • Read the following problem. Mr. Riley's class collected 54 cans for the food drive. Miss Bright's class collected 35 cans. How many cans did the two classes collect?

© Houghton Mifflin Harcourt Publishing Company

Model and Draw

Trace over the quick pictures in the steps.

Step 1 Model 37 + 26. Are there 10 ones to regroup?

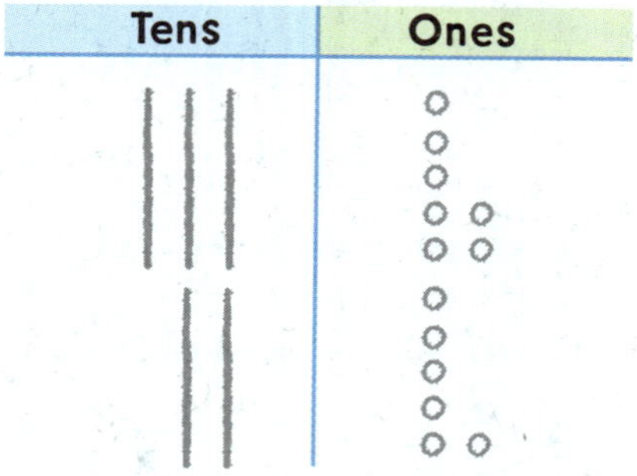

	Tens	Ones
	□	
	3	7
+	2	6

Step 2 Write the regrouped ten. Write how many ones are in the ones place now.

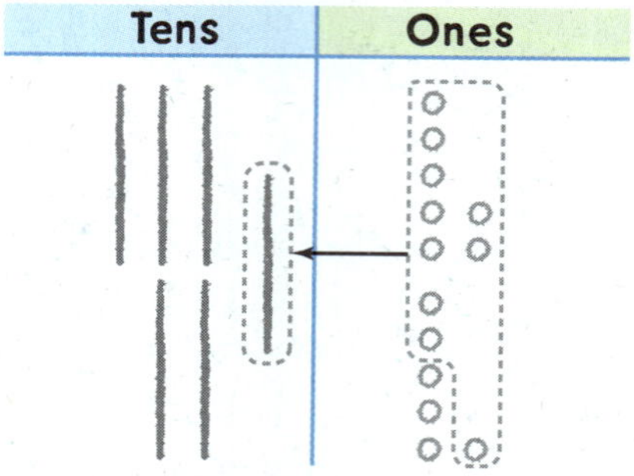

	Tens	Ones
	1	
	3	7
+	2	6
		3

Step 3 How many tens are there? Write how many tens are in the tens place.

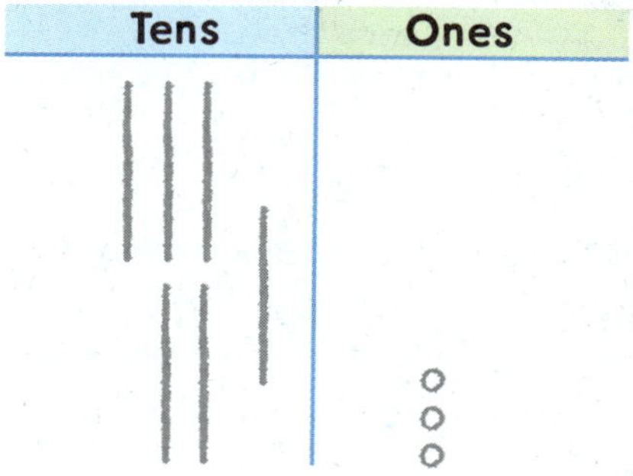

	Tens	Ones
	1	
	3	7
+	2	6
	6	3

Share and Show

Math Board

Draw quick pictures to help you solve. Write the sum.

1.

	Tens	Ones
	□	
	2	6
+	3	2

Tens	Ones

2.

	Tens	Ones
	□	
	5	8
+	2	4

Tens	Ones

© Houghton Mifflin Harcourt Publishing Company

Name ______________________________

On Your Own

Draw quick pictures to help you solve. Write the sum.

3.

	Tens	Ones
	☐	
	3	4
+		9

Tens	Ones

4.

	Tens	Ones
	☐	
	2	7
+	2	4

Tens	Ones

5.

	Tens	Ones
	☐	
	3	5
+	2	3

Tens	Ones

6.

	Tens	Ones
	☐	
	5	9
+		6

Tens	Ones

7.

	Tens	Ones
	☐	
	2	8
+	6	2

Tens	Ones

8.

	Tens	Ones
	☐	
	4	9
+	4	8

Tens	Ones

© Houghton Mifflin Harcourt Publishing Company

PROBLEM SOLVING REAL WORLD

Write Math

Choose a way to solve.
Write or draw to explain.

9. Edna has 35 color pencils. Manny gives her 18 more color pencils. How many color pencils does Edna have now?

______ color pencils

10. H.O.T. Chris and Bianca got 80 points in all in the spelling contest. Each child got more than 20 points. How many points could each child have gotten?

Chris: ______ points

Bianca: ______ points

11. **Test Prep** Ms. Green's students painted 19 pictures. Mr. Lee's students painted 23 pictures. How many pictures did the students paint?

- ○ 32
- ○ 36
- ○ 40
- ○ 42

TAKE HOME ACTIVITY • Write two 2-digit numbers and ask your child if he or she would regroup to find the sum.

FOR MORE PRACTICE:
Standards Practice Book, pp. P87–P88

© Houghton Mifflin Harcourt Publishing Company

Name ____________________

2-Digit Addition

Essential Question How do you record the steps when adding 2-digit numbers?

COMMON CORE STANDARD **CC.2.NBT.5**
Use place value understanding and properties of operations to add and subtract.

Listen and Draw REAL WORLD

Draw quick pictures to model each problem.

Tens	Ones

Tens	Ones

FOR THE TEACHER • Read the following problem and have children draw quick pictures to solve. The animal shelter has 35 dogs and 47 cats for adoption. How many pets are at the shelter? Repeat the activity with this problem. After a pet fair, there are only 18 dogs and 21 cats at the shelter. How many pets are at the shelter now?

Math Talk
Explain when you need to regroup ones.

MATHEMATICAL PRACTICES

© Houghton Mifflin Harcourt Publishing Company

Model and Draw

Add 59 and 24.

Step 1 Add the ones.

9 + 4 = 13

Tens	Ones

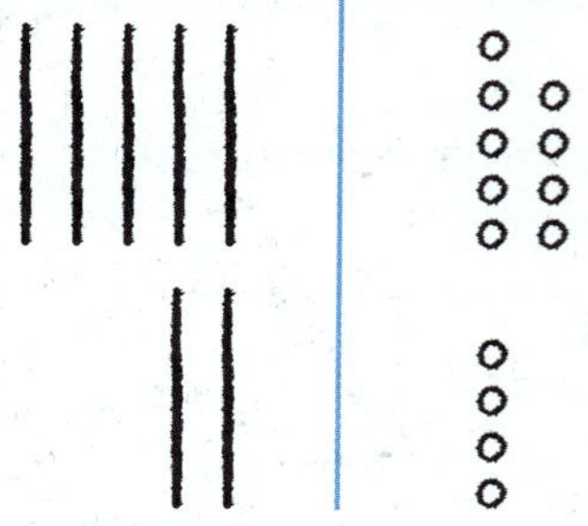

	Tens	Ones
	☐	
	5	9
+	2	4

Step 2 Regroup.
13 ones is the same as 1 ten 3 ones.

Tens	Ones

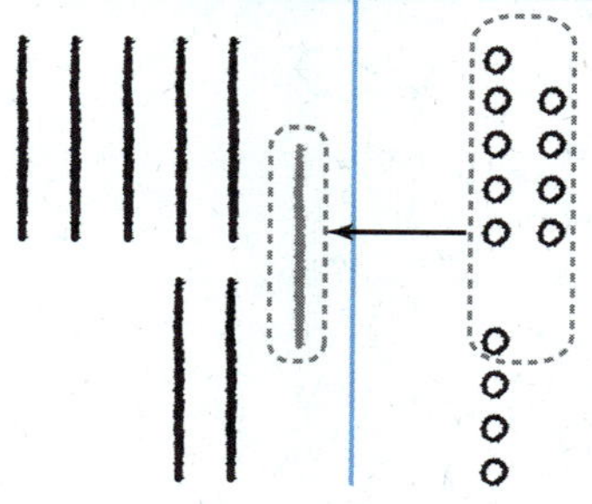

	Tens	Ones
	1	
	5	9
+	2	4
		3

Step 3 Add the tens.

1 + 5 + 2 = 8

Tens	Ones

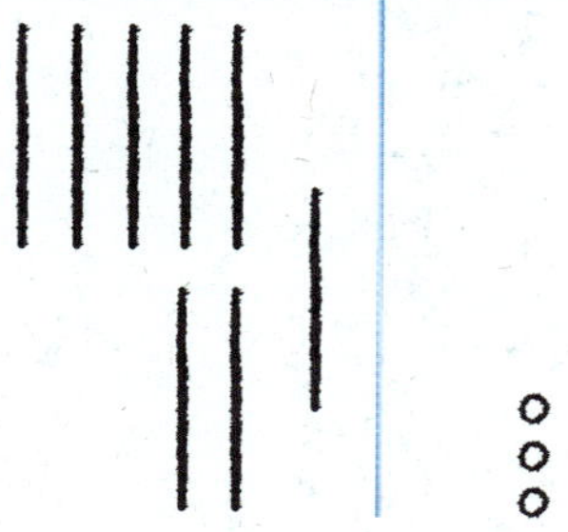

	Tens	Ones
	1	
	5	9
+	2	4
	8	3

Share and Show

Regroup if you need to. Write the sum.

1.

	Tens	Ones
	☐	
	4	2
+	2	9

✓2.

	Tens	Ones
	☐	
	3	1
+	1	4

✓3.

	Tens	Ones
	☐	
	2	7
+	4	5

© Houghton Mifflin Harcourt Publishing Company

Name ____________________

On Your Own

Regroup if you need to. Write the sum.

4.

	Tens	Ones
	□	
	4	8
+		7

5.

	Tens	Ones
	□	
	3	5
+	4	2

6.

	Tens	Ones
	□	
	7	3
+	2	0

7.

	3	3
+	2	7

8.

	5	2
+		5

9.

	3	6
+	5	8

10.

	6	4
+	2	5

11.

	3	5
+	3	8

12.

	3	8
+	5	2

H.O.T. Write the missing digits.

13.

	5	3
+	□	□
	7	8

14.

	□	□
+	4	7
	9	3

15.

	3	□
+	1	9
	□	0

© Houghton Mifflin Harcourt Publishing Company

PROBLEM SOLVING REAL WORLD

Write Math

16. H.O.T. Abby used a different way to add.

35
+ 48
13
+ 70
83

Find the sum, using Abby's way.

$$\begin{array}{r} 57 \\ +\ 29 \\ \hline \end{array}$$

17. Describe Abby's way of adding 2-digit numbers.

____

____

____

____

18. Test Prep Carlos had 68 stamps in his collection. He bought 14 more stamps. How many stamps does he have now?

- ○ 82
- ○ 74
- ○ 72
- ○ 56

TAKE HOME ACTIVITY • Ask your child to show you two ways to add 45 and 38.

FOR MORE PRACTICE: Standards Practice Book, pp. P89–P90

© Houghton Mifflin Harcourt Publishing Company

Name ______________________________

Practice 2-Digit Addition

Essential Question How do you record the steps when adding 2-digit numbers?

COMMON CORE STANDARD CC.2.NBT.5
Use place value understanding and properties of operations to add and subtract.

Listen and Draw REAL WORLD

Choose one way to solve the problem.
Draw or write to show what you did.

Math Talk MATHEMATICAL PRACTICES
Explain why you chose your way of solving the problem.

FOR THE TEACHER • Read the following problem. There were 45 boys and 63 girls who ran in the race. How many children ran in the race?

© Houghton Mifflin Harcourt Publishing Company

Model and Draw

Mrs. Meyers sold 47 snacks before the game. Then she sold 85 snacks during the game. How many snacks did she sell?

Step 1 Add the ones.

$7 + 5 = 12$

Regroup 12 ones as 1 ten 2 ones.

$$\begin{array}{r} {}^{1} \\ 47 \\ +\ 85 \\ \hline 2 \end{array}$$

Step 2 Add the tens.

$1 + 4 + 8 = 13$

$$\begin{array}{r} {}^{1} \\ 47 \\ +\ 85 \\ \hline 2 \end{array}$$

Step 3 13 tens can be regrouped as 1 hundred 3 tens. Write the hundreds digit and the tens digit in the sum.

$$\begin{array}{r} {}^{1} \\ 47 \\ +\ 85 \\ \hline 132 \end{array}$$

Share and Show

Math Board

Write the sum.

1. $\begin{array}{r} 38 \\ +\ 94 \\ \hline \end{array}$

2. $\begin{array}{r} 45 \\ +\ 52 \\ \hline \end{array}$

3. $\begin{array}{r} 83 \\ +\ 76 \\ \hline \end{array}$

4. $\begin{array}{r} 56 \\ +\ 35 \\ \hline \end{array}$

5. $\begin{array}{r} 63 \\ +\ 51 \\ \hline \end{array}$

6. $\begin{array}{r} 74 \\ +\ 49 \\ \hline \end{array}$

© Houghton Mifflin Harcourt Publishing Company

Name ______________________________

On Your Own

Write the sum.

7.
$$\begin{array}{r} 52 \\ +\ 37 \\ \hline \end{array}$$

8.
$$\begin{array}{r} 88 \\ +\ 21 \\ \hline \end{array}$$

9.
$$\begin{array}{r} 74 \\ +\ 67 \\ \hline \end{array}$$

10.
$$\begin{array}{r} 93 \\ +\ 54 \\ \hline \end{array}$$

11.
$$\begin{array}{r} 25 \\ +\ 49 \\ \hline \end{array}$$

12.
$$\begin{array}{r} 92 \\ +\ 78 \\ \hline \end{array}$$

13.
$$\begin{array}{r} 56 \\ +\ 16 \\ \hline \end{array}$$

14.
$$\begin{array}{r} 31 \\ +\ 45 \\ \hline \end{array}$$

15.
$$\begin{array}{r} 43 \\ +\ 72 \\ \hline \end{array}$$

16. H.O.T. Without finding the sums, circle the pairs of addends for which the sum will be greater than 100.

73
18

54
71

47
62

36
59

Explain how you decided which pairs to circle.

____

____

____

TAKE HOME ACTIVITY • Tell your child two 2-digit numbers. Have him or her write the numbers and find the sum.

© Houghton Mifflin Harcourt Publishing Company

FOR MORE PRACTICE:
Standards Practice Book, pp. P91–P92

Name ______________________________

Mid-Chapter Checkpoint

Concepts and Skills

Break apart ones to make a ten.
Then add and write the sum. (CC.2.NBT.6)

1. 37 + 8 = ______

2. 55 + 7 = ______

Break apart the addends to find the sum. (CC.2.NBT.6)

3.
```
  27  →  ______ + ______
+36  →  ______ + ______
        ________________
        ______ + ______ = ______
```

Write the sum. (CC.2.NBT.5)

4.
```
   2 8
+  5 7
------
```

5.
```
   6 7
+  3 1
------
```

6.
```
   7 1
+  1 9
------
```

Test Prep

7. Julia collected 25 cans to recycle. Dan collected 14 cans. How many cans did they collect? (CC.2.NBT.5)

- ○ 39
- ○ 29
- ○ 15
- ○ 11

© Houghton Mifflin Harcourt Publishing Company

Name ______________________________

Rewrite 2-Digit Addition

Essential Question What are two different ways to write addition problems?

COMMON CORE STANDARD CC.2.NBT.5
Use place value understanding and properties of operations to add and subtract.

Listen and Draw REAL WORLD

Write the numbers for each addition problem.

+ ______	+ ______
+ ______	+ ______

Math Talk
Explain why it is important to line up the digits of these addends in columns.

MATHEMATICAL PRACTICES

FOR THE TEACHER • Read the following problem and have children write the addends in vertical format. Juan's family drove 32 miles to his grandmother's house. Then they drove 14 miles to his aunt's house. How many miles did they drive? Repeat for three more problems.

© Houghton Mifflin Harcourt Publishing Company

Model and Draw

Add. 28 + 45 = ?

Step 1 For 28, write the tens digit in the tens column.

Write the ones digit in the ones column.

Repeat for 45.

$$\begin{array}{r} 2\ 8 \\ +\ 4\ 5 \\ \hline \end{array}$$

Step 2 Add the ones.

Regroup if you need to.

Add the tens.

$$\begin{array}{r} 2\ 8 \\ +\ 4\ 5 \\ \hline \end{array}$$

Share and Show

Rewrite the addition problem. Then add.

1. 25 + 8

+ ______

2. 37 + 10

+ ______

3. 25 + 45

+ ______

4. 38 + 29

+ ______

5. 20 + 45

+ ______

6. 63 + 9

+ ______

✓7. 15 + 36

+ ______

✓8. 74 + 18

+ ______

© Houghton Mifflin Harcourt Publishing Company

Name ______________________________

On Your Own

Rewrite the addition problem. Then add.

9. 27 + 54 + ______	10. 34 + 30 + ______	11. 26 − 17 + ______	12. 48 + 38 + ______
13. 50 + 32 + ______	14. 61 + 38 + ______	15. 37 + 43 + ______	16. 79 + 17 + ______
17. 45 + 40 + ______	18. 21 + 52 + ______	19. 17 + 76 + ______	20. 68 + 29 + ______

21. **Explain** how you can solve one of the exercises above without rewriting it.

____

____

____

© Houghton Mifflin Harcourt Publishing Company

PROBLEM SOLVING REAL WORLD

Write Math

Use the table. Write or draw to show how you solved the problems.

Points Scored This Season	
Player	**Number of Points**
Anna	26
Lou	37
Becky	23
Kevin	19

22. How many points did Lou and Becky score?

_______ points

23. H.O.T. Which two players scored 56 points in all? Add to check your answer.

_______ and _______

24. Test Prep John has 29 markers. Claire has 36 markers. How many markers do the two children have?

- ○ 53
- ○ 56
- ○ 65
- ○ 68

TAKE HOME ACTIVITY • Have your child write and solve another problem, using the table above.

FOR MORE PRACTICE: Standards Practice Book, pp. P93–P94

© Houghton Mifflin Harcourt Publishing Company

Name ______________________________

Problem Solving • Addition

PROBLEM SOLVING
Lesson 4.9

Essential Question How can drawing a diagram help when solving addition problems?

COMMON CORE STANDARD **CC.2.OA.1**
Represent and solve problems involving addition and subtraction.

Kendra had 13 crayons. Her dad gave her some more crayons. Then she had 19 crayons. How many crayons did Kendra's dad give her?

Unlock the Problem

What do I need to find?

how many crayons
Kendra's dad gave her

What information do I need to use?

She had _______ crayons.
After he gave her some more crayons, she had _______ crayons.

Show how to solve the problem.

There are 19 crayons in all.

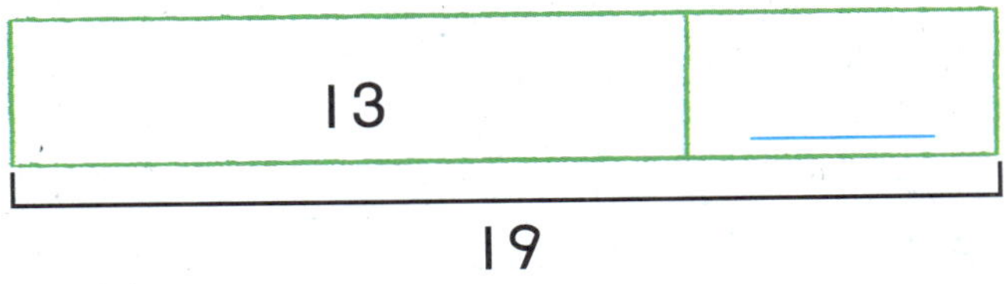

13 + ■ = 19

_______ crayons

HOME CONNECTION • Your child used a bar model and a number sentence to represent the problem. These help show what the missing amount is in order to solve the problem.

© Houghton Mifflin Harcourt Publishing Company

Try Another Problem

Label the bar model. Write a number sentence with a ▒ for the missing number. Solve.

- What do I need to find?
- What information do I need to use?

1. Mr. Kane has 24 red pens. He buys 19 blue pens. How many pens does he have now?

______________________ ______ pens

2. Hannah has 10 pencils. Jim and Hannah have 17 pencils altogether. How many pencils does Jim have?

______________________ ______ pencils

Math Talk

Explain how you know if an amount is a part or the whole in a problem.

MATHEMATICAL PRACTICES

© Houghton Mifflin Harcourt Publishing Company

Name ____________________

Share and Show Math Board

Label the bar model. Write a number sentence with a ▢ for the missing number. Solve.

3. There are 8 owls flying in the forest. There are 15 owls resting in trees. How many owls are there?  ______ owls	______ ______ ______ ____________
4. Aimee and Matthew catch 17 crickets in all. Aimee catches 9 crickets. How many crickets does Matthew catch?  ______ crickets	______ ______ ______ ____________
5. Percy sees a grasshopper jumping in the grass. He counts 16 jumps. Then he counts 15 more jumps. How many jumps does he count?  ______ jumps	______ ______ ______ ____________

© Houghton Mifflin Harcourt Publishing Company

On Your Own

Choose a way to solve.
Write or draw to explain.

Write Math

6. Rita put 5 paper clips in each cup. There are 3 cups in all. How many paper clips are in the cups?

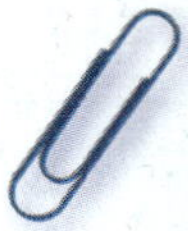

_____ paper clips

7. Jeff has 19 postcards and 2 pens. He buys 20 more postcards. How many postcards does he have now?

_____ postcards

8. H.O.T. Alicia drew 15 flowers. Marie drew 4 more flowers than Alicia drew. How many flowers did they draw?

_____ flowers

9. **Test Prep** There are 23 books in a box. There are 29 books on a shelf. How many books are there?

○ 42
○ 52
○ 56
○ 61

TAKE HOME ACTIVITY • Ask your child to explain how to solve one of the problems above.

FOR MORE PRACTICE:
Standards Practice Book, pp. P95–P96

© Houghton Mifflin Harcourt Publishing Company

Name ______________________________

Algebra • Write Equations to Represent Addition

Essential Question How do you write a number sentence to represent a problem?

COMMON CORE STANDARD CC.2.OA.1

Represent and solve problems involving addition and subtraction.

Listen and Draw REAL WORLD

Draw to show how you found the answer.

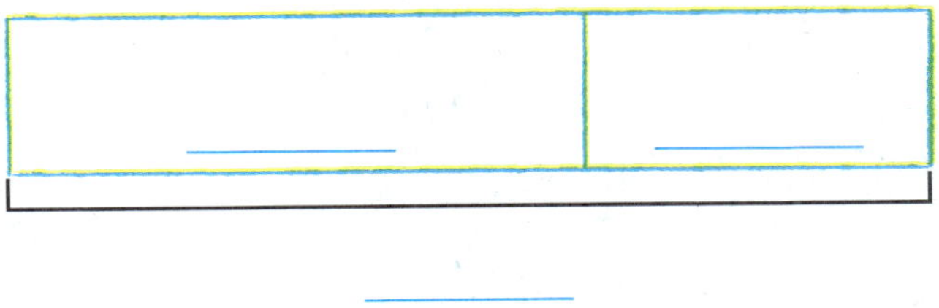

FOR THE TEACHER • Read the following problem and have children choose their own methods for solving. There are 15 children on the bus. Then 9 more children get on the bus. How many children are on the bus now?

Math Talk MATHEMATICAL PRACTICES

Explain how you found the number of children on the bus.

© Houghton Mifflin Harcourt Publishing Company

Model and Draw

You can write a number sentence to show a problem.

Sandy has 16 pencils. Nancy has 13 pencils. How many pencils do the two girls have?

$16 + 13 = \blacksquare$

THINK:

	16 pencils
+	13 pencils
	29 pencils

The two girls have ______ pencils.

Share and Show

Math Board

Write a number sentence for the problem. Use a ■ for the missing number. Then solve.

1. Carl sees 25 melons at the store. 15 are small and the rest are large. How many melons are large?

____

______ melons

2. 83 people went to a movie on Thursday. 53 of them were children and the rest were adults. How many adults were at the movie?

____

______ adults

© Houghton Mifflin Harcourt Publishing Company

Name ________________________________

On Your Own

Write a number sentence for the problem.
Use a ■ for the missing number. Then solve.

3. Chris and his friends went to the zoo. In the Reptile House, they saw 9 snakes and 14 lizards. How many reptiles did they see?

____________________ ________ reptiles

4. Jake had some stamps. Then he bought 20 more stamps. Now he has 56 stamps. How many stamps did Jake have to start?

____________________ ________ stamps

5. H.O.T. Amy has 19 daisies in a bunch. Keisha has 12 more daisies than Amy. How many daisies do Keisha and Amy have?

____________________ ________ daisies

© Houghton Mifflin Harcourt Publishing Company

PROBLEM SOLVING REAL WORLD

Write Math

Read about the field trip. Then solve the problems.

Last week our class went to the park. We counted the plants and animals. We saw 26 oak trees and 14 maple trees. We also saw 13 cardinals and 35 blue jays.

6. How many birds did the class see at the park?

_______ birds

7. H.O.T. Compare the number of trees and the number of birds that the class saw.

_______ ◯ _______

8. Test Prep Mr. Walton baked 54 cookies last week. He baked 38 cookies this week. How many cookies did he bake in the two weeks?

- ○ 92
- ○ 82
- ○ 26
- ○ 16

TAKE HOME ACTIVITY • Have your child explain how he or she solved Exercise 8.

FOR MORE PRACTICE: Standards Practice Book, pp. P97–P98

© Houghton Mifflin Harcourt Publishing Company

Name ______________________________

Algebra • Find Sums for 3 Addends

Essential Question What are some ways to add 3 numbers?

COMMON CORE STANDARD CC.2.NBT.6

Use place value understanding and properties of operations to add and subtract.

Listen and Draw REAL WORLD

Draw to show each problem.

FOR THE TEACHER • Read the following problem and have children draw to show it. Mr. Kim bought 5 blue balloons, 4 red balloons, and 5 yellow balloons. How many balloons did Mr. Kim buy? Repeat for another problem.

Math Talk
Which numbers did you add first in the first problem? **Explain** why.

MATHEMATICAL PRACTICES

© Houghton Mifflin Harcourt Publishing Company

Model and Draw

There are different ways to add three numbers.

How can you add 23, 41, and 17?

Think of different ways to choose digits in the ones column to add first.

You can make a ten first. Then add the other ones digit. Then add the tens.

```
  2 3
  4 1
+ 1 7
-----
```

$3 + 7 = 10$

$10 + 1 = 11$

Add from top to bottom. First add the top two digits in the ones column, then add the next digit. Then add the tens.

```
  2 3
  4 1
+ 1 7
-----
```

$3 + 1 = 4$

$4 + 7 = 11$

Share and Show

Math Board

Add.

1. 33 34 + 32	2. 47 21 + 7	3. 65 13 + 15	4. 58 27 + 22
5. 12 22 + 36	6. 10 42 + 36	✓7. 31 21 + 16	✓8. 30 29 + 48

© Houghton Mifflin Harcourt Publishing Company

Name ______________________________

On Your Own

Add.

9. 22 + 27 + 18	10. 26 + 31 + 19	11. 24 + 11 + 53	12. 33 + 43 + 4
13. 40 + 17 + 32	14. 25 + 25 + 25	15. 19 + 65 + 24	16. 73 + 4 + 16
17. 35 + 24 + 58	18. 32 + 18 + 28	19. 42 + 31 + 12	20. 70 + 18 + 17

21. H.O.T. Circle three numbers in the box that have a sum of 73. Use these clues.

- One number is the sum of 8 and 8.
- One number is between 20 and 30.

13	32
18	
16	49
25	

© Houghton Mifflin Harcourt Publishing Company

PROBLEM SOLVING REAL WORLD

Write Math

Solve. Write or draw to explain.

22. Sophia had 44 marbles. She bought 24 more marbles. Then John gave her 35 marbles. How many marbles does Sophia have now?

______ marbles

23. H.O.T. Write a story problem that could be solved using this number sentence.

$$28 + \blacksquare = 40$$

____

____

____

____

24. **Test Prep** Mrs. Shaw has 23 red notebooks, 15 blue notebooks, and 27 green notebooks. How many notebooks does she have?

- ○ 38
- ○ 42
- ○ 55
- ○ 65

TAKE HOME ACTIVITY • Ask your child to show you two ways to add 17, 13, and 24.

FOR MORE PRACTICE:
Standards Practice Book, pp. P99–P100

© Houghton Mifflin Harcourt Publishing Company

Name ___________________________________

Algebra • Find Sums for 4 Addends

Essential Question What are some ways to add 4 numbers?

COMMON CORE STANDARD CC.2.NBT.6
Use place value understanding and properties of operations to add and subtract.

Listen and Draw REAL WORLD

Show how you solved each problem.

Math Talk MATHEMATICAL PRACTICES
Describe how you found the answer to the first problem.

FOR THE TEACHER • Read this problem and have children choose a way to solve it. Shelly counts 16 ants in her ant farm. Pedro counts 22 ants in his farm. Tara counts 14 ants in her farm. How many ants do the 3 children count? Repeat for another problem.

© Houghton Mifflin Harcourt Publishing Company

Model and Draw

You can add digits in a column in more than one way. Add the ones first. Then add the tens.

Find a sum that you know. Then add to it.

```
  3 1
  1 4 \
  2 7  > 8
+ 2 4 /
-----
```

THINK: 8 + 1 = 9, then add on 7 more. The sum of the ones is 16 ones.

Add pairs of digits first. Then add these sums.

```
  3 1 \
  1 4 / 5
  2 7 \
+ 2 4 / 11
-----
```

THINK: 5 + 11 = 16, so there are 16 ones in all.

Share and Show

Math Board

Add.

1.
```
  23
  11
  22
+ 31
----
```

2.
```
  30
  15
   3
+ 25
----
```

3.
```
  13
  26
  54
+ 12
----
```

4.
```
  27
   2
  23
+ 13
----
```

✓5.
```
  45
  14
  35
+ 51
----
```

✓6.
```
  32
  21
  15
+ 30
----
```

© Houghton Mifflin Harcourt Publishing Company

Name ______________________________

On Your Own

Add.

7. $\begin{array}{r} 36 \\ 12 \\ 21 \\ +\ 26 \\ \hline \end{array}$

8. $\begin{array}{r} 14 \\ 23 \\ 20 \\ +\ 11 \\ \hline \end{array}$

9. $\begin{array}{r} 22 \\ 13 \\ 15 \\ +\ 27 \\ \hline \end{array}$

10. $\begin{array}{r} 45 \\ 12 \\ 41 \\ +\ 22 \\ \hline \end{array}$

11. $\begin{array}{r} 59 \\ 31 \\ 51 \\ +\ 73 \\ \hline \end{array}$

12. $\begin{array}{r} 34 \\ 10 \\ 31 \\ +\ 22 \\ \hline \end{array}$

13. $\begin{array}{r} 14 \\ 40 \\ 51 \\ +\ 32 \\ \hline \end{array}$

14. $\begin{array}{r} 21 \\ 12 \\ 32 \\ +\ 24 \\ \hline \end{array}$

15. $\begin{array}{r} 16 \\ 61 \\ 25 \\ +\ 44 \\ \hline \end{array}$

16. $\begin{array}{r} 60 \\ 15 \\ 3 \\ +\ 21 \\ \hline \end{array}$

17. $\begin{array}{r} 22 \\ 43 \\ 33 \\ +\ 30 \\ \hline \end{array}$

18. $\begin{array}{r} 58 \\ 82 \\ 24 \\ +\ 64 \\ \hline \end{array}$

© Houghton Mifflin Harcourt Publishing Company

PROBLEM SOLVING REAL WORLD

Write Math

Use the table.
Write or draw to show how you solved the problems.

Shells Collected at the Beach	
Child	**Number of Shells**
Katie	34
Paul	15
Noah	26
Laney	21

19. How many shells did the four children collect at the beach?

_____ shells

20. H.O.T. Which two children collected more shells at the beach, Katie and Paul, or Noah and Laney?

_____

21. Test Prep There were 24 red beads, 31 blue beads, and 8 green beads in a jar. Then Sasha put 16 beads into the jar. How many beads are in the jar now?

- ○ 89
- ○ 79
- ○ 69
- ○ 63

TAKE HOME ACTIVITY • Have your child explain how he or she solved Exercise 19.

FOR MORE PRACTICE:
Standards Practice Book, pp. P101–P102

© Houghton Mifflin Harcourt Publishing Company

Name ____________________

Chapter 4 Review/Test

Vocabulary

Use a word in the box to complete each sentence.

sum
regroup
addend

1. When finding the sum for 37 + 14,

____________ 10 ones to make 1 ten. (p. 186)

2. In 46 + 7 = 53, 53 is the ____________. (p. 174)

Concepts and Skills

Draw quick pictures to solve.
Write the sum. (CC.2.NBT.6)

3.

	Tens	Ones
	□	
	2	6
+	3	2

Tens	Ones

4.

	Tens	Ones
	□	
	5	3
+	2	7

Tens	Ones

Add. (CC.2.NBT.6)

5.
$$\begin{array}{r} 44 \\ 23 \\ +\ 16 \\ \hline \end{array}$$

6.
$$\begin{array}{r} 24 \\ 31 \\ +\ 23 \\ \hline \end{array}$$

7.
$$\begin{array}{r} 15 \\ 42 \\ 30 \\ +\ 12 \\ \hline \end{array}$$

© Houghton Mifflin Harcourt Publishing Company

Fill in the bubble for the correct answer choice.

TEST PREP

8. Lauren's family drove to the beach. They saw 14 gulls the first day. The next day they saw 7 more gulls.

How many gulls did they see in the two days? (CC.2.NBT.6)

- ○ 7
- ○ 20
- ○ 21
- ○ 31

9. Mr. O'Brien visited a lighthouse. He climbed 26 stairs. Then he climbed 64 more stairs to the top. How many stairs did he climb at the lighthouse? (CC.2.NBT.6)

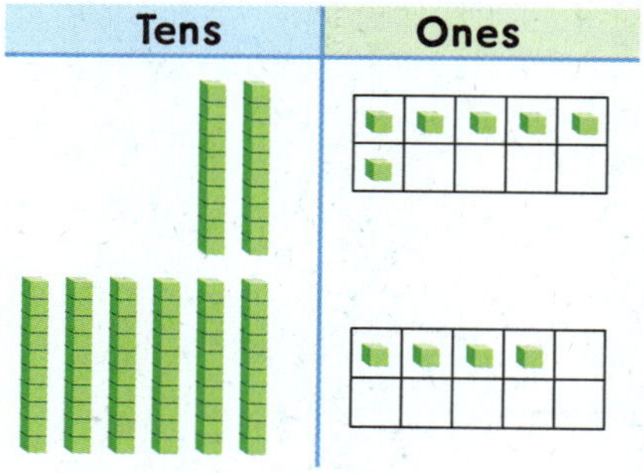

- ○ 90
- ○ 82
- ○ 80
- ○ 42

10. Nicole made a necklace. She used 13 red beads. She used 28 blue beads. How many beads did she use? (CC.2.NBT.6)

- ○ 15
- ○ 31
- ○ 35
- ○ 41

© Houghton Mifflin Harcourt Publishing Company

Name ______________________________

TEST PREP

Fill in the bubble for the correct answer choice.

11. Scott baked 24 muffins. He placed 15 muffins on the plate. How many muffins are not on the plate? (CC.2.OA.1)

- ○ 6
- ○ 8
- ○ 9
- ○ 19

---

12. Carlos is at the museum. There are 23 people in his group. There are 36 people in a second group. There are 44 people in a third group.

How many people are in the three groups? (CC.2.NBT.6)

- ○ 913
- ○ 103
- ○ 80
- ○ 59

---

13. Amy picked 57 strawberries. Her mother picked 34 strawberries. How many strawberries did they pick? (CC.2.NBT.5)

- ○ 91
- ○ 90
- ○ 83
- ○ 81

© Houghton Mifflin Harcourt Publishing Company

Constructed Response

14. Mike saw 17 blue cars and 25 green cars at the toy store. How many cars did he see? Write a number sentence with a ■ for the missing number. Explain how the number sentence shows the problem. (CC.2.OA.1, CC.2.NBT.5)

____

____

____

Performance Task (CC.2.OA.1, CC.2.NBT.5)

15. Ling saw these four signs at the theater.

Section A	Section B	Section C	Section D
35 seats	43 seats	17 seats	23 seats

Which two sections have 58 seats in all?

Draw or write to show how you solved the problem.

Explain how you found the numbers that have a sum of 58.

____

____

____

© Houghton Mifflin Harcourt Publishing Company

Chapter 5

2-Digit Subtraction

Curious About Math with Curious George

There are hundreds of different kinds of dragonflies.
If 52 dragonflies are in a garden and 10 fly away, how many dragonflies are left? How many are left if 10 more fly away?

© Houghton Mifflin Harcourt Publishing Company. Curious George by Margret and H.A. Rey. Copyright (c) 2010 by Houghton Mifflin Harcourt Publishing Company. All rights reserved. The character Curious George®, including without limitation the character's name and the character's likenesses, are registered trademarks of Houghton Mifflin Harcourt Publishing Company.

Name ______________________________

Show What You Know

Subtraction Patterns

Subtract 2. Complete each subtraction sentence.

1. 7 − 2 = 5	4. 4 − ____ = ____
2. 6 − ____ = ____	5. 3 − ____ = ____
3. 5 − ____ = ____	6. 2 − ____ = ____

Subtraction Facts

Write the difference.

7.	8.	9.	10.	11.	12.
8	14	9	16	12	10
− 5	− 6	− 6	− 7	− 6	− 8

Tens and Ones

Write how many tens and ones are in each model.

13. 54

____ tens ____ ones

14. 45

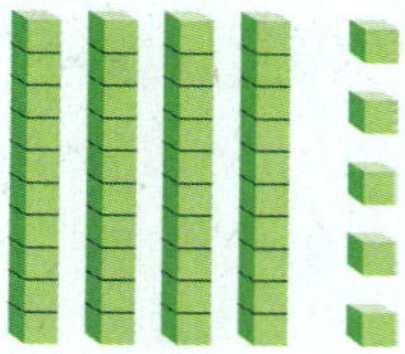

____ tens ____ ones

Family note: This page checks your child's understanding of important skills needed for success in Chapter 5.

GO Online Assessment Options Soar to Success Math

© Houghton Mifflin Harcourt Publishing Company

Name ______________________

Vocabulary Builder

Review Words
difference
regroup
tens
ones
digit

Visualize It

Fill in the boxes of the graphic organizer.

difference

Describe it.

____

____

Examples

$10 - 4 = 6$

____

____

Not Examples

$4 + 6 = 10$

____

____

Understand Vocabulary

Draw a line to complete the sentence.

1. A **digit** can be •
2. You can **regroup** •
3. 20 **ones** are the same •

• as 2 **tens**.

• 0, 1, 2, 3, 4, 5, 6, 7, 8, or 9.

• to trade 10 ones for 1 ten.

© Houghton Mifflin Harcourt Publishing Company

GO Online
• eStudent Edition
• Multimedia eGlossary

Chapter 5

Game Subtraction Search

Materials

- 3 sets of number cards 4–9
- 18 (red counters)

Play with a partner.

1. Shuffle all the cards. Place them face down in one stack.
2. Take one card. Find a square with a subtraction problem with this number as the difference. Your partner checks your answer.
3. If you are correct, place a (red counter) on that square. If there is no match, skip your turn.
4. Take turns. The first player to have (red counters) on all the squares wins.

Player 1

12 − 5	9 − 2	10 − 5
16 − 7	13 − 7	17 − 9
7 − 3	11 − 5	18 − 9

Player 2

8 − 3	15 − 7	11 − 6
17 − 8	9 − 3	16 − 8
13 − 9	6 − 2	14 − 7

© Houghton Mifflin Harcourt Publishing Company

Name ______________________________

Algebra • Break Apart Ones to Subtract

Essential Question How does breaking apart a number make subtracting easier?

COMMON CORE STANDARD CC.2.NBT.5
Use place value understanding and properties of operations to add and subtract.

Listen and Draw

Write two addends for each sum.

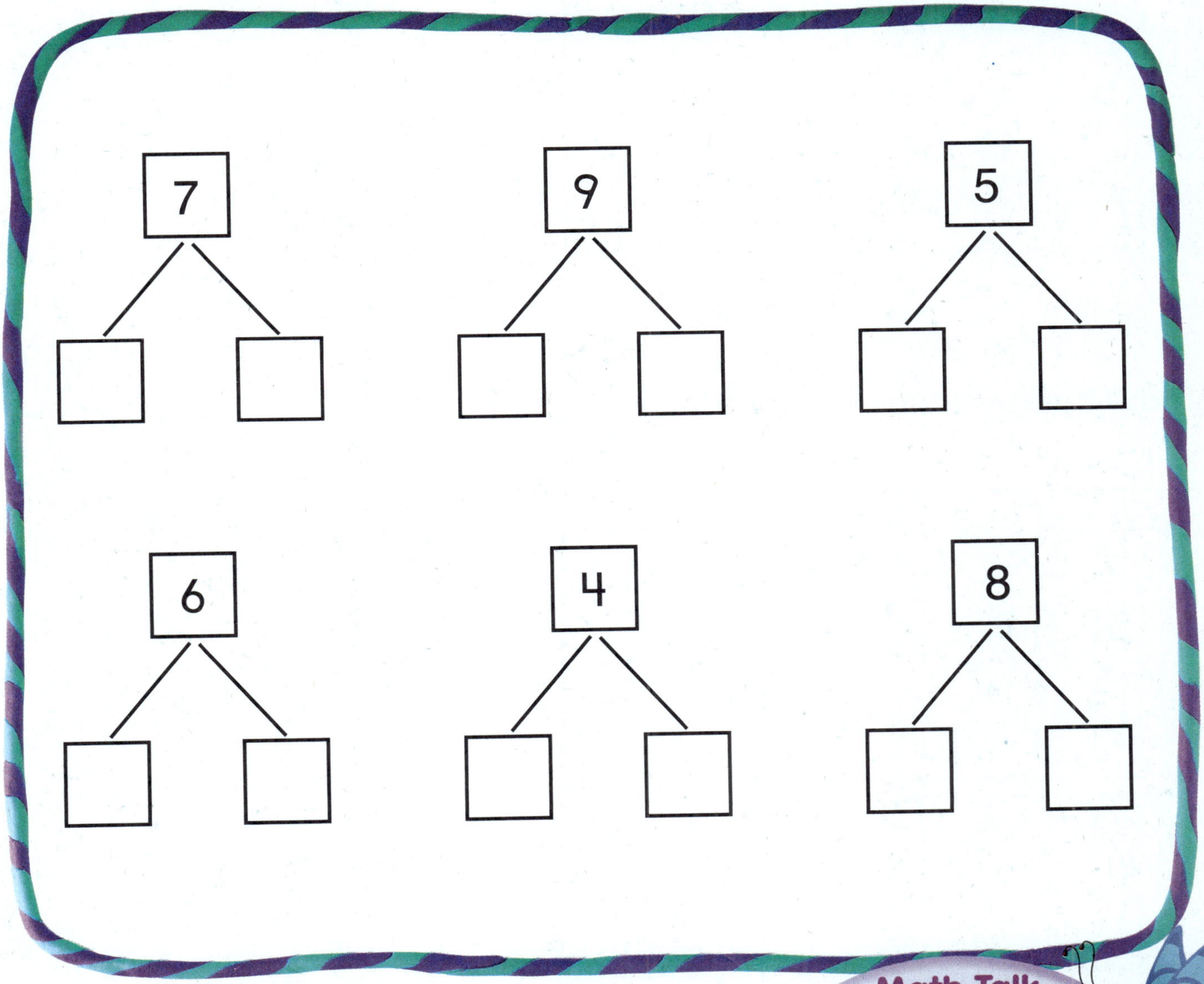

FOR THE TEACHER • After children have recorded addends for each sum, have a class discussion about the different facts that children represented on their papers.

Math Talk
Describe how you chose addends for each sum.

© Houghton Mifflin Harcourt Publishing Company

Model and Draw

Break apart ones. Subtract in two steps.

63 − 7 = ■

3 4

Start at 63. Subtract 3 to get to 60. Then subtract 4 more.

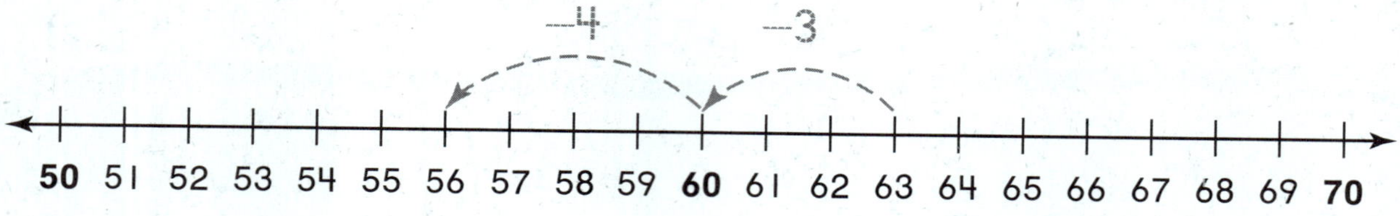

So, 63 − 7 = ______.

Share and Show

Math Board

Break apart ones to subtract. Write the difference.

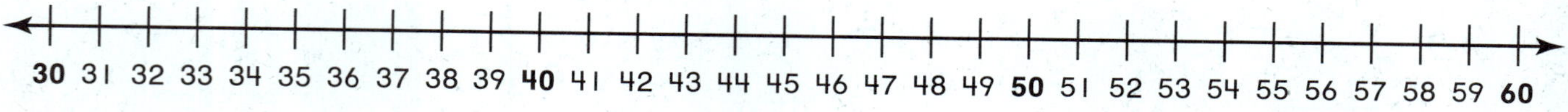

1. 55 − 8 = ______

5 3

2. 42 − 5 = ______

2 3

3. 41 − 9 = ______

4. 53 − 6 = ______

5. 44 − 7 = ______

6. 52 − 8 = ______

© Houghton Mifflin Harcourt Publishing Company

Name ______________________________

On Your Own

Break apart ones to subtract. Write the difference.

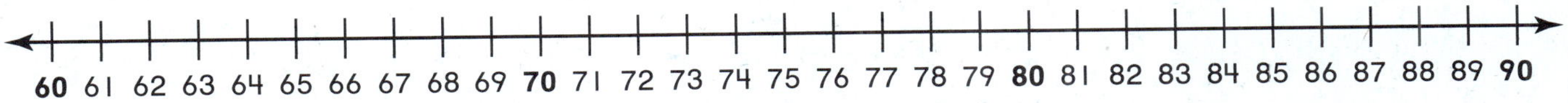

7. 75 − 7 = ______

8. 86 − 8 = ______

9. 82 − 5 = ______

10. 83 − 7 = ______

11. 72 − 7 = ______

12. 76 − 9 = ______

13. 85 − 8 = ______

14. 71 − 6 = ______

H.O.T. Write the differences. Then write the next fact in the pattern.

15. 54 − 5 = 49

54 − 6 = ______

54 − 7 = ______

____

16. 81 − 4 = 77

71 − 4 = ______

61 − 4 = ______

____

© Houghton Mifflin Harcourt Publishing Company

PROBLEM SOLVING REAL WORLD

Write Math

Choose a way to solve.
Write or draw to explain.

17. Cheryl built a toy train with 27 train cars. Then she added 18 more train cars to the train. How many train cars are on the toy train now?

_______ train cars

18. H.O.T. Samuel had 46 marbles. He gave some marbles to a friend and has 9 marbles left. How many marbles did Samuel give to his friend?

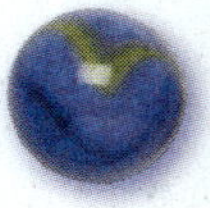

_______ marbles

19. Test Prep Matthew had 73 blocks. He gave 8 blocks to his sister. How many blocks does Matthew have now?

- ○ 81
- ○ 70
- ○ 68
- ○ 65

TAKE HOME ACTIVITY • Ask your child to describe how to find 34 − 6.

© Houghton Mifflin Harcourt Publishing Company

FOR MORE PRACTICE:
Standards Practice Book, pp. P107–P108

Name ______________________________

Algebra • Break Apart Numbers to Subtract

Essential Question How does breaking apart a number make subtracting easier?

COMMON CORE STANDARD **CC.2.NBT.5**

Use place value understanding and properties of operations to add and subtract.

Listen and Draw REAL WORLD

Draw jumps on the number line to show how to break apart the number to subtract.

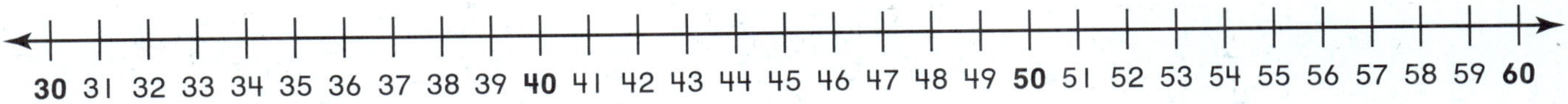

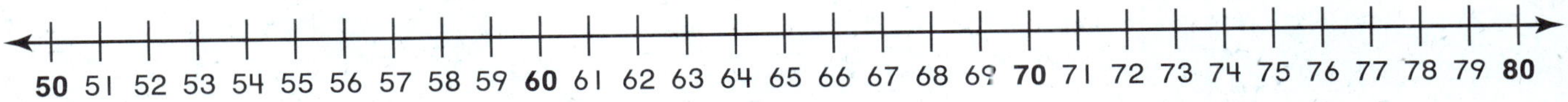

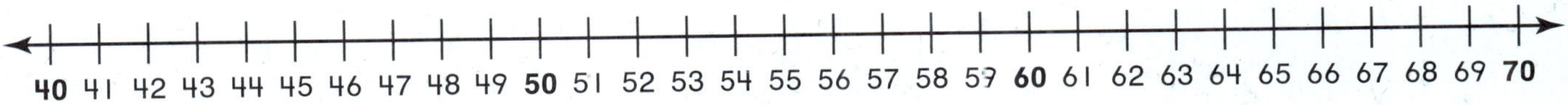

FOR THE TEACHER • Read the following problem. Have children draw jumps on the number line to solve. Mrs. Hill had 45 paintbrushes. She gave 9 paintbrushes to students in her art class. How many paintbrushes does Mrs. Hill have now? Repeat the same problem situation for 72 – 7 and 53 – 6.

Math Talk

For one of the problems, **describe** what you did.

MATHEMATICAL PRACTICES

© Houghton Mifflin Harcourt Publishing Company

Model and Draw

Break apart the number you are subtracting into tens and ones.

Subtract 10.
Next, subtract 2 to get to 60.
Then subtract 5 more.

72 − 17 = ■

10 7

2 5

10 + 2 + 5 = 17

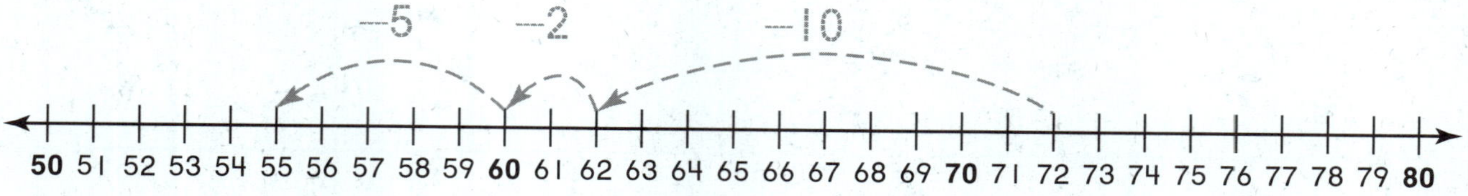

So, 72 − 17 = ______.

Share and Show

Math Board

Break apart the number you are subtracting.
Write the difference.

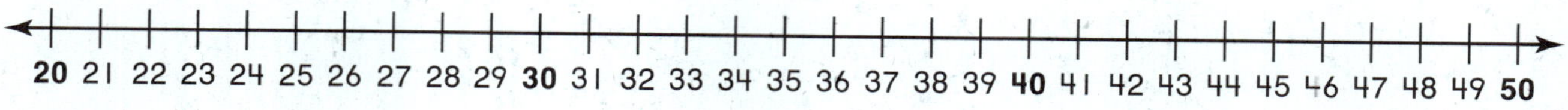

1. 43 − 18 = ______

10 8

3 5

2. 45 − 14 = ______

10 4

3. 46 − 17 = ______

4. 44 − 16 = ______

© Houghton Mifflin Harcourt Publishing Company

Name ______________________________

On Your Own

Break apart the number you are subtracting.
Write the difference.

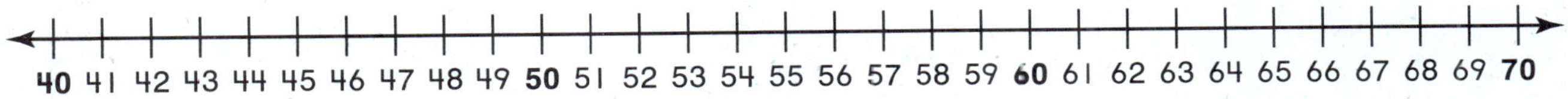

5. 57 − 15 = ______

6. 63 − 17 = ______

7. 68 − 19 = ______

8. 61 − 18 = ______

9. 65 − 13 = ______

10. 59 − 14 = ______

11. 62 − 11 = ______

12. 67 − 18 = ______

13. Look at Tom's steps to solve a problem.
Solve this problem in the same way.

42 − 15 = ?

Tom

35 − 18 = ?

35 − 10 = 25
25 − 5 = 20
20 − 3 = (17)

© Houghton Mifflin Harcourt Publishing Company

PROBLEM SOLVING REAL WORLD

Write Math

Solve. Write or draw to explain.

14. 38 people are in the library. Then 33 more people go into the library. How many people are in the library now?

_______ people

15. H.O.T. Jane has 53 toys in a box. She takes some toys out of the box. Then there are 36 toys in the box. How many toys did she take out of the box?

_______ toys

16. Test Prep There are 32 papers in the first stack. There are 19 papers in the second stack. How many more papers are in the first stack than in the second stack?

- ○ 51
- ○ 27
- ○ 23
- ○ 13

© Houghton Mifflin Harcourt Publishing Company

TAKE HOME ACTIVITY • Ask your child to write a subtraction story that uses 2-digit numbers.

FOR MORE PRACTICE: Standards Practice Book, pp. P109–P110

Name ______________________________

Model Regrouping for Subtraction

Essential Question When do you regroup in subtraction?

COMMON CORE STANDARDS CC.2.NBT.9, CC.2.NBT.5

Use place value understanding and properties of operations to add and subtract.

Listen and Draw REAL WORLD

Use   to model the problem.
Draw quick pictures to show your model.

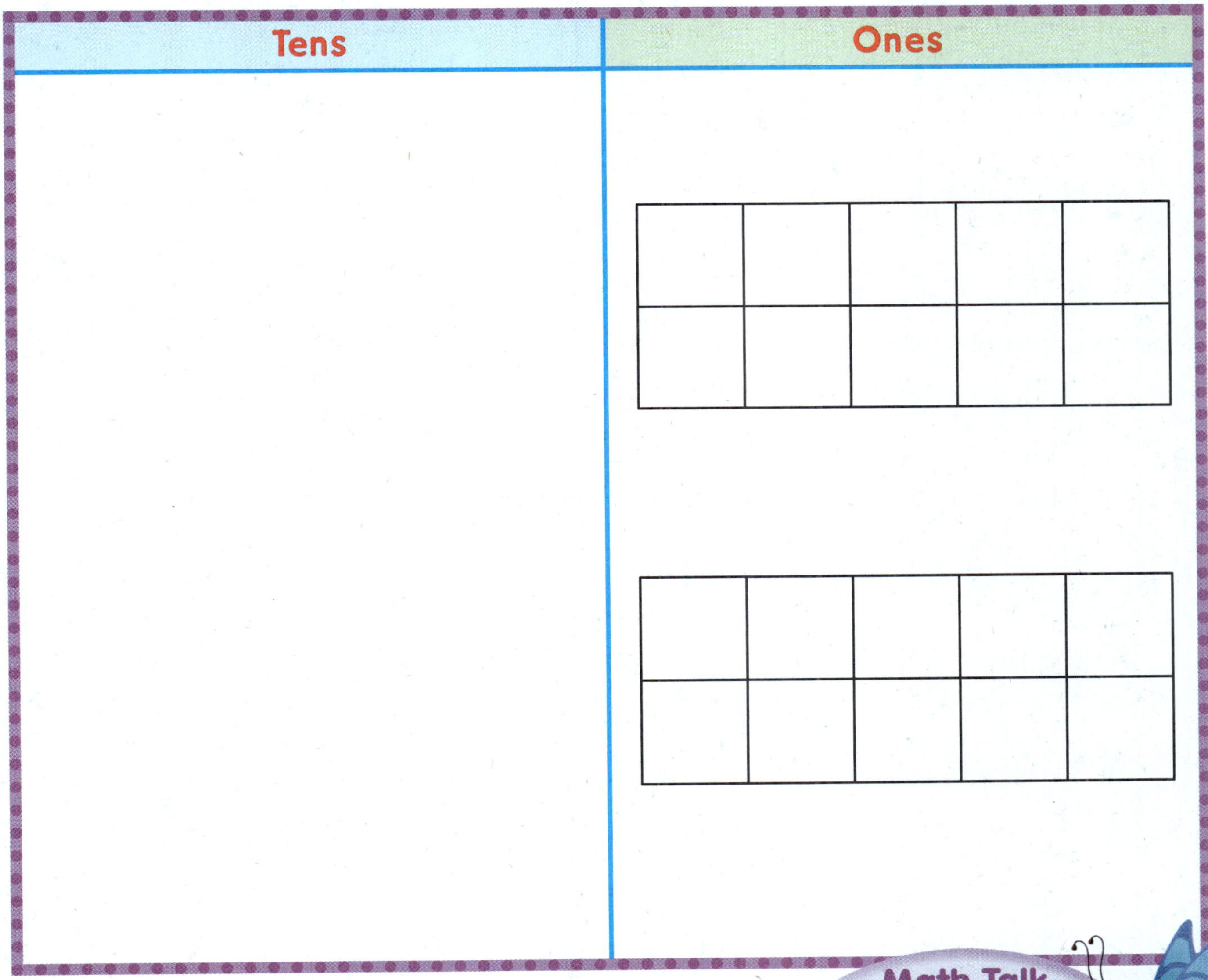

FOR THE TEACHER • Read the following problem. Michelle counted 21 butterflies in her garden. Then 7 butterflies flew away. How many butterflies were still in the garden?

Math Talk **Describe** why you traded a tens block for 10 ones blocks.

MATHEMATICAL PRACTICES

© Houghton Mifflin Harcourt Publishing Company

Model and Draw

How do you subtract 26 from 53?

Step 1 Show 53. Are there enough ones to subtract 6?

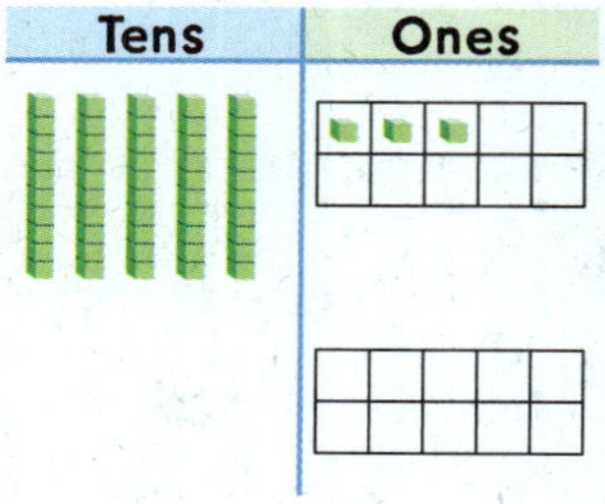

yes   no

Step 2 If there are not enough ones, regroup 1 ten as 10 ones.

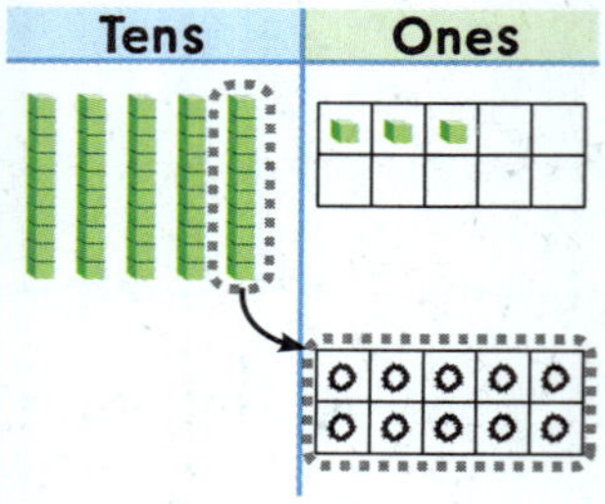

Step 3 Subtract 6 ones from 13 ones.

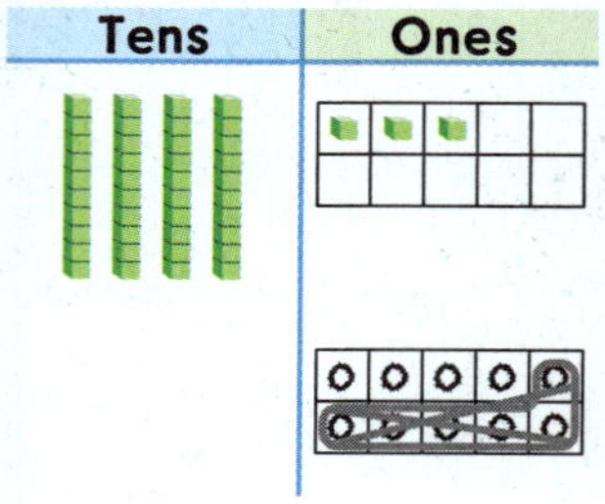

Step 4 Subtract the tens. Write the tens and ones. Write the difference.

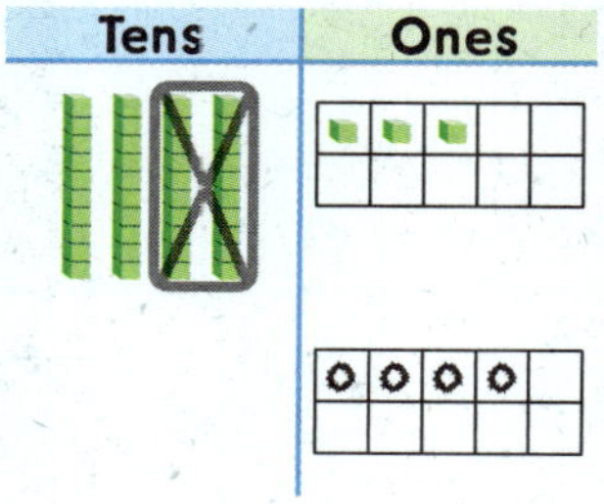

____ tens ____ ones

____

Share and Show

Math Board

Draw to show the regrouping. Write the difference two ways. Write the tens and ones. Write the number.

1. Subtract 13 from 41.

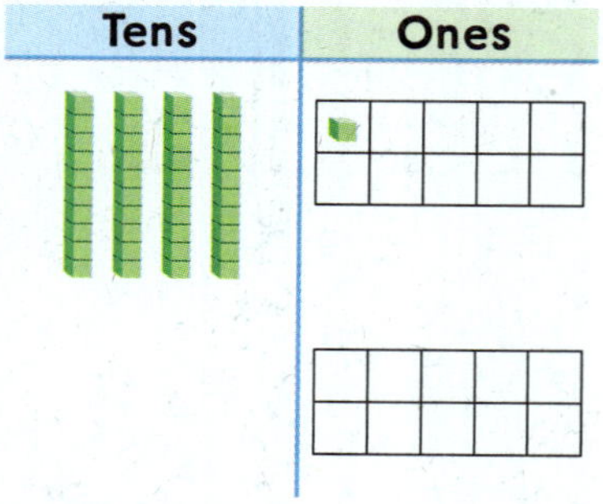

_____ tens _____ ones

____

2. Subtract 9 from 48.

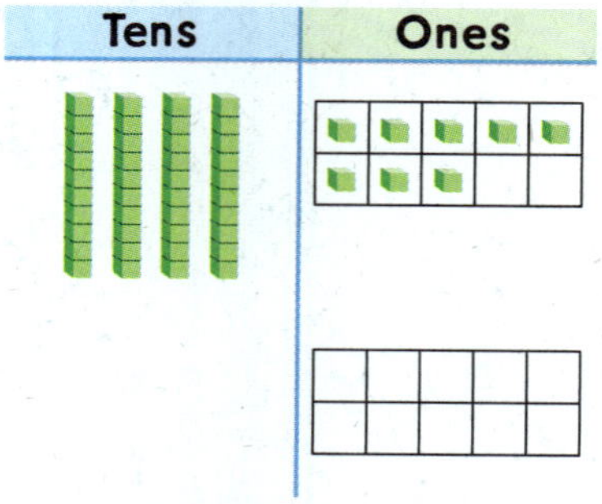

_____ tens _____ ones

____

3. Subtract 28 from 52.

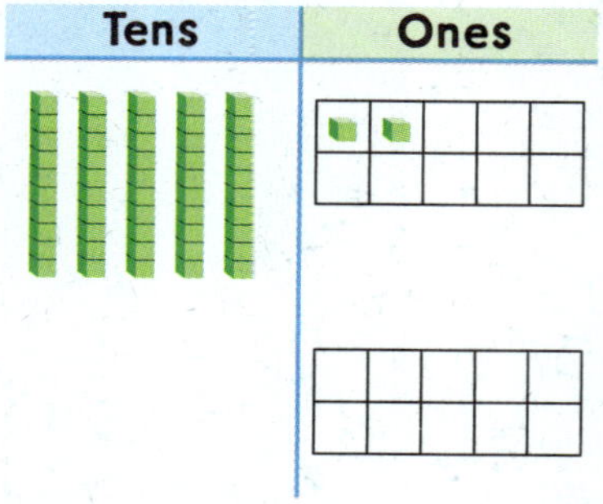

_____ tens _____ ones

____

© Houghton Mifflin Harcourt Publishing Company

Name ______________________________

On Your Own

Draw to show the regrouping. Write the difference two ways. Write the tens and ones. Write the number.

4. Subtract 8 from 23.

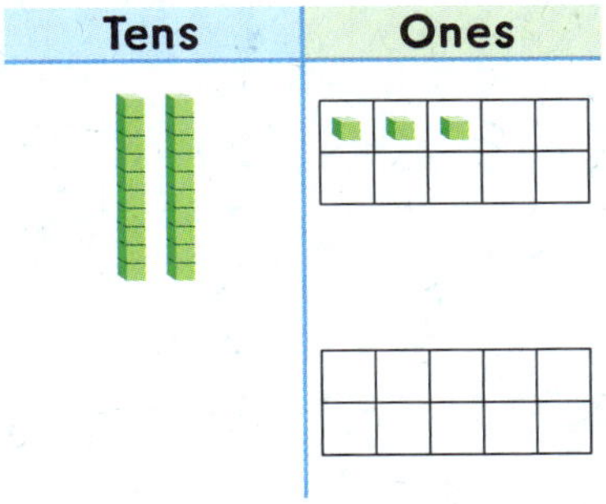

_____ ten _____ ones

____

5. Subtract 36 from 45.

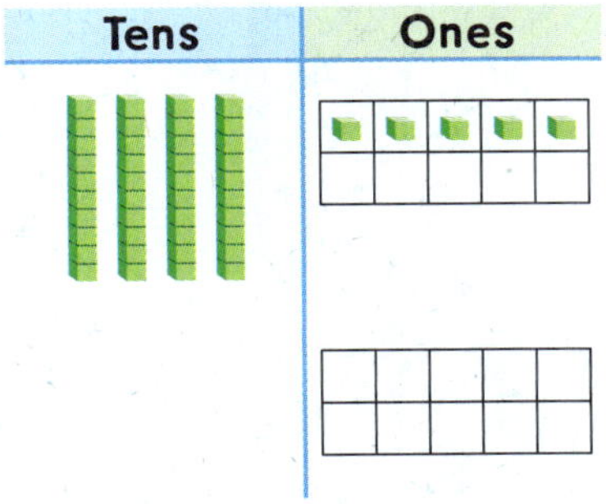

_____ tens _____ ones

____

6. Subtract 6 from 43.

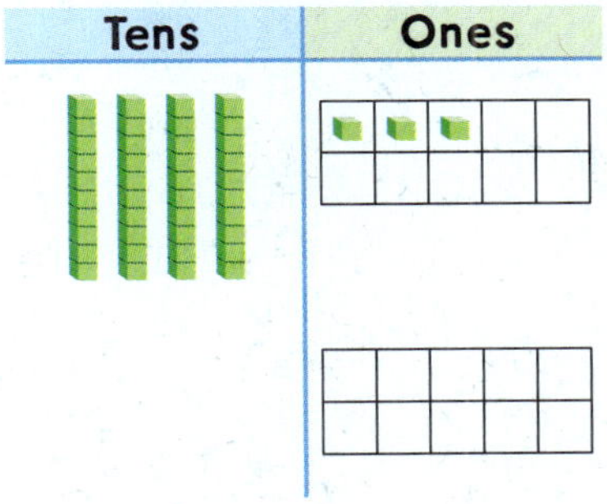

_____ tens _____ ones

____

7. Subtract 39 from 67.

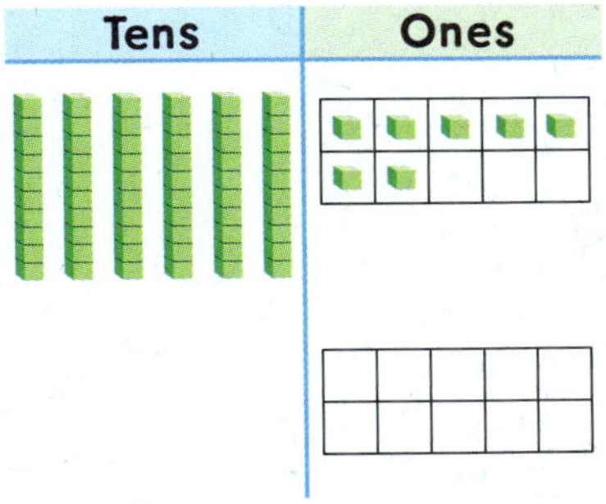

_____ tens _____ ones

____

8. Subtract 21 from 50.

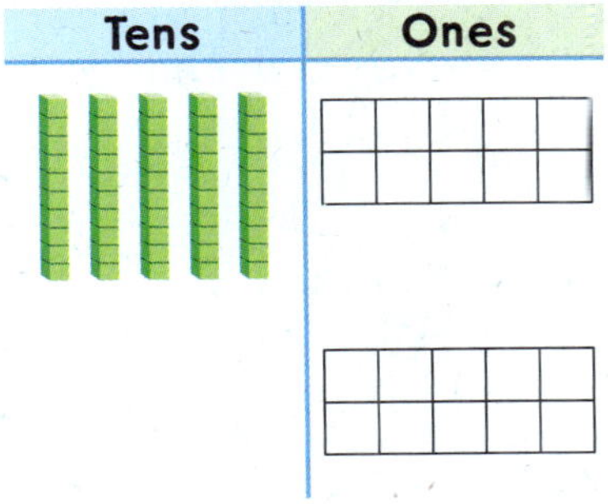

_____ tens _____ ones

____

9. Subtract 29 from 56.

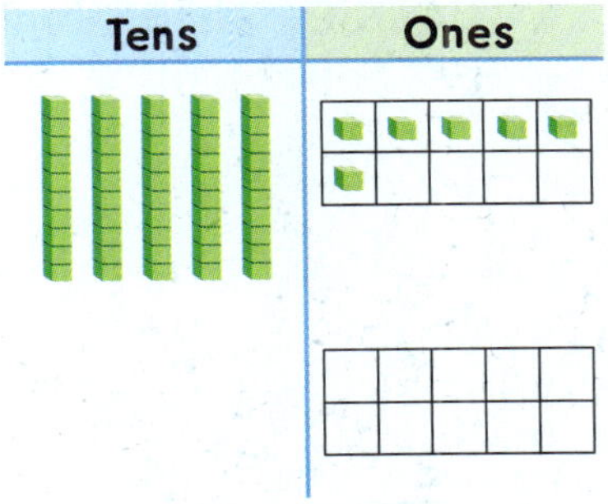

_____ tens _____ ones

____

10. H.O.T. Draw to find what number was subtracted from 53.

Subtract _______ from 53.

3 tens 4 ones

34

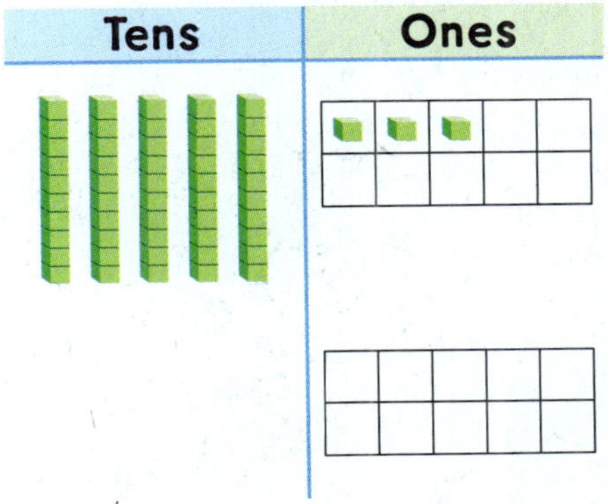

© Houghton Mifflin Harcourt Publishing Company

PROBLEM SOLVING REAL WORLD

Write Math

Choose a way to solve.
Write or draw to explain.

11. Claire's puzzle has 85 pieces. She has used 46 pieces so far. How many puzzle pieces have not been used yet?

______ puzzle pieces

12. H.O.T. Billy has 18 fewer marbles than Sara. Sara has 34 marbles. How many marbles does Billy have?

______ marbles

13. **Test Prep** There were 65 toy animals in the store. Then the clerk sold 17 toy animals. How many toy animals are in the store now?

- ○ 48
- ○ 52
- ○ 78
- ○ 82

TAKE HOME ACTIVITY • Ask your child to write a subtraction story and then explain how to solve it.

FOR MORE PRACTICE: Standards Practice Book, pp. P111–P112

© Houghton Mifflin Harcourt Publishing Company

Name ____________________

Lesson 5.4

Model and Record 2-Digit Subtraction

Essential Question How do you record 2-digit subtraction?

COMMON CORE STANDARD CC.2.NBT.5
Use place value understanding and properties of operations to add and subtract.

Listen and Draw REAL WORLD

Use   to model the problem.
Draw quick pictures to show your model.

Tens	Ones

FOR THE TEACHER • Read the following problem. Mr. Kelly made 47 muffins. His students ate 23 of the muffins. How many muffins were not eaten?

Math Talk
Did you trade blocks in your model? **Explain** why or why not.

MATHEMATICAL PRACTICES

© Houghton Mifflin Harcourt Publishing Company

Model and Draw

Trace over the quick pictures in the steps.

Subtract.

$$\begin{array}{r} 56 \\ -\ 19 \\ \hline \end{array}$$

Step 1 Show 56. Are there enough ones to subtract 9?

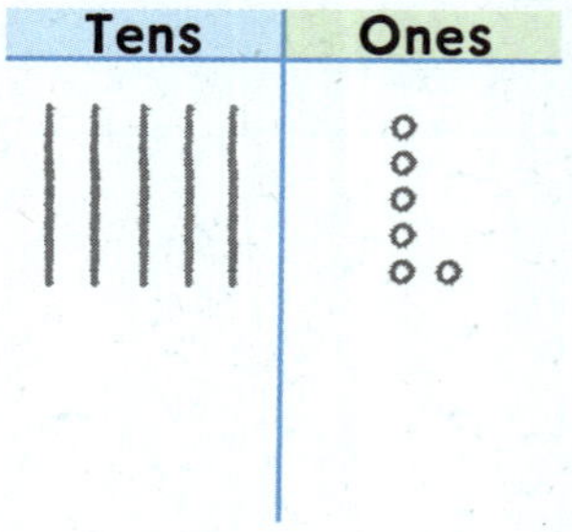

	Tens	Ones
	□	□
	5	6
−	1	9

Step 2 If there are not enough ones, regroup 1 ten as 10 ones.

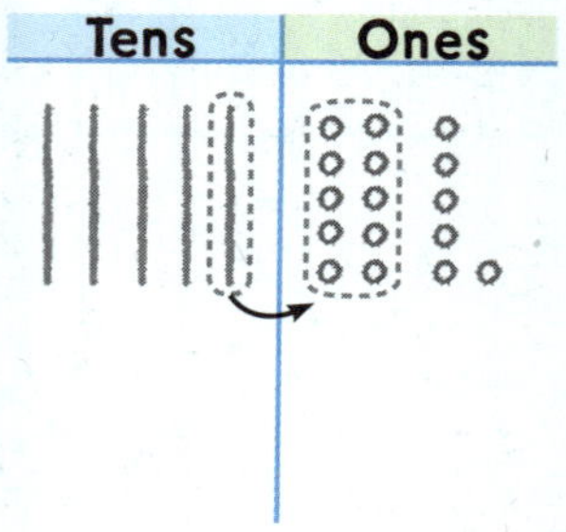

	Tens	Ones
	4	16
	~~5~~	~~6~~
−	1	9

Step 3 Subtract the ones.

16 − 9 = 7

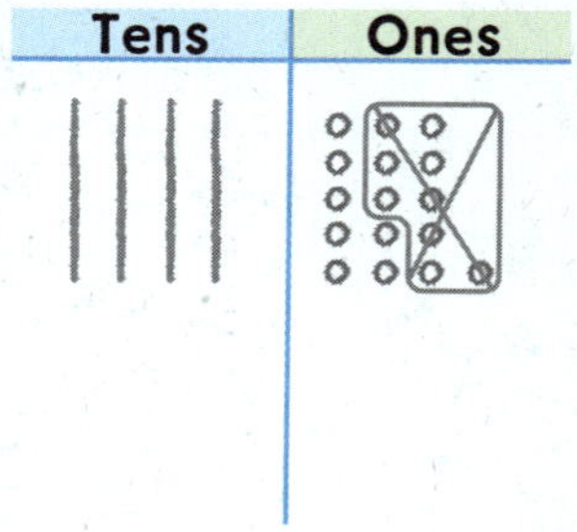

	Tens	Ones
	4	16
	~~5~~	~~6~~
−	1	9
		7

Step 4 Subtract the tens.

4 − 1 = 3

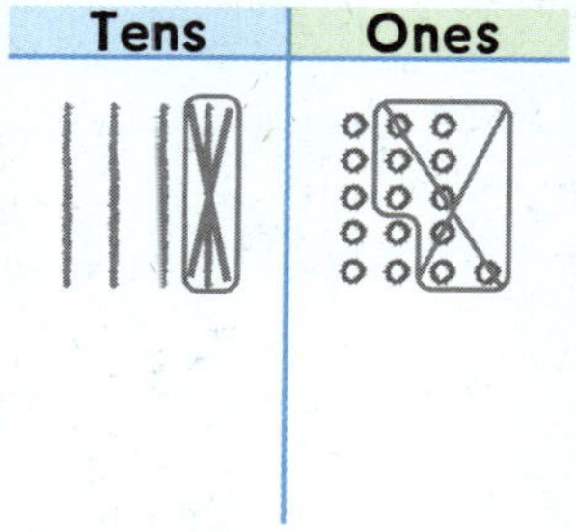

	Tens	Ones
	4	16
	~~5~~	~~6~~
−	1	9
	3	7

Share and Show

Math Board

Draw a quick picture to solve. Write the difference.

✓1.

	Tens	Ones
	□	□
	4	7
−	1	5

Tens	Ones

✓2.

	Tens	Ones
	□	□
	3	2
−	1	8

Tens	Ones

© Houghton Mifflin Harcourt Publishing Company

Name ______________________________

On Your Own

Draw a quick picture to solve. Write the difference.

3.

	Tens	Ones
	☐	☐
	3	5
−	2	9

Tens	Ones

4.

	Tens	Ones
	☐	☐
	2	8
−		5

Tens	Ones

5.

	Tens	Ones
	☐	☐
	5	3
−	2	6

Tens	Ones

6.

	Tens	Ones
	☐	☐
	3	2
−	1	3

Tens	Ones

7.

	Tens	Ones
	☐	☐
	4	4
−	1	7

Tens	Ones

8.

	Tens	Ones
	☐	☐
	3	8
−	1	8

Tens	Ones

© Houghton Mifflin Harcourt Publishing Company

PROBLEM SOLVING REAL WORLD

Write Math

Solve. Write or draw to explain.

9. Sophia got 63 points in the math contest. Dennis got 46 points. How many more points did Sophia get than Dennis?

_______ more points

10. H.O.T. There were some people at the park. 24 people went home. Then there were 19 people at the park. How many people were at the park before?

_______ people

11. **Test Prep** Mr. Sims has a box of 44 erasers. He gives 18 erasers to his students. How many erasers does Mr. Sims have now?

- ○ 22
- ○ 26
- ○ 36
- ○ 62

TAKE HOME ACTIVITY • Write 73 − 28 on a sheet of paper. Ask your child if he or she would regroup to find the difference.

FOR MORE PRACTICE: Standards Practice Book, pp. P113–P114

© Houghton Mifflin Harcourt Publishing Company

Name ______________________________

2-Digit Subtraction

Essential Question How do you record the steps when subtracting 2-digit numbers?

COMMON CORE STANDARD **CC.2.NBT.5**
Use place value understanding and properties of operations to add and subtract.

Listen and Draw REAL WORLD

Draw a quick picture to model each problem.

Tens	Ones

Tens	Ones

FOR THE TEACHER • Read the following problem. Devin had 36 toy robots on his shelf. He moved 12 of the robots to his closet. How many robots are on the shelf now? Repeat the activity with this problem: Devin had 54 toy cars. He gave 9 of them to his brother. How many cars does Devin have now?

Math Talk
Explain how you know when to regroup.

MATHEMATICAL PRACTICES

© Houghton Mifflin Harcourt Publishing Company

Model and Draw

Subtract. $\begin{array}{r} 42 \\ -\ 15 \\ \hline \end{array}$

Step 1 Are there enough ones to subtract 5?

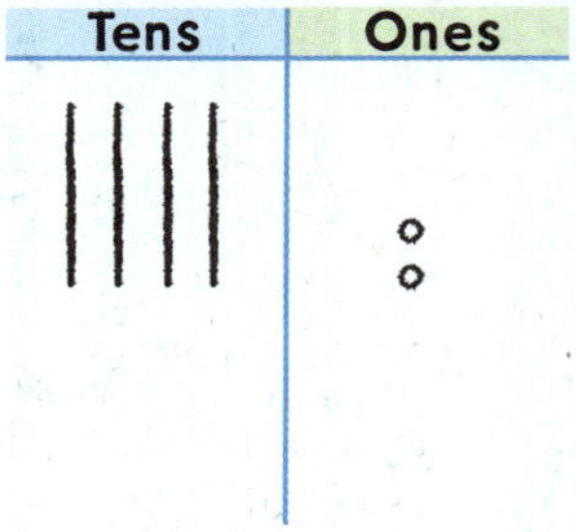

	Tens	Ones
	☐	☐
	4	2
−	1	5

Step 2 Regroup 1 ten as 10 ones.

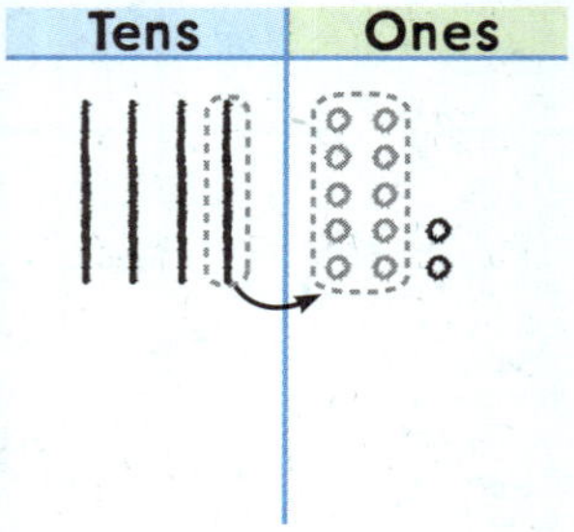

	Tens	Ones
	3	12
	~~4~~	~~2~~
−	1	5

Step 3 Subtract the ones.
$12 - 5 = 7$

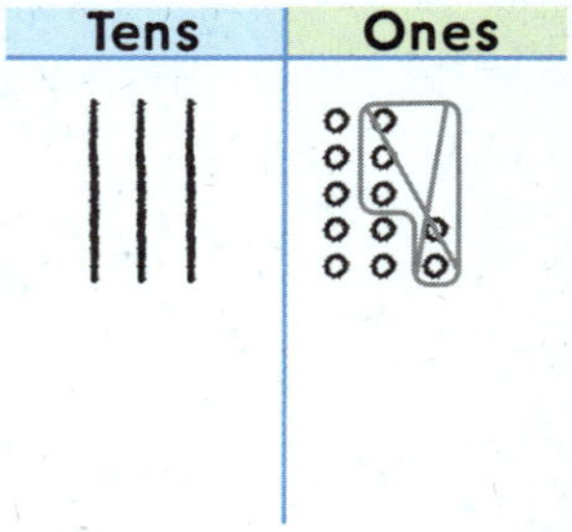

	Tens	Ones
	3	12
	~~4~~	~~2~~
−	1	5
		7

Step 4 Subtract the tens.
$3 - 1 = 2$

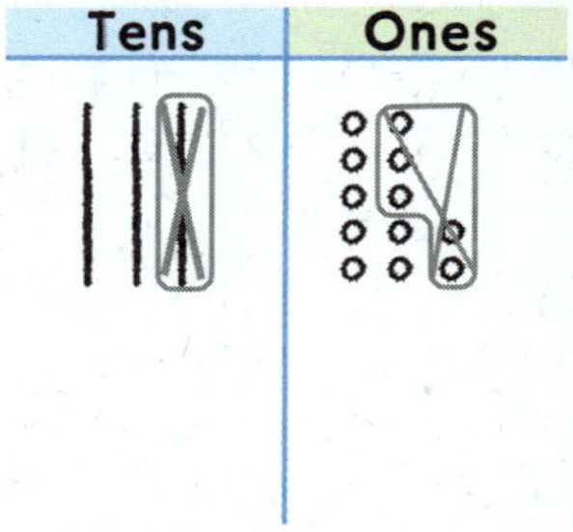

	Tens	Ones
	3	12
	~~4~~	~~2~~
−	1	5
	2	7

Share and Show

Math Board

Regroup if you need to. Write the difference.

1.

	Tens	Ones
	☐	☐
	3	1
−	1	4

✓2.

	Tens	Ones
	☐	☐
	5	6
−	2	1

✓3.

	Tens	Ones
	☐	☐
	7	2
−	3	5

© Houghton Mifflin Harcourt Publishing Company

Name ______________________________

On Your Own

Regroup if you need to. Write the difference.

4.

	Tens	Ones
	□	□
	2	3
−	1	4

5.

	Tens	Ones
	□	□
	8	7
−	5	7

6.

	Tens	Ones
	□	□
	3	4
−	1	8

7.

	Tens	Ones
	□	□
	6	1
−	1	3

8.

	4	5
−	1	8

9.

	5	2
−	3	6

10.

	3	2
−	1	3

11.

	7	5
−	4	3

12.

	5	6
−	2	7

13.

	9	4
−	2	9

14.

	8	7
−	3	9

15.

	8	3
−	4	6

H.O.T. Write the missing numbers.

16.

	6	14
	□	□
−	2	6
	4	8

17.

	3	9
−	□	□
	2	7

18.

	8	11
	□	□
−	5	8
	□	3

© Houghton Mifflin Harcourt Publishing Company

PROBLEM SOLVING REAL WORLD

Write Math

19. H.O.T. This is how Scott found the difference for 83 − 27.

$$\begin{array}{r} 83 \\ -20 \\ \hline 63 \\ -\ 3 \\ \hline 60 \\ -\ 4 \\ \hline 56 \end{array}$$

Find the difference for 92 − 68 using Scott's way.

20. Describe Scott's way of subtracting 2-digit numbers.

____

____

____

____

21. **Test Prep** There are 34 chickens in the barn. If 16 chickens go outside, into the yard, how many chickens will still be in the barn?

- ○ 18
- ○ 22
- ○ 42
- ○ 50

TAKE HOME ACTIVITY • Ask your child to write a 2-digit subtraction problem with no regrouping needed. Have your child explain why he or she chose those numbers.

© Houghton Mifflin Harcourt Publishing Company

FOR MORE PRACTICE: Standards Practice Book, pp. P115–P116

Name ___________________________

Practice 2-Digit Subtraction

Essential Question How do you record the steps when subtracting 2-digit numbers?

COMMON CORE STANDARD CC.2.NBT.5

Use place value understanding and properties of operations to add and subtract.

Listen and Draw REAL WORLD

Choose one way to solve the problem.
Draw or write to show what you did.

FOR THE TEACHER • Read the following problem and have children choose their own methods for solving it. There are 74 books in Mr. Barron's classroom. 19 of the books are about computers. How many of the books are not about computers?

Math Talk

Describe a different way that you could have solved the problem.

MATHEMATICAL PRACTICES

© Houghton Mifflin Harcourt Publishing Company

Model and Draw

Carmen had 50 game cards. Then she gave 16 game cards to Theo. How many game cards does Carmen have now?

Step 1 Look at the ones. There are not enough ones to subtract 6 from 0. So, regroup.

$$\begin{array}{rrr} & 4 & 10 \\ & \not{5} & \not{0} \\ - & 1 & 6 \\ \hline & & \end{array}$$

Step 2 Subtract the ones.

$10 - 6 = 4$

$$\begin{array}{rrr} & 4 & 10 \\ & \not{5} & \not{0} \\ - & 1 & 6 \\ \hline & & 4 \end{array}$$

Step 3 Subtract the tens.

$4 - 1 = 3$

$$\begin{array}{rrr} & 4 & 10 \\ & \not{5} & \not{0} \\ - & 1 & 6 \\ \hline & 3 & 4 \end{array}$$

Share and Show

Math Board

Write the difference.

1. $$\begin{array}{rrr} & 3 & 8 \\ - & 1 & 9 \\ \hline \end{array}$$

2. $$\begin{array}{rrr} & 6 & 5 \\ - & 3 & 2 \\ \hline \end{array}$$

3. $$\begin{array}{rrr} & 5 & 0 \\ - & 1 & 2 \\ \hline \end{array}$$

4. $$\begin{array}{rrr} & 2 & 3 \\ - & & 4 \\ \hline \end{array}$$

5. $$\begin{array}{rrr} & 7 & 0 \\ - & 3 & 8 \\ \hline \end{array}$$

6. $$\begin{array}{rrr} & 5 & 2 \\ - & 1 & 7 \\ \hline \end{array}$$

© Houghton Mifflin Harcourt Publishing Company

Name ____________________

On Your Own

Write the difference.

7. $\begin{array}{r} 41 \\ -\ 24 \\ \hline \end{array}$

8. $\begin{array}{r} 58 \\ -\ 16 \\ \hline \end{array}$

9. $\begin{array}{r} 60 \\ -\ 13 \\ \hline \end{array}$

10. $\begin{array}{r} 52 \\ -\ 47 \\ \hline \end{array}$

11. $\begin{array}{r} 72 \\ -\ 46 \\ \hline \end{array}$

12. $\begin{array}{r} 37 \\ -\ \ 6 \\ \hline \end{array}$

13. $\begin{array}{r} 74 \\ -\ 46 \\ \hline \end{array}$

14. $\begin{array}{r} 90 \\ -\ 18 \\ \hline \end{array}$

15. $\begin{array}{r} 40 \\ -\ \ 7 \\ \hline \end{array}$

16. H.O.T. Write the missing numbers in the subtraction problems. The regrouping for each problem is shown.

$\begin{array}{rr} 6 & 15 \\ \square & \square \\ -\ \square & \square \\ \hline 4 & 7 \end{array}$ $\qquad$ $\begin{array}{rr} 7 & 13 \\ \square & \square \\ -\ \square & \square \\ \hline 2 & 5 \end{array}$

TAKE HOME ACTIVITY • Ask your child to show you one way to find 80 – 34.

© Houghton Mifflin Harcourt Publishing Company

FOR MORE PRACTICE: Standards Practice Book, pp. P117–P118

Name ______________________

Mid-Chapter Checkpoint

Concepts and Skills

Break apart the number you are subtracting. Use the number line to help. Write the difference. (CC.2.NBT.5)

20 21 22 23 24 25 26 27 28 29 **30** 31 32 33 34 35 36 37 38 39 **40** 41 42 43 44 45 46 47 48 49 **50**

1. $34 - 8 =$ ______

2. $45 - 17 =$ ______

Draw a quick picture to solve. Write the difference. (CC.2.NBT.5)

3.

	Tens	Ones
	□	□
	4	2
−	2	9

Tens	Ones

4.

	Tens	Ones
	□	□
	5	4
−	2	3

Tens	Ones

Write the difference. (CC.2.NBT.5)

5.
$$\begin{array}{r} 78 \\ -\,43 \\ \hline \end{array}$$

6.
$$\begin{array}{r} 60 \\ -\,26 \\ \hline \end{array}$$

7.
$$\begin{array}{r} 85 \\ -\,37 \\ \hline \end{array}$$

Test Prep (CC.2.NBT.5)

8. Marissa had 51 toy dinosaurs. She gave 14 toy dinosaurs to her brother. How many toy dinosaurs does she have now?

○ 33
○ 37
○ 47
○ 65

© Houghton Mifflin Harcourt Publishing Company

Name ______________________________

Rewrite 2-Digit Subtraction

Essential Question What are two different ways to write subtraction problems?

COMMON CORE STANDARD CC.2.NBT.5

Use place value understanding and properties of operations to add and subtract.

Listen and Draw REAL WORLD

Write the numbers for each subtraction problem.

− ______	− ______
− ______	− ______

Math Talk **Explain** why it is important to line up the digits of the numbers in columns.

MATHEMATICAL PRACTICES

FOR THE TEACHER • Read the following problem. Have children write the numbers in vertical format. There were 45 children at a party. Then 23 children left the party. How many children were still at the party? Repeat for three more problems.

© Houghton Mifflin Harcourt Publishing Company

Model and Draw

What is 81 − 36?
Rewrite the subtraction problem.
Then find the difference.

Step 1 For 81, write the tens digit in the tens column.

Write the ones digit in the ones column.

Repeat for 36.

$$\begin{array}{rr} 8 & 1 \\ - \; 3 & 6 \\ \hline \end{array}$$

Step 2 Look at the ones. Regroup if you need to.

Subtract the ones.
Subtract the tens.

$$\begin{array}{rr} 7 & 11 \\ \not{8} & \not{1} \\ - \; 3 & 6 \\ \hline \end{array}$$

Share and Show

Math Board

Rewrite the subtraction problem. Then find the difference.

1. 37 − 4
2. 48 − 24
3. 85 − 37
4. 63 − 19
5. 62 − 37
6. 51 − 27
7. 76 − 3
8. 95 − 48

© Houghton Mifflin Harcourt Publishing Company

Name ______________________________

On Your Own

Rewrite the subtraction problem. Then find the difference.

9. 49 − 8	10. 85 − 47	11. 63 − 23	12. 51 − 23
13. 60 − 15	14. 94 − 58	15. 47 − 20	16. 35 − 9
17. 78 − 10	18. 54 − 38	19. 92 − 39	20. 87 − 28

21. **Explain** how you can solve one of the exercises above without rewriting it.

____

____

____

____

© Houghton Mifflin Harcourt Publishing Company

MATHEMATICAL PRACTICES **Model • Reason • Make Sense**

PROBLEM SOLVING REAL WORLD

Write Math

Read about the class trip. Then answer the questions.

Pablo's class went to the art museum. They saw 26 paintings done by children. They saw 53 paintings done by adults. They also saw 18 sculptures and 31 photographs.

22. How many more paintings were done by adults than by children?

_______ more paintings

23. H.O.T. How many more paintings than sculptures did they see?

_______ more paintings

24. ★ **Test Prep** Tom drew 23 pictures last year. Beth drew 14 pictures. How many more pictures did Tom draw than Beth?

- ○ 37
- ○ 19
- ○ 11
- ○ 9

TAKE HOME ACTIVITY • Ask your child to write and solve a subtraction problem about a family trip.

© Houghton Mifflin Harcourt Publishing Company

FOR MORE PRACTICE:
Standards Practice Book, pp. P119–P120

Name ______________________________

Add to Find Differences

Essential Question How can you use addition to solve subtraction problems?

COMMON CORE STANDARD CC.2.NBT.5
Use place value understanding and properties of operations to add and subtract.

Listen and Draw REAL WORLD

Draw pictures to show the problem.
Then write a number sentence for your drawing.

______________________ ________ markers

Now draw pictures to show the next part of the problem.
Write a number sentence for your drawing.

______________________ ________ markers

FOR THE TEACHER • Have children draw pictures to represent this problem. Sophie had 25 markers. She gave 3 markers to Josh. How many markers does Sophie have now? Then ask children: How many markers will Sophie have if Josh gives the 3 markers back to her?

Math Talk
Describe what happens when you add back the number that you had subtracted.

MATHEMATICAL PRACTICES

© Houghton Mifflin Harcourt Publishing Company

Model and Draw

Count up from the number you are subtracting to find the difference.

$$45 - 38 = \blacksquare$$

Start at 38. Count up to 40.

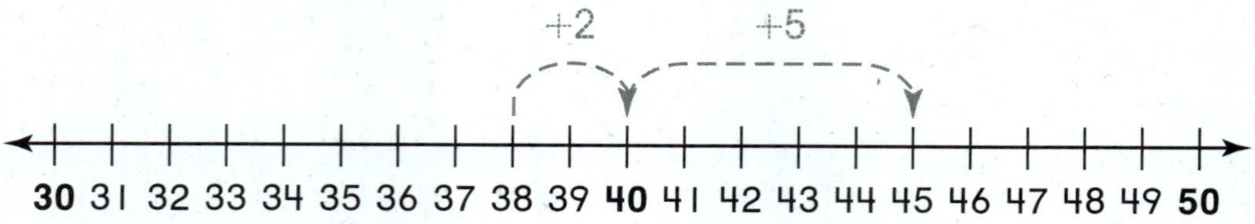

Then count up 5 more to 45.

$2 + 5 = 7$

So, $45 - 38 =$ _____.

Share and Show

Math Board

Use the number line. Count up to find the difference.

1. $36 - 27 =$ _____

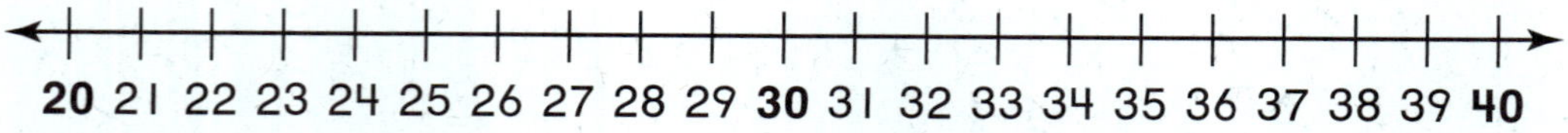

✓2. $56 - 49 =$ _____

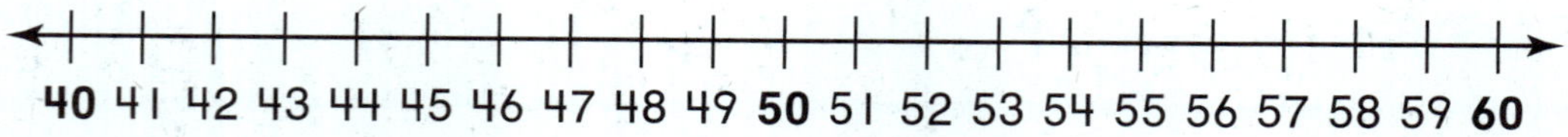

✓3. $64 - 58 =$ _____

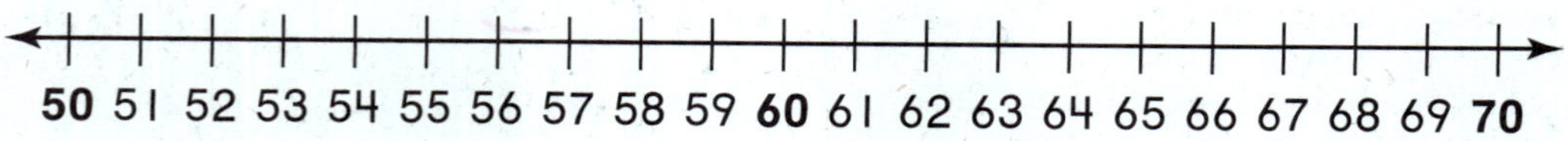

© Houghton Mifflin Harcourt Publishing Company

Name ____________________

On Your Own

Use the number line. Count up to find the difference.

4. 33 − 28 = ____

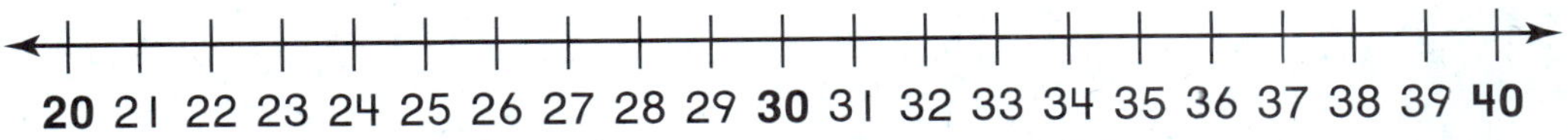

5. 45 − 37 = ____

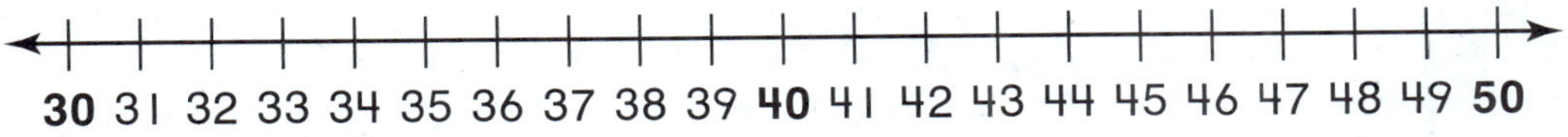

6. 58 − 49 = ____

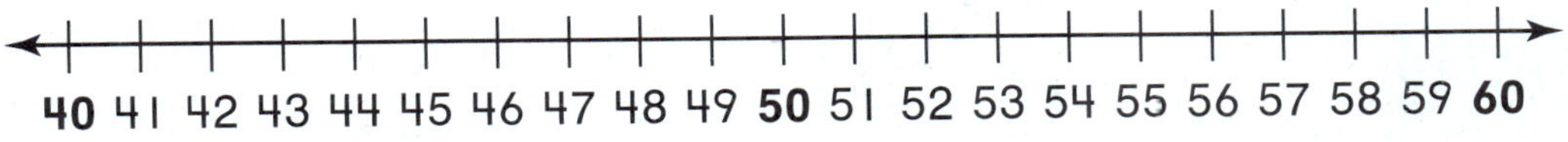

7. 65 − 59 = ____

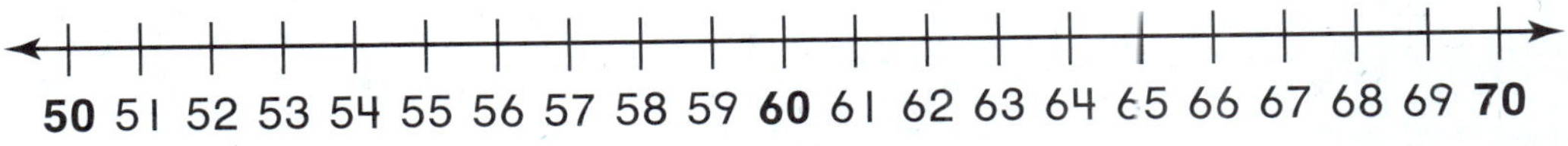

8. 75 − 68 = ____

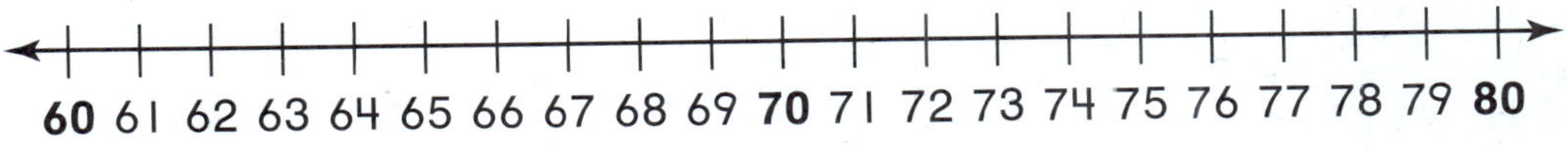

© Houghton Mifflin Harcourt Publishing Company

PROBLEM SOLVING REAL WORLD

Write Math

Solve. You may wish to use the number line to help.

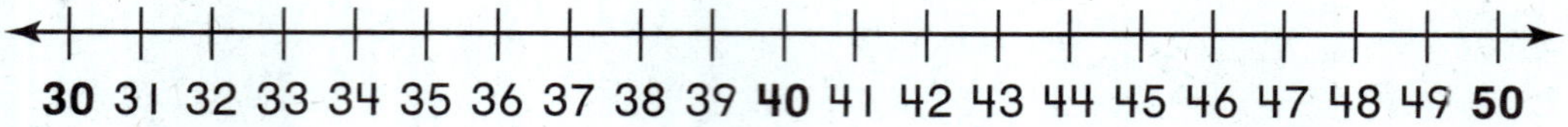

9. There are 46 game pieces in a box. Adam takes 38 game pieces out of the box. How many game pieces are still in the box?

_______ game pieces

10. H.O.T. Spencer wrote 5 fewer stories than Katie. Spencer wrote 18 stories. How many stories did Katie write?

_______ stories

11. Test Prep Rachel had 27 craft sticks. Then she gave 19 craft sticks to Theo. How many craft sticks does Rachel have now?

- ○ 6
- ○ 7
- ○ 8
- ○ 9

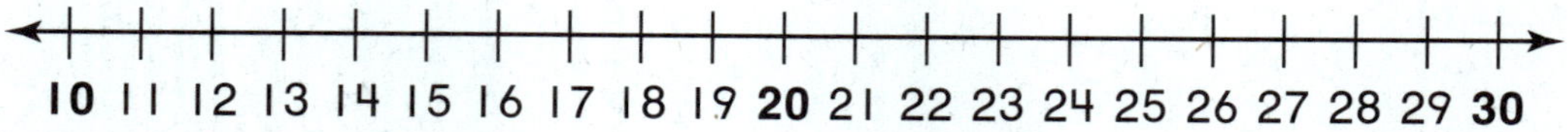

TAKE HOME ACTIVITY • Have your child describe how he or she used a number line to solve one problem in this lesson.

© Houghton Mifflin Harcourt Publishing Company

FOR MORE PRACTICE: Standards Practice Book, pp. P121–P122

Name ______________________

Problem Solving • Subtraction

Essential Question How can drawing a diagram help when solving subtraction problems?

PROBLEM SOLVING
Lesson 5.9

COMMON CORE STANDARD CC.2.OA.1
Represent and solve problems involving addition and subtraction.

Jane and her mom made 33 puppets for the craft fair. They sold 14 puppets. How many puppets do they still have?

Unlock the Problem

What do I need to find?

how many puppets
they still have

What information do I need to use?

They made ________ puppets.

They sold ________ puppets.

Show how to solve the problem.

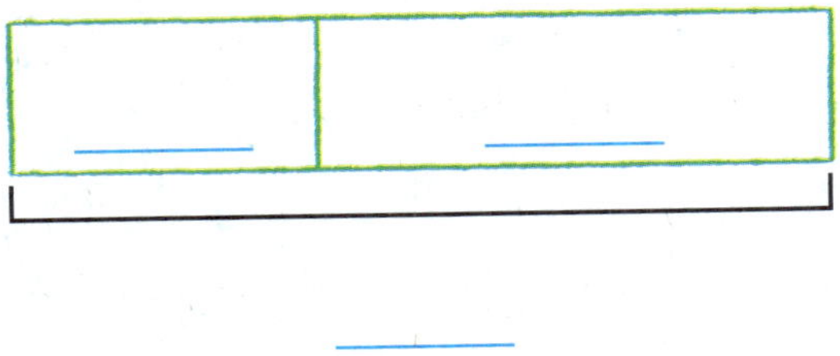

33 − 14 = ■

________ puppets

HOME CONNECTION • Your child used a bar model and a number sentence to represent the problem. Using a bar model helps show what is known and what is needed to solve the problem.

© Houghton Mifflin Harcourt Publishing Company

Try Another Problem

Label the bar model. Write a number sentence with a ■ for the missing number. Solve.

- What do I need to find?
- What information do I need to use?

1. Carlette had a box of 46 craft sticks. She used 28 craft sticks to make a sailboat. How many craft sticks were not used?

______________________ ______ craft sticks

2. Rob's class made 31 clay bowls. Sarah's class made 15 clay bowls. How many more clay bowls did Rob's class make than Sarah's class?

______________________ ______ more clay bowls

Math Talk

Explain how you know that Exercise 1 is a take-away problem.

MATHEMATICAL PRACTICES

© Houghton Mifflin Harcourt Publishing Company

Name ______________________________

Share and Show Math Board

Label the bar model. Write a number sentence with a ■ for the missing number. Solve.

3. Mr. Hayes makes 32 wooden frames. He gives away 15 frames as gifts. How many frames does he still have?

______ frames

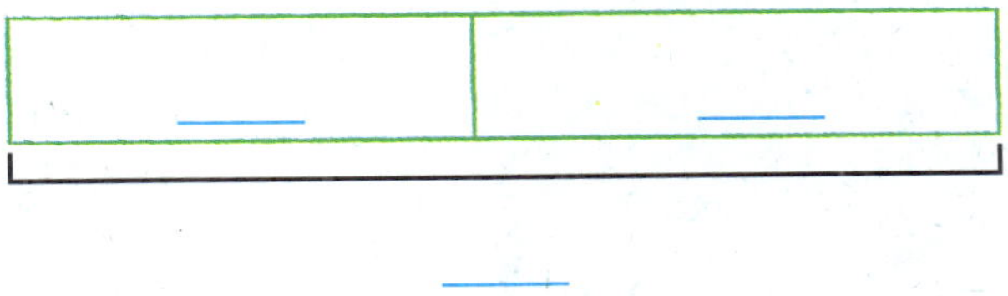

____

4. Wesley has 21 ribbons in a box. He has 15 ribbons on the wall. How many more ribbons does he have in the box than on the wall?

______ more ribbons

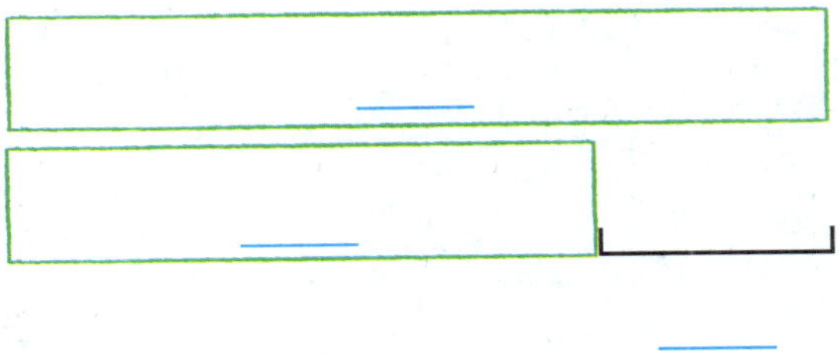

____

5. Jennifer wrote 22 poems. Some of her poems are in her notebook. 7 poems are not in her notebook. How many poems are in her notebook?

______ poems

____

© Houghton Mifflin Harcourt Publishing Company

On Your Own

Choose a way to solve.
Write or draw to explain.

Write Math

6. Fred had 34 rocks in his collection. Then he got 11 more rocks. How many rocks does Fred have now?

_____ rocks

7. Jean has 54 flowers in her garden. Nico has 19 fewer flowers in his garden. How many flowers does Nico have in his garden?

_____ flowers

8. H.O.T. There are 154 tulip plants, 162 daisy plants, and 147 rose plants at the store. Are there more tulip plants or more daisy plants?

more __________ plants

9. **Test Prep** There are 48 crackers in the bag. The children eat 25 crackers. How many crackers are still in the bag?

○ 13
○ 17
○ 23
○ 63

TAKE HOME ACTIVITY • Ask your child to explain how he or she solved one of the problems on this page.

FOR MORE PRACTICE:
Standards Practice Book, pp. P123–P124

© Houghton Mifflin Harcourt Publishing Company

Name ____________________

Algebra • Write Equations to Represent Subtraction

Essential Question How do you write a number sentence to represent a problem?

COMMON CORE STANDARD CC.2.OA.1

Represent and solve problems involving addition and subtraction.

Listen and Draw REAL WORLD

Draw to show the problem. Write a number sentence. Then solve.

____

Math Talk
Describe how your drawing shows the problem.

MATHEMATICAL PRACTICES

FOR THE TEACHER • Read this problem to children. Riley has 53 crayons. He gives some crayons to Courtney. Now Riley has 38 crayons. How many crayons did Riley give to Courtney?

© Houghton Mifflin Harcourt Publishing Company

Model and Draw

You can write a number sentence to show a problem.

Liza has 65 postcards. She gives 24 postcards to Wesley. How many postcards does Liza have now?

$65 - 24 = \blacksquare$

THINK:
65 postcards
−24 postcards
41 postcards

Liza has ______ postcards now.

Share and Show

Write a number sentence for the problem.
Use a ■ for the missing number. Then solve.

1. There were 32 birds in the trees. Then 18 birds flew away. How many birds are in the trees now?

____

______ birds

2. Carla read 43 pages in her book. Joe read 32 pages in his book. How many more pages did Carla read than Joe?

____

______ more pages

© Houghton Mifflin Harcourt Publishing Company

Name ______________________________

On Your Own

Write a number sentence for the problem.
Use a ■ for the missing number. Then solve.

3. There were 40 ants on a rock. Some ants moved to the grass. Now there are 26 ants on the rock. How many ants moved to the grass?

____

______ ants

4. Keisha had a box of ribbons. She took 29 ribbons out of the box. Then there were 17 ribbons still in the box. How many ribbons were in the box to start?

____

______ ribbons

5. **H.O.T.** There are 50 bees in a hive. Some bees fly out. If fewer than 20 bees are still in the hive, how many bees could have flown out?

______ bees

Use subtraction to prove your answer.

© Houghton Mifflin Harcourt Publishing Company

PROBLEM SOLVING REAL WORLD

Write Math

Solve. Write or draw to explain.

6. Haley had some stickers. John gave her 15 more stickers. Now Haley has 44 stickers. How many stickers did she have to start with?

_______ stickers

7. H.O.T. Brendan made this number line to find a difference. What was he subtracting from 100? Explain your answer.

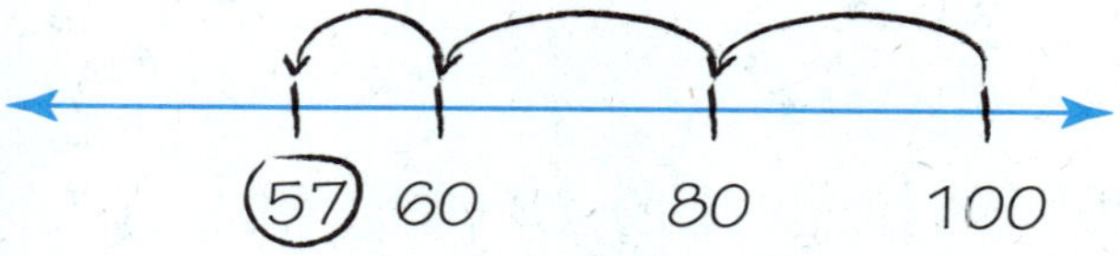

____

____

____

8. **Test Prep** There are 48 pictures on the zoo wall. Of these, 25 are wild cats and the rest are birds. How many of the pictures are birds?

- ○ 63
- ○ 37
- ○ 23
- ○ 13

TAKE HOME ACTIVITY • Have your child explain how he or she solved one problem in this lesson.

FOR MORE PRACTICE: Standards Practice Book, pp. P125–P126

© Houghton Mifflin Harcourt Publishing Company

Name ____________________

Solve Multistep Problems

Essential Question How do you decide what steps to do to solve a problem?

COMMON CORE STANDARD CC.2.OA.1
Represent and solve problems involving addition and subtraction.

Listen and Draw REAL WORLD

Label the bar model to show each problem. Then solve.

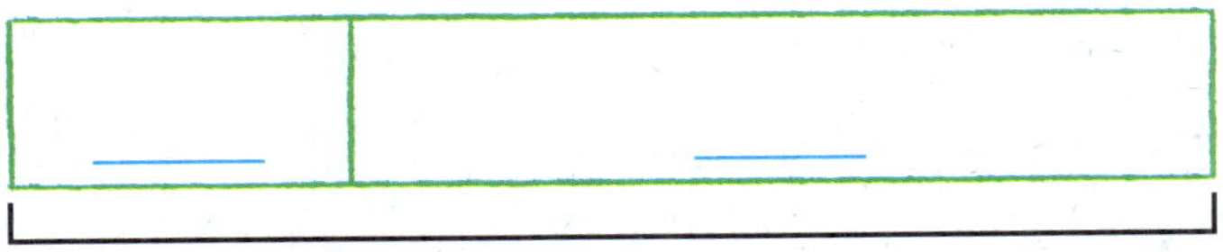

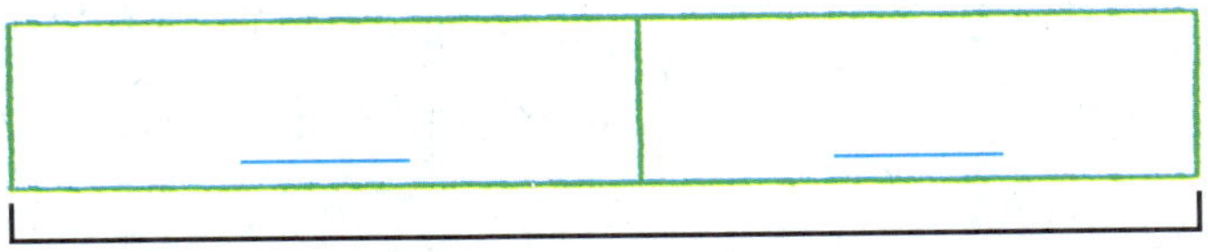

FOR THE TEACHER • Read this 1st problem for children. Cassie has 32 sheets of paper. She gives Jeff 9 sheets of paper. How many sheets of paper does Cassie have now? After children solve, read this 2nd problem. Cassie draws 18 pictures. Jeff draws 16 pictures. How many pictures do they draw?

Math Talk

Describe how the two bar models are different.

MATHEMATICAL PRACTICES

© Houghton Mifflin Harcourt Publishing Company

Model and Draw

Bar models help you know what to do to solve a problem.

Ali has 27 stamps. Matt has 38 stamps. How many more stamps are needed so they will have 91 stamps?

27	38

_____

First, find how many stamps they have now.

They have _______ stamps now.

_____	_____

91

Next, find how many more stamps they need.

They need _______ more stamps.

Share and Show

Math Board

Complete the bar models for the steps you do to solve the problem.

THINK: What do you need to find first?

1. Jen has 93 beads. Ana has 46 red beads and 29 blue beads. How many more beads does Ana need to have 93 beads also?

_______ more beads

© Houghton Mifflin Harcourt Publishing Company

Name ______________________________

On Your Own

Complete the bar models for the steps you do to solve the problem.

2. Max has 35 trading cards. He buys 22 more cards. Then he gives 14 cards to Rudy. How many cards does Max have now?

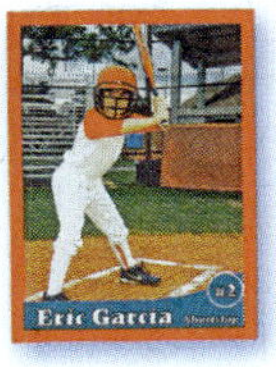

________ cards

3. Drew has 32 toy cars. He trades 7 of those cars for 11 other toy cars. How many toy cars does Drew have now?

________ toy cars

4. Marta and Debbie each have 17 ribbons. They buy 1 package with 8 ribbons in it. How many ribbons do they have now?

________ ribbons

© Houghton Mifflin Harcourt Publishing Company

PROBLEM SOLVING REAL WORLD

Write Math

Solve. Write or draw to explain.

5. Shelby had 32 rocks. She finds 33 more rocks at the park and gives 28 rocks to George. How many rocks does she have now?

_______ rocks

6. H.O.T. Benjamin finds 31 pinecones at the park. Together, Jenna and Ellen find the same number of pinecones as Benjamin. How many pinecones could each girl have found?

Jenna: _______ pinecones

Ellen: _______ pinecones

7. **Test Prep** Tanya finds 22 leaves. Maurice finds 5 more leaves than Tanya finds. How many leaves do the two children find?

- ○ 59
- ○ 49
- ○ 27
- ○ 17

TAKE HOME ACTIVITY • Have your child explain how he or she would solve Exercise 6 if the number 31 was changed to 42.

FOR MORE PRACTICE:
Standards Practice Book, pp. P127–P128

© Houghton Mifflin Harcourt Publishing Company

Name ______________________________

Chapter 5 Review/Test

Vocabulary

Use a word from the box to complete the sentence.

ones
tens
regroup

1. In 64 − 8, you could break apart ______________ in the number 8 before you subtract. (p. 230)

2. You can trade 1 ten for 10 ones when you ______________. (p. 238)

Concepts and Skills

Break apart the number you are subtracting. Use the number line to help. Write the difference. (CC.2.NBT.5)

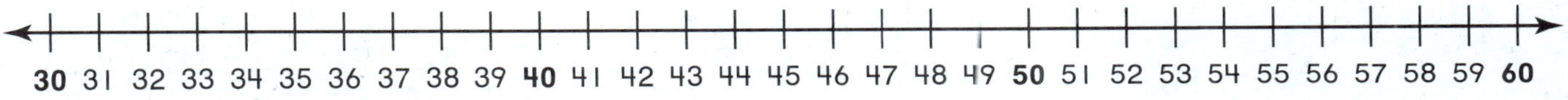

3. 43 − 7 = ______

4. 48 − 9 = ______

5. 51 − 16 = ______

6. 55 − 18 = ______

Draw a quick picture to solve. Write the difference. (CC.2.NBT.5)

7.

	Tens	Ones
	□	□
	4	2
−	1	5

Tens	Ones

8.

	Tens	Ones
	□	□
	5	4
−	3	1

Tens	Ones

© Houghton Mifflin Harcourt Publishing Company

Fill in the bubble for the correct answer choice.

TEST PREP

9. Amanda bought 43 stickers. She gave 16 stickers to her sister. How many stickers does Amanda have now? (CC.2.OA.1)

- ○ 17
- ○ 27
- ○ 39
- ○ 59

10. This year there were 34 sailboats in a race. Last year there were 19 sailboats in a race. How many more sailboats were in the race this year than last year? (CC.2.NBT.5)

- ○ 15
- ○ 25
- ○ 33
- ○ 53

11. Jorge had 40 favorite games saved on his computer. He erased 12 of the games. How many favorite games does he have saved now? (CC.2.NBT.9, CC.2.NBT.5)

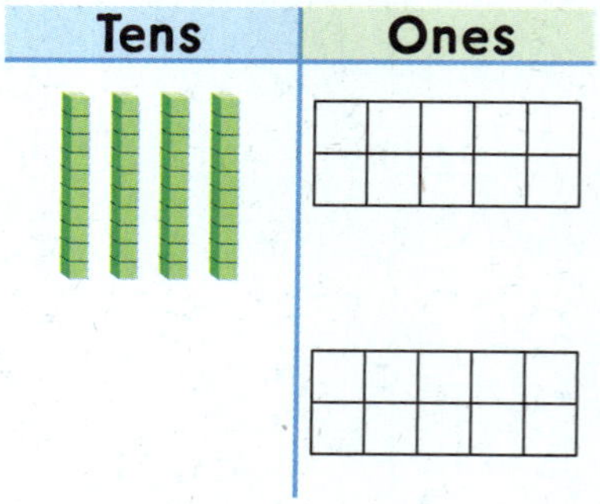

- ○ 28
- ○ 32
- ○ 48
- ○ 52

© Houghton Mifflin Harcourt Publishing Company

Name ______________________________

Fill in the bubble for the correct answer choice.

TEST PREP

12. Caleb baked 36 muffins. He brought them to school to share with his class. 29 muffins were eaten. How many muffins were not eaten? (CC.2.OA.1)

- ○ 65
- ○ 55
- ○ 17
- ○ 7

13. On Monday, 52 children played basketball. On Friday, 19 children played baseball and 27 children played basketball.

How many more children played games on Monday than on Friday? (CC.2.OA.1)

- ○ 25
- ○ 16
- ○ 11
- ○ 6

14. Lauren needs 30 objects for a treasure hunt. She has collected some objects, but still needs 11 more objects. How many objects has she collected so far? (CC.2.NBT.5)

- ○ 9
- ○ 19
- ○ 21
- ○ 41

© Houghton Mifflin Harcourt Publishing Company

Constructed Response

15. Linda had 63 shells. She gave 34 shells to Joe. How many shells does she have now? Write a number sentence with a ■ for the missing number. Explain how the number sentence shows the problem. (CC.2.OA.1, CC.2.NBT.5)

____

____

____

____

Performance Task (CC.2.OA.1, CC.2.NBT.5)

16. At the bike store, there are 42 bikes in all. There are large bikes and small bikes. 18 bikes are small.

How many bikes are large?
Draw or write to show how you found your answer.

How many more large bikes than small bikes are there?
Draw or write to show how you found your answer.

© Houghton Mifflin Harcourt Publishing Company

Chapter 6

3-Digit Addition and Subtraction

Curious About Math with Curious George

Monarch butterflies roost together during migration.

If you count 83 butterflies on one tree and 72 on another, how many butterflies have you counted altogether?

© Houghton Mifflin Harcourt Publishing Company
Curious George by Margret and H.A. Rey. Copyright © 2010 by Houghton Mifflin Harcourt Publishing Company. All rights reserved. The character Curious George®, including without limitation the character's name and the character's likenesses, are registered trademarks of Houghton Mifflin Harcourt Publishing Company.

Name ______________________________

Show What You Know

Model Subtracting Tens

Write the difference.

1. 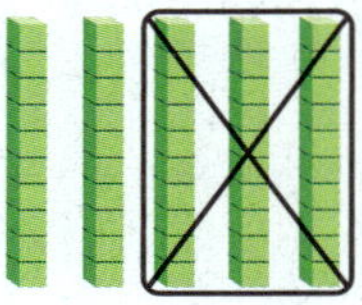

5 tens − 3 tens = ____ tens

50 − 30 = _____

2. 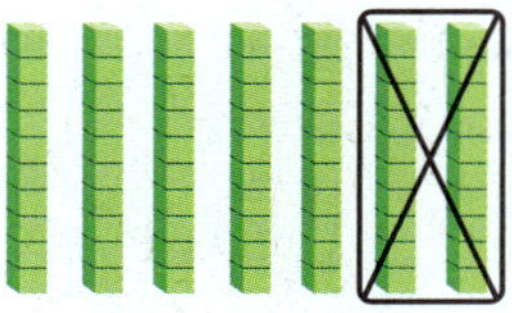

7 tens − 2 tens = ____ tens

70 − 20 = _____

2-Digit Addition

Write the sum.

3. $\begin{array}{r} 54 \\ +\ 25 \\ \hline \end{array}$

4. $\begin{array}{r} 35 \\ +\ 18 \\ \hline \end{array}$

5. $\begin{array}{r} 82 \\ +\ 67 \\ \hline \end{array}$

6. $\begin{array}{r} 29 \\ +\ 81 \\ \hline \end{array}$

Hundreds, Tens, and Ones

Write the hundreds, tens, and ones shown. Write the number.

7. 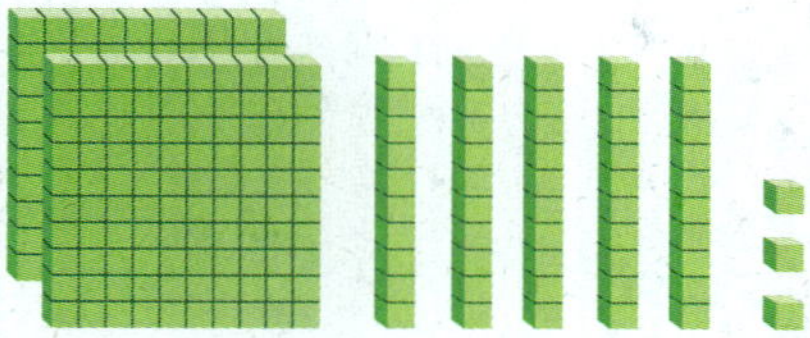

Hundreds	Tens	Ones

_____

8. 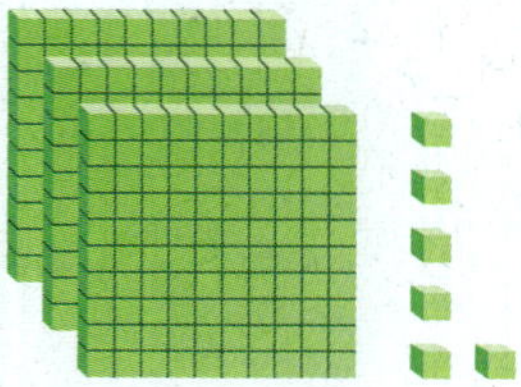

Hundreds	Tens	Ones

_____

Family note: This page checks your child's understanding of important skills needed for success in Chapter 6.

GO Online Assessment Options Soar to Success Math

© Houghton Mifflin Harcourt Publishing Company

Name ______________________

Vocabulary Builder

Review Words
- regroup
- sum
- difference
- hundreds

Visualize It

Fill in the graphic organizer by writing examples of ways to **regroup**.

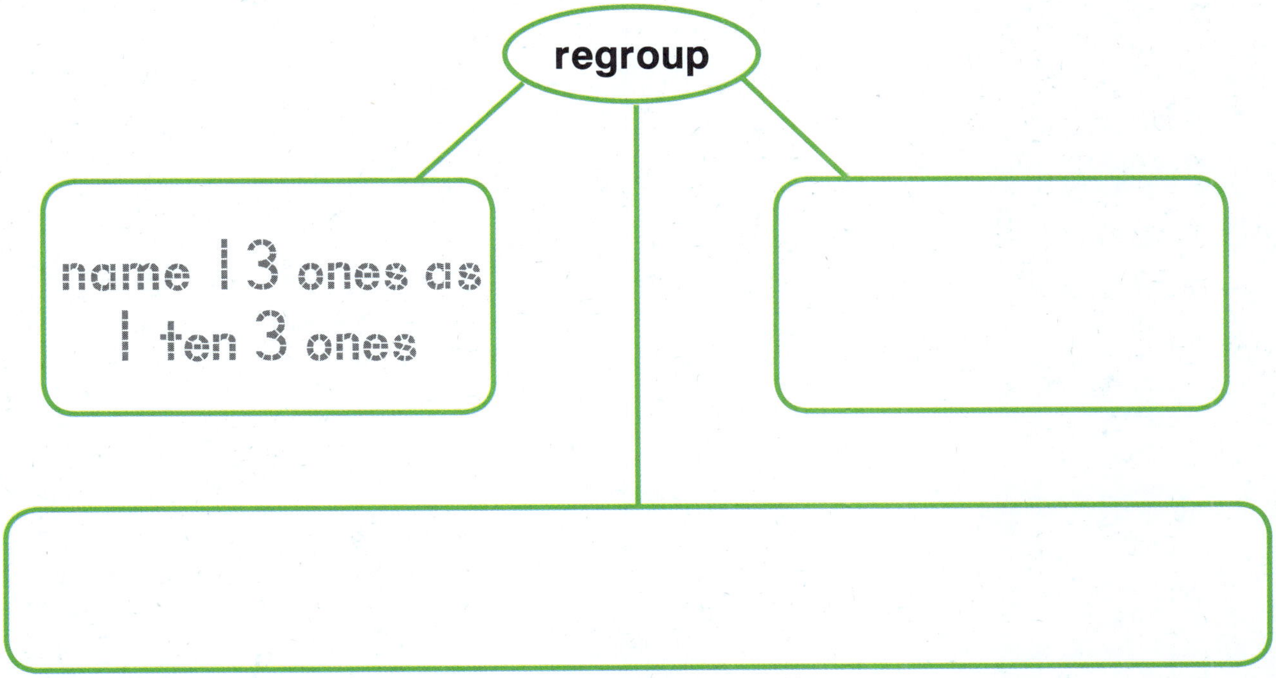

Understand Vocabulary

1. Write a number that has a **hundreds** digit that is greater than its tens digit. ______

2. Write an addition sentence that has a **sum** of 20. ______________

3. Write a subtraction sentence that has a **difference** of 10. ______________

GO Online
- eStudent Edition
- Multimedia eGlossary

© Houghton Mifflin Harcourt Publishing Company

Chapter 6

Game 2-Digit Shuffle

Materials

- number cards 10–50
- 15 
- 15 

Play with a partner.

1. Shuffle the number cards. Place them face down in a pile.
2. Take two cards. Say the sum of the two numbers.
3. Your partner checks your sum.
4. If your sum is correct, place a counter on a button. If you regrouped to solve, place a counter on another button.
5. Take turns. Cover all the buttons. The player with more counters on the board wins.
6. Repeat the game, saying the difference between the two numbers for each turn.

© Houghton Mifflin Harcourt Publishing Company

Name ________________________________

Draw to Represent 3-Digit Addition

Essential Question How do you draw quick pictures to show adding 3-digit numbers?

COMMON CORE STANDARD CC.2.NBT.7
Use place value understanding and properties of operations to add and subtract.

Listen and Draw REAL WORLD

Draw quick pictures to model the problem.
Then solve.

Tens	Ones

________ pages

Math Talk MATHEMATICAL PRACTICES

Explain how your quick pictures show the problem.

FOR THE TEACHER • Read this problem to children. Manuel read 45 pages in a book. Then he read 31 more pages. How many pages did Manuel read? Have children draw quick pictures to solve the problem.

© Houghton Mifflin Harcourt Publishing Company

Model and Draw

Add 234 and 141.

Hundreds	Tens	Ones

3 hundreds 7 tens 5 ones

375

Share and Show

Math Board

Draw quick pictures. Write how many hundreds, tens, and ones in all. Write the number.

1. Add 125 and 344.

Hundreds	Tens	Ones

_____ hundreds _____ tens _____ ones

____

2. Add 307 and 251.

Hundreds	Tens	Ones

_____ hundreds _____ tens _____ ones

____

© Houghton Mifflin Harcourt Publishing Company

Name ______________________________

On Your Own

Draw quick pictures. Write how many hundreds, tens, and ones in all. Write the number.

3. Add 231 and 218.

Hundreds	Tens	Ones

_____ hundreds _____ tens _____ ones

____

4. Add 232 and 150.

Hundreds	Tens	Ones

_____ hundreds _____ tens _____ ones

____

5. Add 173 and 205.

Hundreds	Tens	Ones

_____ hundreds _____ tens _____ ones

____

© Houghton Mifflin Harcourt Publishing Company

PROBLEM SOLVING REAL WORLD

Write Math

Solve. Write or draw to explain.

6. There are 125 poems in Carrie's book and 143 poems in Angie's book. How many poems are in these two books?

______ poems

7. H.O.T. The baker made 85 bagels. He sold 47 bagels in the morning and 23 bagels in the afternoon. How many bagels were not sold?

______ bagels

8. Describe how you solved Exercise 7.

____

____

____

____

9. **Test Prep** There are 452 girls and 310 boys at the game. How many children are at the game?

- ○ 862
- ○ 772
- ○ 762
- ○ 742

TAKE HOME ACTIVITY • Write 145 + 122. Have your child explain how he or she can draw quick pictures to find the sum.

FOR MORE PRACTICE:
Standards Practice Book, pp. P133–P134

© Houghton Mifflin Harcourt Publishing Company

Name ______________________________

Lesson 6.2

Break Apart 3-Digit Addends

Essential Question How do you break apart addends to add hundreds, tens, and then ones?

COMMON CORE STANDARD CC.2.NBT.7

Use place value understanding and properties of operations to add and subtract.

Listen and Draw

Write the number. Draw a quick picture for the number. Then write the number in different ways.

____

____ hundreds ____ tens ____ ones

______ + ______ + ______

____

____ hundreds ____ tens ____ ones

______ + ______ + ______

FOR THE TEACHER • Have children write 258 on the blank in the left corner of the first box. Have children draw a quick picture for this number and then complete the other two forms for the number. Repeat the activity for 325.

Math Talk

What number can be written as 400 + 20 + 9?

MATHEMATICAL PRACTICES

© Houghton Mifflin Harcourt Publishing Company

Model and Draw

Break apart the addends into hundreds, tens, and ones.
Add the hundreds, the tens, and the ones.
Then find the total sum.

538 → 500 + 30 + 8

+216 → 200 + 10 + 6

700 + ___ + ___ = ______

Share and Show

Math Board

Break apart the addends to find the sum.

1. 321 → ______ + ______ + ______

+457 → ______ + ______ + ______

______ + ______ + ______ = ______

2. 744 → ______ + ______ + ______

+162 → ______ + ______ + ______

______ + ______ + ______ = ______

3. 254 → ______ + ______ + ______

+536 → ______ + ______ + ______

______ + ______ + ______ = ______

© Houghton Mifflin Harcourt Publishing Company

Name ____________________

On Your Own

Break apart the addends to find the sum.

4.

374 → ____ + ____ + ____

+518 → ____ + ____ + ____

____ + ____ + ____ = ____

5.

425 → ____ + ____ + ____

+232 → ____ + ____ + ____

____ + ____ + ____ = ____

6.

849 → ____ + ____ + ____

+123 → ____ + ____ + ____

____ + ____ + ____ = ____

7. H.O.T. Write the missing numbers in the problem.

412 → ____ + ____ + ____

+ ____ → 500 + 60 + ____

____ + ____ + 10 = ____

© Houghton Mifflin Harcourt Publishing Company

PROBLEM SOLVING REAL WORLD

Write Math

Solve. Write or draw to explain.

8. Mr. Jones has 158 sheets of art paper and 231 sheets of plain paper. How many sheets of paper does he have?

_______ sheets of paper

9. H.O.T. Wesley added in a different way.

```
  327
+ 468
-----
  700    7 hundreds
   80    8 tens
+  15    15 ones
-----
  795
```

Use Wesley's way to find the sum.

```
  539
+ 247
-----
```

10. ★ **Test Prep** There are 324 children at Theo's school. There are 419 children at Latasha's school. How many children are at the two schools?

- ○ 733
- ○ 743
- ○ 745
- ○ 825

TAKE HOME ACTIVITY • Write 347 + 215. Have your child break apart the numbers and then find the sum.

FOR MORE PRACTICE: Standards Practice Book, pp. P135–P136

© Houghton Mifflin Harcourt Publishing Company

Name ______________________________

3-Digit Addition: Regroup Ones

Essential Question When do you regroup ones in addition?

COMMON CORE STANDARD CC.2.NBT.7

Use place value understanding and properties of operations to add and subtract.

Listen and Draw REAL WORLD

Use  to model the problem.
Draw quick pictures to show what you did.

Hundreds	Tens	Ones

FOR THE TEACHER • Read the following problem and have children model it with blocks. There were 213 people at the show on Friday and 156 people at the show on Saturday. How many people were at the show on the two nights? Have children draw quick pictures to show how they solved the problem.

Math Talk

Describe how you modeled the problem.

MATHEMATICAL PRACTICES

© Houghton Mifflin Harcourt Publishing Company

Model and Draw

Add the ones.

$6 + 7 = 13$

Regroup 13 ones as 1 ten 3 ones.

	Hundreds	Tens	Ones
		1	
	2	4	6
+	1	1	7
			3

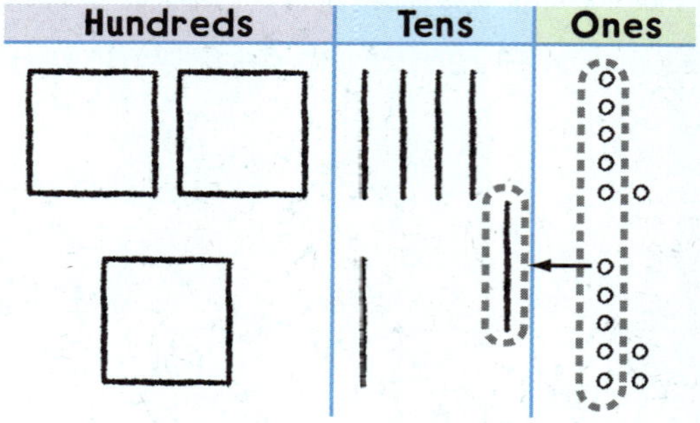

Add the tens.

$1 + 4 + 1 = 6$

	Hundreds	Tens	Ones
		1	
	2	4	6
+	1	1	7
		6	3

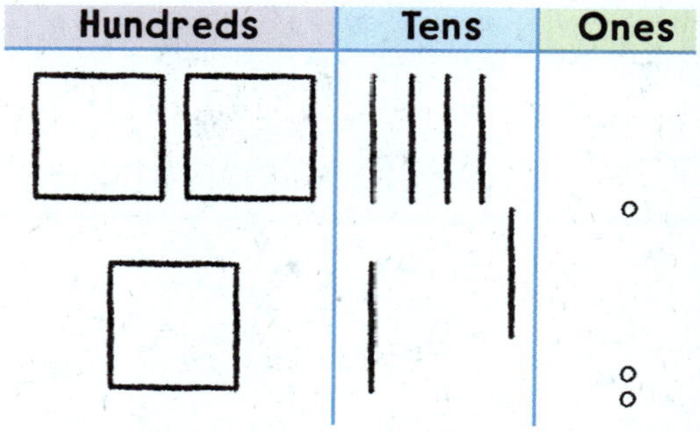

Add the hundreds.

$2 + 1 = 3$

	Hundreds	Tens	Ones
		1	
	2	4	6
+	1	1	7
	3	6	3

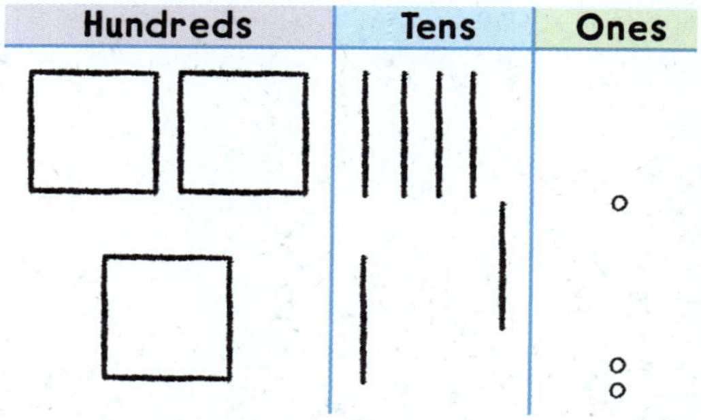

Share and Show

Math Board

Write the sum.

1.

	Hundreds	Tens	Ones
		□	
	3	2	8
+	1	3	4

2.

	Hundreds	Tens	Ones
		□	
	4	4	5
+		2	3

© Houghton Mifflin Harcourt Publishing Company

Name ______________________________

On Your Own

Write the sum.

3.

	Hundreds	Tens	Ones
		☐	
	5	2	6
+	1	0	3

4.

	Hundreds	Tens	Ones
		☐	
	3	4	8
+		1	9

5.

	Hundreds	Tens	Ones
		☐	
	6	2	8
+	3	4	7

6.

	Hundreds	Tens	Ones
		☐	
	2	3	5
+	2	5	7

7.

	Hundreds	Tens	Ones
		☐	
	5	6	2
+	3	2	9

8.

	Hundreds	Tens	Ones
		☐	
	1	4	7
+	1	2	5

9.

	Hundreds	Tens	Ones
		☐	
	4	3	5
+	2	1	4

10.

	Hundreds	Tens	Ones
		☐	
	3	2	9
+	2	4	8

© Houghton Mifflin Harcourt Publishing Company

PROBLEM SOLVING REAL WORLD

Write Math

Solve. Write or draw to explain.

11. The gift shop is 140 steps away from the zoo entrance. The train stop is 235 steps away from the gift shop. How many total steps is this?

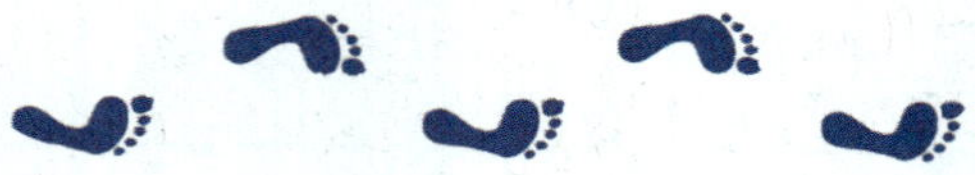

_______ steps

12. H.O.T. On Thursday, there were 326 visitors at the zoo. There were 200 more visitors at the zoo on Friday than on Thursday. How many visitors were at the zoo on both days?

_______ visitors

13. **Test Prep** On Thursday, 175 drinks were sold at the zoo. On Friday, 219 drinks were sold. How many drinks were sold on both days?

- ○ 484
- ○ 464
- ○ 404
- ○ 394

TAKE HOME ACTIVITY • Ask your child to explain why he or she regrouped in only some of the problems in this lesson.

© Houghton Mifflin Harcourt Publishing Company

FOR MORE PRACTICE:
Standards Practice Book, pp. P137–P138

Name ______________________________

3-Digit Addition: Regroup Tens

Essential Question When do you regroup tens in addition?

COMMON CORE STANDARD CC.2.NBT.7

Use place value understanding and properties of operations to add and subtract.

Listen and Draw REAL WORLD

Use 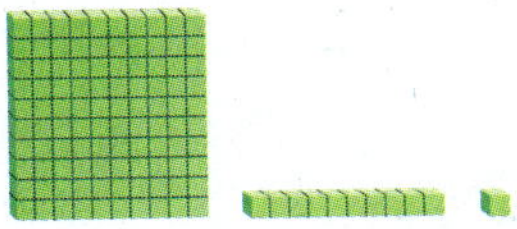 to model the problem.
Draw quick pictures to show what you did.

Hundreds	Tens	Ones

FOR THE TEACHER • Read the following problem and have children model it with blocks. On Monday, 253 children visited the aquarium. On Tuesday, 324 children visited the aquarium. How many children visited the aquarium those two days? Have children draw quick pictures to show how they solved the problem.

Math Talk

Explain how your quick pictures show what happened in the problem.

MATHEMATICAL PRACTICES

© Houghton Mifflin Harcourt Publishing Company

Model and Draw

Add the ones.

$2 + 5 = 7$

	Hundreds	Tens	Ones
	☐	☐	
	1	4	2
+	2	8	5
			7

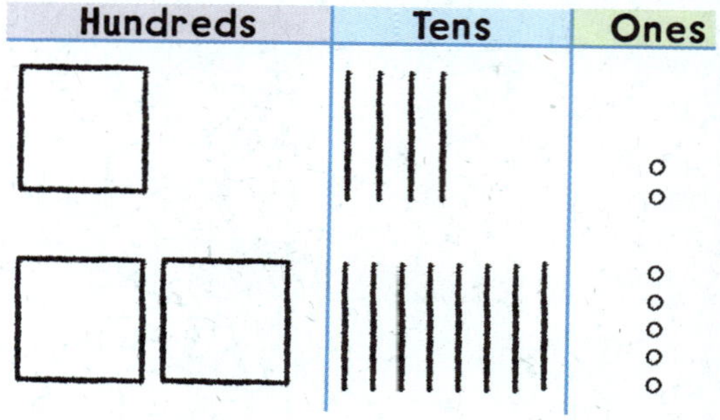

Add the tens.

$4 + 8 = 12$

Regroup 12 tens as 1 hundred 2 tens.

	Hundreds	Tens	Ones
	1	☐	
	1	4	2
+	2	8	5
		2	7

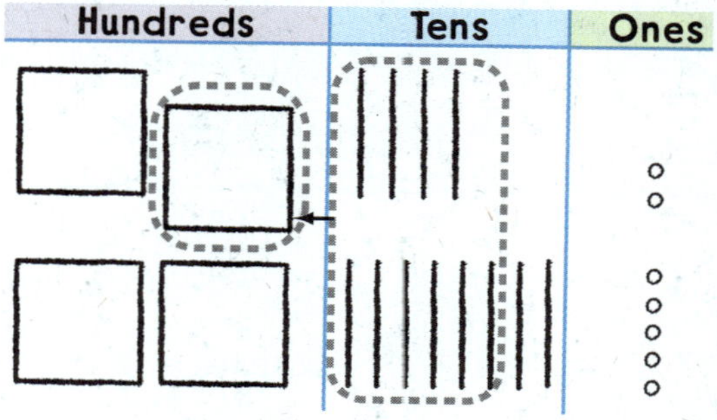

Add the hundreds.

$1 + 1 + 2 = 4$

	Hundreds	Tens	Ones
	1	☐	
	1	4	2
+	2	8	5
	4	2	7

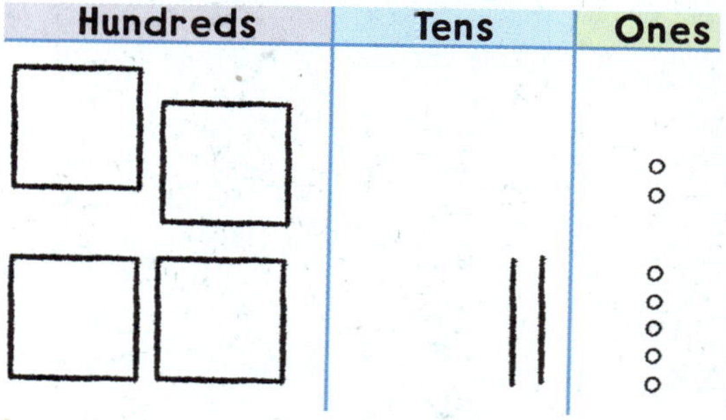

Share and Show

Math Board

Write the sum.

1.

	Hundreds	Tens	Ones
	☐	☐	
	3	4	7
+	2	9	1

✓2.

	Hundreds	Tens	Ones
	☐	☐	
	1	6	5
+	3	5	4

✓3.

	Hundreds	Tens	Ones
	☐	☐	
	5	3	8
+	1	4	0

© Houghton Mifflin Harcourt Publishing Company

Name ______________________

On Your Own

Write the sum.

4.

Hundreds	Tens	Ones
□	□	
1	5	6
+	4	2

5.

Hundreds	Tens	Ones
□	□	
7	6	4
+ 1	5	3

6.

Hundreds	Tens	Ones
□	□	
3	7	2
+ 1	8	5

7.

2	2	4
+ 1	5	7

8.

2	5	4
+ 4	0	5

9.

6	4	4
+	9	2

10. 132 + 258 = ____

11. 314 + 435 = ____

12. 753 + 152 = ____

Rewrite the numbers. Then add.

13. 760 + 178

14. 216 + 346

15. 423 + 285

© Houghton Mifflin Harcourt Publishing Company

PROBLEM SOLVING REAL WORLD

Write Math

These lists show the pieces of fruit that Mr. Olson and Mr. Lee sold at the market.

Mr. Olson	Mr. Lee
257 apples	314 pears
281 plums	229 peaches

Write or draw to explain.

16. How many pieces of fruit did Mr. Olson sell?

_______ pieces of fruit

17. H.O.T. Who sold more pieces of fruit? How many more?

____

_______ more pieces of fruit

18. **Test Prep** There are 465 oranges packed in boxes. There are 253 oranges in baskets. How many oranges are there?

- ○ 718
- ○ 708
- ○ 698
- ○ 612

© Houghton Mifflin Harcourt Publishing Company

TAKE HOME ACTIVITY • Have your child choose a new combination of two fruits on this page and find the total number of pieces of the two types of fruit.

FOR MORE PRACTICE: Standards Practice Book, pp. P139–P140

Name ______________________________

Addition: Regroup Ones and Tens

Essential Question How do you know when to regroup in addition?

COMMON CORE STANDARD CC.2.NBT.7
Use place value understanding and properties of operations to add and subtract.

Listen and Draw REAL WORLD

Write an addition problem to find each answer. Draw quick pictures to prove that each sum is correct.

FOR THE TEACHER • Read the following problem and have children solve it. There are 259 girls and 304 boys at Elm Street School. How many children are at Elm Street School? Repeat the activity for 462 + 374.

Math Talk
Did you regroup in the same way for both problems? **Explain.**

MATHEMATICAL PRACTICES

© Houghton Mifflin Harcourt Publishing Company

Model and Draw

Sometimes you will regroup more than once in addition problems.

$$\begin{array}{r} \scriptstyle 1\ 1 \\ 2\ 5\ 9 \\ +\ 4\ 7\ 6 \\ \hline 7\ 3\ 5 \end{array}$$

9 ones + 6 ones = 15 ones, or 1 ten 5 ones

1 ten + 5 tens + 7 tens = 13 tens, or 1 hundred 3 tens

1 hundred + 2 hundreds + 4 hundreds = 7 hundreds

THINK:
Are there 10 or more ones?
Are there 10 or more tens?

Share and Show

Math Board

Write the sum.

1. $\begin{array}{r} 1\ 8\ 4 \\ +\ 3\ 2\ 9 \\ \hline \end{array}$

2. $\begin{array}{r} 5\ 4\ 6 \\ +\ 2\ 7\ 8 \\ \hline \end{array}$

3. $\begin{array}{r} 3\ 2\ 7 \\ +\ 3\ 5\ 3 \\ \hline \end{array}$

4. $\begin{array}{r} 2\ 3\ 4 \\ +\ 1\ 5\ 2 \\ \hline \end{array}$

✓5. $\begin{array}{r} 3\ 7\ 5 \\ +\ 2\ 7\ 2 \\ \hline \end{array}$

✓6. $\begin{array}{r} 1\ 8\ 9 \\ +\ 6\ 2\ 3 \\ \hline \end{array}$

© Houghton Mifflin Harcourt Publishing Company

Name ______________________________

On Your Own

Write the sum.

7.
```
  5 7 4
+ 2 8 1
-------
```

8.
```
  4 1 6
+ 4 8 3
-------
```

9.
```
  3 4 6
+ 5 9 7
-------
```

10.
```
  3 6 5
+ 2 8 3
-------
```

11.
```
  6 4 7
+ 1 0 9
-------
```

12.
```
  5 4 6
+ 3 5 6
-------
```

13.
```
  3 4 8
+ 6 3 1
-------
```

14.
```
  4 5 5
+ 1 3 9
-------
```

15.
```
  5 6 3
+ 2 4 5
-------
```

H.O.T. Write the missing digits.

16.
```
  ☐ ☐ 6
+ 4 5 ☐
-------
  6 9 0
```

17.
```
  6 ☐ 7
+ 2 3 ☐
-------
  ☐ 6 2
```

18.
```
  1 3 4
+ ☐ 7 ☐
-------
  5 ☐ 3
```

TAKE HOME ACTIVITY • Have your child write a 3-digit addition problem and then solve it.

© Houghton Mifflin Harcourt Publishing Company

FOR MORE PRACTICE: Standards Practice Book, pp. P141–P142

Name ________________________

Mid-Chapter Checkpoint

Concepts and Skills

Break apart the addends to find the sum. (CC.2.NBT.7)

1.
$$\begin{array}{r} 567 \\ +324 \\ \hline \end{array}$$

567 → ______ + ______ + ______

+324 → ______ + ______ + ______

______ + ______ + ______ = ______

Write the sum. (CC.2.NBT.7)

2.
$$\begin{array}{r} 248 \\ +\ 346 \\ \hline \end{array}$$

3.
$$\begin{array}{r} 610 \\ +\ 264 \\ \hline \end{array}$$

4.
$$\begin{array}{r} 391 \\ +\ 537 \\ \hline \end{array}$$

Test Prep

5. There are 148 small sand dollars and 119 large sand dollars at the store. How many sand dollars are at the store? (CC.2.NBT.7)

- ○ 257
- ○ 267
- ○ 357
- ○ 367

© Houghton Mifflin Harcourt Publishing Company

Name ______________________________

Problem Solving • 3-Digit Subtraction

Essential Question How can making a model help when solving subtraction problems?

COMMON CORE STANDARD **CC.2.NBT.7**
Use place value understanding and properties of operations to add and subtract.

There were 436 people at the art show. 219 people left the art show early. How many people stayed at the art show?

Unlock the Problem

What do I need to find?

how many people ______________________________
stayed at the art show

What information do I need to use?

________ people were at the art show.

Then, ________ people left the show.

Show how to solve the problem.

Make a model. Then draw a quick picture of your model.

________ people

HOME CONNECTION • Your child used a model and a quick picture to represent and solve a subtraction problem.

© Houghton Mifflin Harcourt Publishing Company

Try Another Problem

Make a model to solve. Then draw a quick picture of your model.

- What do I need to find?
- What information do I need to use?

1. There are 532 pieces of art at the show. 319 pieces of art are paintings. How many pieces of art are not paintings?

_______ pieces of art

2. 245 children go to the face-painting event. 114 of the children are boys. How many of the children are girls?

_______ girls

Math Talk **Explain** how you solved the first problem on this page.

MATHEMATICAL PRACTICES

© Houghton Mifflin Harcourt Publishing Company

Name ______________________________

Share and Show

Math Board

Make a model to solve. Then draw a quick picture of your model.

3. There were 237 books on the shelves. Miss Lane took 126 books off the shelves. How many books were still on the shelves? 	________ books
4. 164 children and 31 adults saw the movie in the morning. 125 children saw the movie in the afternoon. How many fewer children saw the movie in the afternoon than in the morning?	________ fewer children
5. There were 232 postcards on the table. Janet used 118 postcards to cover the bulletin board. How many postcards were not used? 	________ postcards

© Houghton Mifflin Harcourt Publishing Company

On Your Own

Choose a way to solve. Write or draw to explain.

Write Math

6. There were some grapes in a bowl. Clancy's friends ate 24 of the grapes. Then there were 38 grapes in the bowl. How many grapes were in the bowl before?

_______ grapes

7. H.O.T. Maria has 127 animal cards. Ellen has twice that number of cards. How many animal cards do the girls have?

_______ animal cards

8. **Test Prep** Mr. Grant had 350 balloons. He sold 133 balloons at the park. How many balloons does he have now?

○ 217
○ 223
○ 423
○ 483

TAKE HOME ACTIVITY • Ask your child to choose one of the problems in this lesson and solve it in a different way.

© Houghton Mifflin Harcourt Publishing Company

FOR MORE PRACTICE: Standards Practice Book, pp. P143–P144

Name ______________________________

3-Digit Subtraction: Regroup Tens

Essential Question When do you regroup tens in subtraction?

COMMON CORE STANDARD CC.2.NBT.7
Use place value understanding and properties of operations to add and subtract.

Listen and Draw REAL WORLD

Use  to model the problem.
Draw a quick picture to show what you did.

Hundreds	Tens	Ones

FOR THE TEACHER • Read the following problem and have children model it with blocks. 473 people went to the football game. 146 people were still there at the end of the game. How many people left before the end of the game? Have children draw quick pictures of their models.

Math Talk
Describe what to do when there are not enough ones to subtract from.

MATHEMATICAL PRACTICES

© Houghton Mifflin Harcourt Publishing Company

Model and Draw

354 − 137 = ?

Are there enough ones to subtract 7?

yes (no)

Regroup 1 ten as 10 ones.

	Hundreds	Tens	Ones
		4	14
	3	5	4
−	1	3	7

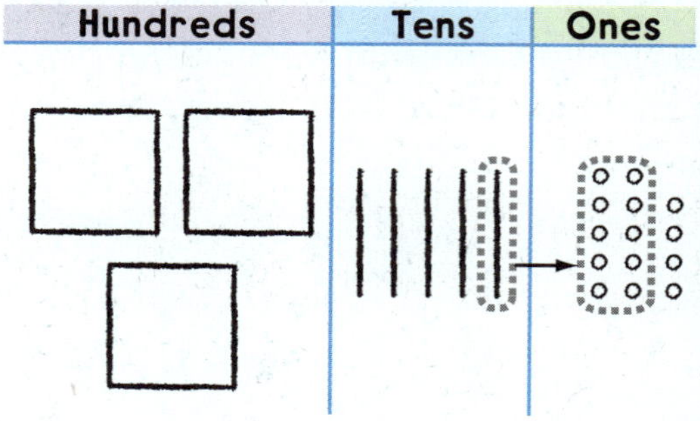

Now there are enough ones.

Subtract the ones.

14 − 7 = 7

	Hundreds	Tens	Ones
		4	14
	3	5	4
−	1	3	7
			7

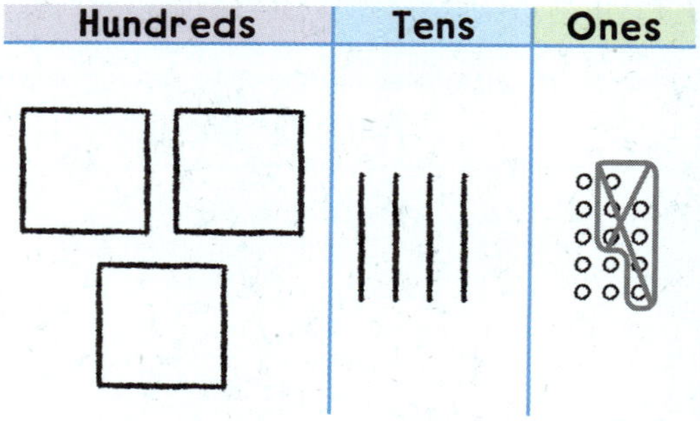

Subtract the tens.

4 − 3 = 1

Subtract the hundreds.

3 − 1 = 2

	Hundreds	Tens	Ones
		4	14
	3	5	4
−	1	3	7
	2	1	7

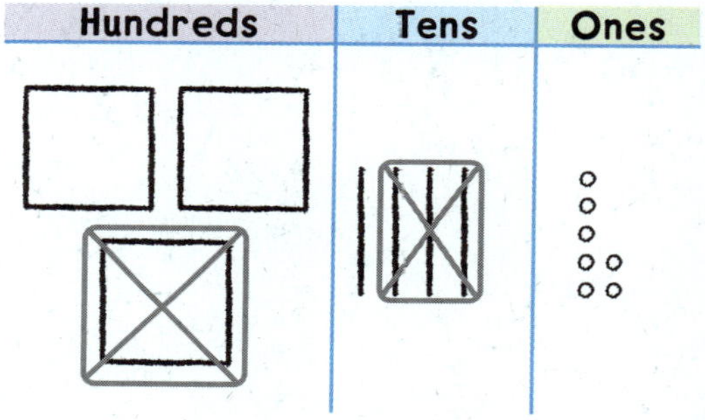

Share and Show

Math Board

Solve. Write the difference.

1.

	Hundreds	Tens	Ones
		☐	☐
	4	3	1
−	3	2	6

2.

	Hundreds	Tens	Ones
		☐	☐
	6	5	8
−	2	3	7

© Houghton Mifflin Harcourt Publishing Company

Name ______________________________

On Your Own

Solve. Write the difference.

3.

	Hundreds	Tens	Ones
		☐	☐
	7	2	8
−	1	0	7

4.

	Hundreds	Tens	Ones
		☐	☐
	4	5	2
−	2	1	6

5.

	Hundreds	Tens	Ones
		☐	☐
	9	6	5
−	2	3	8

6.

	Hundreds	Tens	Ones
		☐	☐
	4	8	9
−	1	4	9

7.

	Hundreds	Tens	Ones
		☐	☐
	6	4	5
−	2	2	7

8.

	Hundreds	Tens	Ones
		☐	☐
	6	7	0
−	1	3	8

9.

	Hundreds	Tens	Ones
		☐	☐
	8	7	4
−	4	3	8

10.

	Hundreds	Tens	Ones
		☐	☐
	9	8	4
−	7	1	5

© Houghton Mifflin Harcourt Publishing Company

PROBLEM SOLVING REAL WORLD

Write Math

Solve. Write or draw to explain.

11. There are 235 whistles and 42 bells in the store. Ryan counts 128 whistles on the shelf. How many whistles are not on the shelf?

_______ whistles

12. H.O.T. There were 287 music books in the store. After some of the music books were sold, there are 159 music books left. How many music books were sold?

_______ music books

13. **Test Prep** Ms. Watson has 254 stickers. She gives 123 stickers to her students. How many stickers does she still have?

○ 121
○ 127
○ 131
○ 137

TAKE HOME ACTIVITY • Ask your child to explain why he or she regrouped in only some of the problems in this lesson.

© Houghton Mifflin Harcourt Publishing Company

FOR MORE PRACTICE:
Standards Practice Book, pp. P145–P146

Name ____

3-Digit Subtraction: Regroup Hundreds

Essential Question When do you regroup hundreds in subtraction?

COMMON CORE STANDARD **CC.2.NBT.7**
Use place value understanding and properties of operations to add and subtract.

Listen and Draw REAL WORLD

Draw quick pictures to show the problem.

Hundreds	Tens	Ones

FOR THE TEACHER • Read the following problem and have children model it with quick pictures. The Reading Club collected 349 books. 173 books were fiction books. The other books were nonfiction books. How many nonfiction books were there?

Math Talk

Describe what to do when there are not enough tens to subtract from.

MATHEMATICAL PRACTICES

© Houghton Mifflin Harcourt Publishing Company

Model and Draw

428 − 153 = ?

Subtract the ones.

8 − 3 = 5

	Hundreds	Tens	Ones
	4	2	8
−	1	5	3
			5

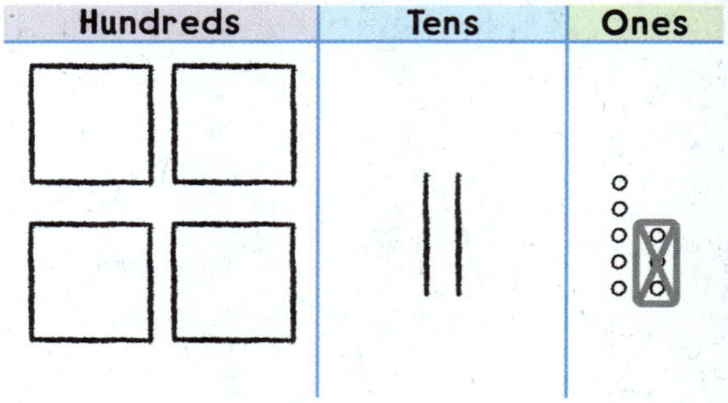

There are not enough tens to subtract from.

Regroup 1 hundred.
4 hundreds 2 tens is now 3 hundreds 12 tens.

	Hundreds	Tens	Ones
	3	12	
	~~4~~	~~2~~	8
−	1	5	3
			5

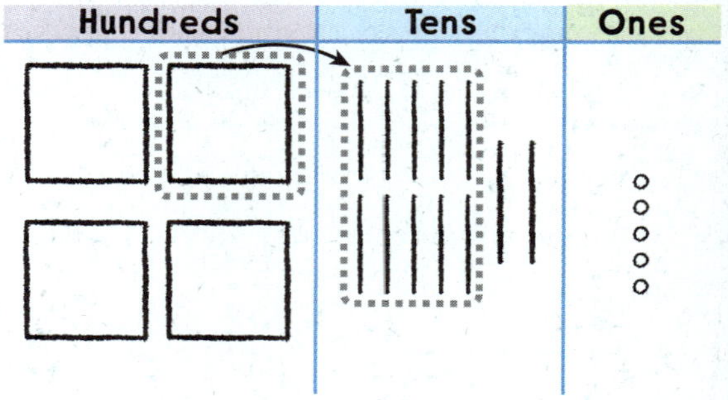

Subtract the tens.

12 − 5 = 7

Subtract the hundreds.

3 − 1 = 2

	Hundreds	Tens	Ones
	3	12	
	~~4~~	~~2~~	8
−	1	5	3
	2	7	5

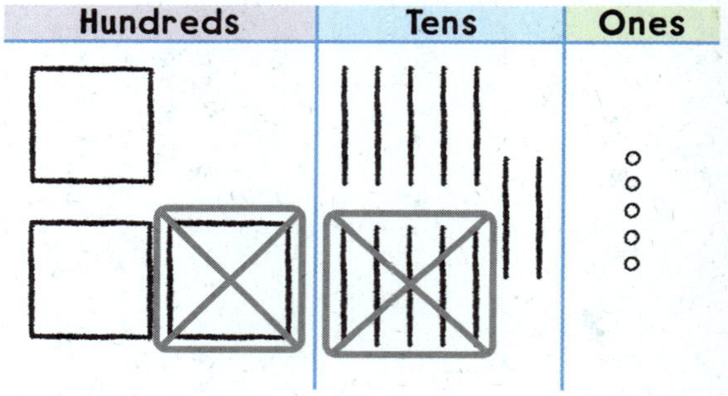

Share and Show

Math Board

Solve. Write the difference.

1.

	Hundreds	Tens	Ones
	4	7	8
−	3	5	6

2.

	Hundreds	Tens	Ones
	8	1	4
−	2	6	3

© Houghton Mifflin Harcourt Publishing Company

Name ___________________________

On Your Own

Solve. Write the difference.

3.

	Hundreds	Tens	Ones
	☐	☐	☐
	6	2	9
−	4	8	2

4.

	Hundreds	Tens	Ones
	☐	☐	☐
	9	3	6
−	1	7	3

5.

	4	3	5
−	1	9	2

6.

	3	8	7
−		4	7

7.

$$\begin{array}{r} 588 \\ -\ 450 \\ \hline \end{array}$$

8.

$$\begin{array}{r} 345 \\ -\ 263 \\ \hline \end{array}$$

Rewrite the numbers. Then subtract.

9. 567 − 183

−
____

10. 718 − 467

−
____

© Houghton Mifflin Harcourt Publishing Company

PROBLEM SOLVING REAL WORLD

Write Math

Solve. Write or draw to explain.

11. There were 375 puzzle pieces in the box. Liz took 190 pieces out of the box. How many puzzles pieces are still in the box?

_________ puzzle pieces

12. H.O.T. Sam built two towers. He used 139 blocks for the first tower. He used 276 blocks in all. For which tower did he use more blocks?

____

Explain how you solved the problem.

____

____

____

13. Test Prep Mr. Simms has 315 paper hats. He gives 140 paper hats to students in the parade. How many paper hats does he have now?

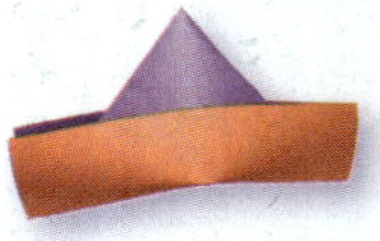

- ○ 255
- ○ 235
- ○ 215
- ○ 175

TAKE HOME ACTIVITY • Have your child explain how to find the difference for 745 − 341.

FOR MORE PRACTICE: Standards Practice Book, pp. P147–P148

© Houghton Mifflin Harcourt Publishing Company

Name ______________________________

Subtraction: Regroup Hundreds and Tens

Essential Question How do you know when to regroup in subtraction?

COMMON CORE STANDARD CC.2.NBT.7

Use place value understanding and properties of operations to add and subtract.

Listen and Draw REAL WORLD

Write a subtraction problem to find each answer. Draw a quick picture to prove that each difference is correct.

FOR THE TEACHER • Read the following problem and have children solve. There are 128 adults and 431 children at the museum. How many more children than adults are there? Repeat the activity for 738 – 275.

Math Talk
Did you regroup in the same way for each problem? **Explain.**

MATHEMATICAL PRACTICES

© Houghton Mifflin Harcourt Publishing Company

Model and Draw

Sometimes you will regroup more than once in subtraction problems.

		11	
	6	~~1~~	15
	~~7~~	~~2~~	~~5~~
−	3	4	9
	3	7	6

Regroup 2 tens 5 ones as 1 ten 15 ones. Subtract the ones.

↓

Regroup 7 hundreds 1 ten as 6 hundreds 11 tens. Subtract the tens.

↓

Subtract the hundreds.

Share and Show

Math Board

Solve. Write the difference.

1.
$$\begin{array}{r} 421 \\ -\ 138 \\ \hline \end{array}$$

2.
$$\begin{array}{r} 274 \\ -\ 182 \\ \hline \end{array}$$

3.
$$\begin{array}{r} 546 \\ -\ 267 \\ \hline \end{array}$$

4.
$$\begin{array}{r} 859 \\ -\ 57 \\ \hline \end{array}$$

✓ 5.
$$\begin{array}{r} 747 \\ -\ 159 \\ \hline \end{array}$$

✓ 6.
$$\begin{array}{r} 938 \\ -\ 370 \\ \hline \end{array}$$

© Houghton Mifflin Harcourt Publishing Company

Name ______________________________

On Your Own

Solve. Write the difference.

7.

$$\begin{array}{rrrr} & 3 & 4 & 2 \\ - & 1 & 3 & 8 \\ \hline \end{array}$$

8.

$$\begin{array}{rrrr} & 4 & 6 & 3 \\ - & 2 & 8 & 1 \\ \hline \end{array}$$

9.

$$\begin{array}{rrrr} & 8 & 5 & 5 \\ - & 4 & 9 & 7 \\ \hline \end{array}$$

10.

$$\begin{array}{rrrr} & 6 & 5 & 7 \\ - & 3 & 8 & 4 \\ \hline \end{array}$$

11.

$$\begin{array}{rrrr} & 5 & 2 & 1 \\ - & 1 & 4 & 6 \\ \hline \end{array}$$

12.

$$\begin{array}{rrrr} & 7 & 5 & 8 \\ - & 5 & 3 & 7 \\ \hline \end{array}$$

13.

$$\begin{array}{rrrr} & 5 & 4 & 2 \\ - & 1 & 6 & 8 \\ \hline \end{array}$$

14.

$$\begin{array}{rrrr} & 8 & 2 & 3 \\ - & 6 & 7 & 3 \\ \hline \end{array}$$

15.

$$\begin{array}{rrrr} & 9 & 4 & 7 \\ - & 5 & 7 & 9 \\ \hline \end{array}$$

H.O.T. Write the missing digits.

16.

$$\begin{array}{rrrr} & \square & 5 & 8 \\ - & 2 & \square & 2 \\ \hline & 5 & 1 & \square \end{array}$$

17.

$$\begin{array}{rrrr} & & 4 & 15 \\ & 9 & \square & \square \\ - & 6 & 2 & 8 \\ \hline & 3 & 2 & 7 \end{array}$$

18.

$$\begin{array}{rrrr} & 7 & 13 & \\ & \square & \square & 7 \\ - & 1 & 5 & \square \\ \hline & 6 & 8 & 1 \end{array}$$

© Houghton Mifflin Harcourt Publishing Company

PROBLEM SOLVING REAL WORLD

Write Math

Solve.

19. H.O.T. This is how Walter found the difference for 617 − 350.

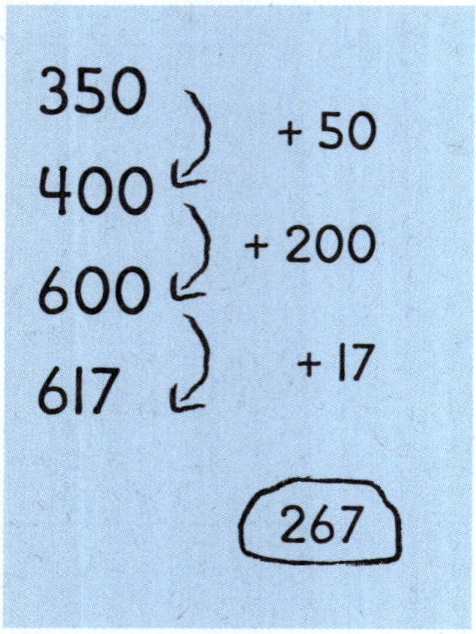

Find the difference for 843 − 270 using Walter's way.

20. ★ **Test Prep** There are 471 children at Caleb's school. 256 children ride buses to get to school.

How many children do not ride buses to get to school?

- ○ 127
- ○ 215
- ○ 225
- ○ 227

TAKE HOME ACTIVITY • Ask your child to find the difference when subtracting 182 from 477.

FOR MORE PRACTICE:
Standards Practice Book, pp. P149–P150

© Houghton Mifflin Harcourt Publishing Company

Name ____________________

Regrouping with Zeros

Essential Question How do you regroup when there are zeros in the number you start with?

COMMON CORE STANDARD **CC.2.NBT.7**

Use place value understanding and properties of operations to add and subtract.

Listen and Draw REAL WORLD

Draw or write to show how you solved the problem.

FOR THE TEACHER • Read the following problem and have children solve. There were 403 cookies in the bakery. 159 of the cookies are sold. How many cookies were not sold? Encourage children to discuss and show different ways to solve the problem.

Math Talk
Describe another way that you could solve the problem.

© Houghton Mifflin Harcourt Publishing Company

Model and Draw

Ms. Dean has a book with 504 pages in it. She has read 178 pages so far. How many more pages does she still have to read?

$$\begin{array}{r} 504 \\ -\,178 \\ \hline \end{array}$$

Step 1 There are not enough ones to subtract from.

Since there are 0 tens, regroup 5 hundreds as 4 hundreds 10 tens.

$$\begin{array}{rrr} \scriptstyle 4 & \scriptstyle 10 & \\ \not{5} & \not{0} & 4 \\ -\,1 & 7 & 8 \\ \hline \end{array}$$

Step 2 Next, regroup 10 tens 4 ones as 9 tens 14 ones.

Now there are enough ones to subtract from.

$14 - 8 = 6$

$$\begin{array}{rrr} & \scriptstyle 9 & \\ \scriptstyle 4 & \scriptstyle \not{10} & \scriptstyle 14 \\ \not{5} & \not{0} & \not{4} \\ -\,1 & 7 & 8 \\ \hline & & 6 \end{array}$$

Step 3 Subtract the tens.

$9 - 7 = 2$

Subtract the hundreds.

$4 - 1 = 3$

$$\begin{array}{rrr} & \scriptstyle 9 & \\ \scriptstyle 4 & \scriptstyle \not{10} & \scriptstyle 14 \\ \not{5} & \not{0} & \not{4} \\ -\,1 & 7 & 8 \\ \hline 3 & 2 & 6 \end{array}$$

Share and Show

Math Board

Solve. Write the difference.

1.

$$\begin{array}{r} 308 \\ -\,259 \\ \hline \end{array}$$

2.

$$\begin{array}{r} 755 \\ -\,438 \\ \hline \end{array}$$

3.

$$\begin{array}{r} 801 \\ -\,375 \\ \hline \end{array}$$

© Houghton Mifflin Harcourt Publishing Company

Name ___________________________

On Your Own

Solve. Write the difference.

4.
$$\begin{array}{r} 563 \\ -\,182 \\ \hline \end{array}$$

5.
$$\begin{array}{r} 904 \\ -\,568 \\ \hline \end{array}$$

6.
$$\begin{array}{r} 705 \\ -\,231 \\ \hline \end{array}$$

7.
$$\begin{array}{r} 603 \\ -\,328 \\ \hline \end{array}$$

8.
$$\begin{array}{r} 442 \\ -\,238 \\ \hline \end{array}$$

9.
$$\begin{array}{r} 901 \\ -\,675 \\ \hline \end{array}$$

10.
$$\begin{array}{r} 702 \\ -\,426 \\ \hline \end{array}$$

11.
$$\begin{array}{r} 684 \\ -\,219 \\ \hline \end{array}$$

12.
$$\begin{array}{r} 479 \\ -\,137 \\ \hline \end{array}$$

H.O.T. First, solve for the difference. Then use addition to check your work.

13.
$$\begin{array}{r} 304 \\ -\,138 \\ \hline \end{array} \qquad + \underline{\qquad\qquad}$$

14.
$$\begin{array}{r} 905 \\ -\,756 \\ \hline \end{array} \qquad + \underline{\qquad\qquad}$$

© Houghton Mifflin Harcourt Publishing Company

PROBLEM SOLVING REAL WORLD

Write Math

15. Miguel has 125 more baseball cards than Chad. Miguel has 435 baseball cards. How many baseball cards does Chad have?

_______ baseball cards

16. H.O.T. Claire has 250 pennies. Some pennies are in a box and some are in her bank. There are more than 100 pennies in each place. How many pennies could be in each place?

_______ pennies in a box

_______ pennies in her bank

Explain how you solved the problem.

____

____

____

____

17. **Test Prep** There are 403 cats and dogs at the Pet Fair. There are 227 dogs. How many cats are there?

- ○ 186
- ○ 184
- ○ 176
- ○ 164

TAKE HOME ACTIVITY • Ask your child to explain how he or she solved one of the problems in this lesson.

© Houghton Mifflin Harcourt Publishing Company

FOR MORE PRACTICE: Standards Practice Book, pp. P151–P152

Name ______________________________

Chapter 6 Review/Test

Vocabulary

Use a word in the box to complete each sentence.

sum
regroup
difference

1. You can ______________ 7 hundreds 1 ten as 6 hundreds 1 1 tens. (p. 310)

2. In 235 − 108 = 127, 127 is the ______________. (p. 306)

Concepts and Skills

Draw quick pictures. Write how many hundreds, tens, and ones in all. Write the number. (CC.2.NBT.7)

3. Add 246 and 132.

Hundreds	Tens	Ones

____ hundreds ____ tens ____ ones

____

Break apart the addends to find the sum. (CC.2.NBT.7)

4.
  413 → ______ + ______ + ______
+278 → ______ + ______ + ______

______ + ______ + ______ = ______

© Houghton Mifflin Harcourt Publishing Company

Fill in the bubble for the correct answer choice.

TEST PREP

5. Mr. Kent's art class used 234 craft sticks. Ms. Reed's art class used 358 craft sticks. How many craft sticks were used by the two classes? (CC.2.NBT.7)

- ○ 524
- ○ 582
- ○ 592
- ○ 692

6. At the marine park, 563 people were at the dolphin show. 281 people were at the otter show.

How many people were at the two shows? (CC.2.NBT.7)

- ○ 844
- ○ 854
- ○ 944
- ○ 954

7. 116 girls and 122 boys saw the school play. How many children saw the school play? (CC.2.NBT.7)

- ○ 338
- ○ 238
- ○ 234
- ○ 226

© Houghton Mifflin Harcourt Publishing Company

Name ________________________________

TEST PREP

Fill in the bubble for the correct answer choice.

8. Mr. Brown had 542 baseball cards in his collection. He sold 128 of the cards. How many cards does he have now? (CC.2.NBT.7)

- ○ 676
- ○ 670
- ○ 426
- ○ 414

9. At the library, there are 668 books and magazines. There are 565 books at the library. How many magazines are there? (CC.2.NBT.7)

- ○ 13
- ○ 103
- ○ 403
- ○ 1,233

10. Mrs. Preston had 509 leaves. She gave 274 leaves to her students.

How many leaves does she still have? (CC.2.NBT.7)

- ○ 225
- ○ 235
- ○ 335
- ○ 375

© Houghton Mifflin Harcourt Publishing Company

Constructed Response

11. Find the sum for each problem.

$$\begin{array}{r} 156 \\ +\ 408 \\ \hline \end{array} \qquad \begin{array}{r} 572 \\ +\ 135 \\ \hline \end{array}$$

Describe how these problems are different. (CC.2.NBT.7)

____

____

Performance Task (CC.2.NBT.7)

12. This is how many blocks each child used.

How many blocks did Anna and Terry use?
Draw or write to show how you found your answer.

How many more blocks did Terry use than Rafael?
Draw or write to show how you found your answer.

© Houghton Mifflin Harcourt Publishing Company

Making a Kite

by Kathryn Krieger and Christine Ruiz

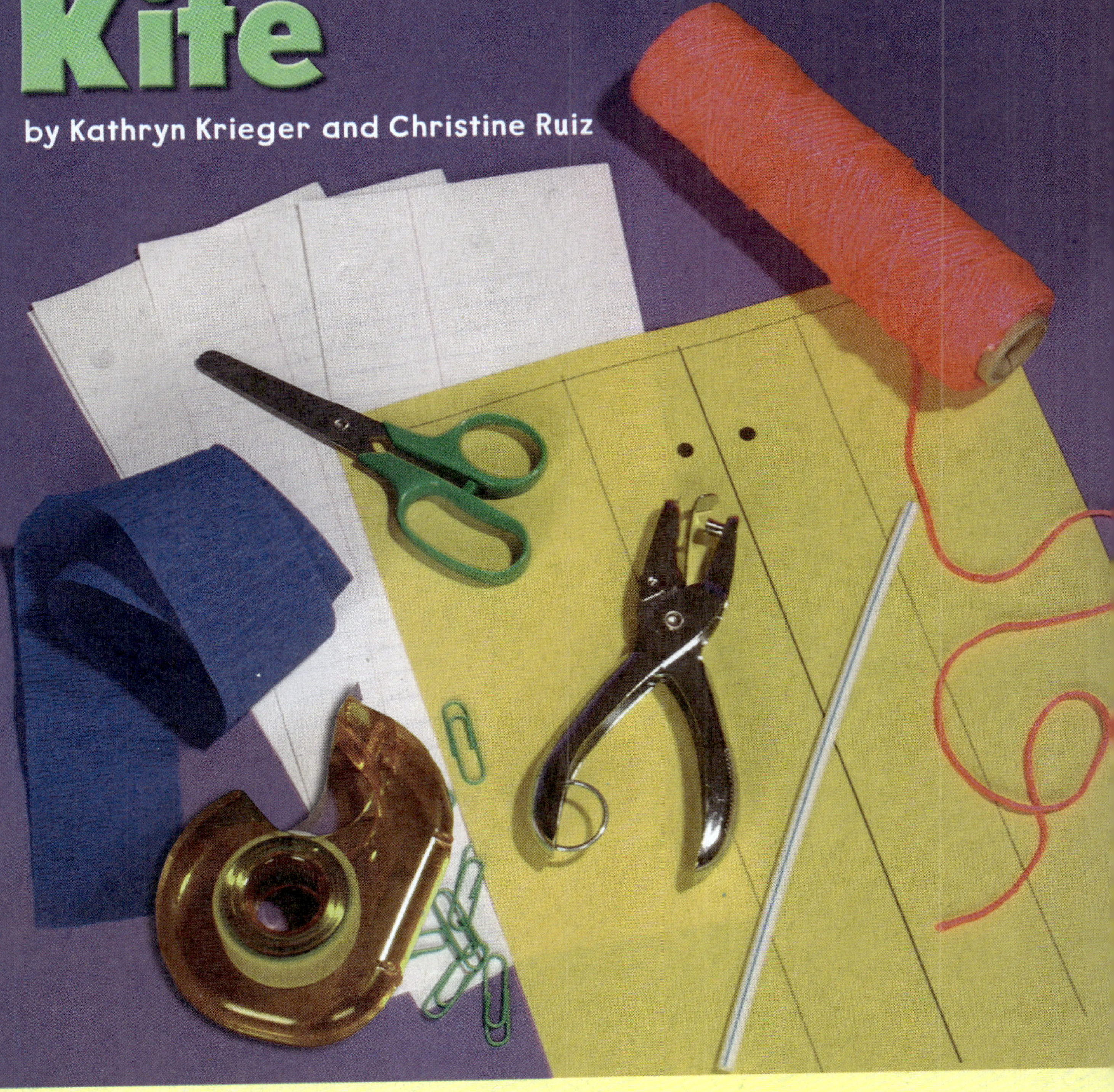

© Houghton Mifflin Harcourt Publishing Company

COMMON CORE

CRITICAL AREA Using standard units of measure

Ellie and Mike get the materials to make a kite. Then they make the body of the kite.

Materials

- paper kite pattern
- tape
- straw
- 10 small paper clips
- scissors
- hole punch
- string
- 3 sheets of paper
- streamer paper

1 

Fold the pattern in half.

2 

Fold along both dashed lines.

3 

Tape on each end.

© Houghton Mifflin Harcourt Publishing Company

What are the parts of a kite?

Mike does not want the front of the kite to bend too much. He uses a straw to make the kite stronger.

4

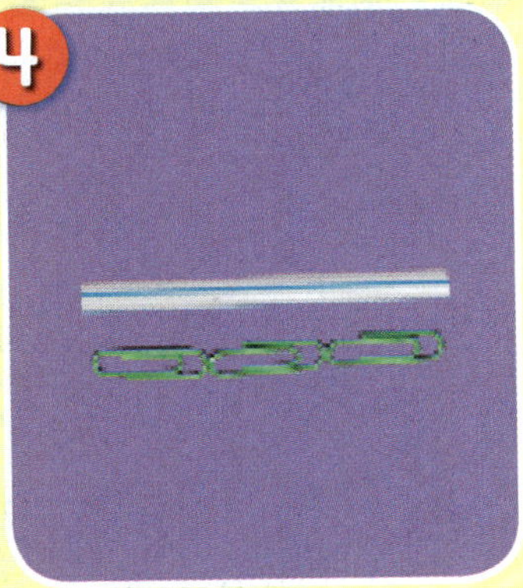

Measure 3 paper clips long. Cut.

5

Tape the straw on the line.

© Houghton Mifflin Harcourt Publishing Company

Why is a straw used as part of the kite?

The kite must have a string for Ellie or Mike to hold. If the kite does not have a string, it will blow away. Ellie will tie the string onto the kite.

6

Punch one hole.

7

Measure 3 paper-lengths of string. Cut.

8

Put the string through the hole and tie it.

Science

Why is a string needed on a kite?

© Houghton Mifflin Harcourt Publishing Company

A tail will help the kite fly straight. Mike measures streamer paper and will tape it to the kite. Then the kite will be finished!

Measure 10 paper-clip-lengths of streamer paper. Cut.

Tape the streamer to the kite as a tail.

© Houghton Mifflin Harcourt Publishing Company

Why is a tail needed on a kite?

You can make a kite too.
Start at the beginning of
this story. Follow the steps.

© Houghton Mifflin Harcourt Publishing Company

Science

How do all of the parts help the kite fly?

Name ____________________

Write About the Story

Draw and write a story about making a kite. Explain how to measure the parts of the kite in your story.

Vocabulary Review

measure

length

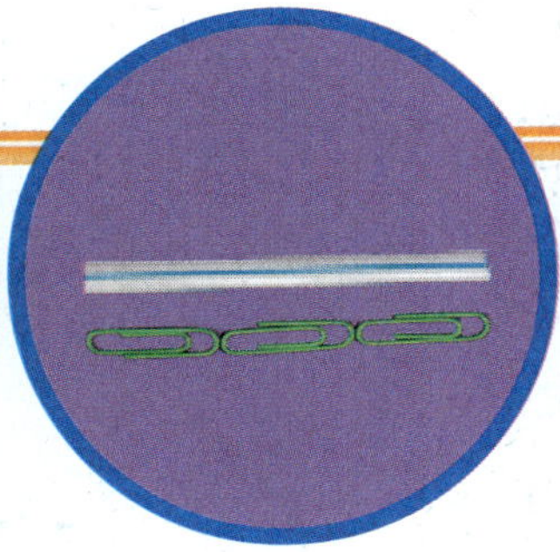

Write Math

____

____

____

____

____

© Houghton Mifflin Harcourt Publishing Company

What is the length?

Estimate the length of each straw. Then measure the length of each straw using small paper clips.

1. Estimate: about _____ paper clips long

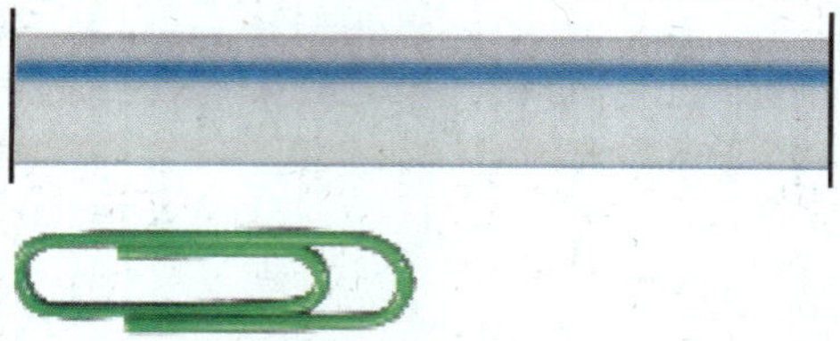

Measure: about _____ paper clips long

2. Estimate: about _____ paper clips long

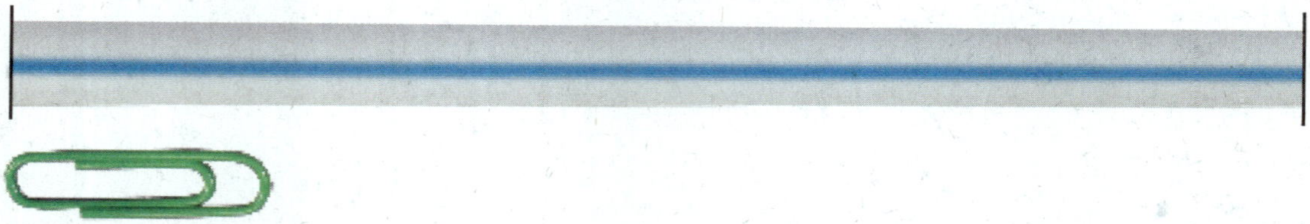

Measure: about _____ paper clips long

3. Estimate: about _____ paper clips long

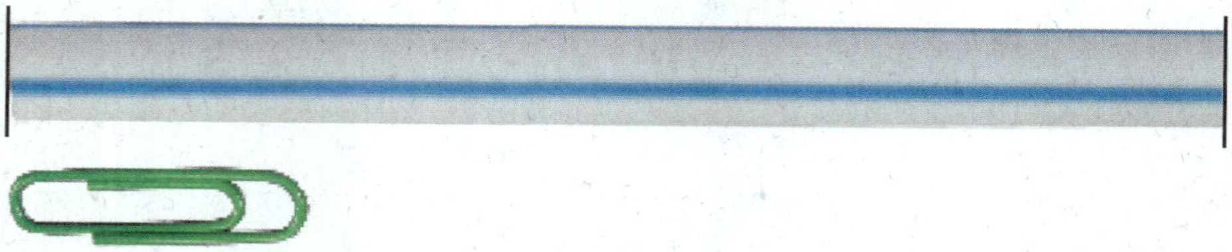

Measure: about _____ paper clips long

Math Board Look around the classroom. Find other objects to measure. Measure the length of each object using small paper clips.

© Houghton Mifflin Harcourt Publishing Company

Chapter 7

Money and Time

Curious About Math with Curious George

A sundial shows the time using the position of the sun. It has numbers around it, like a clock face. What numbers are on a clock face?

© Houghton Mifflin Harcourt Publishing Company.
Curious George by Margret and H.A. Rey. Copyright (c) 2010 by Houghton Mifflin Harcourt Publishing Company.
All rights reserved. The character Curious George®, including without limitation the character's name and the character's likenesses, are registered trademarks of Houghton Mifflin Harcourt Publishing Company.

Name ______________________________

Show What You Know

Order Numbers to 100 on a Number Line

Write the number that is just before, between, or just after.

1. 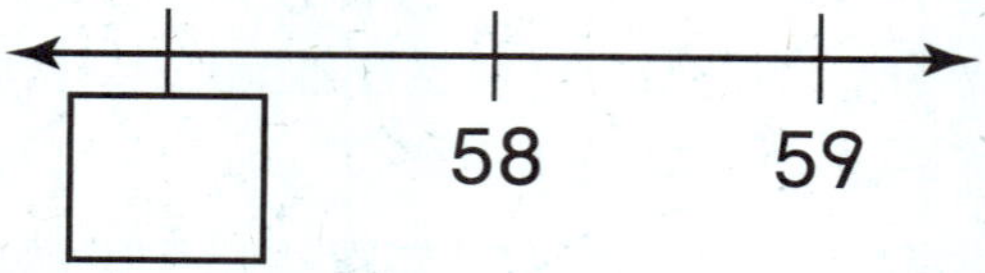

2. 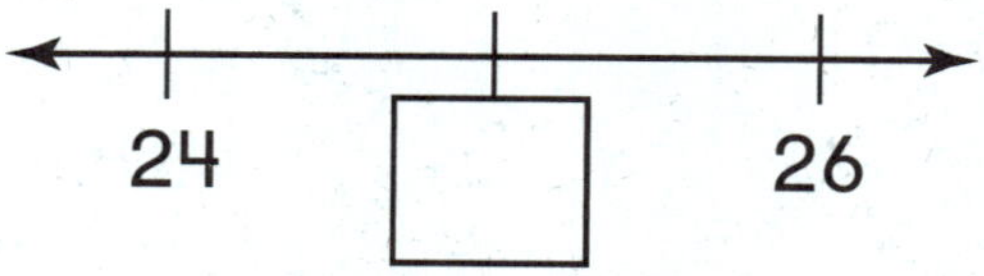

Skip Count by Fives and Tens

3. Count by fives. Write how many in all.

______________________________ ________ paints in all

4. Count by tens. Write how many in all.

______________________________ ________ paints in all

Time to the Hour

Write the time shown on the clock.

5. 

6. 

Family note: This page checks your child's understanding of important skills needed for success in Chapter 7.

GO Online Assessment Options Soar to Success Math

© Houghton Mifflin Harcourt Publishing Company

Name ______________________________

Vocabulary Builder

Review Words
- count
- pattern
- count on

Visualize It

Fill in the graphic organizer.
Show ways to **count on**.

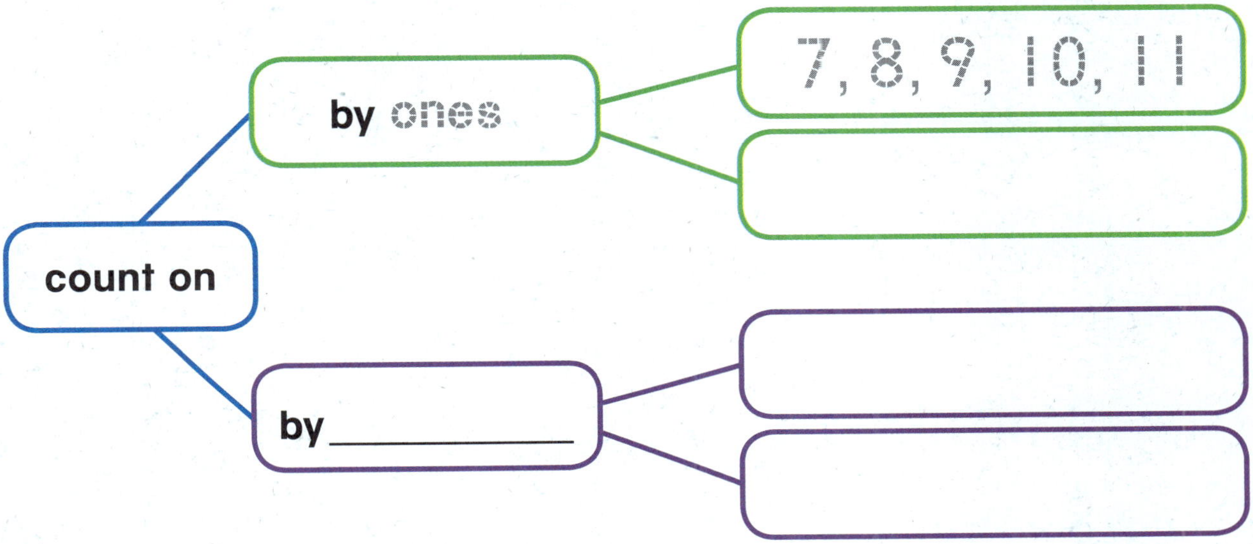

Understand Vocabulary

Write the missing numbers in each counting **pattern.**

1. **Count** by ones. 40, ____, ____, ____, 44, ____, 46, ____

2. **Count** by fives. 10, 15, ____, ____, ____, 35, ____, ____

3. **Count** by tens. 20, ____, ____, 50, ____, ____, 80, ____

© Houghton Mifflin Harcourt Publishing Company

GO Online
- eStudent Edition
- Multimedia eGlossary

Chapter **7**

Game

5 and 10 Count

Materials • 1 blue cube • 1 red cube • spinner

Play with a partner.

1. Spin the pointer on the spinner for your starting number. Put your cube on that number.
2. Spin the pointer. Count on by that number two times.
3. Take turns. The first player to get to 100 wins. Play again.

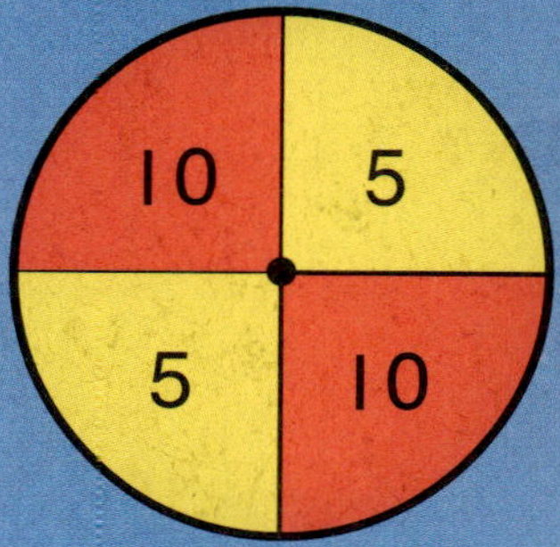

1	2	3	4	**5**	6	7	8	9	**10**
11	12	13	14	**15**	16	17	18	19	**20**
21	22	23	24	**25**	26	27	28	29	**30**
31	32	33	34	**35**	36	37	38	39	**40**
41	42	43	44	**45**	46	47	48	49	**50**
51	52	53	54	**55**	56	57	58	59	**60**
61	62	63	64	**65**	66	67	68	69	**70**
71	72	73	74	**75**	76	77	78	79	**80**
81	82	83	84	**85**	86	87	88	89	**90**
91	92	93	94	**95**	96	97	98	99	**100**

© Houghton Mifflin Harcourt Publishing Company

Name ______________________________

Dimes, Nickels, and Pennies

Essential Question How do you find the total value of a group of dimes, nickels, and pennies?

COMMON CORE STANDARD **CC.2.MD.8**
Work with time and money.

Listen and Draw REAL WORLD

Sort the coins. Then draw the coins.

FOR THE TEACHER • Distribute play coins of dimes, nickels, and pennies and discuss their values. Have children sort the coins and draw them inside the three circles. Have children label the drawings with the numbers *1*, *5*, or *10* to indicate the cent value of each coin drawn.

Math Talk
A nickel has the same value as how many pennies? **Explain.**

© Houghton Mifflin Harcourt Publishing Company

Model and Draw

10 cents
10¢

dime

5 cents
5¢

nickel

1 cent
1¢

penny

¢ is the **cent sign**.

Count dimes by tens.

10¢, 20¢, 30¢

Count nickels by fives.

5¢, 10¢, 15¢

Count by tens. Count by fives. Count by ones.

10¢, 20¢, 25¢, 30¢, 31¢, 32¢

32¢ total value

Share and Show

Math Board

Count on to find the total value.

1.

______________________ total value

2.

______________________ total value

© Houghton Mifflin Harcourt Publishing Company

Name ______________________________

On Your Own

Remember:
Write the cent sign
after the number.

Count on to find the total value.

3.

____

total value

4.

____

total value

5.

total value

6.

total value

7.

total value

8.

total value

© Houghton Mifflin Harcourt Publishing Company

PROBLEM SOLVING REAL WORLD

Write Math

Solve. Write or draw to explain.

9. Maggie had 5 nickels. She gave 2 nickels to her sister. What is the total value of the nickels that Maggie has now?

____

10. Jackson has 4 pennies and 3 dimes. How much money does Jackson have?

____

11. H.O.T. Draw two ways to show 25¢. You can use dimes, nickels, and pennies.

12. Test Prep Sue has these coins. How much money is this?

- ○ 4¢
- ○ 20¢
- ○ 40¢
- ○ 80¢

TAKE HOME ACTIVITY • Draw pictures of five coins, using dimes, nickels, and pennies. Ask your child to find the total value.

FOR MORE PRACTICE:
Standards Practice Book, pp. P157–P158

© Houghton Mifflin Harcourt Publishing Company

Name ____

Quarters

Essential Question How do you find the total value of a group of coins?

COMMON CORE STANDARD CC.2.MD.8
Work with time and money.

Listen and Draw REAL WORLD

Sort the coins. Then draw the coins.

FOR THE TEACHER • Distribute play coins of quarters, dimes, and nickels and discuss their values. Have children sort the coins and draw them inside the three boxes. Have them label the drawings with *5¢*, *10¢*, or *25¢*.

Math Talk

Describe how the value of a quarter is greater than the value of a dime.

MATHEMATICAL PRACTICES

© Houghton Mifflin Harcourt Publishing Company

Model and Draw

A **quarter** has a value of 25 cents.

25¢

Count by twenty-fives. Count by tens. Count by ones.

25¢, 50¢, 60¢, 70¢, 71¢, 72¢

72¢

total value

Share and Show

Math Board

Remember:
¢ is the cent sign.

Count on to find the total value.

1. 

total value

2. 

total value

3. 

total value

© Houghton Mifflin Harcourt Publishing Company

Name ________________________________

On Your Own

Count on to find the total value.

4.

____

total value

5.

____

total value

6.

total value

7.

total value

8.

total value

© Houghton Mifflin Harcourt Publishing Company

MATHEMATICAL PRACTICES Model • Reason • Make Sense

PROBLEM SOLVING REAL WORLD

Write Math

Read the clue. Choose the name of a coin from the box to answer the question.

nickel	dime
quarter	penny

9. I have the same value as 5 pennies.

   What coin am I?

   ____

10. I have the same value as 25 pennies.

    What coin am I?

    ____

11. I have the same value as 2 nickels.

    What coin am I?

    ____

12. H.O.T. I have the same value as a group of 4 nickels and 5 pennies.

    What coin am I?

    ____

13. **Test Prep** Tom gives these coins to his brother.

How much money does Tom give to his brother?

- ○ 80¢
- ○ 65¢
- ○ 50¢
- ○ 25¢

TAKE HOME ACTIVITY • Have your child draw two quarters, two dimes, and two nickels, and then find the total value.

FOR MORE PRACTICE: Standards Practice Book, pp. P159–P160

© Houghton Mifflin Harcourt Publishing Company

Name ____________________________________

Count Collections

Essential Question How do you order coins to help find the total value of a group of coins?

COMMON CORE STANDARD CC.2.MD.8
Work with time and money.

Listen and Draw REAL WORLD

Line up the coins from greatest value to least value. Then draw the coins in that order.

greatest | least

greatest | least

FOR THE TEACHER • Give each child a mixture of four play coins. Have children order their coins and then draw them. Have children trade sets of coins and repeat.

Math Talk **Describe** how the values of the different kinds of coins compare.

MATHEMATICAL PRACTICES

© Houghton Mifflin Harcourt Publishing Company

Model and Draw

Order the coins from greatest value to least value.
Then find the total value.

25¢ 25¢ 10¢ 1¢ 1¢

Count the cents.
25, 50, 60, 61, 62

____
total value

Share and Show

Math Board

Remember: Write the cent sign.

Draw and label the coins from greatest to least value. Find the total value.

1.

____

✓ 2.

____

✓ 3.

____

© Houghton Mifflin Harcourt Publishing Company

Name ____________________

On Your Own

Draw and label the coins from greatest to least value. Find the total value.

4.

____

5.

____

6.

____

7.

____

8.

____

© Houghton Mifflin Harcourt Publishing Company

PROBLEM SOLVING REAL WORLD

Write Math

Solve. Write or draw to explain.

9. Paulo had these coins.

He spent 1 quarter. How much money does he have now? ________

10. Rachel has 2 quarters, 3 dimes, and 1 nickel in her bank. How much money is in Rachel's bank? ________

11. H.O.T. Blake has only nickels and dimes. He has twice as many nickels as dimes. The total value of his coins is 60¢. What coins does Blake have?

________ nickels ________ dimes

12. **Test Prep** Tyler has these coins in his pocket. What is the total value of these coins?

- ○ 65¢
- ○ 60¢
- ○ 55¢
- ○ 50¢

TAKE HOME ACTIVITY • Have your child draw and label coins with a total value of 32¢.

FOR MORE PRACTICE: Standards Practice Book, pp. P161–P162

© Houghton Mifflin Harcourt Publishing Company

Name ________________________________

Show Amounts in Two Ways

Essential Question How do you choose coins to show a money amount in different ways?

HANDS ON
Lesson 7.4

COMMON CORE STANDARD CC.2.MD.8
Work with time and money.

Listen and Draw REAL WORLD

Show the amount with coins. Draw the coins. Write the amount.

FOR THE TEACHER • Distribute play coins. Tell children to use coins to show 27 cents. Then have them draw the coins and write the amount. Repeat the activity for 51 cents.

Math Talk
Can you show 10¢ with 3 coins? **Explain** how you know.

MATHEMATICAL PRACTICES

© Houghton Mifflin Harcourt Publishing Company

Model and Draw

Here are two ways to show 30¢.

Look at Matthew's way. If you trade 2 dimes and 1 nickel for 1 quarter, the coins will show Alicia's way.

Count the cents. Start with the dimes.

Count the cents. Start with the quarter.

Matthew

30¢

Alicia

30¢

Share and Show

Math Board

Use coins. Show the amount in two ways. Draw and label the coins.

1. 61¢		
2. 36¢		

© Houghton Mifflin Harcourt Publishing Company

Name ___________________________________

On Your Own

Use coins. Show the amount in two ways.
Draw and label the coins.

3. 55¢		
4. 90¢		
5. 75¢		
6. 42¢		

© Houghton Mifflin Harcourt Publishing Company

PROBLEM SOLVING REAL WORLD

Write Math

Use coins to solve.

7. Lee buys a pen for 50¢. Draw coins to show two different ways to pay 50¢.

8. H.O.T. Delia used 4 coins to buy a book for 40¢. Draw coins to show two ways to pay 40¢ with 4 coins.

9. **Test Prep** Rex buys an eraser that costs 20¢. Which group of coins has a total value of 20¢?

- ○ 2 nickels and 10 pennies
- ○ 1 dime and 1 nickel
- ○ 3 nickels and 1 dime
- ○ 1 quarter and 5 pennies

TAKE HOME ACTIVITY • With your child, take turns drawing different collections of coins to show 57¢.

© Houghton Mifflin Harcourt Publishing Company

FOR MORE PRACTICE: Standards Practice Book, pp. P163–P164

Name ____________________

One Dollar

Essential Question How can you show the value of one dollar with coins?

COMMON CORE STANDARD CC.2.MD.8
Work with time and money.

Listen and Draw REAL WORLD

Draw the coins. Write the total value.

____

____

Math Talk How many pennies have the same value as 80¢? **Explain.**

MATHEMATICAL PRACTICES

FOR THE TEACHER • In the first box, have children draw eight nickels and then count to find the total value. In the second box, have children draw eight dimes and then count to find the total value.

© Houghton Mifflin Harcourt Publishing Company

Model and Draw

One **dollar** has the same value as 100 cents.

$1.00 = 100¢

dollar sign → $ **decimal point** → .

The decimal point separates the dollars from the cents.

Share and Show

Math Board

Draw the coins to show $1.00. Write the total value.

Count 100 cents for one dollar.

1. nickels

$1.00

2. quarters

______

3. dimes

______

© Houghton Mifflin Harcourt Publishing Company

Name ____________________

On Your Own

Circle coins to make $1.00.
Cross out the coins you do not use.

4.

5.

6.

7. H.O.T. Draw more coins to show $1.00.

© Houghton Mifflin Harcourt Publishing Company

TAKE HOME ACTIVITY • Have your child draw a group of coins to show $1.00.

FOR MORE PRACTICE:
Standards Practice Book, pp. P165–P166

Name ______________________________

Mid-Chapter Checkpoint

Concepts and Skills

Count on to find the total value. (CC.2.MD.8)

1. 

[ ] total value

2. 

[ ] total value

Use coins. Show the amount in two ways.
Draw and label the coins. (CC.2.MD.8)

3. 31¢

4. **Test Prep** Mary used these coins to buy a folder. What is the total value of these coins? (CC.2.MD.8)

- ○ 30¢
- ○ 35¢
- ○ 60¢
- ○ 70¢

© Houghton Mifflin Harcourt Publishing Company

Lesson 7.6

Name ______________________________

Amounts Greater Than $1

Essential Question How do you show money amounts greater than one dollar?

COMMON CORE STANDARD CC.2.MD.8
Work with time and money.

Listen and Draw REAL WORLD

Draw and label the coins.
Write the total value.

______ total value

FOR THE TEACHER • Read the following problem: Dominic has 1 quarter, 2 dimes, 3 nickels, and 1 penny in his coin bank. How much money is in Dominic's bank? Have children draw and label coins to help them solve the problem.

Math Talk
Explain how you found the total value of the coins in the coin bank.

MATHEMATICAL PRACTICES

© Houghton Mifflin Harcourt Publishing Company

Model and Draw

When you write amounts greater than one dollar, use a dollar sign and a decimal point.

$1.00

$1.27
total value

$1.50
total value

Share and Show

Math Board

Circle the money that makes $1.00. Then write the total value of the money shown.

1.

_____

2.

_____

© Houghton Mifflin Harcourt Publishing Company

Name ______________________________

On Your Own

Circle the money that makes $1.00. Then write the total value of the money shown.

3.

____

4.

____

5.

____

6.

____

© Houghton Mifflin Harcourt Publishing Company

PROBLEM SOLVING REAL WORLD

Write Math

Solve. Write or draw to explain.

7. Martin used 3 quarters and 7 dimes to pay for a kite. How much money did he use?

____

8. H.O.T. Pam has fewer than 9 coins. The coins have a total value of $1.15. What coins could she have?

Draw the coins. Then write a list of her coins.

____

____

9. Test Prep Jason put this money in his bank. What is the total value of this money?

- ○ $1.10
- ○ $1.25
- ○ $1.30
- ○ $1.35

TAKE HOME ACTIVITY • With your child, take turns drawing coins or a $1 bill and coins with a total value of $1.23.

FOR MORE PRACTICE: Standards Practice Book, pp. P167–P168

© Houghton Mifflin Harcourt Publishing Company

Name ______________________________

Problem Solving • Money

Essential Question How does acting it out help when solving problems about money?

COMMON CORE STANDARD CC.2.MD.8
Work with time and money.

Kendra gave 2 dimes, 2 nickels, 1 quarter, and two $1 bills to the clerk for a puzzle. How much money did Kendra give the clerk?

Unlock the Problem

What do I need to find?

how much money
Kendra gave the
clerk

What information do I need to use?

Kendra gave the clerk
2 dimes, ______________________________
____
____

Show how to solve the problem.

Draw to show the money that Kendra used.

Kendra gave the clerk ____________.

HOME CONNECTION • Your child used play money to act out the problem. Representing problems with materials can be a useful strategy for children to use to solve problems.

© Houghton Mifflin Harcourt Publishing Company

Try Another Problem

Use play coins and bills to solve.
Draw to show what you did.

- What do I need to find?
- What information do I need to use?

1. Jacob has two $1 bills, 2 dimes, and 3 pennies in his pocket. How much money does Jacob have in his pocket?

____

2. Amber used 2 quarters, 1 nickel, 1 dime, and three $1 bills to buy a toy. How much money did Amber use to buy the toy?

____

Math Talk

Explain how you found the amount of money in Jacob's pocket.

MATHEMATICAL PRACTICES

© Houghton Mifflin Harcourt Publishing Company

Name ______________________

Share and Show

Math Board

Use play coins and bills to solve.
Draw to show what you did.

3. Val used 3 quarters, 2 nickels, 2 pennies, and one $1 bill to buy a book. How much money did Val use to buy the book? __________

4. Derek has two $1 bills, 2 quarters, and 6 dimes. How much money does he have? __________

5. Katy gave the clerk 3 quarters, 2 nickels, 2 dimes, and 3 pennies. How much money did she give to the clerk? __________

© Houghton Mifflin Harcourt Publishing Company

On Your Own

Solve. Write or draw to explain.

Write Math

6. Mr. Murphy has 120 fewer stickers than Miss Chen. Mr. Murphy has 364 stickers. How many stickers does Miss Chen have?

_________ stickers

7. H.O.T. Mia found 38 shells at the beach on Monday and 45 shells on Tuesday. She gave 26 shells to her sister. How many shells does Mia have now?

_________ shells

Describe how you solved the problem.

____

____

____

____

8. **Test Prep** Ross has 2 quarters, 1 dime, and two $1 bills. How much money does Ross have?

- ○ $2.60
- ○ $2.55
- ○ $2.35
- ○ $1.60

TAKE HOME ACTIVITY • Ask your child to explain how he or she solved the problem in Exercise 8.

© Houghton Mifflin Harcourt Publishing Company

FOR MORE PRACTICE:
Standards Practice Book, pp. P169–P170

Name ______________________________

Time to the Hour and Half Hour

Essential Question How do you tell time to the hour and half hour on a clock?

COMMON CORE STANDARD CC.2.MD.7
Work with time and money.

Listen and Draw REAL WORLD

Draw the hour hand to show each time.

FOR THE TEACHER • Call out times to the hour and to the half hour. Begin with 3:00. Have children draw the hour hand to show the time. Repeat the activity for half past 5:00, 11:00, and half past 8:00.

Math Talk
Describe where the hour hand points to show half past 4:00.

MATHEMATICAL PRACTICES

© Houghton Mifflin Harcourt Publishing Company

Model and Draw

It takes 5 **minutes** for the minute hand to move from one number to the next number on a clock face.

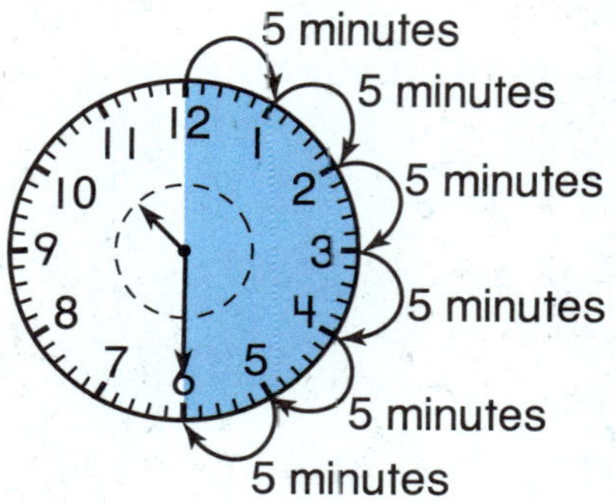

The clock hands on these clocks show 4:00 and 4:30. Write the times below the clocks.

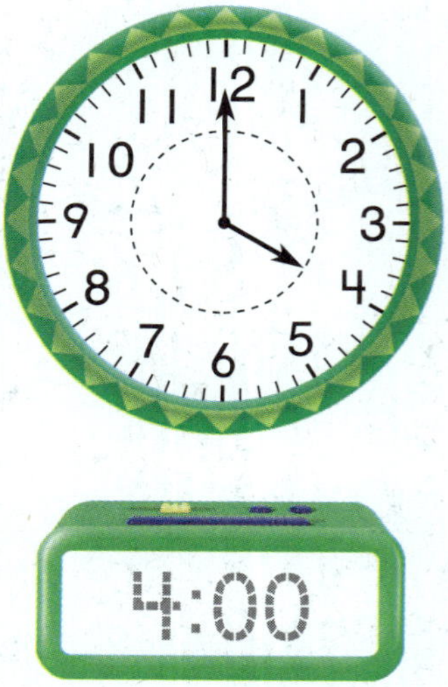

The 30 tells you that the time is 30 minutes after the hour.

Share and Show

Math Board

Look at the clock hands. Write the time.

1.

2.

3.

© Houghton Mifflin Harcourt Publishing Company

Name ______________________________

On Your Own

Look at the clock hands. Write the time.

4.

5.

6.

7.

8.

9.

H.O.T. Look at the time. Draw the hour hand and the minute hand to show the same time.

10.

11.

12.

© Houghton Mifflin Harcourt Publishing Company

PROBLEM SOLVING REAL WORLD

Write Math

13. H.O.T. Allie eats lunch when the hour hand points halfway between the 11 and the 12, and the minute hand points to the 6. When does Allie eat lunch? Show the time on both clocks.

How do you know what time to write in the digital clock? Explain.

____

____

____

14. **Test Prep** Reggie's guitar lesson starts at 10:30. Which clock shows this time?

○ 

○ 

○ 

○ 

TAKE HOME ACTIVITY • Have your child explain how he or she completed the exercises on this page.

© Houghton Mifflin Harcourt Publishing Company

FOR MORE PRACTICE: Standards Practice Book, pp. P171–P172

Name ___________________________

Time to 5 Minutes

Essential Question How do you tell and show time to five minutes?

COMMON CORE STANDARD CC.2.MD.7

Work with time and money.

Listen and Draw REAL WORLD

Draw the hour hand and the minute hand to show the time.

FOR THE TEACHER • Read the following story and have children draw the hour and minute hands to show each time. Sofia goes to music at 10:30. She goes to the playground at 11:00. She eats lunch at 11:30. Show the times Sofia does these things.

Math Talk

Describe where the minute hand points to show half past the hour.

MATHEMATICAL PRACTICES

© Houghton Mifflin Harcourt Publishing Company

Model and Draw

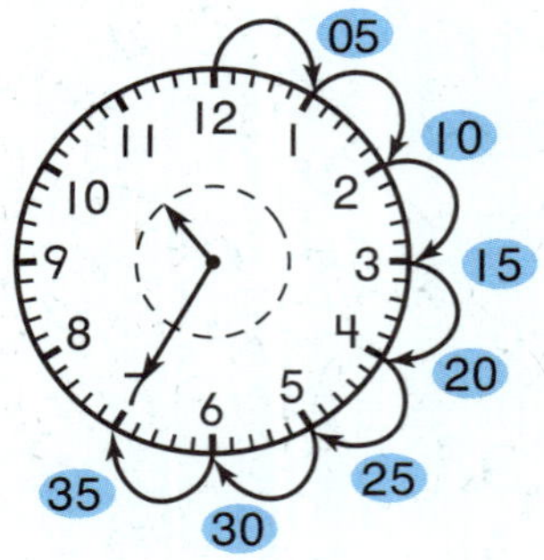

What does it mean when the minute hand points to the 7?

Count by fives until you reach the 7.

Remember:
The minute hand moves from one number to the next in 5 minutes.

The hour hand points between the 10 and the 11. The minute hand points to the 7.

The time is 10:35.

Share and Show

Math Board

Look at the clock hands. Write the time.

1.

2.

3.

4.

5.

6.

© Houghton Mifflin Harcourt Publishing Company

Name ______________________________

On Your Own

Look at the clock hands. Write the time.

7.

8.

9.

10.

11.

12.

H.O.T. Look at the time. Draw the minute hand to show the same time.

13.

14.

15.

© Houghton Mifflin Harcourt Publishing Company

MATHEMATICAL PRACTICES **Model • Reason • Make Sense**

PROBLEM SOLVING REAL WORLD

Write Math

Draw the minute hand to show the time.
Then write the time.

16. My hour hand points between the 8 and the 9. My minute hand points to the 5. What time do I show?

17. H.O.T. How many minutes does it take for the minute hand to travel around the clock from the 12 to the 12?

18. **Test Prep** What time is shown on this clock?

- ○ 1:45
- ○ 12:45
- ○ 12:09
- ○ 9:05

TAKE HOME ACTIVITY • Have your child draw a large blank clock face and use two pencils as clock hands to show some different times.

© Houghton Mifflin Harcourt Publishing Company

Name ____________________

Practice Telling Time

Essential Question What are the different ways you can read the time on a clock?

Lesson 7.10

COMMON CORE STANDARD CC.2.MD.7
Work with time and money.

Listen and Draw REAL WORLD

Write the times on the digital clocks.
Then label the clocks with the children's names.

____

____

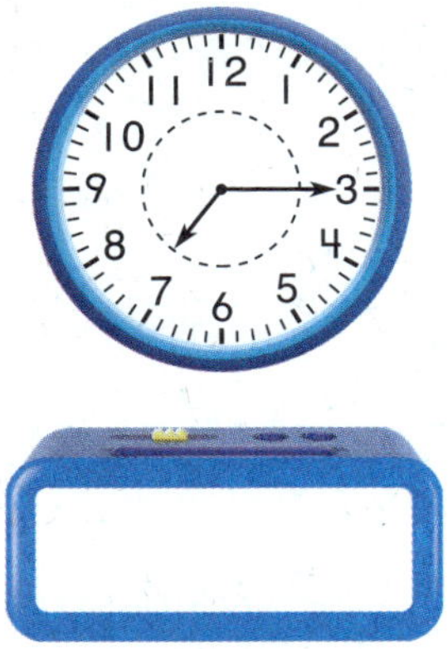

____

____

Math Talk Where would the minute hand point to show 15 minutes after the hour? **Explain.**

MATHEMATICAL PRACTICES

FOR THE TEACHER • First have children write the time for each analog clock. Then write *Luke, Beth, Kelly,* and *Mike* on the board. Tell chilcren to listen for each name to label the different times with. Luke plays football at 3:25. Beth eats lunch at 11:45. Kelly reads a book at 6:10. Mike eats breakfast at 7:15.

© Houghton Mifflin Harcourt Publishing Company

Model and Draw

These are different ways to write and say the time.

15 minutes after 8
quarter past 8

30 minutes after 8
half past 8

Share and Show

Math Board

Draw the minute hand to show the time. Write the time.

1. 15 minutes after 1

2. half past 9

3. quarter past 5

4. quarter past 10

✓5. 40 minutes after 3

✓6. half past 7

© Houghton Mifflin Harcourt Publishing Company

Name ______________________________

On Your Own

Draw the minute hand to show the time.
Write the time.

7. 15 minutes after 11

8. quarter past 4

9. 25 minutes after 8

10. 10 minutes after 6

11. half past 2

12. 45 minutes after 3

13. 5 minutes after 7

14. 30 minutes after 12

15. quarter past 10

© Houghton Mifflin Harcourt Publishing Company

PROBLEM SOLVING REAL WORLD

Write Math

16. Lily eats lunch at quarter past 12. Meg eats lunch at 12:30. Katie eats lunch at 12:15. Which girls eat lunch at the same time?

_____________ and _____________

17. Austin arrives at school at half past 8. Draw clock hands to show half past 8. Then write the time.

18. H.O.T. Soccer practice starts at 4:30. Gabe arrives at soccer practice at 4:15. Does he arrive before or after practice starts? Explain.

____

____

____

19. Test Prep What time is shown on this clock?

- ○ half past 4
- ○ half past 5
- ○ 6 minutes after 4
- ○ quarter past 5

TAKE HOME ACTIVITY • Name a time to 5 minutes. Ask your child to describe where the clock hands point at this time.

© Houghton Mifflin Harcourt Publishing Company

FOR MORE PRACTICE: Standards Practice Book, pp. P175–P176

Name ______________________________

A.M. and P.M.

Essential Question How do you use A.M. and P.M. to describe times?

COMMON CORE STANDARD CC.2.MD.7
Work with time and money.

Listen and Draw REAL WORLD

Draw the clock hands to show each time.
Then write each time.

Morning	Evening
	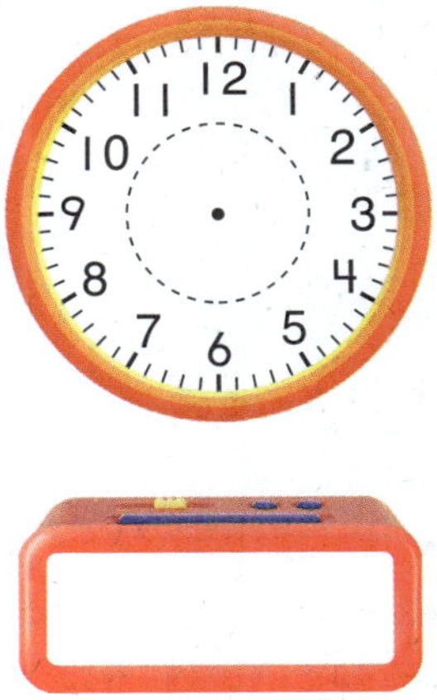

Math Talk MATHEMATICAL PRACTICES
Describe some activities that you do in both the morning and in the evening.

FOR THE TEACHER • Have children draw a picture and write a label for the picture for an activity they do in the morning and for an activity they do in the evening. Then have them show the time they do each activity on the clocks.

© Houghton Mifflin Harcourt Publishing Company

Model and Draw

Noon is 12:00 in the daytime.

Midnight is 12:00 at night.

Times after midnight and before noon are written with **A.M.**

11:00 A.M. is in the morning.

Times after noon and before midnight are written with **P.M.**

11:00 P.M. is in the evening.

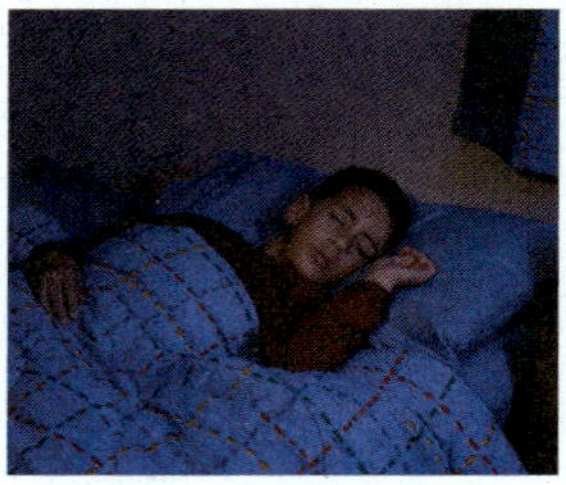

Share and Show

Math Board

Write the time. Then circle **A.M.** or **P.M.**

1. eat breakfast

A.M.

P.M.

2. go to art class

A.M.

P.M.

3. do homework

A.M.

P.M.

4. arrive at school

A.M.

P.M.

© Houghton Mifflin Harcourt Publishing Company

Name ______________________________

On Your Own

Write the time. Then circle **A.M.** or **P.M.**

5. go to the library

A.M.

P.M.

6. wake up

A.M.

P.M.

7. eat lunch

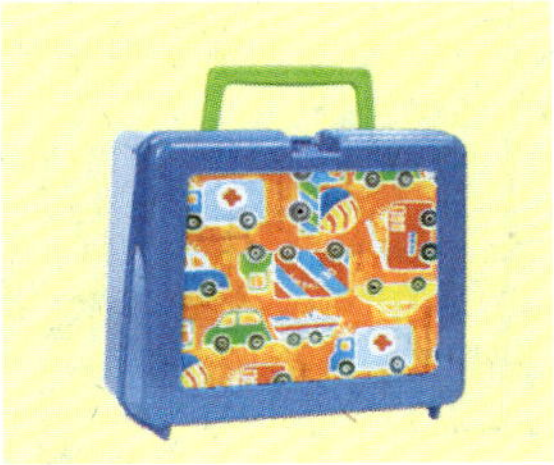

A.M.

P.M.

8. leave school

A.M.

P.M.

9. go to science class

A.M.

P.M.

10. look at the moon

A.M.

P.M.

© Houghton Mifflin Harcourt Publishing Company

PROBLEM SOLVING REAL WORLD

Write Math

11. Use the times in the list. Complete the story.

Don got to school at ________________.

His class went to the library

at ________________. After school,

Don read a book at ________________.

10:15 A.M.
3:20 P.M.
8:30 A.M.

12. H.O.T. Some times are shown on this time line. Write a label for each dot that names something you do at school during that part of the day.

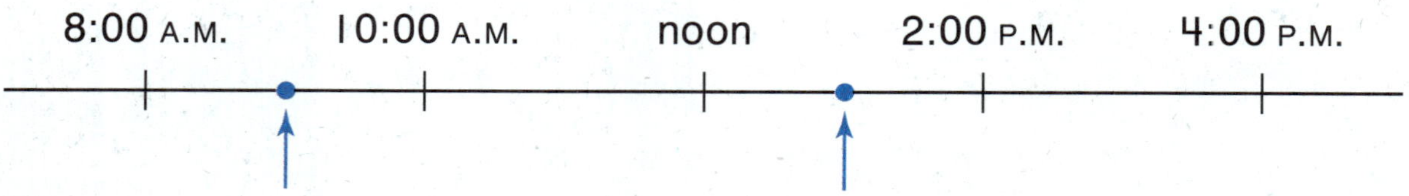

________________ ________________

At what times would you say the dots are placed on the time line?

________________ and ________________

13. **Test Prep** The clock shows the time that Jane went to recess. At what time did she go to recess?

- ○ 6:00 A.M.
- ○ 11:30 A.M.
- ○ 6:30 P.M.
- ○ 11:30 P.M.

TAKE HOME ACTIVITY • Name some activities and times. Have your child say A.M. or P.M. for the times.

© Houghton Mifflin Harcourt Publishing Company

FOR MORE PRACTICE: Standards Practice Book, pp. P177–P178

Name ________________________________

Chapter 7 Review/Test

Vocabulary

Use a word in the box to complete each sentence.

dime
dollar
A.M.
P.M.

1. One ________________ has the same value as 100 cents. (p. 354)

2. The value of one ________________ is 10 cents. (p. 338)

3. Times after noon and before midnight are written with ________________. (p. 378)

Concepts and Skills

Count on to find the total value. (CC.2.MD.8)

4.

[ ] total value

Use coins. Show the amount in two ways.
Draw and label the coins. (CC.2.MD.8)

5.

42¢

© Houghton Mifflin Harcourt Publishing Company

Fill in the bubble for the correct answer choice.

TEST PREP

6. The clock shows the time that the museum opens. What time is shown? (CC.2.MD.7)

- ○ 8:00
- ○ 9:00
- ○ 10:00
- ○ 12:00

7. The play begins at 8:30. Which clock shows 8:30? (CC.2.MD.7)

○ 

○ 

○ 

○ 

8. The clock shows the time that music class starts. At what time does music class start? (CC.2.MD.7)

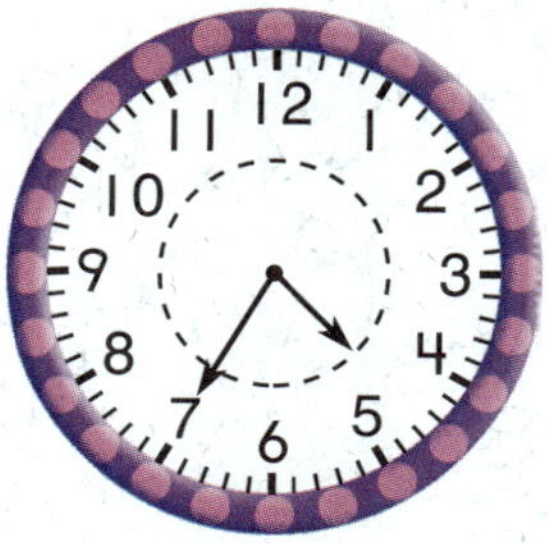

- ○ 7:25 A.M.
- ○ 7:25 P.M.
- ○ 4:35 A.M.
- ○ 4:35 P.M.

© Houghton Mifflin Harcourt Publishing Company

Name ______________________________

TEST PREP

Fill in the bubble for the correct answer choice.

9. Lindsey wants to buy lemonade that costs one dollar. Which coins could she use to buy the lemonade? (CC.2.MD.8)

   ○ 4 quarters
   ○ 4 dimes
   ○ 4 nickels
   ○ 4 pennies

10. Pete uses these coins to buy a marker. How much money is this? (CC.2.MD.8)

   ○ 45¢
   ○ 50¢
   ○ 55¢
   ○ 65¢

11. Chris used this money to buy a book. How much money is this? (CC.2.MD.8)

   ○ $1.50
   ○ $1.65
   ○ $1.75
   ○ $1.80

© Houghton Mifflin Harcourt Publishing Company

Constructed Response

12. Wes has 4 nickels and 10 pennies. Draw to show this amount using a different group of coins.

Explain how you decided what coins to draw. (CC.2.MD.8)

____

____

____

Performance Task (CC.2.MD.7)

13. The clocks show when Rachel started each activity. Write the time for each activity.

ate a snack

played soccer

read a book

Do you think these are A.M. times or P.M. times? Explain.

____

____

____

© Houghton Mifflin Harcourt Publishing Company

Chapter **8**

Length in Customary Units

Curious About Math with Curious George

The Missouri River is the longest river in the United States.

What is the longest piece of furniture in your classroom? How would you find out?

© Houghton Mifflin Harcourt Publishing Company
Curious George by Margret and H.A. Rey. Copyright (c) 2010 by Houghton Mifflin Harcourt Publishing Company. All rights reserved. The character Curious George, including without limitation the character's name and the character's likenesses, are registered trademarks of Houghton Mifflin Harcourt Publishing Company.

Name ____________________

Show What You Know

Compare Lengths

1. Order the pencils from shortest to longest.
Write 1, 2, 3.

____
____
____

Use Nonstandard Units to Measure Length

Use real objects and ■ to measure.

2. 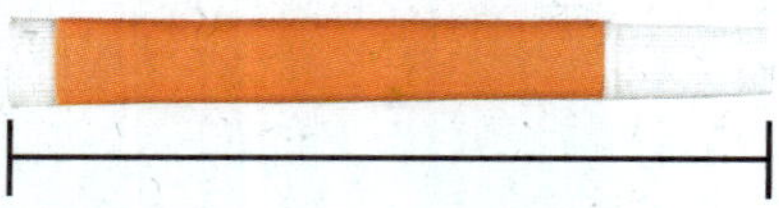

about ______ ■

3. 

about ______ ■

Measure Length Twice: Nonstandard Units

Use paper clips first. Then use cubes.
Measure the length of the pencil.

4. about ______ paper clips

5. about ______ cubes

Family note: This page checks your child's understanding of important skills needed for success in Chapter 8.

GO Online Assessment Options Soar to Success Math

© Houghton Mifflin Harcourt Publishing Company

Name ______________________________

Vocabulary Builder

Review Words

length
longer
shorter
longest
shortest

Visualize It

Fill in the graphic organizer to describe the lengths of different objects.

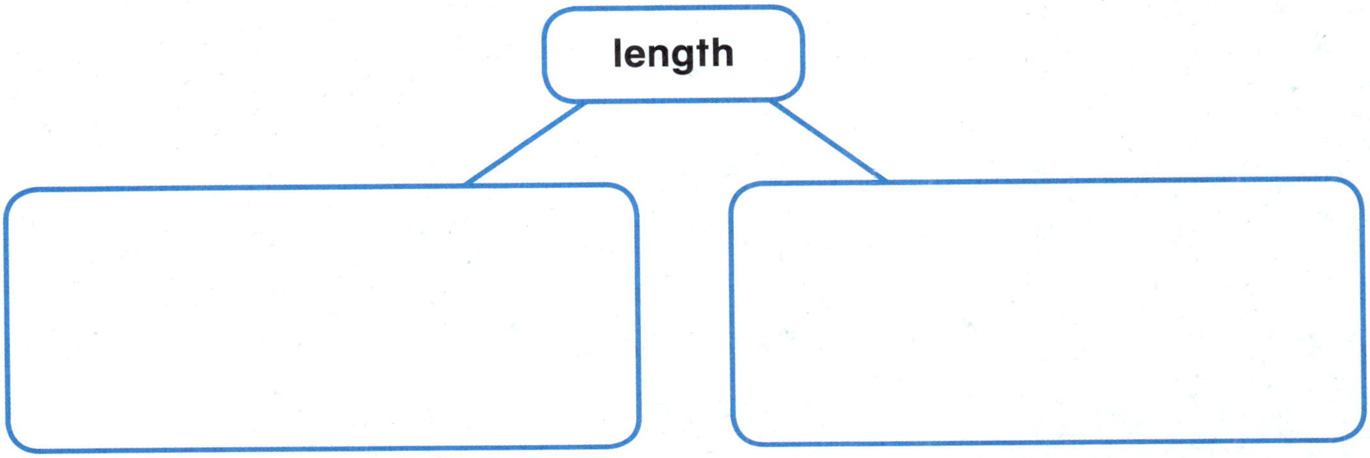

Understand Vocabulary

Use review words. Complete the sentences.

1. The blue pencil is the ________________ pencil.

2. The red pencil is the ________________ pencil.

3. The red pencil is ________________ than the yellow pencil.

4. The blue pencil is ________________ than the yellow pencil.

© Houghton Mifflin Harcourt Publishing Company

GO Online
• eStudent Edition
• Multimedia eGlossary

Game

Longer or Shorter?

Materials

- 9
- 9
-

Play with a partner.

1. Each player chooses a picture on the board and then finds a real object that matches that picture.
2. Place the objects next to each other to find which is longer and which is shorter. If the objects are the same length, choose another object.
3. Spin the pointer on the spinner. The player with the object that matches the spinner puts a cube on that picture on the board.
4. Take turns until all the pictures have cubes. The player with more cubes on the board wins.

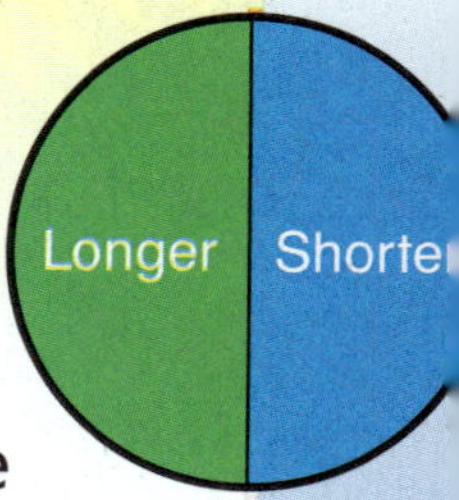

© Houghton Mifflin Harcourt Publishing Company

Name ______________________________

Measure with Inch Models

HANDS ON
Lesson 8.1

Essential Question How can you use inch models to measure length?

COMMON CORE STANDARD CC.2.MD.1
Measure and estimate lengths in standard units.

Listen and Draw REAL WORLD

Use color tiles to measure the length.

_______ color tiles

_______ color tiles

_______ color tiles

Math Talk
Describe how to use color tiles to measure the length of an object.

HOME CONNECTION • Your child used color tiles as an introduction to measurement of length before using standard measurement tools.

© Houghton Mifflin Harcourt Publishing Company

Model and Draw

A color tile is about 1 **inch** long.

About how many inches long is this string?

Count the color tiles to find how many inches long the string is.

The string is 4 color tiles long.

So, the string is about __4__ inches long.

Share and Show

Math Board

Use color tiles. Measure the length of the object in inches.

1\.

about ______ inches

2\.

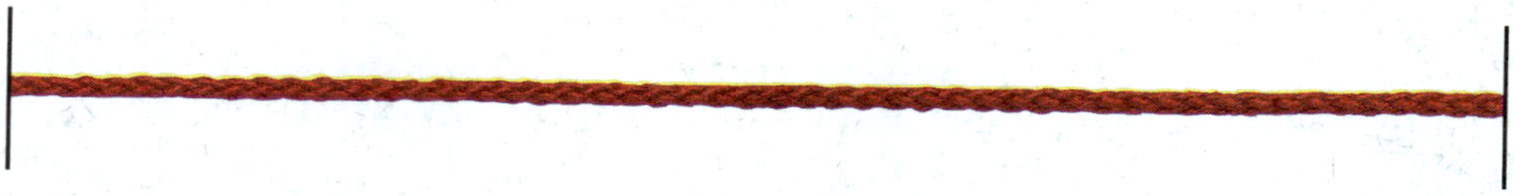

about ______ inches

3\.

about ______ inches

4\.

about ______ inches

© Houghton Mifflin Harcourt Publishing Company

Name ______________________________

On Your Own

Use color tiles. Measure the length of the object in inches.

5. 

about ________ inches

6. 

about ________ inches

7. 

about ________ inches

8. 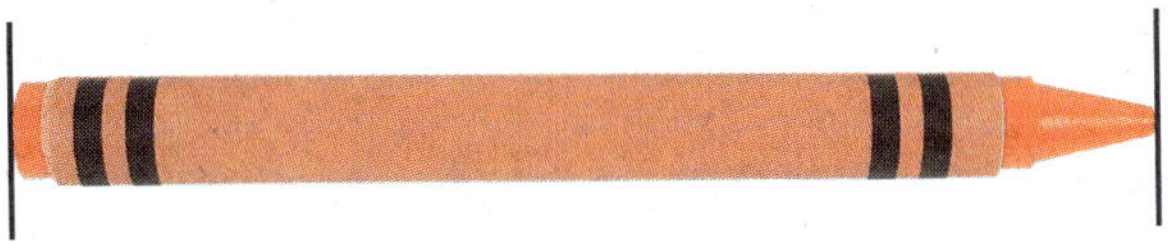

about ________ inches

9. 

about ________ inches

10. 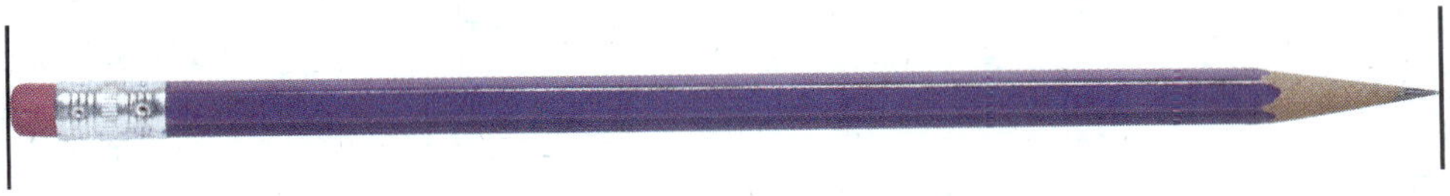

about ________ inches

© Houghton Mifflin Harcourt Publishing Company

PROBLEM SOLVING REAL WORLD

Write Math

Look in your classroom. Find two objects that are about 2 inches long. Draw and label the objects.

11. ____________________

12. ____________________

13. H.O.T. Liza has a piece of ribbon that is 12 inches long. She needs to cut it into pieces that are each 4 inches long. How many pieces can she make?

_______ pieces

14. Test Prep Jeremy used color tiles to measure a string. Which is the best choice for the length of the string?

- ○ about 1 inch
- ○ about 2 inches
- ○ about 3 inches
- ○ about 4 inches

TAKE HOME ACTIVITY • Have your child use several of the same small item (such as paper clips) to measure the lengths of some objects at home.

FOR MORE PRACTICE: Standards Practice Book, pp. P183–P184

© Houghton Mifflin Harcourt Publishing Company

Name ______________________________

Make and Use a Ruler

Essential Question Why is using a ruler similar to using a row of color tiles to measure length?

COMMON CORE STANDARD CC.2.MD.1
Measure and estimate lengths in standard units.

Listen and Draw REAL WORLD

Use color tiles. Make the given length. Trace along the edge to show the length.

4 inches

2 inches

3 inches

Math Talk

Describe how you knew how many color tiles to use for each length.

MATHEMATICAL PRACTICES

HOME CONNECTION • Your child used color tiles as 1-inch models to show different lengths. This activity helps to make inch units a more familiar concept.

© Houghton Mifflin Harcourt Publishing Company

Model and Draw

Use a color tile to make a ruler on a paper strip.
Color 6 parts that are each about 1 inch long.

How to use your ruler:
Line up the left edge of an object with the first mark.

Share and Show

Math Board

Measure the length with your ruler.
Count the inches.

1.

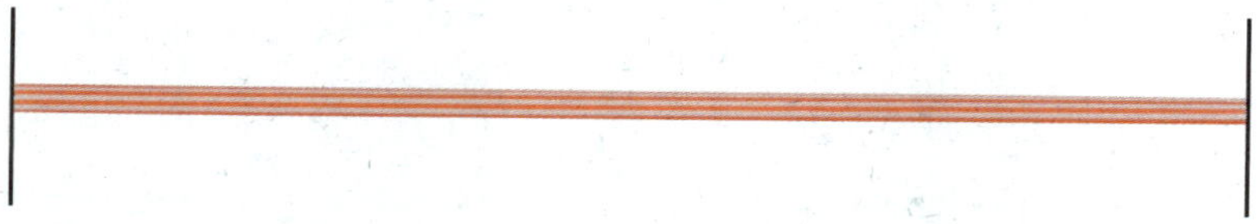

about ______ inches

2.

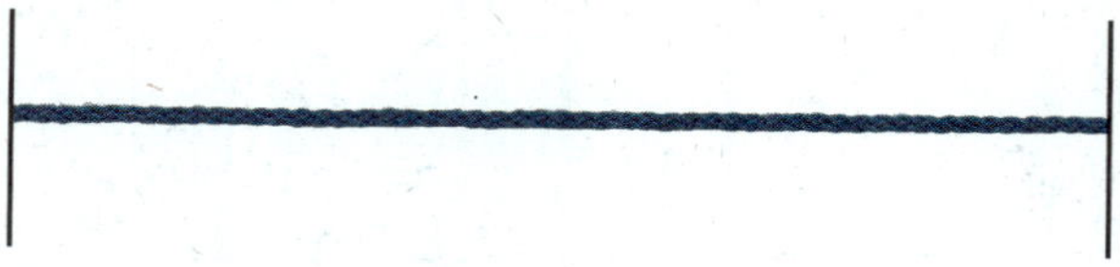

about ______ inches

3.

about ______ inches

© Houghton Mifflin Harcourt Publishing Company

Name ________________________________

On Your Own

Measure the length with your ruler.
Count the inches.

4. 

about _______ inches

5. 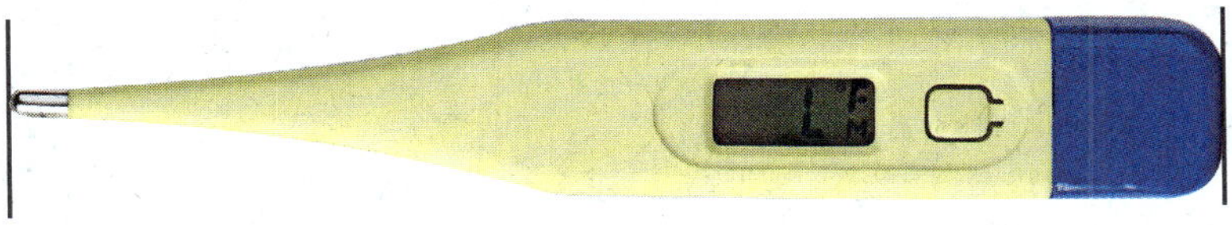

about _______ inches

6. 

about _______ inches

7. 

about _______ inches

8. 

about _______ inches

© Houghton Mifflin Harcourt Publishing Company

PROBLEM SOLVING REAL WORLD

Write Math

Work with a classmate.

9. H.O.T. Together, use both of your rulers to measure the length of a bulletin board or a window. What is the length?

about _______ inches

10. Describe what you did in Exercise 9. How did you measure a length that is longer than your rulers?

____

____

____

____

11. **Test Prep** Use your ruler. What is the best choice for the length of this piece of yarn?

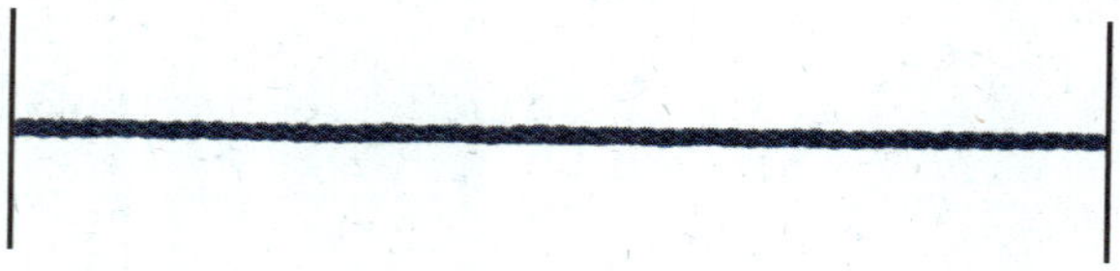

○ about 6 inches

○ about 5 inches

○ about 4 inches

○ about 3 inches

TAKE HOME ACTIVITY • Choose one object in this lesson. Have your child find objects that are longer, about the same length, and shorter.

FOR MORE PRACTICE: Standards Practice Book, pp. P185–P186

© Houghton Mifflin Harcourt Publishing Company

Name ______________________________

Estimate Lengths in Inches

Essential Question How do you estimate the lengths of objects in inches?

COMMON CORE STANDARD CC.2.MD.3
Measure and estimate lengths in standard units.

Listen and Draw REAL WORLD

Choose three objects. Measure their lengths with your ruler. Draw the objects and write their lengths.

about ______ inches

about ______ inches

about ______ inches

FOR THE TEACHER • Provide a collection of small objects, 2 to 6 inches in length, for children to measure. Have them select one object, measure it, and return it before selecting another object.

Math Talk

Describe how the three lengths compare. Which is the longest object?

© Houghton Mifflin Harcourt Publishing Company

Model and Draw

The bead is 1 inch long. Use this bead to help find how many beads will fit on the string. Which is the best estimate for the length of the string?

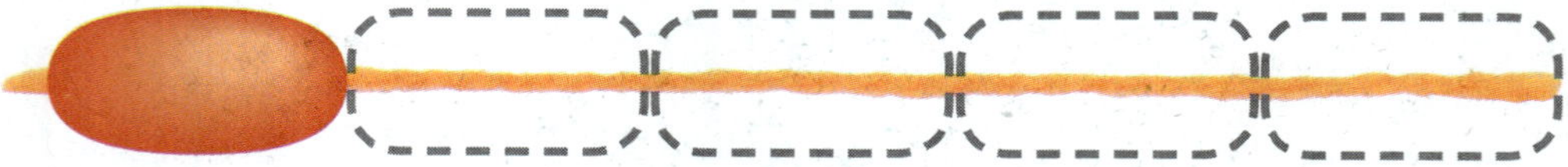

2 inches   5 inches   8 inches

2 inches is too short.   5 inches is about right.   8 inches is too long.

Share and Show

Math Board

Circle the best estimate for the length of the string.

1.

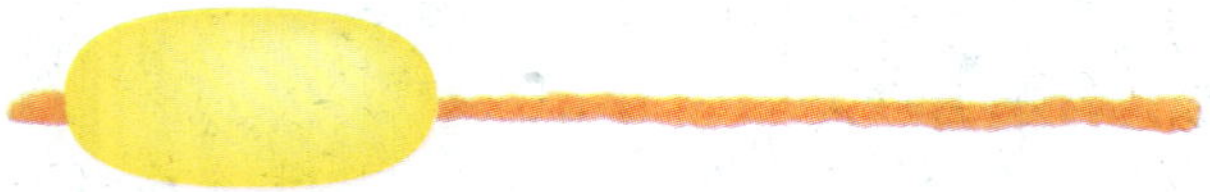

1 inch   3 inches   5 inches

2.

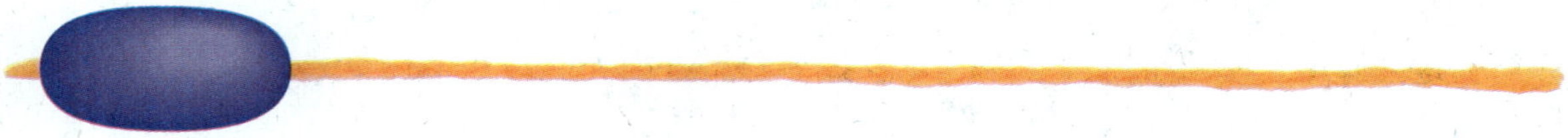

2 inches   4 inches   6 inches

3.

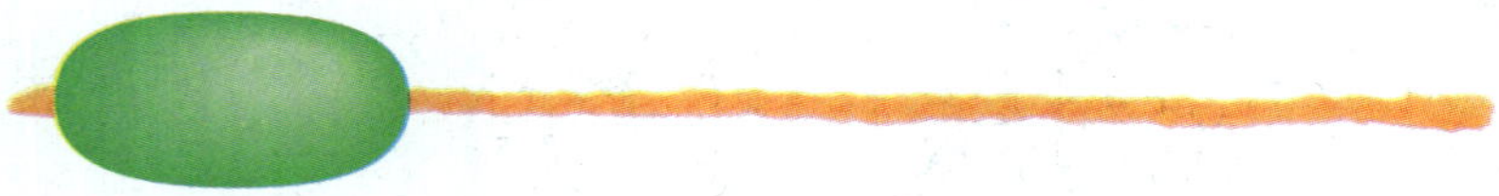

4 inches   6 inches   8 inches

© Houghton Mifflin Harcourt Publishing Company

Name ______________________________

On Your Own

Circle the best estimate for the length of the string.

4.

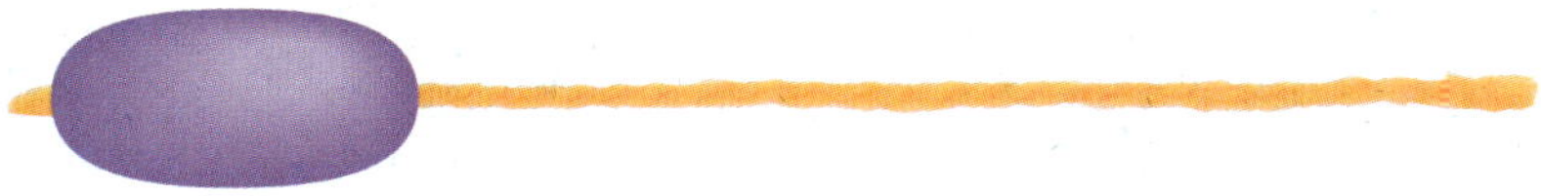

4 inches   7 inches   10 inches

5.

3 inches   6 inches   9 inches

6.

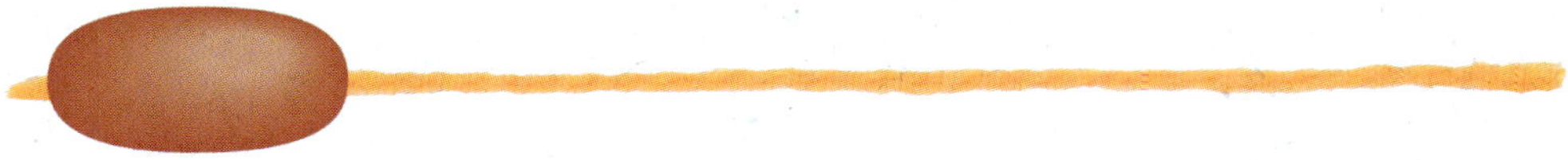

1 inch   3 inches   5 inches

7. Use the 1-inch mark. Estimate the length of each ribbon.

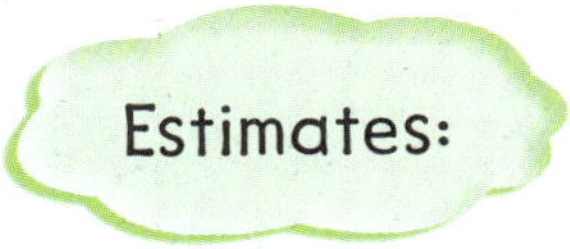

red ribbon: about ______ inches

blue ribbon: about ______ inches

© Houghton Mifflin Harcourt Publishing Company

PROBLEM SOLVING REAL WORLD

Write Math

Solve. Write or draw to explain.

8. Sasha has a string that is the length of 5 beads. Each bead is 2 inches long. What is the length of the string?

_______ inches

9. H.O.T. Maurice has a string that is 15 inches long. He has beads that are each 3 inches long. How many beads will fit on the string?

_______ beads

10. **Test Prep** Tameka has this string. She has many beads that are 1 inch long, like this blue bead.

Which is the best estimate for the length of the string?

- ○ 10 inches
- ○ 5 inches
- ○ 2 inches
- ○ 1 inch

TAKE HOME ACTIVITY • With your child, estimate the lengths in inches of some small objects, such as books.

FOR MORE PRACTICE: Standards Practice Book, pp. P187–P188

© Houghton Mifflin Harcourt Publishing Company

Name ______________________________

Measure with an Inch Ruler

HANDS ON Lesson 8.4

Essential Question How do you use an inch ruler to measure lengths?

COMMON CORE STANDARD CC.2.MD.1

Measure and estimate lengths in standard units.

Listen and Draw REAL WORLD

Draw each caterpillar to match the given length.

FOR THE TEACHER • Have children use the rulers that they made in Lesson 8.2 to draw a caterpillar that is 1 inch long. Have children use the 1-inch-long caterpillar as a guide to draw a caterpillar that is 2 inches long and a caterpillar that is 3 inches long, without using their rulers.

Math Talk

Describe how you decided how long to draw the 2-inch and 3-inch caterpillars.

© Houghton Mifflin Harcourt Publishing Company

Model and Draw

What is the length of the string to the nearest inch?

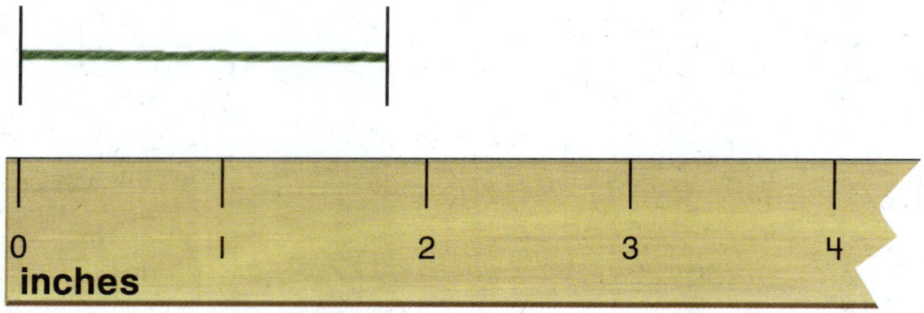

Step 1

Line up the end of the string with the zero mark on the ruler.

Step 2

Find the inch mark that is closest to the other end of the string.

___2___ inches

Share and Show

Math Board

Measure the length to the nearest inch.

1.

_______ inches

2.

_______ inches

3.

_______ inches

4.

_______ inches

© Houghton Mifflin Harcourt Publishing Company

Name ______________________________

On Your Own

Measure the length to the nearest inch.

5.

______ inches

6.

______ inches

7.

______ inches

8.

______ inches

9.

______ inches

10.

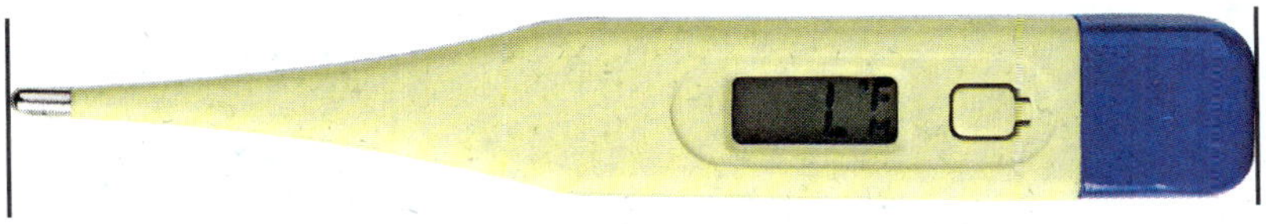

______ inches

© Houghton Mifflin Harcourt Publishing Company

PROBLEM SOLVING REAL WORLD

Write Math

Solve.

11. Measure. What is the total length?

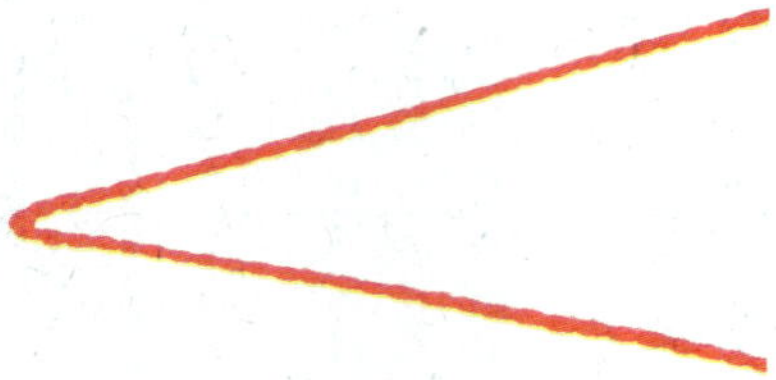

_______ inches

12. Measure. What is the total length?

_______ inches

13. H.O.T. How much longer is the red string than the blue string?

_______ inches longer

14. H.O.T. If the red and blue strings were straight and placed end to end, what would the total length be?

_______ inches

15. **Test Prep** Use an inch ruler. What is the length of the pencil to the nearest inch?

- ○ 1 inch
- ○ 2 inches
- ○ 3 inches
- ○ 5 inches

TAKE HOME ACTIVITY • Have your child measure the lengths of some objects to the nearest inch using a ruler or a similar measuring tool.

FOR MORE PRACTICE:
Standards Practice Book, pp. P189–P190

© Houghton Mifflin Harcourt Publishing Company

Name ________________________________

Problem Solving • Add and Subtract in Inches

COMMON CORE STANDARDS CC.2.MD.5, CC.2.MD.6
Relate addition and subtraction to length.

Essential Question How can drawing a diagram help when solving problems about length?

There is a paper clip chain that is 16 inches long. Ann removes 9 inches of paper clips from the chain. How long is the paper clip chain now?

Unlock the Problem REAL WORLD

What do I need to find?

how long the paper clip chain is now

What information do I need to use?

The chain is ______ inches long.

______ inches of paper clips are removed from the chain.

Show how to solve the problem.

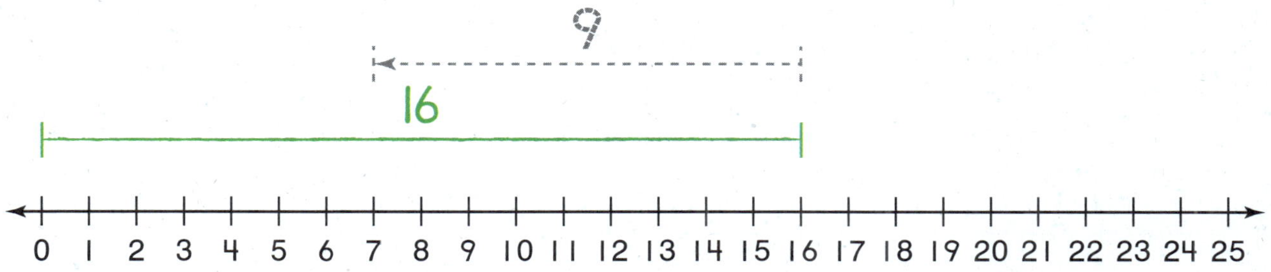

____

The paper clip chain is ______ inches long now.

HOME CONNECTION • Your child drew a diagram to represent a problem about lengths. The diagram can be used to choose the operation for solving the problem.

© Houghton Mifflin Harcourt Publishing Company

Try Another Problem

Draw a diagram. Write a number sentence using a ▢ for the missing number. Solve.

- What do I need to find?
- What information do I need to use?

1. Carmen has a string that is 13 inches long and a string that is 8 inches long. How many inches of string does she have?

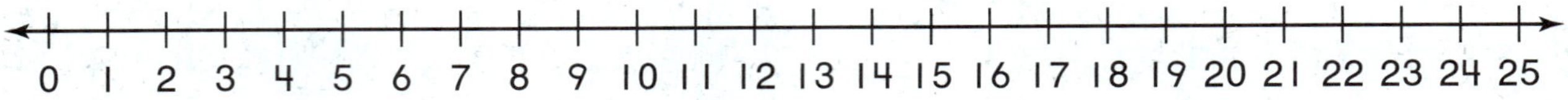

____

Carmen has _______ inches of string.

2. Eli has a cube train that is 24 inches long. He removes 9 inches of cubes from the train. How long is Eli's cube train now?

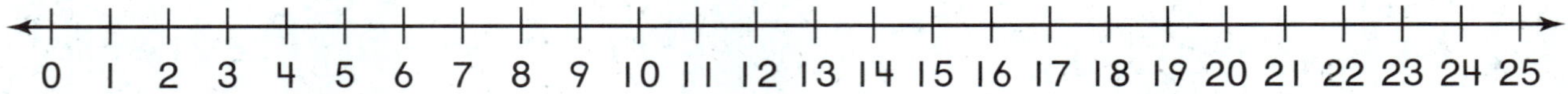

____

Eli's cube train is _______ inches long now.

Math Talk
Describe how your diagram shows what happened in the second problem.

MATHEMATICAL PRACTICES

© Houghton Mifflin Harcourt Publishing Company

Name ______________________________

Share and Show

Math Board

Draw a diagram. Write a number sentence using a ▒ for the missing number. Solve.

3. Lee has a paper strip chain that is 25 inches long. He unhooks 13 inches from the chain. How long is Lee's paper strip chain now?

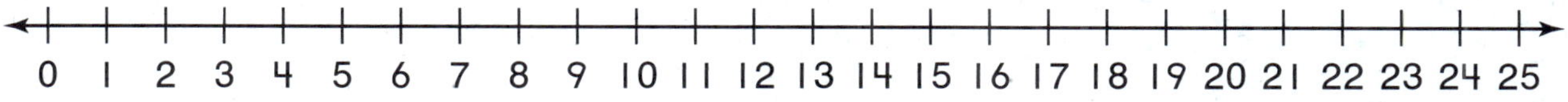

____

Lee's paper strip chain is ______ inches long now.

4. H.O.T. Sue has two ribbons that have the same length. She has 18 inches of ribbon in all. How long is each ribbon?

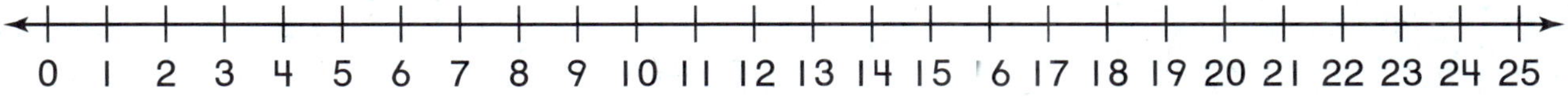

____

Each ribbon is ______ inches long.

TAKE HOME ACTIVITY • Have your child explain how he or she used a diagram to solve Exercise 4.

© Houghton Mifflin Harcourt Publishing Company

FOR MORE PRACTICE:
Standards Practice Book, pp. P191–P192

Name ______________________________

Mid-Chapter Checkpoint

Concepts and Skills

Use color tiles. Measure the length of the object in inches. (CC.2.MD.1)

1. 

about _____ inches

The bead is one inch long. Circle the best estimate for the length of the string. (CC.2.MD.3)

2. 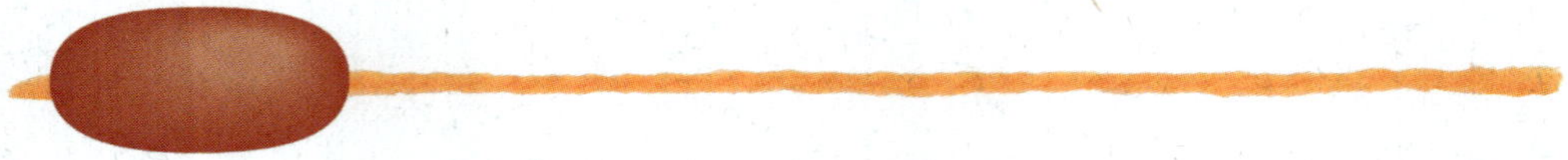

1 inch   2 inches   5 inches

Draw a diagram. Write a number sentence using a ■ for the missing number. Solve.

3. A mark is 17 inches long. Katy erases 9 inches from the mark. How long is the mark now? (CC.2.MD.5, CC.2.MD.6)

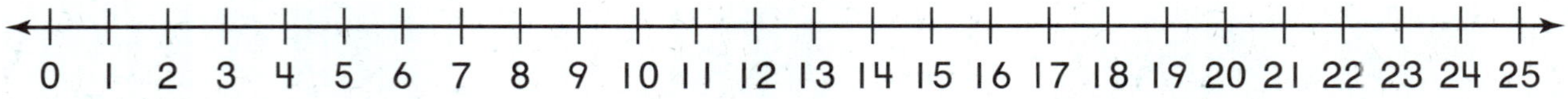

____

The mark is ________ inches long now.

4. **Test Prep** Use an inch ruler. What is the length of the string to the nearest inch? (CC.2.MD.1)

- ○ 1 inch
- ○ 2 inches
- ○ 3 inches
- ○ 5 inches

© Houghton Mifflin Harcourt Publishing Company

Name ______________________________________

Measure in Inches and Feet

Essential Question Why is measuring in feet different from measuring in inches?

HANDS ON
Lesson 8.6

COMMON CORE STANDARD CC.2.MD.2
Measure and estimate lengths in standard units.

Listen and Draw REAL WORLD

Draw or write to describe how you did each measurement.

First measurement

Second measurement

Math Talk
Describe how the length of a sheet of paper and the length of a paper clip are different.

MATHEMATICAL PRACTICES

FOR THE TEACHER • Have pairs of children stand apart and measure the distance between them with sheets of paper folded in half lengthwise. Then have them measure the same distance using large paper clips.

© Houghton Mifflin Harcourt Publishing Company

Model and Draw

12 inches is the same as 1 **foot**.
A 12-inch ruler is about 1 foot long.
You can measure lengths in inches and also in feet.

The real table is about 60 inches long.
The real table is also about 5 feet long.

Share and Show

Math Board

Measure to the nearest inch.
Then measure to the nearest foot.

	Find the real object.	Measure.
1.	desk 	______ inches ______ feet
2.	window 	______ inches ______ feet
3.	door 	______ inches ______ feet

© Houghton Mifflin Harcourt Publishing Company

Name ______________________________

On Your Own

Measure to the nearest inch.
Then measure to the nearest foot.

	Find the real object.	Measure.
4.	**chalkboard** 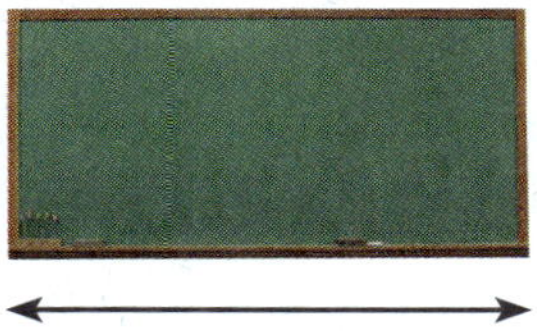	______ inches ______ feet
5.	**poster** 	______ inches ______ feet
6.	**teacher's desk** 	______ inches ______ feet
7.	**easel** 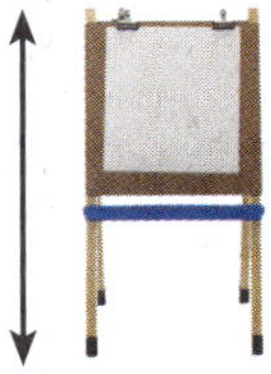	______ inches ______ feet
8.	**bulletin board** 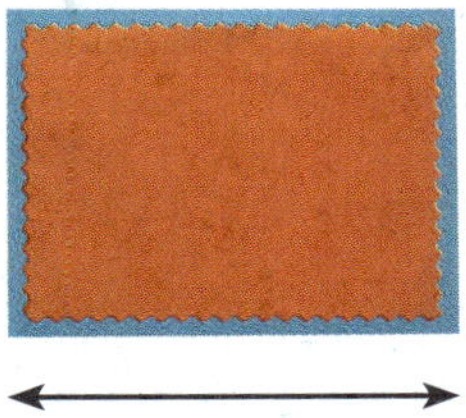	______ inches ______ feet

© Houghton Mifflin Harcourt Publishing Company

MATHEMATICAL PRACTICES Model • Reason • Make Sense

PROBLEM SOLVING REAL WORLD

Write Math

9. Use a ruler to measure the length of a real shelf in inches and in feet.

Measurements: ______ inches

______ feet

10. H.O.T. Look at your measurements for the shelf. Why is the number of inches different from the number of feet?

____

____

____

____

11. **Test Prep** Stephen is telling his brother about using a ruler. Which sentence is true?

- ○ 1 inch is the same length as 1 foot.
- ○ 1 foot is a greater length than 1 inch.
- ○ 1 inch is a greater length than 1 foot.
- ○ Inches are not used to measure length.

TAKE HOME ACTIVITY • Have your child measure the distance of a few footsteps in inches and then in feet.

FOR MORE PRACTICE: Standards Practice Book, pp. P193–P194

© Houghton Mifflin Harcourt Publishing Company

Name ______________________________

Estimate Lengths in Feet

Essential Question How do you estimate the lengths of objects in feet?

Lesson 8.7

COMMON CORE STANDARD CC.2.MD.3
Measure and estimate lengths in standard units.

Listen and Draw

Look for 3 classroom objects that are about the same length as an inch ruler. Draw and label the objects.

Math Talk Which objects have a greater length than the ruler? **Explain.**

MATHEMATICAL PRACTICES

FOR THE TEACHER • Provide a collection of objects for children to choose from. Set a 12-inch ruler on the table with the objects for children to use as a visual comparison.

© Houghton Mifflin Harcourt Publishing Company

Model and Draw

Estimate how many 12-inch rulers will be about the same length as this bulletin board.

Think about how many rulers will fit end-to-end.

______ rulers, or ______ feet

Share and Show

Math Board

Find each object. Estimate how many 12-inch rulers will be about the same length as the object.

1. bookshelf

Estimate: ______ rulers, or ______ feet

2. chair

Estimate: ______ rulers, or ______ feet

© Houghton Mifflin Harcourt Publishing Company

Name ________________________________

On Your Own

Find each object. Estimate how many 12-inch rulers will be about the same length as the object.

3. desktop

Estimate: ______ rulers, or ______ feet

4. wall map

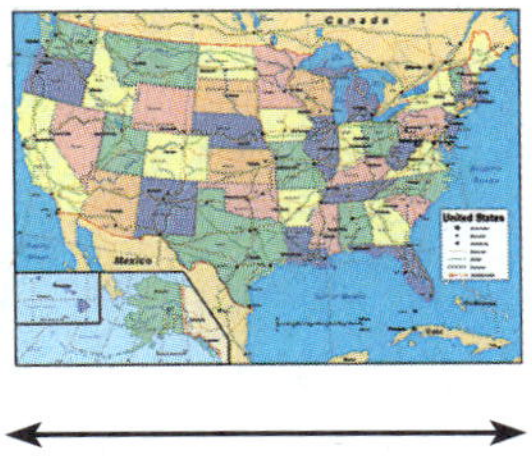

Estimate: ______ rulers, or ______ feet

5. window

Estimate: ______ rulers, or ______ feet

6. teacher's desk

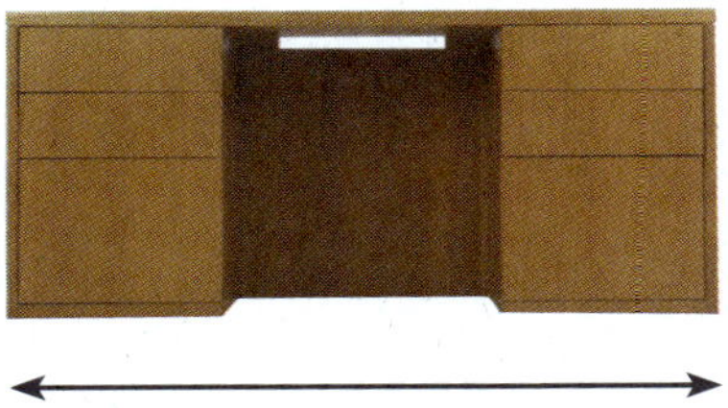

Estimate: ______ rulers, or ______ feet

© Houghton Mifflin Harcourt Publishing Company

PROBLEM SOLVING REAL WORLD

Write Math

Solve. Write or draw to explain.

7. Jorge and Nina place 12-inch rulers end-to-end along the entire length of a window. They each use 2 rulers. About how many feet long is the window?

about _______ feet

8. H.O.T. Estimate the distance from your desk to the door in feet. Then estimate the same distance in inches.

_______ feet

_______ inches

Explain how you made your estimates for the number of feet and for the number of inches.

____

____

____

____

9. **Test Prep** Which is the best estimate for the length of a real bat?

○ 1 foot
○ 3 feet
○ 6 feet
○ 10 feet

TAKE HOME ACTIVITY • With your child, estimate the lengths of some objects in feet.

© Houghton Mifflin Harcourt Publishing Company

FOR MORE PRACTICE:
Standards Practice Book, pp. P195–P196

Name ______________________________

Choose a Tool

Essential Question How do you choose a measuring tool to use when measuring lengths?

COMMON CORE STANDARD CC.2.MD.1
Measure and estimate lengths in standard units.

Listen and Draw REAL WORLD

Draw or write to describe how you measured the distances with the yarn.

Distance 1

Distance 2

FOR THE TEACHER • Have each small group use a 1-yard piece of yarn to measure a distance marked on the floor with masking tape. Have groups repeat the activity to measure another distance that is different from the first one.

Math Talk
Which distance was longer? **Explain** how you know.

MATHEMATICAL PRACTICES

© Houghton Mifflin Harcourt Publishing Company

Model and Draw

You can use different tools to measure lengths and distances.

inch ruler

An inch ruler can be used to measure shorter lengths.

yardstick

A **yardstick** shows 3 feet. It can be used to measure greater lengths and distances.

measuring tape

A **measuring tape** can be used to measure lengths and distances that are not flat or straight.

Share and Show

Math Board

Choose the best tool for measuring the real object. Then measure and record the length or distance.

inch ruler
yardstick
measuring tape

1. the length of a book

Tool: ______________________

Length: ______________________

2. the distance around a cup

Tool: ______________________

Distance: ______________________

© Houghton Mifflin Harcourt Publishing Company

Name ______________________________

On Your Own

inch ruler
yardstick
measuring tape

Choose the best tool for measuring the real object. Then measure and record the length or distance.

3. the length of a chalkboard

Tool: ______________________________

Length: ______________________________

4. the length of a marker

Tool: ______________________________

Length: ______________________________

5. the distance around a globe

Tool: ______________________________

Distance: ______________________________

6. the length of a classroom wall

Tool: ______________________________

Length: ______________________________

© Houghton Mifflin Harcourt Publishing Company

MATHEMATICAL PRACTICES **Model • Reason • Make Sense**

PROBLEM SOLVING REAL WORLD

Write Math

Choose the better tool for measuring.
Explain your choice.

7. Rachel wants to measure the length of a sidewalk. Should she use an inch ruler or a yardstick? Explain.

Rachel should use ____________________ because

____

____

____

8. H.O.T. What is an object that you would measure with a measuring tape? Explain why you would use this tool.

____

____

____

9. **Test Prep** Jim wants to measure some books to find a book that is 9 inches long. Which is the best tool for Jim to use?

- ○ large paper clip
- ○ cup
- ○ yarn
- ○ inch ruler

TAKE HOME ACTIVITY • Have your child name some objects that he or she would measure using a yardstick.

FOR MORE PRACTICE:
Standards Practice Book, pp. P197–P198

© Houghton Mifflin Harcourt Publishing Company

Name ______________________________

Display Measurement Data

Essential Question How can a line plot be used to show measurement data?

COMMON CORE STANDARD CC.2.MD.9
Represent and interpret data.

Listen and Draw REAL WORLD

Use an inch ruler. Measure and record each length.

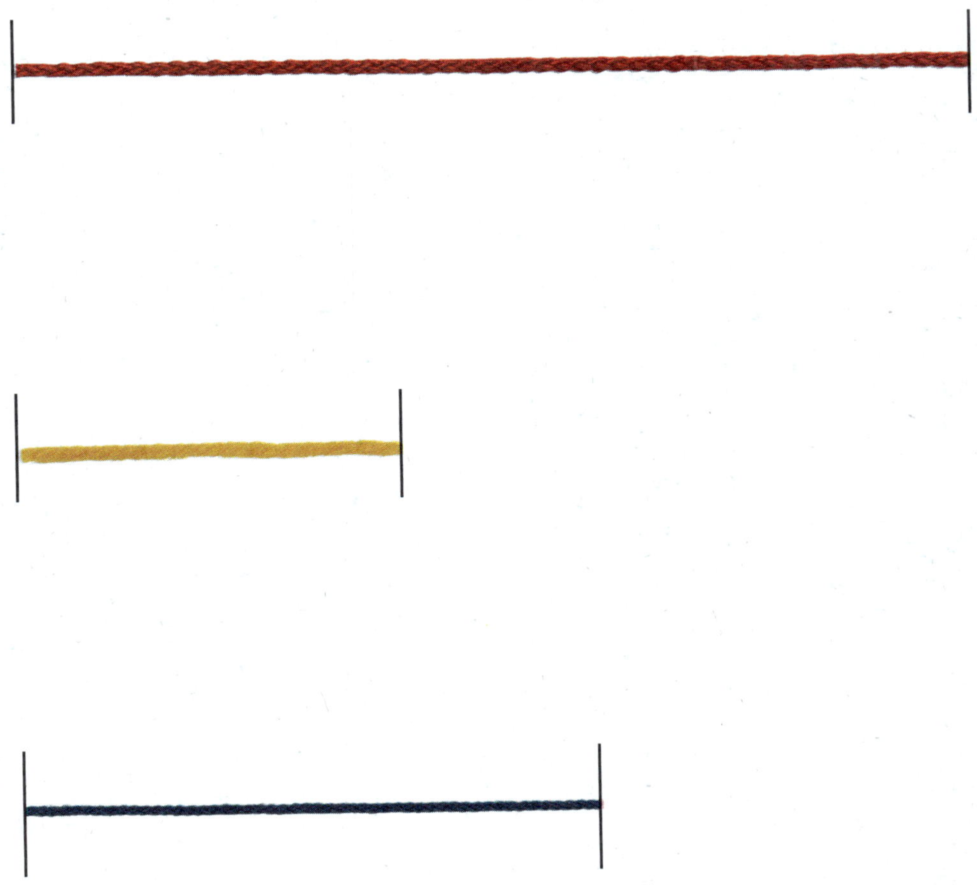

______ inches

______ inches

______ inches

Math Talk **Describe** how the lengths of the three strings are different.

MATHEMATICAL PRACTICES

HOME CONNECTION • Your child practiced measuring different lengths in inches in preparation for collecting measurement data in this lesson.

© Houghton Mifflin Harcourt Publishing Company

Model and Draw

A **line plot** is a way to show data.
On this line plot, each ***X*** stands for the length of one paintbrush in inches.

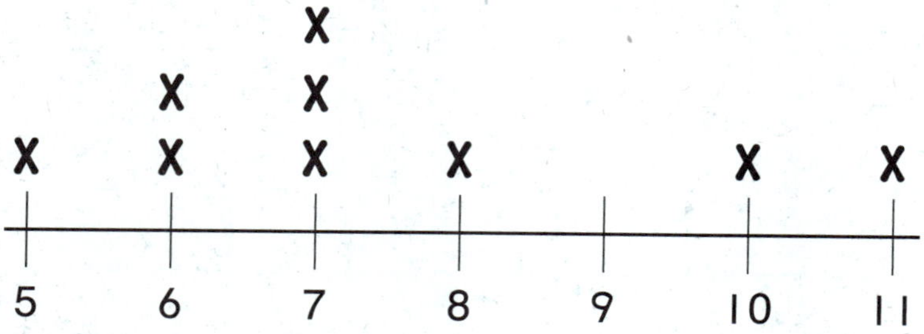

Lengths of Paintbrushes in Inches

How many paintbrushes are just 6 inches long? How many different paintbrushes are shown in this data?

Share and Show

Math Board

1. Use an inch ruler. Measure and record the lengths of 5 books in inches.

1st book: ______ inches	
2nd book: ______ inches	
3rd book: ______ inches	
4th book: ______ inches	
5th book: ______ inches	

2. Write a title for the line plot. Then write the numbers and draw the ***X***s.

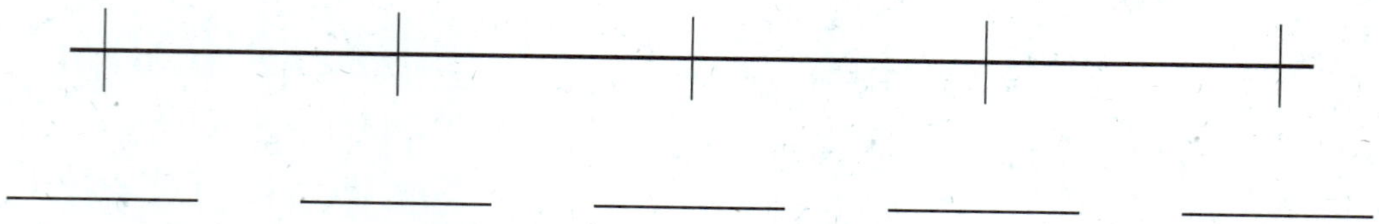

____

© Houghton Mifflin Harcourt Publishing Company

Name ______________________________

On Your Own

3. Use an inch ruler. Measure and record the lengths of 5 pencils in inches.

4. Write a title for the line plot. Then write the numbers and draw the ***X***s.

1st pencil: _______ inches
2nd pencil: _______ inches
3rd pencil: _______ inches
4th pencil: _______ inches
5th pencil: _______ inches

_______ _______ _______ _______ _______

____

5. Use an inch ruler. Measure and record the lengths of 4 crayons in inches. Then complete the line plot.

1st crayon: _______ inches
2nd crayon: _______ inches
3rd crayon: _______ inches
4th crayon: _______ inches

_______ _______ _______ _______

____

© Houghton Mifflin Harcourt Publishing Company

PROBLEM SOLVING REAL WORLD

Write Math

6. Use the data in the list to complete the line plot.

Lengths of Ribbons
6 inches
5 inches
8 inches
7 inches
6 inches

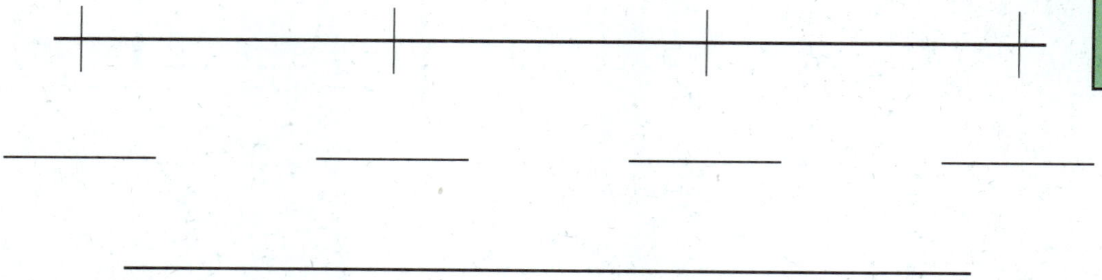

7. H.O.T. Suppose there were two more ribbons that were each 7 inches long. How would you change the line plot above to include this data?

____

____

8. ★ **Test Prep** Use the line plot.
How many leaves are 4 inches long?

- ○ 2
- ○ 3
- ○ 5
- ○ 8

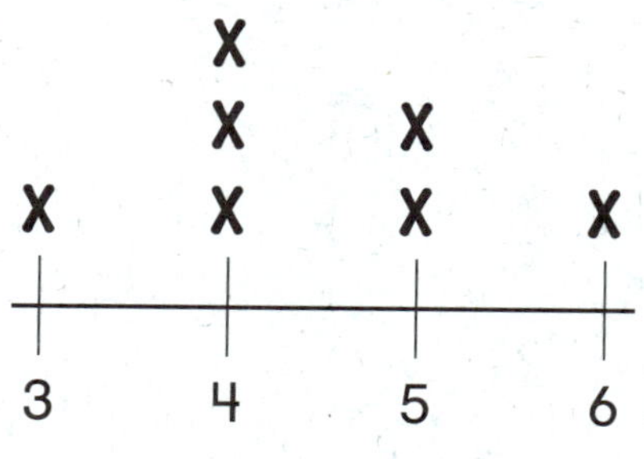

Lengths of Leaves in Inches

© Houghton Mifflin Harcourt Publishing Company

TAKE HOME ACTIVITY • Have your child describe the information found in the line plot in Exercise 8.

FOR MORE PRACTICE:
Standards Practice Book, pp. P199–P200

Name ______________________________

Chapter 8 Review/Test

Vocabulary

Use a word in the box to complete each sentence.

foot
yardstick
inch

1. A ________________ is the same length as 12 inches. (p. 410)

2. An ________________ is shorter than a foot. (p. 410)

Concepts and Skills

Use color tiles. Measure the length of the object in inches. (CC.2.MD.1)

3.

about _______ inches

Draw a diagram. Write a number sentence using a ▢ for the missing number. Solve. (CC.2.MD.5, CC.2.MD.6)

4. Paula has two ribbons. One ribbon is 11 inches long and the other ribbon is 9 inches long. How many inches of ribbon does Paula have?

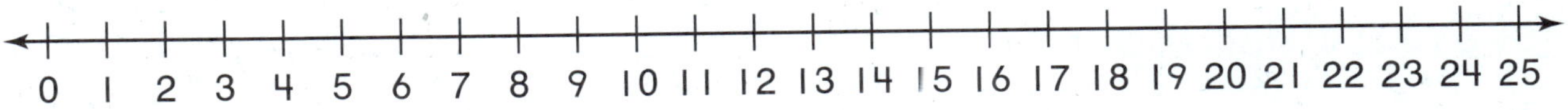

____

Paula has _______ inches of ribbon.

© Houghton Mifflin Harcourt Publishing Company

Fill in the bubble for the correct answer choice.

TEST PREP

5. Use an inch ruler. Measure the length of the pen to the nearest inch.

Which is the best choice for the length of the pen? (CC.2.MD.1)

- ○ 10 inches
- ○ 6 inches
- ○ 3 inches
- ○ 1 inch

6. The bead is one inch long. Which is the best estimate for the length of the string? (CC.2.MD.3)

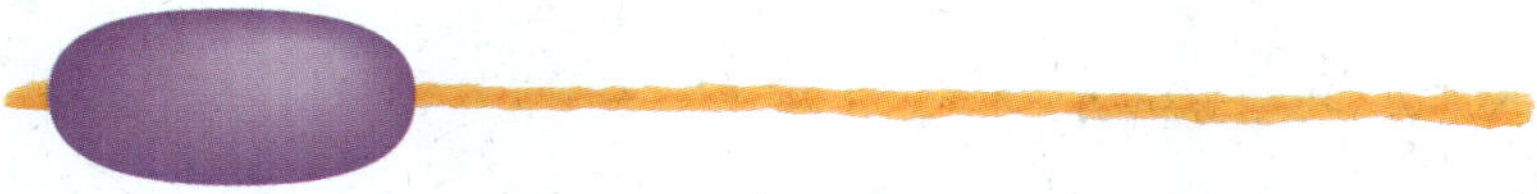

- ○ 4 inches
- ○ 7 inches
- ○ 9 inches
- ○ 10 inches

7. Which is the best estimate for the length of a real bulletin board? (CC.2.MD.3)

- ○ 300 feet
- ○ 30 feet
- ○ 3 feet
- ○ 1 foot

© Houghton Mifflin Harcourt Publishing Company

Name ____________________________________

TEST PREP

Fill in the bubble for the correct answer choice.

8. Use an inch ruler to measure. What is the length of the ribbon to the nearest inch? (CC.2.MD.1)

- ○ 2 inches
- ○ 5 inches
- ○ 8 inches
- ○ 12 inches

9. The bead is one inch long. Which is the best estimate for the length of the string? (CC.2.MD.3)

- ○ 9 inches
- ○ 6 inches
- ○ 3 inches
- ○ 1 inch

10. Use the line plot. How many books are 8 inches long? (CC.2.MD.9)

- ○ 3
- ○ 4
- ○ 6
- ○ 10

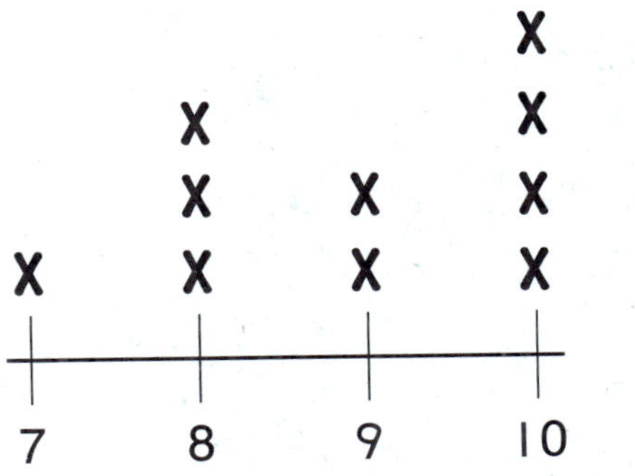

Lengths of Books in Inches

© Houghton Mifflin Harcourt Publishing Company

Constructed Response

11. Janet wants to measure the length of a wall in inches and in feet. Describe how these two measurements will be different. (CC.2.MD.2)

____

____

____

Performance Task (CC.2.MD.5, CC.2.MD.1)

12. Dustin will use the red string and the blue string for a project. How many inches of string will he use?

blue string: 15 inches
red string: 8 inches
green string: 6 inches

Draw or write to show how you found your answer.

____

Suppose Dustin has some yellow string for his project. Should he use an inch ruler, a measuring tape, or a yardstick to measure the length of the string? Explain your choice.

____

____

____

____

© Houghton Mifflin Harcourt Publishing Company

Chapter 9

Length in Metric Units

Curious About Math with Curious George

A wind farm is a group of wind turbines used to make electricity. One way to measure the distance between two wind turbines is by counting footsteps. What is another way?

© Houghton Mifflin Harcourt Publishing Company
Curious George by Margret and H.A. Rey. Copyright © 2010 by Houghton Mifflin Harcourt Publishing Company. All rights reserved. The character Curious George®, including without limitation the character's name and the character's likenesses, are registered trademarks of Houghton Mifflin Harcourt Publishing Company.

Name ______________________________

Show What You Know

Compare Lengths

1. Order the strings from shortest to longest.
Write 1, 2, 3.

____

____

____

Use Nonstandard Units to Measure Length

Use real objects and ■ to measure.

2.  about ______ ■

3.  about ______ ■

Measure Length Twice: Nonstandard Units

Use ■ first. Then use paper clip.
Measure the length of the ribbon.

4. about ______ ■

5. about ______ paper clip

Family note: This page checks your child's understanding of important skills needed for success in Chapter 9.

GO Online Assessment Options
Soar to Success Math

© Houghton Mifflin Harcourt Publishing Company

Name ____________________

Review Words
measure
length
estimate

Vocabulary Builder

Visualize It
Fill in the graphic organizer. Think of an object and write about how you can **measure** the **length** of that object.

length

____
____

____
____

Understand Vocabulary
Use the color tiles to **estimate** the length of each straw.

1. 

about _______ tiles

2. 

about _______ tiles

© Houghton Mifflin Harcourt Publishing Company

GO Online • eStudent Edition • Multimedia eGlossary

Game

Estimating Length

Materials

- 12 (red counters)
- 12 (yellow counters)
- 15 (green cubes)
- 15 (blue cubes)

Play with a partner.

1. Take turns choosing a picture. Find the real object.
2. Each player estimates the length of the object in cubes and then makes a cube train for his or her estimate.
3. Compare the cube trains to the length of the object. The player with the closer estimate puts a counter on the picture. If there is a tie, both players put a counter on the picture.
4. Repeat until all pictures are covered. The player with more counters on the board wins.

© Houghton Mifflin Harcourt Publishing Company

Name ________________________________

Measure with a Centimeter Model

HANDS ON
Lesson 9.1

Essential Question How do you use a centimeter model to measure the lengths of objects?

COMMON CORE STANDARD CC.2.MD.1
Measure and estimate lengths in standard units.

Listen and Draw REAL WORLD

Use to measure the length.

_____ unit cubes

_____ unit cubes

_____ unit cubes

Math Talk
Describe how to use unit cubes to measure an object's length.

MATHEMATICAL PRACTICES

HOME CONNECTION • Your child used unit cubes as an introduction to measurement of length before using metric measurement tools.

© Houghton Mifflin Harcourt Publishing Company

Model and Draw

A unit cube is about 1 **centimeter** long.

About how many centimeters long is this string?

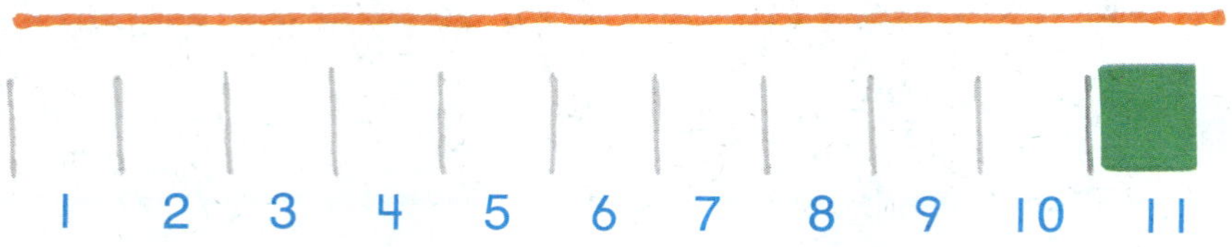

You can make a mark for each centimeter to keep track and to count.

The string is about __11__ centimeters long.

Share and Show

Math Board

Use a unit cube. Measure the length in centimeters.

1.

about ______ centimeters

2.

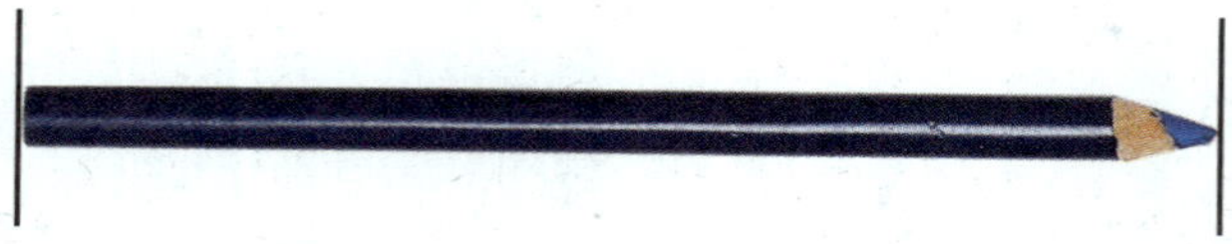

about ______ centimeters

3.

about ______ centimeters

© Houghton Mifflin Harcourt Publishing Company

Name ________________________________

On Your Own

Use a unit cube. Measure the length in centimeters.

4.

about ______ centimeters

5.

about ______ centimeters

6.

about ______ centimeters

7.

about ______ centimeters

8.

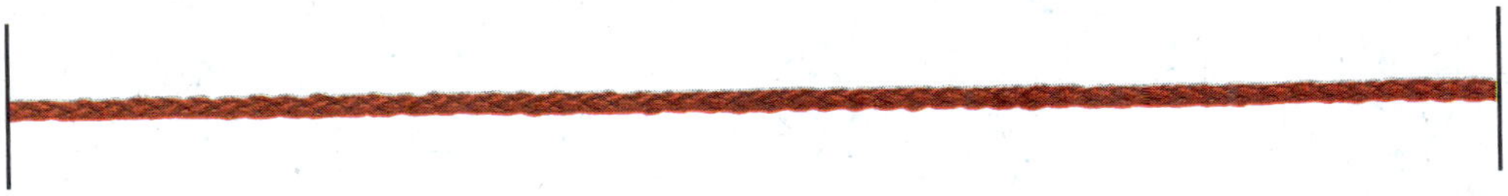

about ______ centimeters

© Houghton Mifflin Harcourt Publishing Company

PROBLEM SOLVING REAL WORLD

Write Math

Solve. Write or draw to explain.

9. H.O.T. Mrs. Duncan measured the lengths of a crayon and a pencil. The pencil is twice as long as the crayon. The sum of their lengths is 24 centimeters. What are their lengths?

crayon: ____________________

pencil: ____________________

10. **Test Prep** Marita used unit cubes to measure the length of a straw.

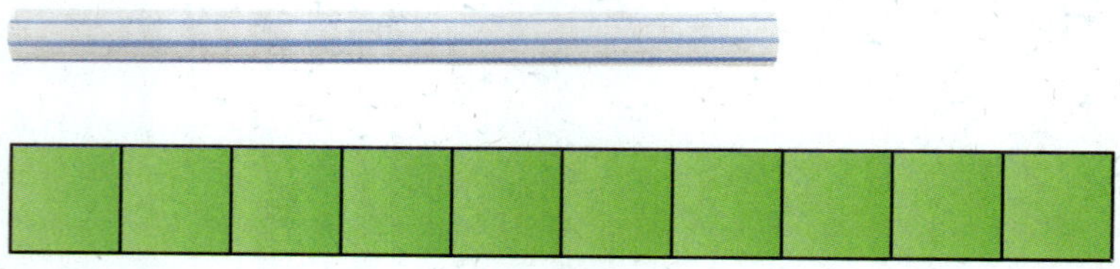

Which is the best choice for the length of the straw?

- ○ 1 centimeter
- ○ 3 centimeters
- ○ 7 centimeters
- ○ 10 centimeters

TAKE HOME ACTIVITY • Have your child compare the lengths of other objects to those in this lesson.

FOR MORE PRACTICE: Standards Practice Book, pp. P205–P206

© Houghton Mifflin Harcourt Publishing Company

Name ____________________________

Estimate Lengths in Centimeters

Essential Question How do you use known lengths to estimate unknown lengths?

COMMON CORE STANDARD CC.2.MD.3
Measure and estimate lengths in standard units.

Listen and Draw REAL WORLD

Find three classroom objects that are shorter than your 10-centimeter strip. Draw the objects. Write estimates for their lengths.

about _____ centimeters

about _____ centimeters

about _____ centimeters

Math Talk Which object has a length closest to 10 centimeters? **Explain.**

MATHEMATICAL PRACTICES

HOME CONNECTION • Your child used a 10-centimeter strip of paper to practice estimating the lengths of some classroom objects.

© Houghton Mifflin Harcourt Publishing Company

Model and Draw

This pencil is about 10 centimeters long.
Which is the most reasonable estimate for the length of the ribbon?

7 centimeters

13 centimeters

20 centimeters

The ribbon is longer than the pencil. 7 centimeters is not reasonable.

The ribbon is not twice as long as the pencil. 20 centimeters is not reasonable.

The ribbon is a little longer than the pencil.
So, 13 centimeters is the most reasonable estimate.

Share and Show

Math Board

1. The yarn is about 5 centimeters long. Circle the best estimate for the length of the crayon.

10 centimeters

15 centimeters

20 centimeters

2. The string is about 12 centimeters long.
Circle the best estimate for the length of the straw.

3 centimeters

7 centimeters

11 centimeters

© Houghton Mifflin Harcourt Publishing Company

Name ______________________________

On Your Own

3. The rope is about 8 centimeters long. Circle the best estimate for the length of the paper clip.

2 centimeters

4 centimeters

8 centimeters

4. The pencil is about 11 centimeters long. Circle the best estimate for the length of the chain.

6 centimeters

10 centimeters

13 centimeters

5. The hair clip is about 7 centimeters long. Circle the best estimate for the length of the yarn.

10 centimeters

17 centimeters

22 centimeters

6. The ribbon is about 13 centimeters long. Circle the best estimate for the length of the string.

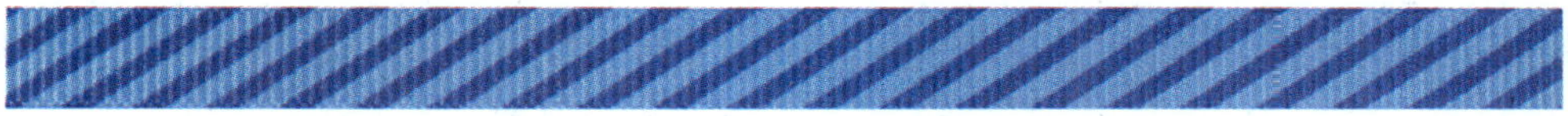

5 centimeters

11 centimeters

17 centimeters

© Houghton Mifflin Harcourt Publishing Company

PROBLEM SOLVING REAL WORLD

Write Math

Circle the best estimate.

7. About how long is a new crayon?

5 centimeters

10 centimeters

20 centimeters

8. About how long is a new pencil?

20 centimeters

40 centimeters

50 centimeters

9. H.O.T. Mr. Lott has 250 more centimeters of tape than Mrs. Simon. Mr. Lott has 775 centimeters of tape. How many centimeters of tape does Mrs. Simon have?

_______ centimeters

10. Test Prep The length of the feather is about 7 centimeters.

Which is the best estimate for the length of the yarn?

○ 5 centimeters
○ 7 centimeters
○ 14 centimeters
○ 70 centimeters

TAKE HOME ACTIVITY • Give your child an object that is about 5 centimeters long. Have him or her use it to estimate the lengths of some other objects.

FOR MORE PRACTICE: Standards Practice Book, pp. P207–P208

© Houghton Mifflin Harcourt Publishing Company

Name ________________________________

Measure with a Centimeter Ruler

Essential Question How do you use a centimeter ruler to measure lengths?

COMMON CORE STANDARD CC.2.MD.1
Measure and estimate lengths in standard units.

Listen and Draw REAL WORLD

Find three small objects in the classroom.
Use unit cubes to measure their lengths.
Draw the objects and write their lengths.

______ centimeters

______ centimeters

______ centimeters

Math Talk

Describe how the three lengths compare. Which object is shortest?

MATHEMATICAL PRACTICES

HOME CONNECTION • Your child used unit cubes to measure the lengths of some classroom objects as an introduction to measuring lengths in centimeters.

© Houghton Mifflin Harcourt Publishing Company

Model and Draw

What is the length of the crayon to the nearest centimeter?

Remember: Line up the left edge of the object with the zero mark on the ruler.

9 centimeters

Share and Show

Measure the length to the nearest centimeter.

1.

_____ centimeters

2.

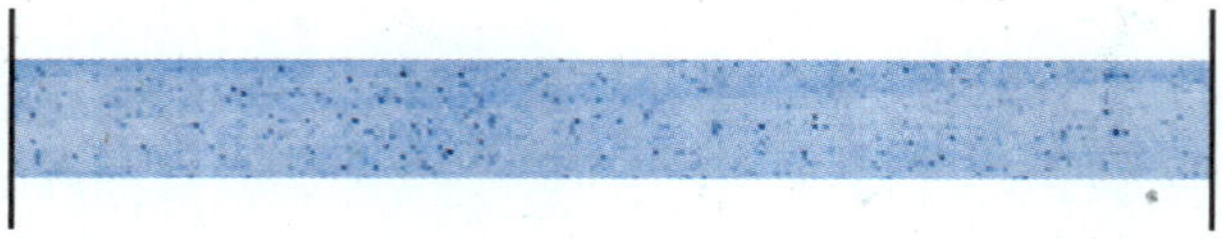

_____ centimeters

3.

_____ centimeters

© Houghton Mifflin Harcourt Publishing Company

Name ______________________________

On Your Own

Measure the length to the nearest centimeter.

4.

_____ centimeters

5.

_____ centimeters

6.

_____ centimeters

7.

_____ centimeters

8.

_____ centimeters

© Houghton Mifflin Harcourt Publishing Company

PROBLEM SOLVING REAL WORLD

Write Math

9. H.O.T. The crayon was on the table next to the centimeter ruler. The left edge of the crayon was not lined up with the zero mark on the ruler.

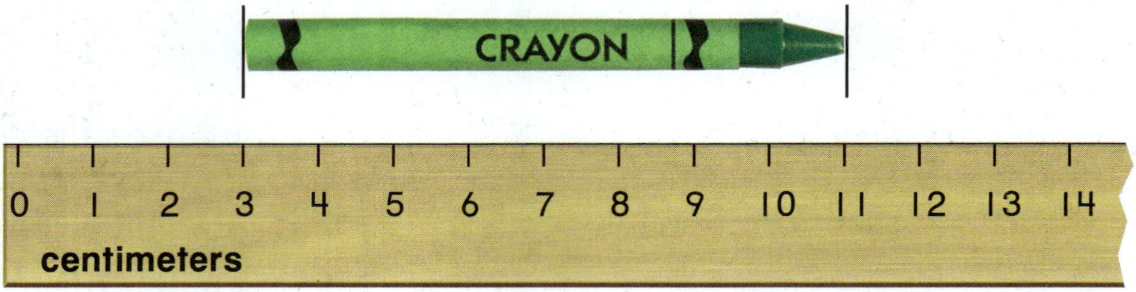

What is the length of the crayon?

about ____________________

Explain how you found your answer.

____

____

____

10. ★ **Test Prep** Use a centimeter ruler. Which is the best choice for the length of this string?

- ○ 1 centimeter
- ○ 4 centimeters
- ○ 7 centimeters
- ○ 10 centimeters

TAKE HOME ACTIVITY • Have your child measure the lengths of some objects using a centimeter ruler.

© Houghton Mifflin Harcourt Publishing Company

FOR MORE PRACTICE:
Standards Practice Book, pp. P209–P210

Name ______________________________

Problem Solving • Add and Subtract Lengths

Essential Question How can drawing a diagram help when solving problems about lengths?

COMMON CORE STANDARDS CC.2.MD.6, CC.2.MD.5
Relate addition and subtraction to length.

Nate had 23 centimeters of string.
He gave 9 centimeters of string to Myra.
How much string does Nate have now?

Unlock the Problem REAL WORLD

What do I need to find?

how much string
Nate has now

What information do I need to use?

Nate had ______ centimeters of string.

He gave ______ centimeters of string to Myra.

Show how to solve the problem.

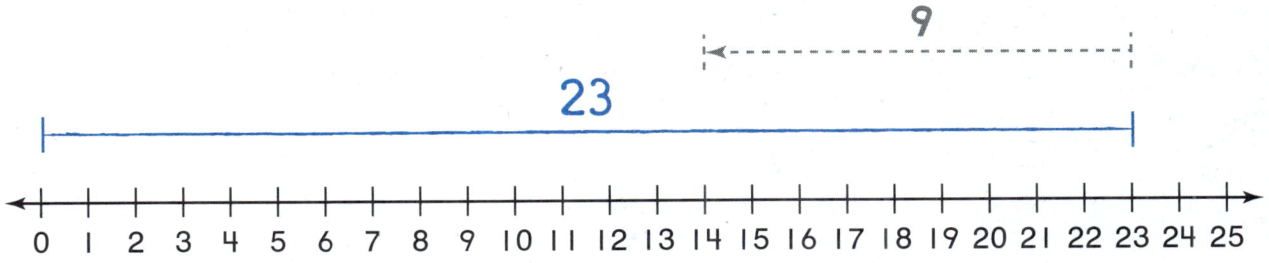

____

Nate has ______ centimeters of string now.

HOME CONNECTION • Your child drew a diagram to represent a problem about lengths. The diagram can be used to choose the operation for solving the problem.

© Houghton Mifflin Harcourt Publishing Company

Try Another Problem

Draw a diagram. Write a number sentence using a ■ for the missing number. Then solve.

- What do I need to find?
- What information do I need to use?

1. Ellie has a ribbon that is 12 centimeters long. Gwen has a ribbon that is 9 centimeters long. How many centimeters of ribbon do they have?

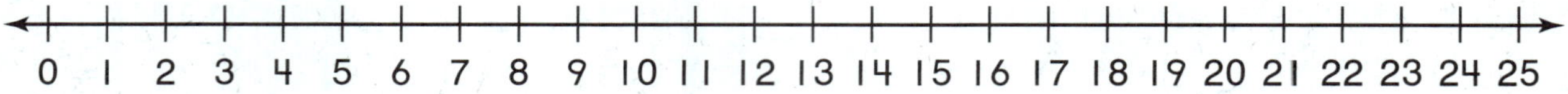

____

They have ______ centimeters of ribbon.

2. A strip of paper is 24 centimeters long. Justin tears 8 centimeters off of the strip. How long is the strip of paper now?

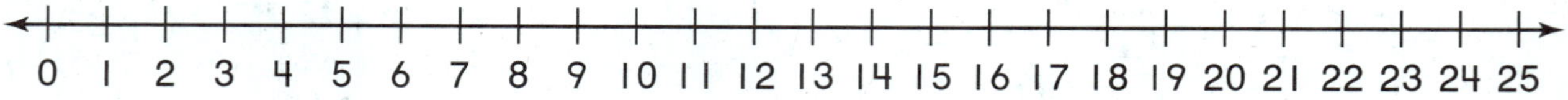

____

Now the strip of paper is ______ centimeters long.

Math Talk

Explain how your diagram shows what happened in the first problem.

MATHEMATICAL PRACTICES

© Houghton Mifflin Harcourt Publishing Company

Name ______________________________

Share and Show

Draw a diagram. Write a number sentence using a ■ for the missing number. Then solve.

✓3. A chain of paper clips is 18 centimeters long. Sondra adds 6 centimeters of paper clips to the chain. How long is the chain now?

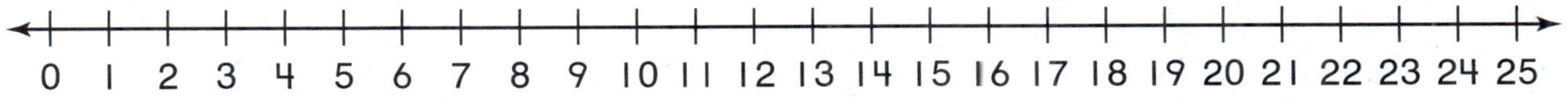

____

The chain is ______ centimeters long now.

4. H.O.T. A chalk mark was 22 centimeters long. Then Greg erased part of the mark and it was 5 centimeters long. How many centimeters of the mark did Greg erase?

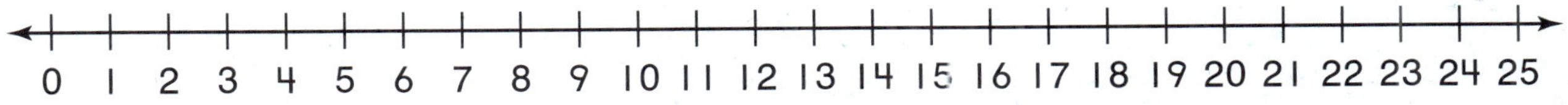

____

Greg erased ______ centimeters of the mark.

© Houghton Mifflin Harcourt Publishing Company

TAKE HOME ACTIVITY • Have your child explain how he or she used a diagram to solve Exercise 3.

FOR MORE PRACTICE:
Standards Practice Book, pp. P211–P212

Name ______________________________

Mid-Chapter Checkpoint

Concepts and Skills

Use a unit cube. Measure the length in centimeters. (CC.2.MD.1)

1.

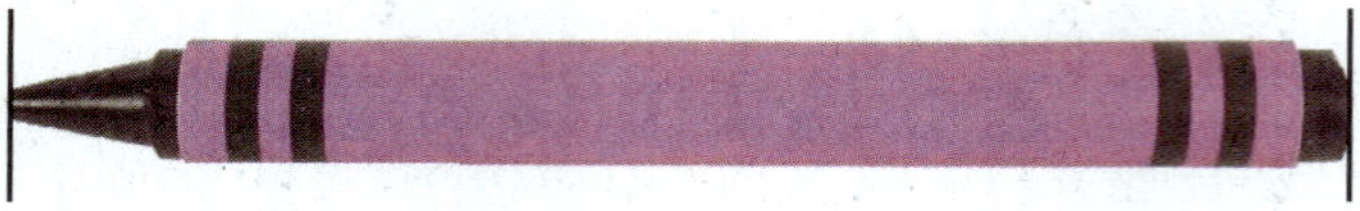

about _____ centimeters

2.

about _____ centimeters

3. The pencil is about 11 centimeters long. Circle the best estimate for the length of the string. (CC.2.MD.3)

7 centimeters

10 centimeters

16 centimeters

4. **Test Prep** Use a centimeter ruler. What is the length of this ribbon to the nearest centimeter? (CC.2.MD.1)

- ○ 18 centimeters
- ○ 13 centimeters
- ○ 9 centimeters
- ○ 5 centimeters

© Houghton Mifflin Harcourt Publishing Company

Name ____________________

Centimeters and Meters

Essential Question How is measuring in meters different from measuring in centimeters?

COMMON CORE STANDARD CC.2.MD.2
Measure and estimate lengths in standard units.

Listen and Draw REAL WORLD

Draw or write to describe how you did each measurement.

1st measurement

2nd measurement

FOR THE TEACHER • Have each small group use a 1-meter piece of yarn to measure a distance marked on the floor with masking tape. Then have them measure the same distance using a sheet of paper folded in half lengthwise.

Math Talk

Describe how the lengths of the yarn and the sheet of paper are different.

MATHEMATICAL PRACTICES

© Houghton Mifflin Harcourt Publishing Company

Model and Draw

I **meter** is the same as 100 centimeters.

The real door is about 200 centimeters tall.
The real door is also about 2 meters tall.

Share and Show

Math Board

Measure to the nearest centimeter.
Then measure to the nearest meter.

	Find the real object.	Measure.
1.	chair 	______ centimeters ______ meters
2.	teacher's desk 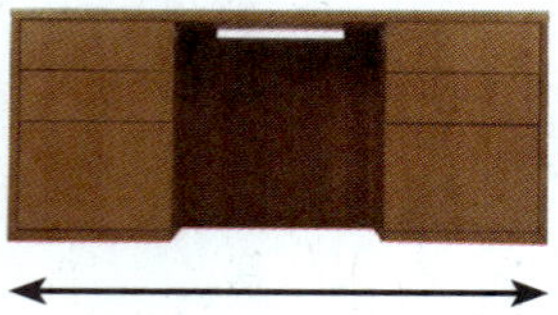	______ centimeters ______ meters
3.	wall 	______ centimeters ______ meters

© Houghton Mifflin Harcourt Publishing Company

Name ______________________________

On Your Own

Measure to the nearest centimeter.
Then measure to the nearest meter.

	Find the real object.	Measure.
4.	chalkboard 	_______ centimeters _______ meters
5.	bookshelf 	_______ centimeters _______ meters
6.	table 	_______ centimeters _______ meters
7.	bulletin board 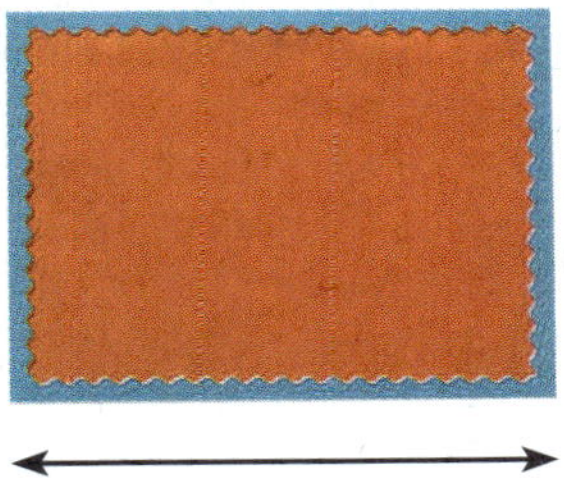	_______ centimeters _______ meters

© Houghton Mifflin Harcourt Publishing Company

PROBLEM SOLVING REAL WORLD

Write Math

8. H.O.T. Jason and his dad are walking next to a barn. They want to measure the length of the barn. Would the length be a greater number of centimeters or a greater number of meters?

____

Explain your answer.

____

____

____

____

9. **Test Prep** Use a centimeter ruler to measure.

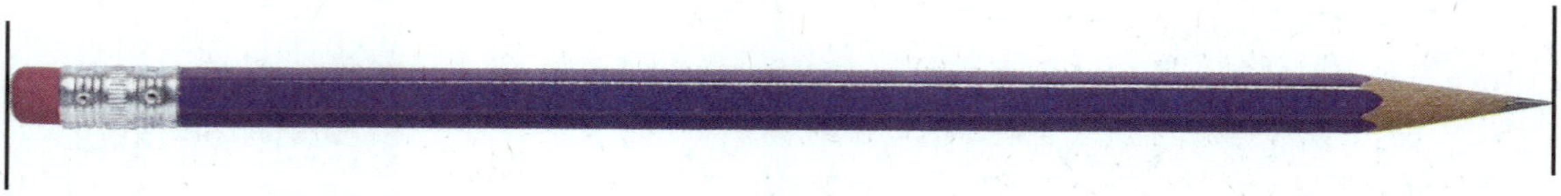

Which is the best choice for the length of the pencil?

- ○ 30 centimeters
- ○ 25 centimeters
- ○ 20 centimeters
- ○ 15 centimeters

TAKE HOME ACTIVITY • Have your child describe how centimeters and meters are different.

FOR MORE PRACTICE: Standards Practice Book, pp. P213–P214

© Houghton Mifflin Harcourt Publishing Company

Name ______________________________

Estimate Lengths in Meters

Essential Question How do you estimate the lengths of objects in meters?

COMMON CORE STANDARD CC.2.MD.3

Measure and estimate lengths in standard units.

Listen and Draw REAL WORLD

Find a writing tool that is about 10 centimeters long. Draw and label it.

Is there a classroom object that is about 50 centimeters long? Draw and label it.

Math Talk **Describe** how the lengths of the two real objects compare.

MATHEMATICAL PRACTICES

FOR THE TEACHER • Provide a collection of objects for children to choose from. Above the table of displayed objects, draw and label a 10-centimeter line segment and a 50-centimeter line segment.

© Houghton Mifflin Harcourt Publishing Company

Model and Draw

Estimate. About how many meter sticks will match the width of a door?

A 1-meter measuring stick is about 100 centimeters long.

about ______ meters

Share and Show

Find the real object.
Estimate its length in meters.

1. bookshelf

about ______ meters

2. bulletin board

about ______ meters

© Houghton Mifflin Harcourt Publishing Company

Name ______________________________

On Your Own

Find the real object.
Estimate its length in meters.

3. teacher's desk

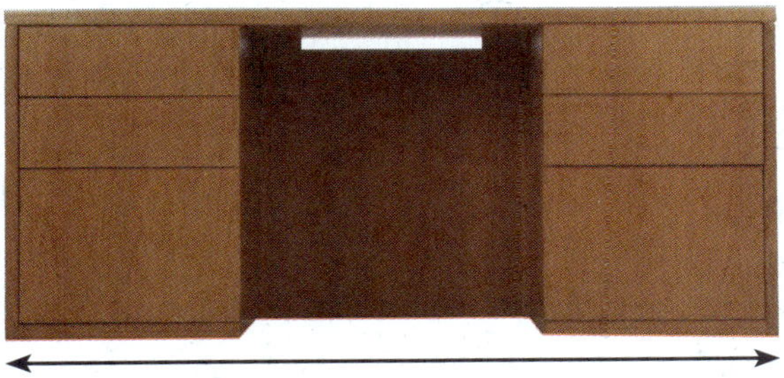

about ______ meters

4. wall

about ______ meters

5. window

about ______ meters

6. chalkboard

about ______ meters

© Houghton Mifflin Harcourt Publishing Company

PROBLEM SOLVING REAL WORLD

Write Math

Solve. Write or draw to explain.

7. Tim and Erin each placed 3 meter sticks end-to-end along the length of the bicycle rack. About how long is the bicycle rack?

about _______ meters long

8. H.O.T. In meters, estimate the distance from your teacher's desk to the door of your classroom.

about _______ meters

Explain how you made your estimate.

____

____

____

____

9. Test Prep Which is the best estimate for the length of an adult's bicycle?

- ○ 2 meters
- ○ 5 meters
- ○ 8 meters
- ○ 20 meters

TAKE HOME ACTIVITY • With your child, estimate the lengths of some objects in meters.

© Houghton Mifflin Harcourt Publishing Company

FOR MORE PRACTICE: Standards Practice Book, pp. P215–P216

Name ____________________

Measure and Compare Lengths

Essential Question How do you find the difference between the lengths of two objects?

HANDS ON
Lesson 9.7

COMMON CORE STANDARD CC.2.MD.4
Measure and estimate lengths in standard units.

Listen and Draw REAL WORLD

Measure and record each length.

_______ centimeters

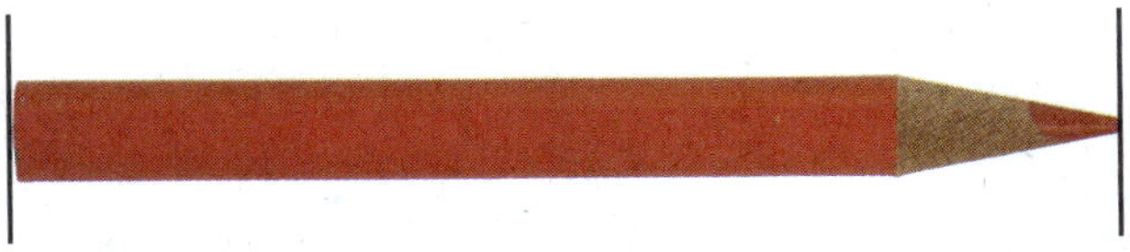

_______ centimeters

Math Talk Name a classroom object that is longer than the paintbrush. **Explain** how you know.

MATHEMATICAL PRACTICES

TAKE HOME ACTIVITY • Your child measured these lengths as an introduction to measuring and then comparing lengths.

© Houghton Mifflin Harcourt Publishing Company

Model and Draw

How much longer is the pencil than the crayon?

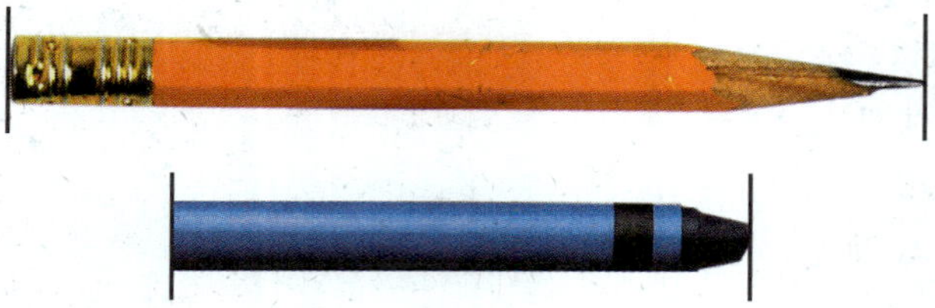

8 centimeters

5 centimeters

8 centimeters − 5 centimeters = ______ centimeters

The pencil is ______ centimeters longer than the crayon.

Share and Show

Math Board

Measure the length of each object. Write a number sentence to find the difference between the lengths.

1.

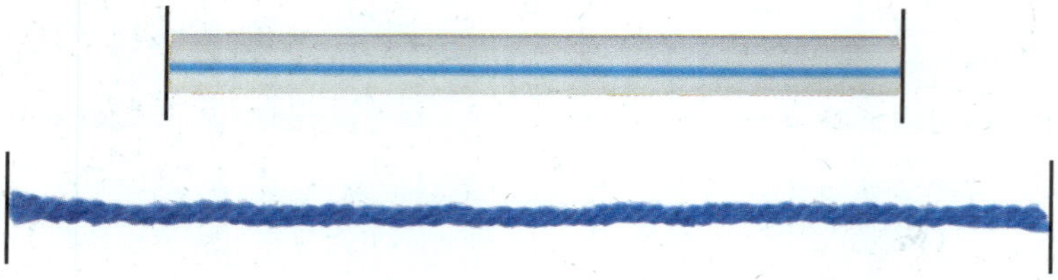

______ centimeters

______ centimeters

______ centimeters − ______ centimeters = ______ centimeters

The string is ______ centimeters longer than the straw.

2.

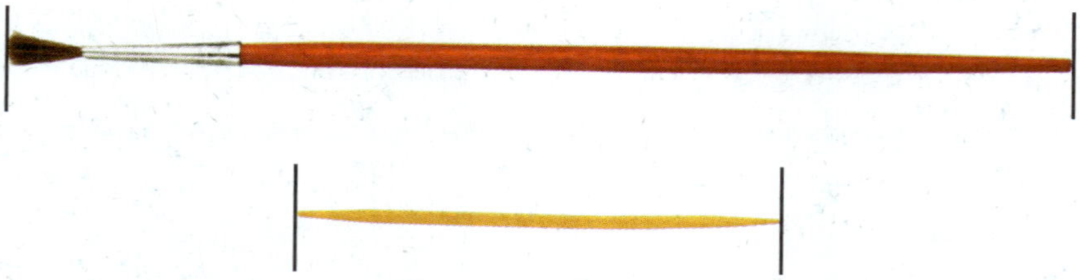

______ centimeters

______ centimeters

______ centimeters − ______ centimeters = ______ centimeters

The paintbrush is ______ centimeters longer than the toothpick.

© Houghton Mifflin Harcourt Publishing Company

Name ______________________________

On Your Own

Measure the length of each object. Write a number sentence to find the difference between the lengths.

3. 

______ centimeters

______ centimeters

______ centimeters − ______ centimeters = ______ centimeters

The yarn is ______ centimeters longer than the crayon.

4. 

______ centimeters

______ centimeters

______ centimeters − ______ centimeters = ______ centimeters

The string is ______ centimeters longer than the paper clip.

5. H.O.T. Use a centimeter ruler. Measure the length of your desk and the length of a book.

desk: ______ centimeters

book: ______ centimeters

Which is shorter? ______________________

How much shorter is it? ______________________

© Houghton Mifflin Harcourt Publishing Company

PROBLEM SOLVING REAL WORLD

Write Math

Solve. Write or draw to explain.

6. Mark has a paper strip chain that is 23 centimeters long. He unhooks 15 centimeters from the chain. What is the length of the paper strip chain now?

_______ centimeters

7. H.O.T. The yellow ribbon is 15 centimeters longer than the green ribbon. The green ribbon is 29 centimeters long. What is the length of the yellow ribbon?

_______ centimeters

8. **Test Prep** Measure the length of each object.

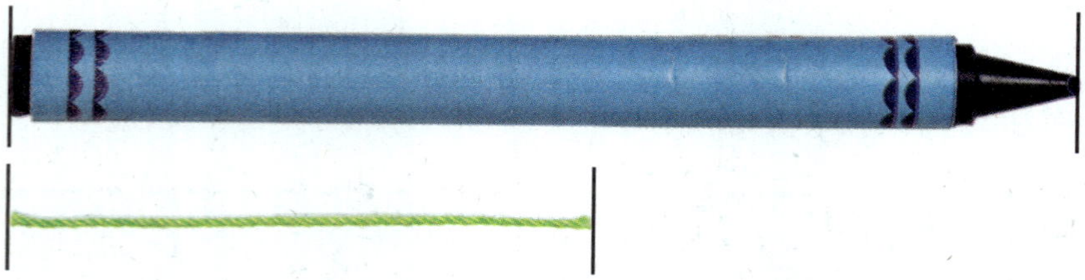

How much longer is the crayon than the string?

○ 17 centimeters longer
○ 11 centimeters longer
○ 8 centimeters longer
○ 5 centimeters longer

TAKE HOME ACTIVITY • Have your child tell you how he or she solved one of the problems on this page.

FOR MORE PRACTICE: Standards Practice Book, pp. P217–P218

© Houghton Mifflin Harcourt Publishing Company

Name ______________________________

Chapter 9 Review/Test

Vocabulary

Use the words in the box to complete the sentence.

centimeter
meter

1. One ______________ is longer than

one ______________. (p. 450)

Concepts and Skills

Draw a diagram. Write a number sentence using a ■ for the missing number. Then solve. (CC.2.MD.6, CC.2.MD.5)

2. Mrs. Cook has a poster board that is 21 centimeters long. She cuts off 8 centimeters from the poster board. How long is the poster board now?

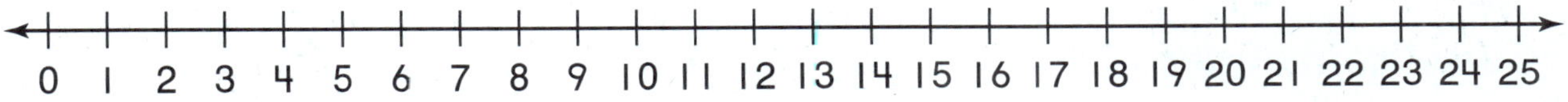

____

The poster board is ______ centimeters long now.

Measure the real object to the nearest centimeter. Then measure to the nearest meter. (CC.2.MD.2)

3. bulletin board

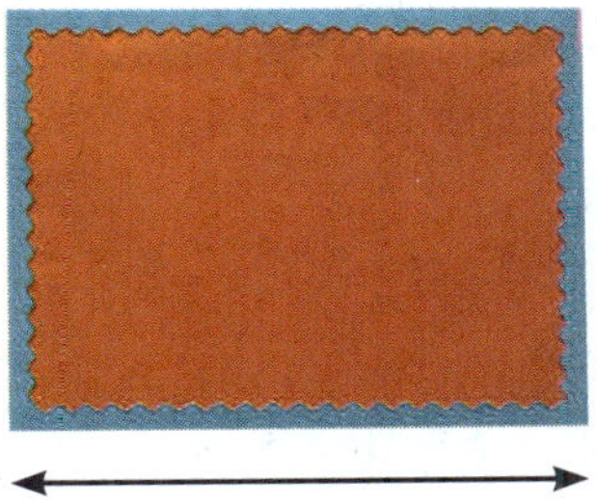

______ centimeters

______ meters

© Houghton Mifflin Harcourt Publishing Company

Fill in the bubble for the correct answer choice.

TEST PREP

4. Which is the best estimate for the length of a real desk? (CC.2.MD.3)

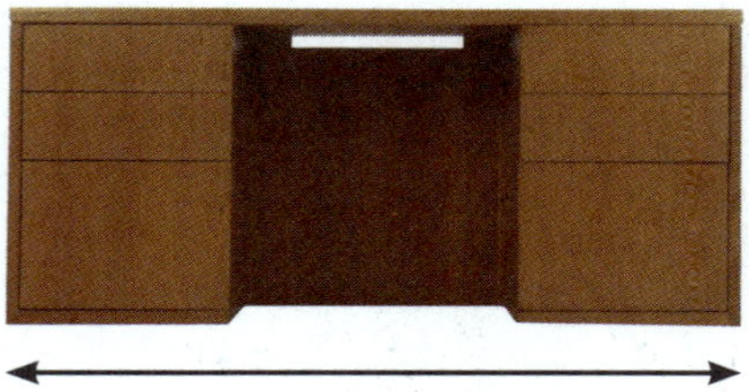

- ○ 2 meters
- ○ 10 meters
- ○ 50 meters
- ○ 100 meters

5. Use a centimeter ruler.

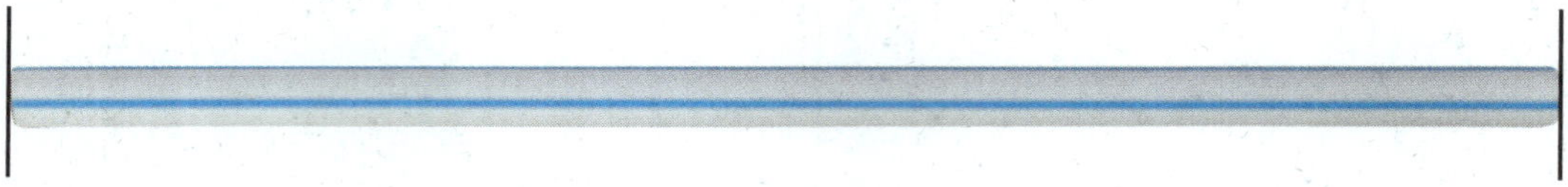

How much longer is the straw than the yarn? (CC.2.MD.4)

- ○ 20 centimeters longer
- ○ 12 centimeters longer
- ○ 8 centimeters longer
- ○ 3 centimeters longer

6. Use a centimeter ruler. Which is the best choice for the length of the toothpick? (CC.2.MD.1)

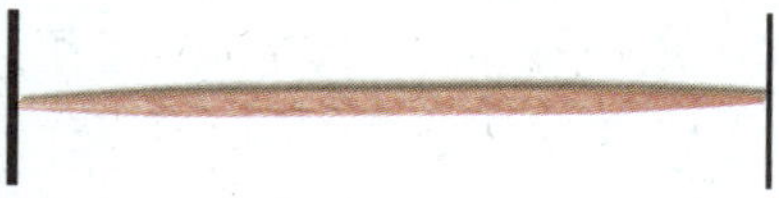

- ○ 10 centimeters
- ○ 9 centimeters
- ○ 7 centimeters
- ○ 5 centimeters

© Houghton Mifflin Harcourt Publishing Company

Name ____________________

Fill in the bubble for the correct answer choice.

TEST PREP

7. Use a centimeter ruler to measure the length of the paintbrush to the nearest centimeter.

Which is the best choice for the length of the paintbrush? (CC.2.MD.1)

- ○ 13 centimeters
- ○ 18 centimeters
- ○ 21 centimeters
- ○ 23 centimeters

8. The paper clip is about 4 centimeters long. Which is the best estimate for the length of the string? (CC.2.MD.3)

- ○ 20 centimeters
- ○ 9 centimeters
- ○ 4 centimeters
- ○ 3 centimeters

© Houghton Mifflin Harcourt Publishing Company

Constructed Response

9. The craft stick is about 12 centimeters long.
Circle the best estimate for the length of the string.

6 centimeters

9 centimeters

11 centimeters

Explain how you chose your estimate. (CC.2.MD.3)

____

____

____

Performance Task (CC.2.MD.5, CC.2.MD.2)

10. Mrs. Dillon has 2 posters. The first poster is 75 centimeters long. The second poster is 58 centimeters long. How much longer is the first poster than the second poster?
Draw or write to show how you solved the problem.

_____ centimeters longer

If Mrs. Dillon measures the length of her bulletin board in centimeters and in meters, how will the number of centimeters and the number of meters be different? Explain.

____

____

____

© Houghton Mifflin Harcourt Publishing Company

Chapter

10 Data

Curious About Math with Curious George

Look at the different kinds of balloons.

What are some ways you can sort these balloons?

© Houghton Mifflin Harcourt Publishing Company
Curious George by Margret and H.A. Rey. Copyright © 2010 by Houghton Mifflin Harcourt Publishing Company. All rights reserved. The character Curious George®, including without limitation the character's name and the character's likenesses, are registered trademarks of Houghton Mifflin Harcourt Publishing Company.

Name ______________________

Show What You Know

Read a Picture Graph

Use the picture graph.

Fruit We Like				
orange	orange	orange	orange	orange
pear	pear	pear		

1. How many children chose pear? _______ children

2. Circle the fruit that more children chose.

Read a Tally Chart

Complete the tally chart.

Color We Like		Total
green	III	
red	~~IIII~~ I	
blue	~~IIII~~ III	

3. How many children chose red?

_______ children

4. Which color did the fewest children choose?

____

Addition and Subtraction Facts

Write the sum or difference.

5. $10 - 4 =$ ______	6. $4 + 5 =$ ______	7. $6 + 5 =$ ______
8. $9 - 3 =$ ______	9. $5 + 7 =$ ______	10. $11 - 3 =$ ______

Family note: This page checks your child's understanding of important skills needed for success in Chapter 10.

GO Online Assessment Options Soar to Success Math

© Houghton Mifflin Harcourt Publishing Company

Name ______________________

Review Words

tally marks
more than
fewer than

Vocabulary Builder

Visualize It

Draw **tally marks** to show each number.

tally marks

7

4

10

13

Understand Vocabulary

Write a number to complete the sentence.

1. 10 apples is **more than** _______ apples.

2. 6 bananas is **fewer than** _______ bananas.

3. _______ grapes is **more than** 6 grapes.

4. _______ oranges is **fewer than** 5 oranges.

GO Online
- eStudent Edition
- Multimedia eGlossary

© Houghton Mifflin Harcourt Publishing Company

Game

Making Tens

Materials • • 25
• small bag

Play with a partner.

1. Put 25 in a bag.
2. Toss the . Take that many and put them on your ten frame. Take turns.
3. When you have 10 on your ten frame, make a tally mark on the tally chart. Then put the 10 back in the bag.
4. The first player to make 10 tally marks wins.

Player 1

Player 2

Making Tens

Player	Tally
Player 1	
Player 2	

© Houghton Mifflin Harcourt Publishing Company

Name ______________________________

Lesson 10.1

Collect Data

Essential Question How do you use a tally chart to record data from a survey?

COMMON CORE STANDARD CC.2.MD.10
Represent and interpret data.

Listen and Draw

Take turns pulling a cube from the bag.
Draw a tally mark in the chart for each cube.

Cube Colors	
Color	**Tally**
blue	
red	
green	

HOME CONNECTION • Your child made tally marks to record the color of cubes pulled from a bag. This activity prepares children for using and recording data in this chapter.

Math Talk

Explain how tally marks help you keep track of what has been pulled.

MATHEMATICAL PRACTICES

© Houghton Mifflin Harcourt Publishing Company

Model and Draw

You can take a **survey** to collect **data**.
You can record the data with tally marks.

Greg asked his classmates which lunch is their favorite.

Favorite Lunch	
Lunch	**Tally**
pizza	𝍷𝍷𝍷𝍷
sandwich	𝍸 𝍷
salad	𝍷𝍷𝍷
pasta	𝍸

> The tally marks in the tally chart show the children's answers. Each tally mark stands for one child's choice.

Share and Show

1. Take a survey. Ask 10 classmates which pet is their favorite. Use tally marks to show their choices.

Favorite Pet	
Pet	**Tally**
cat	
dog	
fish	
bird	

2. How many classmates chose dog?

_______ classmates

3. Which pet did the fewest classmates choose?

____

4. Did more classmates choose cat or dog? _______________

How many more? _______ more classmates

© Houghton Mifflin Harcourt Publishing Company

Name ______________________________

On Your Own

5. Take a survey. Ask 10 classmates which indoor game is their favorite. Use tally marks to show their choices.

Favorite Indoor Game

Game	Tally
board	
card	
computer	
puzzle	

6. How many classmates chose board game?

_______ classmates

7. Which game did the most classmates choose?

____

8. Did more classmates choose a card game or a computer game?

____

How many more? _______ more classmates

9. Which game did the fewest classmates choose?

____

10. How many classmates did not choose a board game or a puzzle? **Explain** how you know.

____

____

____

____

© Houghton Mifflin Harcourt Publishing Company

PROBLEM SOLVING REAL WORLD

Write Math

Claire asked her classmates to choose their favorite subject. She made this tally chart.

Favorite Subject

Subject	Tally
reading	𝍸 |
math	𝍸 ||||
science	𝍸 𝍸

11. How many more classmates chose math than reading?

_______ more classmates

12. How many classmates did Claire ask?

_______ classmates

13. H.O.T. Write a new question about the data in the chart. Then write the answer to your question.

____

____

____

14. **Test Prep** Use the tally chart. Which statement is true?

Favorite Meal

Meal	Tally
breakfast	𝍸 |||
lunch	𝍸 𝍸
dinner	𝍸 𝍸 ||

- ○ 13 children voted for breakfast.
- ○ 35 children voted in all.
- ○ 12 children voted for dinner.
- ○ Fewer children voted for lunch than for breakfast.

TAKE HOME ACTIVITY • With your child, take a survey about favorite games and make a tally chart to show the data.

© Houghton Mifflin Harcourt Publishing Company

FOR MORE PRACTICE: Standards Practice Book, pp. P223 P224

Name ______________________________

Read Picture Graphs

Essential Question How do you use a picture graph to show data?

COMMON CORE STANDARD CC.2.MD.10
Represent and interpret data.

Listen and Draw REAL WORLD

Use the tally chart to solve the problem.
Draw or write to show what you did.

Favorite Hobby

Hobby	Tally
crafts	𝍸 |
reading	||||
music	𝍸
sports	𝍸 ||

_______ more children

Math Talk Can the chart be used to find how many girls chose music? **Explain.**

MATHEMATICAL PRACTICES

FOR THE TEACHER • Read the following problem. Mr. Martin's class made this tally chart. How many more children in his class chose sports than chose reading as their favorite hobby?

© Houghton Mifflin Harcourt Publishing Company

Model and Draw

A **picture graph** uses pictures to show data.

Key: Each ⚽ stands for 1 game.

A key tells how many each picture stands for.

Share and Show

Math Board

Use the picture graph to answer the questions.

Key: Each ☺ stands for 1 child.

1. Which snack was chosen by the fewest children? ________________

2. How many more children chose pretzels than apples? ______ more children

© Houghton Mifflin Harcourt Publishing Company

Name ______________________________

On Your Own

Use the picture graph to answer the questions.

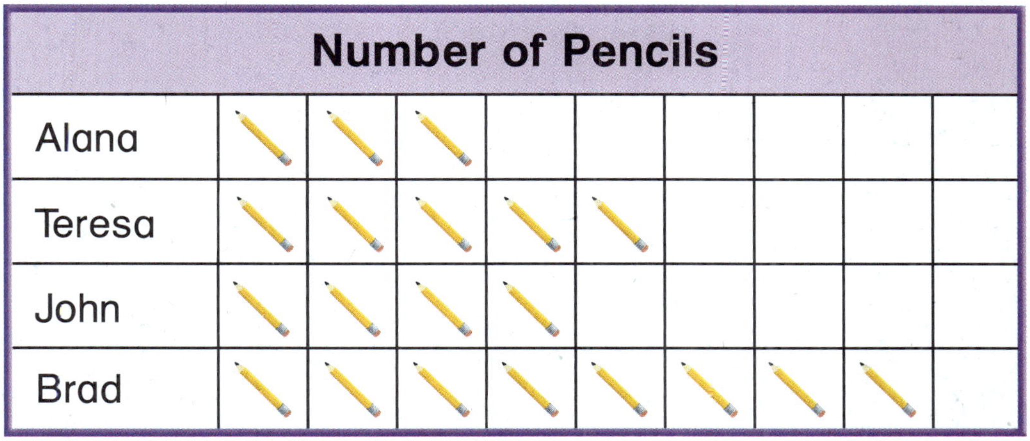

Key: Each ✏ **stands for 1 pencil.**

3. How many pencils do Alana and Brad have? _______ pencils

4. How many more pencils does Teresa have than Alana has? _______ more pencils

5. How many pencils do the four children have? _______ pencils

6. Christy has 7 pencils. Write two sentences to describe how her number of pencils compares to the data in the picture graph.

____

____

____

____

____

© Houghton Mifflin Harcourt Publishing Company

PROBLEM SOLVING REAL WORLD

Write Math

Favorite Balloon Color								
green	🎈	🎈	🎈	🎈				
blue	🎈	🎈	🎈	🎈	🎈			
red	🎈	🎈	🎈	🎈	🎈	🎈	🎈	
purple	🎈	🎈	🎈	🎈				

Key: Each 🎈 stands for 1 child.

7. How many children chose the color blue or chose the color green? _______ children

8. H.O.T. Which three colors were chosen by a total of 13 children?

____

9. **Test Prep** Use the picture graph. How many pets do the three children have?

○ 6
○ 5
○ 4
○ 3

Number of Pets				
Scott	◆	◆	◆	
Andre	◆			
Maddie	◆	◆		

Key: Each ◆ stands for 1 pet.

TAKE HOME ACTIVITY • Have your child explain how he or she solved Exercise 9.

FOR MORE PRACTICE:
Standards Practice Book, pp. P225–P226

© Houghton Mifflin Harcourt Publishing Company

Name ______________________________

Make Picture Graphs

Essential Question How do you make a picture graph to show data in a tally chart?

COMMON CORE STANDARD **CC.2.MD.10**
Represent and interpret data.

Listen and Draw

Take turns pulling a cube from the bag.
Draw a smiley face in the graph for each cube.

Cube Colors					
blue					
red					
green					
orange					

Key: Each ☺ stands for 1 cube.

HOME CONNECTION • Your child made a graph by recording smiley faces for the colors of cubes taken from a bag. This activity prepares children for working with picture graphs in this lesson.

Math Talk
Explain how you know that the number of smiley faces for blue matches the number of blue cubes.

MATHEMATICAL PRACTICES

© Houghton Mifflin Harcourt Publishing Company

Model and Draw

Each picture in the graph stands for 1 flower.
Draw pictures to show the data in the tally chart.

Number of Flowers Picked	
Name	**Tally**
Jessie	III
Inez	𝍸
Paulo	IIII

Number of Flowers Picked					
Jessie	⬭	⬭	⬭		
Inez					
Paulo					

Key: Each ⬭ stands for 1 flower.

Share and Show

1. Use the tally chart to complete the picture graph.
Draw a ☺ for each child.

Favorite Sandwich	
Sandwich	**Tally**
cheese	𝍸
ham	II
tuna	IIII
turkey	III

Favorite Sandwich					
cheese					
ham					
tuna					
turkey					

Key: Each ☺ stands for 1 child.

2. How many children chose tuna? ______ children

3. How many more children chose cheese than ham? ______ more children

© Houghton Mifflin Harcourt Publishing Company

Name ________________________________

On Your Own

4. Use the tally chart to complete the picture graph.
Draw a ☺ for each child.

Favorite Fruit	
Fruit	**Tally**
apple	||||
plum	||
banana	~~||||~~
orange	|||

Favorite Fruit					
apple					
plum					
banana					
orange					

Key: Each ☺ stands for 1 child.

5. How many children chose banana? _______ children

6. How many fewer children chose plum than banana? _______ fewer children

7. Which fruit did the most children choose? _______________

8. How many more children chose banana than orange? _______ more children

9. H.O.T. Which three fruits were chosen by a total of 10 children?

____

TAKE HOME ACTIVITY • **Ask your child to explain how to read the picture graph on this page.**

© Houghton Mifflin Harcourt Publishing Company

FOR MORE PRACTICE:
Standards Practice Book, pp. P227–P228

Name ______________________________

Mid-Chapter Checkpoint

Concepts and Skills

Use the picture graph to answer the questions. (CC.2.MD.10)

Favorite Season									
spring	☺	☺	☺	☺	☺	☺			
summer	☺	☺	☺	☺	☺	☺	☺	☺	
fall	☺	☺	☺	☺					
winter	☺	☺	☺	☺	☺	☺	☺		

Key: Each ☺ stands for 1 child.

1. Which season did the fewest children choose? ______________

2. How many more children chose spring than fall? ______ more children

3. How many children chose a season that was not winter? ______ children

Test Prep (CC.2.MD.10)

4. James took a survey. 5 children chose green as their favorite color. Which group of tally marks should James use to show this?

   ○ |||

   ○ ||||

   ○ 𝍸

   ○ 𝍸 |

© Houghton Mifflin Harcourt Publishing Company

Name ______________________________

Read Bar Graphs

Essential Question How is a bar graph used to show data?

Lesson 10.4

COMMON CORE STANDARD CC.2.MD.10
Represent and interpret data.

Listen and Draw REAL WORLD

Use the picture graph to solve the problem.
Draw or write to show what you did.

Red Trucks Seen Last Week

Morgan	■	■	■					
John	■	■	■	■	■	■		
Cindy	■	■	■	■	■	■	■	■
Carlos	■	■	■	■				

Key: Each ■ stands for 1 red truck.

________ red trucks

FOR THE TEACHER • Read this problem to children. Morgan made a picture graph to show the number of red trucks that she and her friends saw last week. How many red trucks did the four children see last week?

Math Talk

Describe how the data in the graph for John and for Cindy are different.

MATHEMATICAL PRACTICES

© Houghton Mifflin Harcourt Publishing Company

Model and Draw

A **bar graph** uses bars to show data.
Look at where the bars end.
This tells how many.

There are 8 children playing soccer.

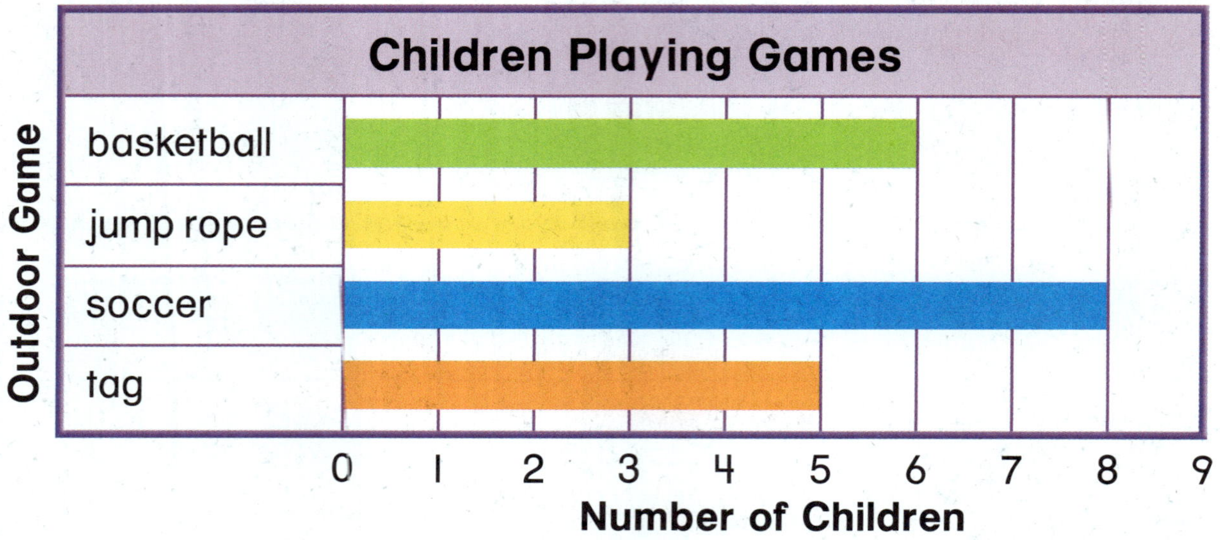

Share and Show

Use the bar graph.

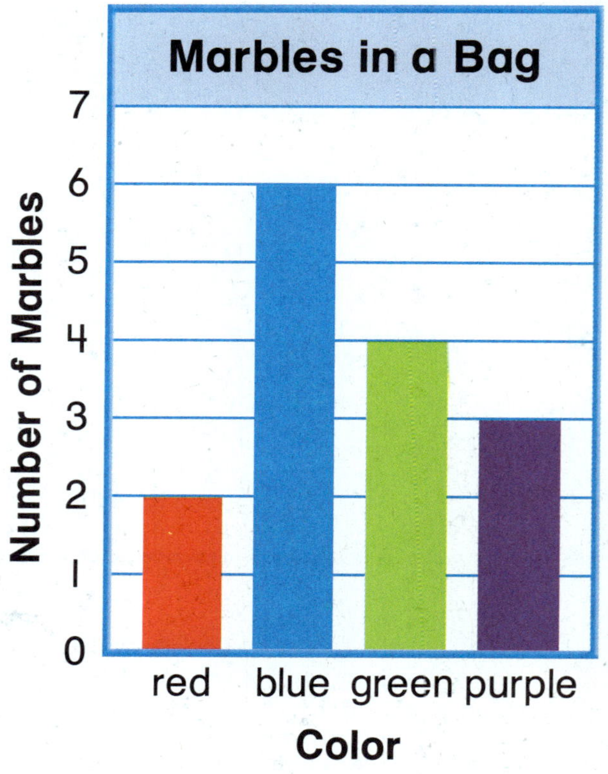

1. How many green marbles are in the bag?

   _______ green marbles

2. How many more blue marbles than purple marbles are in the bag?

   _______ more blue marbles

3. How many marbles are in the bag?

   _______ marbles

© Houghton Mifflin Harcourt Publishing Company

Name ______________________________

On Your Own

Use the bar graph.

4. How many children chose the beach?

_______ children

5. Which place did the fewest children choose?

____

6. How many more children chose the zoo than the aquarium?

_______ more children

7. How many children chose a place that was not the zoo?

_______ children

8. Find the number of children who chose the aquarium and the beach. Then find the number of children who chose the zoo and the museum. Describe how these two numbers are different.

____

____

____

____

© Houghton Mifflin Harcourt Publishing Company

PROBLEM SOLVING REAL WORLD

Write Math

Use the bar graph.

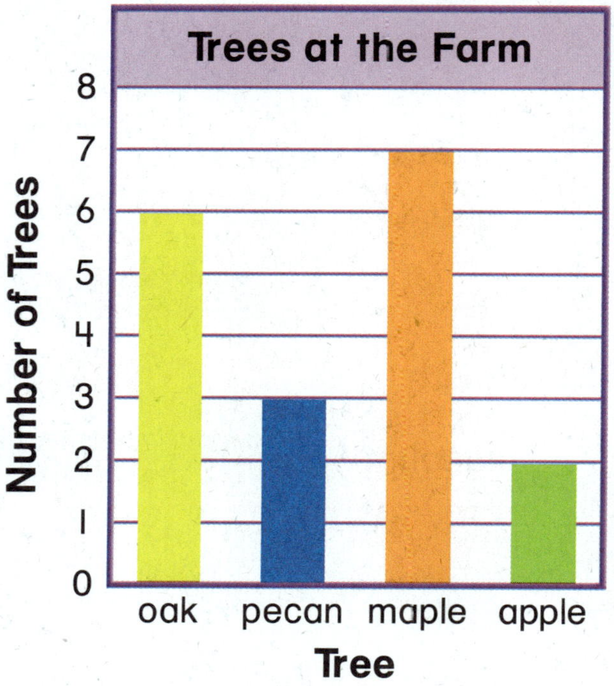

9. How many maple trees are there?

_______ maple trees

10. How many fewer apple trees than oak trees are there?

_______ fewer apple trees

11. How many trees are not apple trees?

_______ trees

12. H.O.T. Suppose 7 more trees are brought to the farm. How many trees would be at the farm then? Explain.

____

____

____

13. **Test Prep** Look at the bar graph above. How many oak trees are at the farm?

- ○ 3
- ○ 6
- ○ 7
- ○ 8

TAKE HOME ACTIVITY • Ask your child to explain how he or she solved Exercise 10.

FOR MORE PRACTICE:
Standards Practice Book, pp. P229–P230

© Houghton Mifflin Harcourt Publishing Company

Name ______________________________

Make Bar Graphs

Essential Question How do you make a bar graph to show data?

COMMON CORE STANDARD CC.2.MD.10
Represent and interpret data.

Listen and Draw REAL WORLD

Use the bar graph to solve the problem. Draw or write to show what you did.

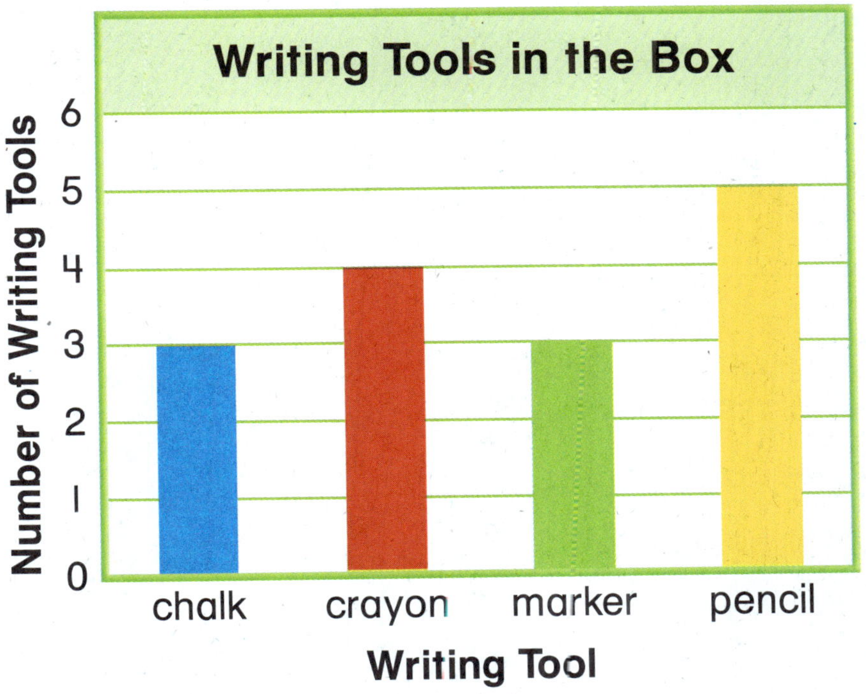

_________ writing tools

Math Talk **Describe** how the information in the graph for crayon and for marker is different.

MATHEMATICAL PRACTICES

FOR THE TEACHER • Read the following problem. Barry made this bar graph. How many writing tools are in the box?

© Houghton Mifflin Harcourt Publishing Company

Model and Draw

Abel read 2 books, Brad read 4 books, Cara read 1 book, and Lynn read 3 books.

Complete the bar graph to show this data.

Share and Show

Math Board

Ella is making a bar graph to show the kinds of pets her classmates have.

- 5 classmates have a dog.
- 7 classmates have a cat.
- 2 classmates have a bird.
- 3 classmates have fish.

1. Write labels and draw bars to complete the graph.

2. How will the graph change if one more child gets a bird?

____

____

____

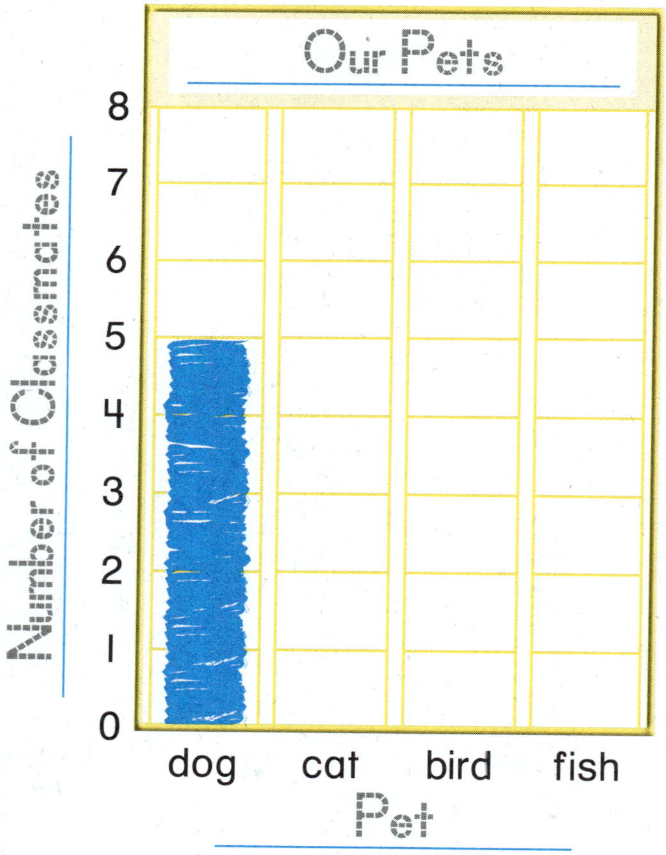

© Houghton Mifflin Harcourt Publishing Company

Name ____________________

On Your Own

Dexter asked his classmates which pizza topping is their favorite.

- 4 classmates chose peppers.
- 7 classmates chose meat.
- 5 classmates chose mushrooms.
- 2 classmates chose olives.

3. Write a title and labels for the bar graph.

4. Draw bars in the graph to show the data.

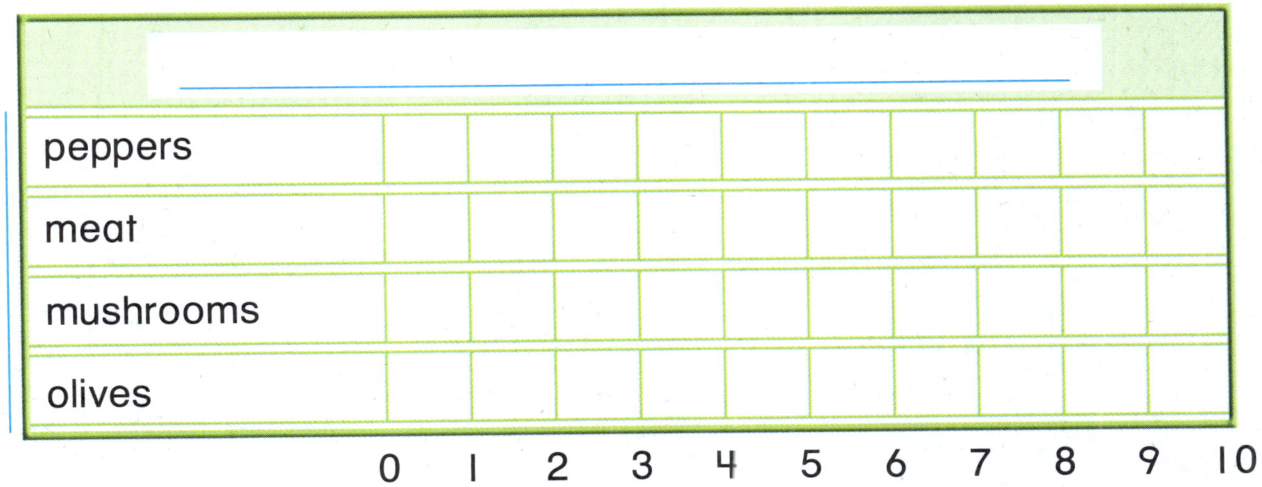

5. Which topping did the most classmates choose? ____________

6. H.O.T. Did more classmates choose peppers and olives than meat? **Explain.**

____

____

____

© Houghton Mifflin Harcourt Publishing Company

PROBLEM SOLVING REAL WORLD

Write Math

Cody asked his classmates which zoo animal is their favorite.

- 6 classmates chose bear.
- 4 classmates chose lion.
- 7 classmates chose tiger.
- 3 classmates chose zebra.

Use the data to complete the bar graph.

7. Write a title and labels. Draw bars.

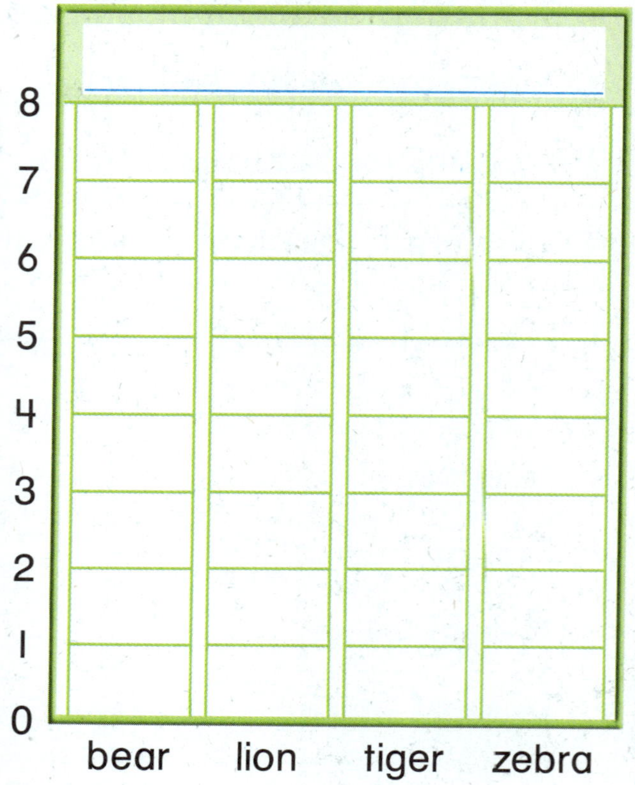

8. How many more classmates chose bear than zebra?

_______ more classmates

9. H.O.T. How many fewer classmates chose lion than classmates that chose the other zoo animals?

_______ fewer classmates

10. **Test Prep** Look at the bar graph above. Which animal did the most classmates choose?

- ○ bear
- ○ tiger
- ○ lion
- ○ zebra

TAKE HOME ACTIVITY • Ask your child to describe how he or she used the favorite zoo animal data to complete the bar graph.

© Houghton Mifflin Harcourt Publishing Company

FOR MORE PRACTICE: Standards Practice Book, pp. P231–P232

Name ______________________________

Problem Solving • Display Data

PROBLEM SOLVING
Lesson 10.6

Essential Question How does making a bar graph help when solving problems about data?

COMMON CORE STANDARD CC.2.MD.10
Represent and interpret data.

Maria recorded the rainfall in her town for four months. How did the amount of rainfall change from September to December?

September	4 inches
October	3 inches
November	2 inches
December	1 inch

Unlock the Problem

What do I need to find?

how the amount of rainfall changed from September to December

What information do I need to use?

the amount of rainfall in each of the four months

Show how to solve the problem.

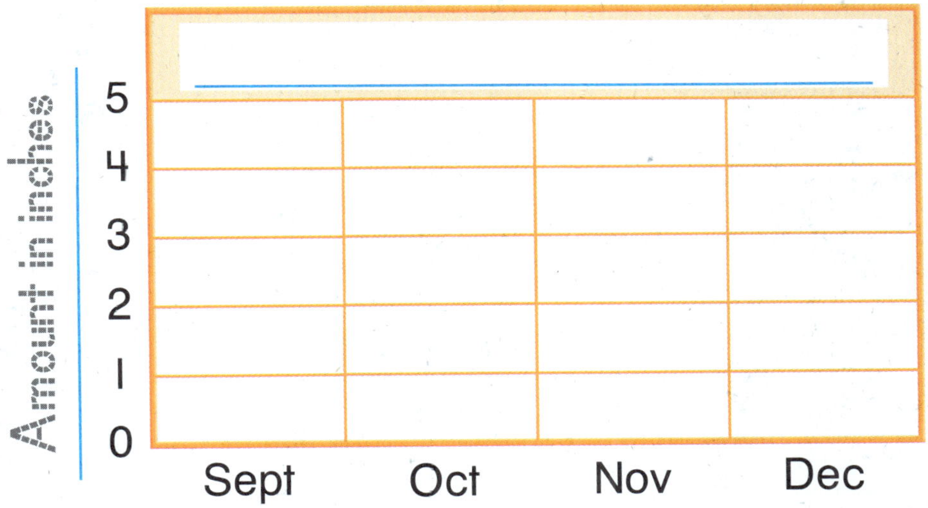

The amount of rainfall ______________________________

____

HOME CONNECTION • Your child made a bar graph to show the data. Making a graph helps your child organize data to solve problems.

© Houghton Mifflin Harcourt Publishing Company

Try Another Problem

Make a bar graph to solve the problem.

- What do I need to find?
- What information do I need to use?

1. Matthew measured the height of his plant once a week for four weeks. Describe how the height of the plant changed from May 1 to May 22.

May 1	2 inches
May 8	3 inches
May 15	5 inches
May 22	7 inches

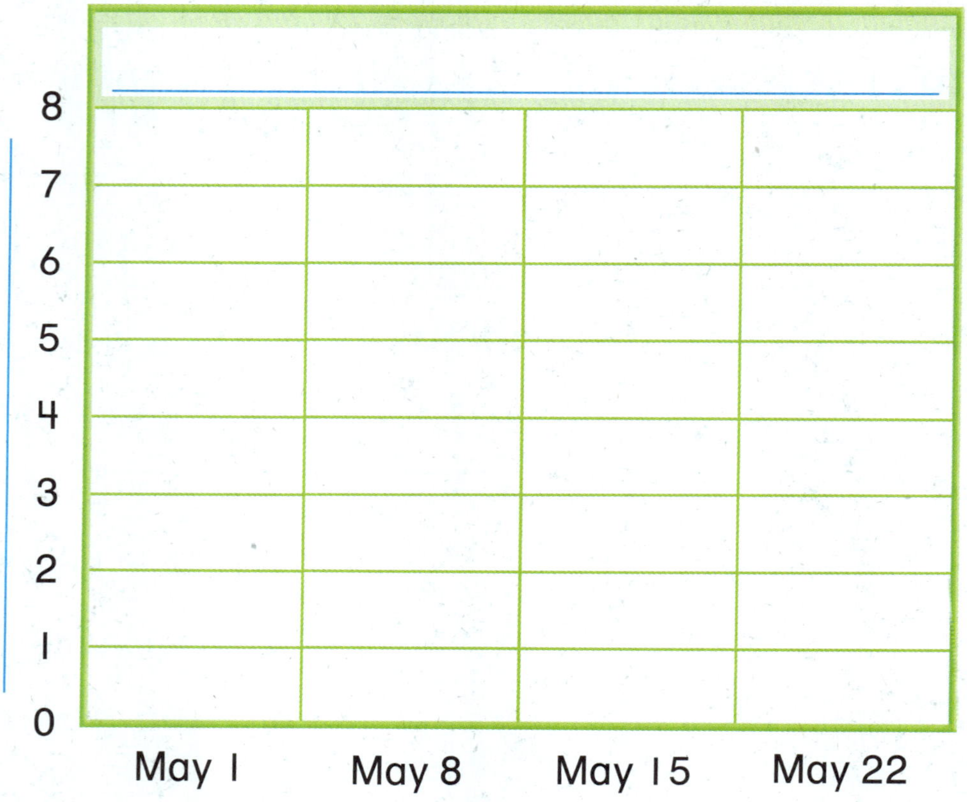

The height of the plant ______________________________

____

Math Talk
How many inches did the plant grow from May 1 to May 22? **Explain.**

© Houghton Mifflin Harcourt Publishing Company

Name ______________________________

Share and Show

Make a bar graph to solve the problem.

2. Bianca wrote the number of hours that she practiced playing guitar in June. Describe how the amount of practice time changed from Week 1 to Week 4.

Week 1	1 hour
Week 2	2 hours
Week 3	4 hours
Week 4	5 hours

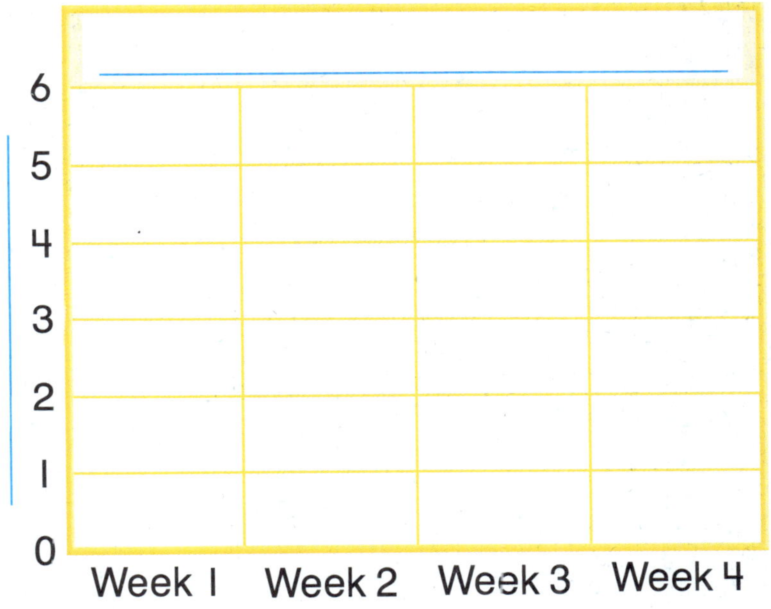

____

The amount of practice time ______________________________

____

3. If Bianca's practice time is 4 hours in Week 5, how does her practice time change from Week 1 to Week 5?

____

____

____

© Houghton Mifflin Harcourt Publishing Company

On Your Own

Solve.

Write Math

4. How many strings are 9 inches long?

_______ strings

5. H.O.T. How many strings are more than 6 inches long?

_______ strings

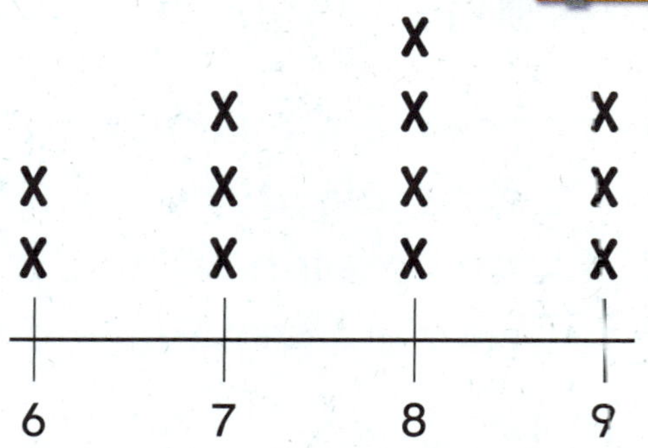

Lengths of Strings in Inches

6. **Test Prep** Use the bar graph. How did the amount of snowfall change from Week 1 to Week 4?

- ○ The amount of snowfall stayed the same.
- ○ The amount of snowfall increased.
- ○ The amount of snowfall decreased.
- ○ The amount of snowfall decreased and then increased.

TAKE HOME ACTIVITY • Have your child explain how he or she solved Exercise 5.

FOR MORE PRACTICE:
Standards Practice Book, pp. P233–P234

© Houghton Mifflin Harcourt Publishing Company

Name ______________________________

✓ Chapter 10 Review/Test

Vocabulary

Use a word in the box to complete each sentence.

bar graph
picture graph
data

1. You can take a survey to collect ______________. (p. 470)

2. A ______________ uses pictures to show data in a graph. (p. 474)

Concepts and Skills

Use the tally chart to complete the picture graph.
Draw a ☺ for each bird. (CC.2.MD.10)

Birds Counted at the Park

Child	Tally
Reggie	IIII
Kate	𝍸
Ted	II
Mandy	IIII

Birds Counted at the Park

Reggie					
Kate					
Ted					
Mandy					

Key: Each ☺ stands for 1 bird.

3. Which child counted the most birds? ______________

4. How many fewer birds did Ted count than Reggie counted? ______ fewer birds

5. How many birds did the four children count? ______ birds

© Houghton Mifflin Harcourt Publishing Company

Fill in the bubble for the correct answer choice.

TEST PREP

6. Use the tally chart.
How many children chose apple muffins? (CC.2.MD.10)

- ○ 13
- ○ 8
- ○ 7
- ○ 5

Favorite Muffin

Muffin	Tally
banana	|||
blueberry	𝍸 𝍸	
apple	𝍸 |||

7. Use the bar graph.
How many more yellow toy cars than green toy cars were sold? (CC.2.MD.10)

- ○ 1
- ○ 3
- ○ 4
- ○ 5

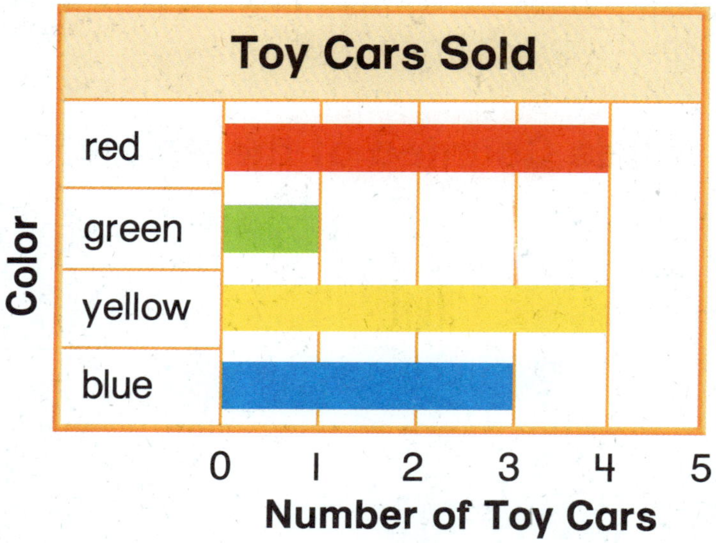

8. Use the picture graph.
How many stickers do Megan and Lin have? (CC.2.MD.10)

- ○ 4
- ○ 5
- ○ 6
- ○ 7

Stickers We Have

Shane	☺	☺	☺		
Megan	☺	☺			
Lin	☺	☺	☺	☺	
Elroy	☺	☺	☺		

Key: Each ☺ stands for 1 sticker.

© Houghton Mifflin Harcourt Publishing Company

Name ________________________________

TEST PREP

Fill in the bubble for the correct answer choice.

9. Use the picture graph.
How many fewer books did Joy read than Tony? (CC.2.MD.10)

- ○ 1
- ○ 2
- ○ 3
- ○ 5

Key: Each [book] stands for 1 book.

---

10. Use the tally chart. How many children chose truck? (CC.2.MD.10)

- ○ 5
- ○ 8
- ○ 10
- ○ 12

Favorite Toy

Toy	Tally
ball	𝍸
truck	𝍸 𝍸 ||
doll	𝍸 |||

---

11. Use the bar graph.
How many more mums than roses are in the basket? (CC.2.MD.10)

- ○ 1
- ○ 2
- ○ 3
- ○ 8

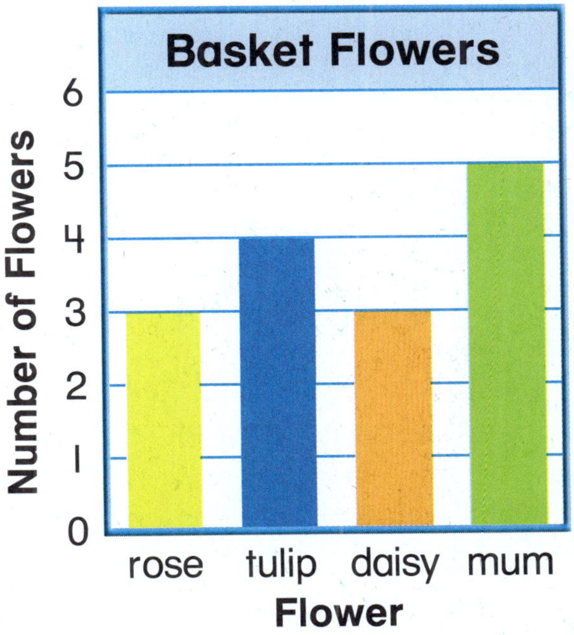

© Houghton Mifflin Harcourt Publishing Company

Constructed Response

12. The data for grape juice is not shown in the picture graph. If 13 children voted in all, how many pictures should there be for grape juice?

_______ pictures

Explain your answer. (CC.2.MD.10)

Key: Each [cup] stands for 1 child.

____

____

Performance Task (CC.2.MD.10)

13. In a survey for favorite vegetable, 3 children chose squash, 4 children chose beans, 6 children chose corn, and 5 children chose carrots. Write labels and draw bars to complete the graph.

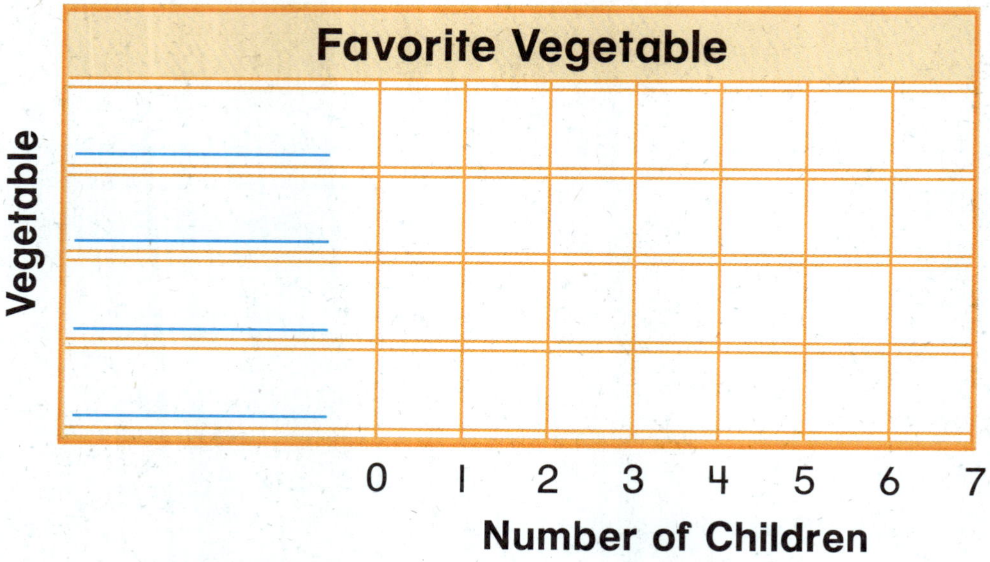

Write a sentence to describe the data in the graph.

____

____

© Houghton Mifflin Harcourt Publishing Company

A Farmer's Job

by Tami Morton

CRITICAL AREA Describing and analyzing shapes

COMMON CORE

© Houghton Mifflin Harcourt Publishing Company

A farmer's job is never done. Farmers are busy during all of the seasons of the year. They grow fruits and vegetables for people to eat.
What shapes do you see?

____

Social Studies

Why is a farmer's work important?

© Houghton Mifflin Harcourt Publishing Company

In the spring, farmers get the fields ready.

They plow the fields and fertilize the soil.

They plant their seeds.

What shapes do you see?

____

Social Studies

How is a farmer's work today different from long ago?

© Houghton Mifflin Harcourt Publishing Company

In the summer, farmers take care of their crops. They make sure that the plants have enough water when it does not rain. What shapes do you see?

____

Social Studies

Why does a farmer need to know about changes in the weather?

© Houghton Mifflin Harcourt Publishing Company

In the fall, farmers harvest many fruits and vegetables. They sell most of these fruits and vegetables to other people. What shapes do you see?

____

Social Studies

Why does a farmer grow more fruits and vegetables than his or her family can eat?

© Houghton Mifflin Harcourt Publishing Company

In the winter, farmers clear the fields and get ready for the next season. They plan what they are going to plant. They check their machines. A farmer's job is never done. What shapes do you see?

____

Social Studies

Why are the seasons important to a farmer?

© Houghton Mifflin Harcourt Publishing Company

Name ______________________________

Write About the Story

Look at the pictures of the farm objects. Draw a picture and write your own story about the objects. Tell about the shapes that the objects look like.

Vocabulary Review

cylinder	cube
cone	circle
sphere	triangle
square	rectangle
rectangular prism	

Write Math

____

____

____

____

____

© Houghton Mifflin Harcourt Publishing Company

What shape do you see?

Draw a line to match the shape with the name.

cylinder   rectangular prism   circle

Circle each shape that has a curved surface.

cylinder
rectangular prism
cube
cone
sphere

Math Board

Write a riddle about a shape. Ask a classmate to read the riddle and name the shape.

© Houghton Mifflin Harcourt Publishing Company

Chapter 11

Geometry and Fraction Concepts

Curious About Math with Curious George

Hot air rises. A balloon filled with hot air will float up into the sky.

Some balloons look as though they have two-dimensional shapes on them. Name some two-dimensional shapes. Then draw some examples of them.

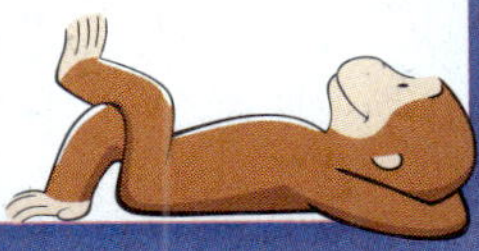

© Houghton Mifflin Harcourt Publishing Company.
Curious George by Margret and H.A. Rey. Copyright (c) 2010 by Houghton Mifflin Harcourt Publishing Company.
All rights reserved. The character Curious George®, including without limitation the character's name and the character's likenesses, are registered trademarks of Houghton Mifflin Harcourt Publishing Company.

Name ______________________________

Show What You Know

Equal Parts

Circle the shape that has two equal parts.

1. 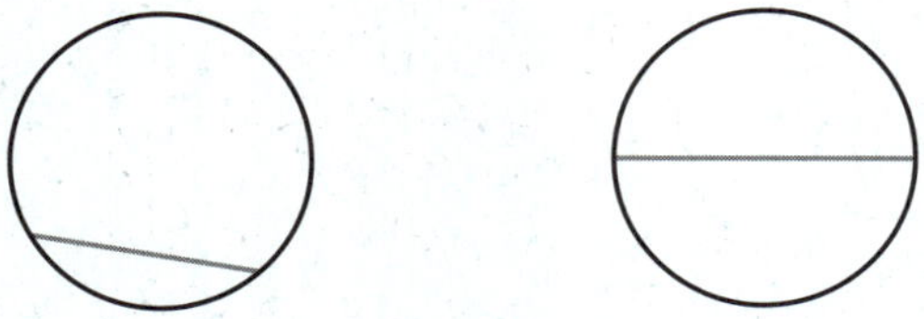

2. 

Identify Three-Dimensional Shapes

3. Circle each (sphere).

4. Circle each (cube).

Identify Shapes

Circle all the shapes that match the shape name.

5. triangle 

6. rectangle 

Family note: This page checks your child's understanding of important skills needed for success in Chapter 11.

GO Online Assessment Options Soar to Success Math

© Houghton Mifflin Harcourt Publishing Company

Name ______________________________

Review Words
- equal parts
- shape
- rectangle
- triangle
- square

Vocabulary Builder

Visualize It
Draw pictures to complete the graphic organizer.

equal parts

Examples	Not Examples

Understand Vocabulary
Draw a **shape** to match the shape name.

rectangle	triangle	square

GO Online
- eStudent Edition
- Multimedia eGlossary

© Houghton Mifflin Harcourt Publishing Company

Game: Count the Sides

Materials • 1 [number cube] • 10 [red counters] • 10 [yellow counters]

Play with a partner.

1. Toss the [number cube]. If you toss a 1 or a 2, toss the [number cube] again.
2. Look for a shape that has the same number of sides as the number you tossed.
3. Put one of your counters on that shape.
4. Take turns. Cover all the shapes. The player with more counters on the board wins.

© Houghton Mifflin Harcourt Publishing Company

Name ______________________________________

Three-Dimensional Shapes

Essential Question What objects match three-dimensional shapes?

COMMON CORE STANDARD CC.2.G.1
Reason with shapes and their attributes.

Listen and Draw REAL WORLD

Draw a picture of an object that has the shape shown.

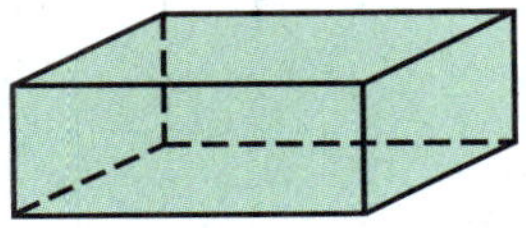

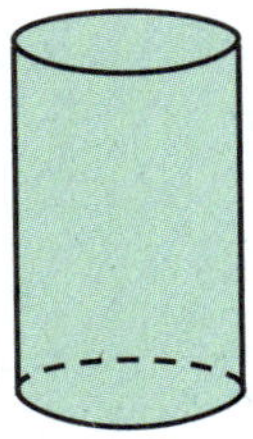

FOR THE TEACHER • Have children look at the first shape and name some real objects that have this shape, such as a cereal box. Have each child draw a picture of a real-life object that has the same shape. Repeat for the second shape.

Math Talk

Describe how the shapes are alike. **Describe** how they are different.

MATHEMATICAL PRACTICES

© Houghton Mifflin Harcourt Publishing Company

Model and Draw

These are three-dimensional shapes.

cube	rectangular prism
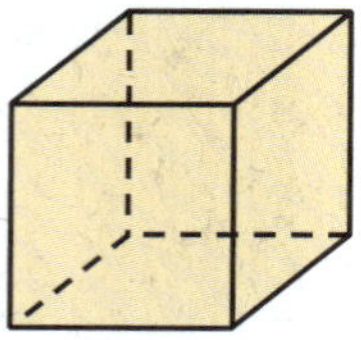	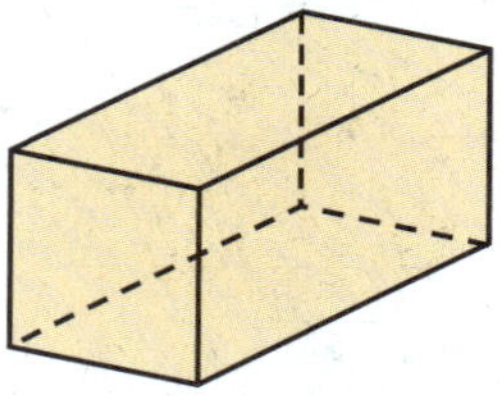

sphere	cylinder	cone
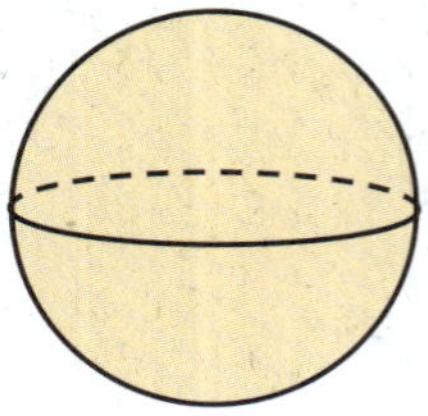		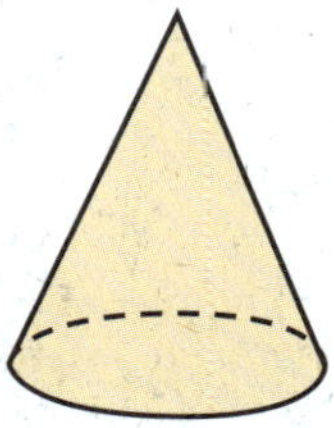

Which of these objects has the shape of a cube?

Share and Show

Math Board

Circle the objects that match the shape name.

1. sphere

2. cube

© Houghton Mifflin Harcourt Publishing Company

Name ____________________

On Your Own

Circle the objects that match the shape name.

3. cylinder

4. rectangular prism

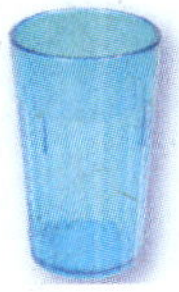

5. cone

6. cube

7. H.O.T. Circle the shapes that roll.
Draw an X on the shapes that do not roll.

© Houghton Mifflin Harcourt Publishing Company

PROBLEM SOLVING REAL WORLD

Write Math

8. Reba traced around the bottom of each block. Match each block with the shape Reba drew.

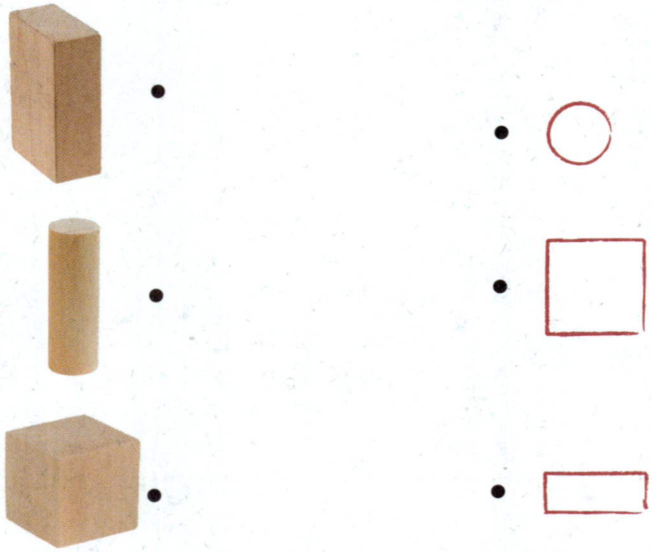

9. H.O.T. Julio used cardboard squares as the flat surfaces of a cube. How many squares did he use?

_______ squares

10. Test Prep Which of these shapes is a cube?

○ ○ ○ ○

TAKE HOME ACTIVITY • Ask your child to name an object that has the shape of a cube.

© Houghton Mifflin Harcourt Publishing Company

FOR MORE PRACTICE: Standards Practice Book, pp. P239–P240

Name ________________________

Attributes of Three-Dimensional Shapes

COMMON CORE STANDARD CC.2.G.1
Reason with shapes and their attributes.

Essential Question How would you describe the faces of a rectangular prism and the faces of a cube?

Listen and Draw

Circle the cones. Draw an X on the sphere.

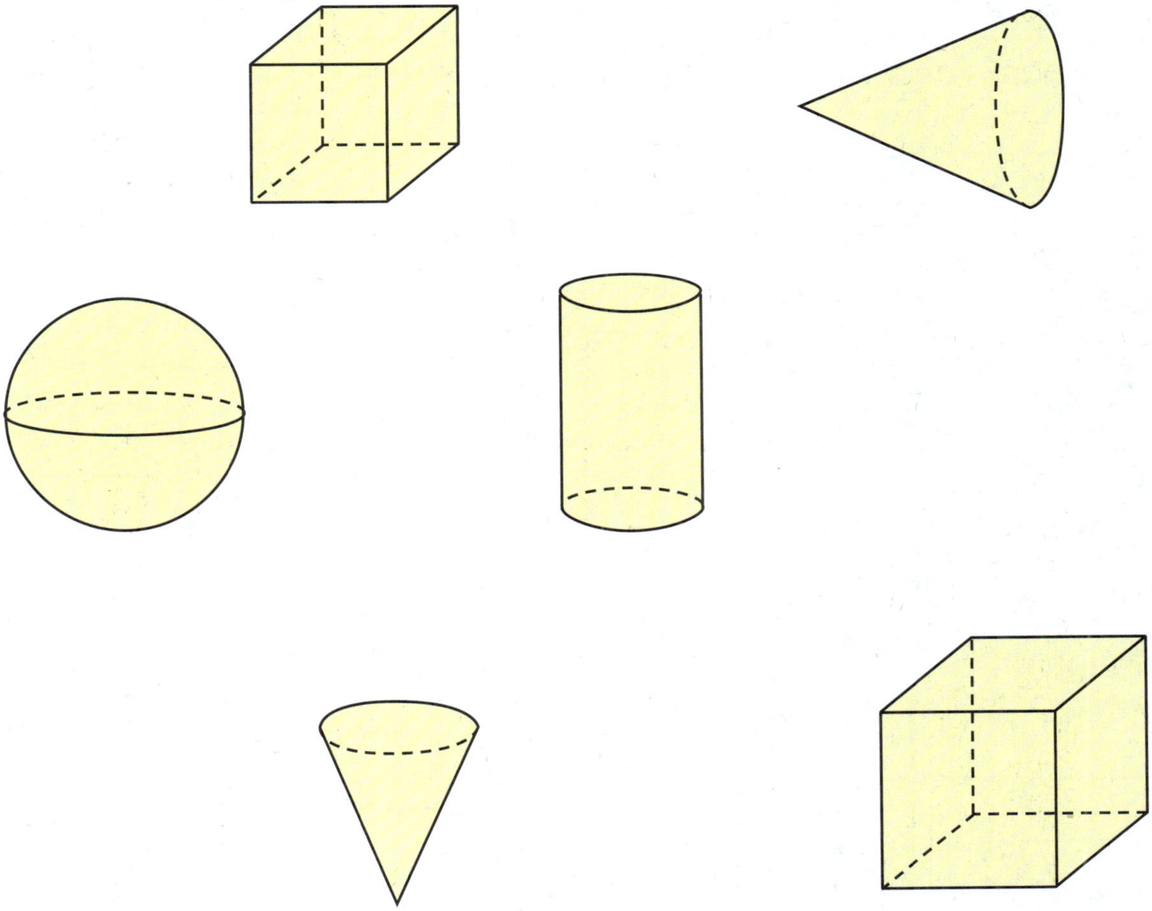

Math Talk

Name the other shapes on this page. **Describe** how they are different.

MATHEMATICAL PRACTICES

HOME CONNECTION • Your child identified the shapes on this page to review some of the different kinds of three-dimensional shapes.

© Houghton Mifflin Harcourt Publishing Company

Model and Draw

The **faces** of a cube are squares.

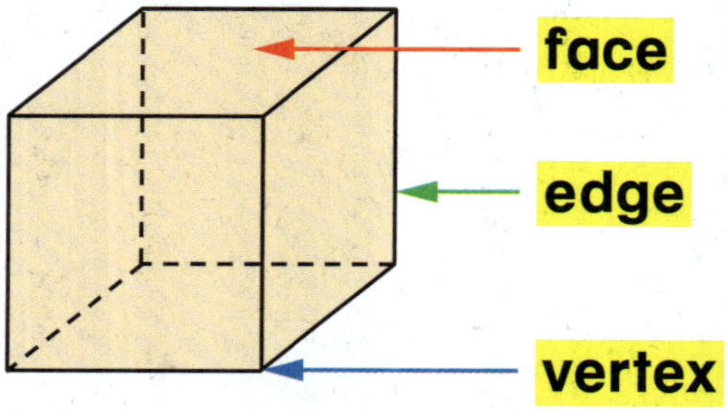

The **vertices** are the corner points of the cube.

Share and Show

Math Board

Write how many for each.

	faces	edges	vertices
1. 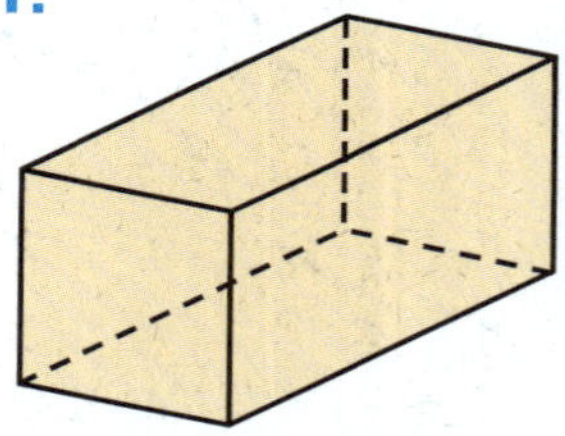 rectangular prism	___	___	___
2. 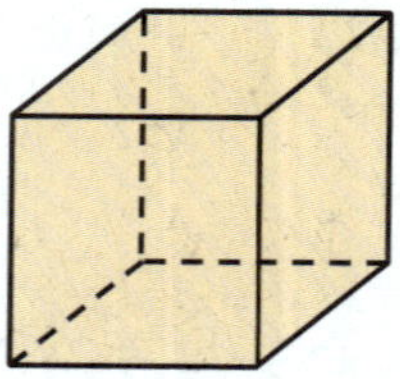 cube	___	___	___

© Houghton Mifflin Harcourt Publishing Company

Name ______________________________

On Your Own

Circle the set of shapes that are the faces of the three-dimensional shape.

3.

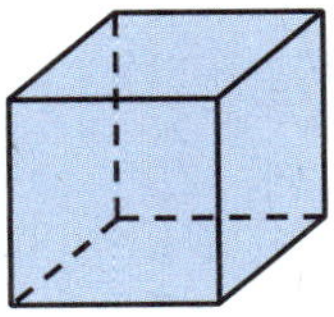

cube

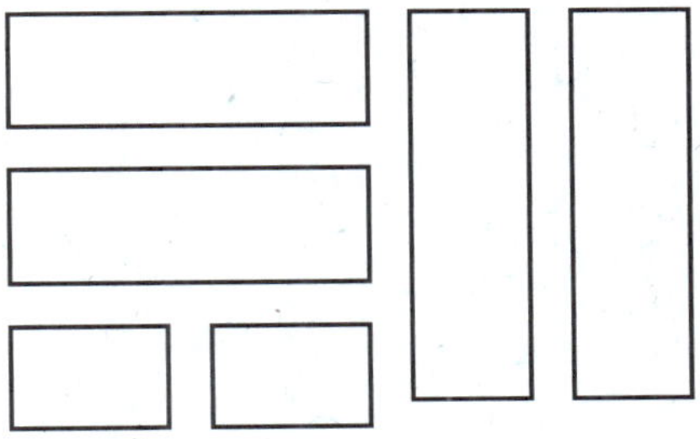

4.

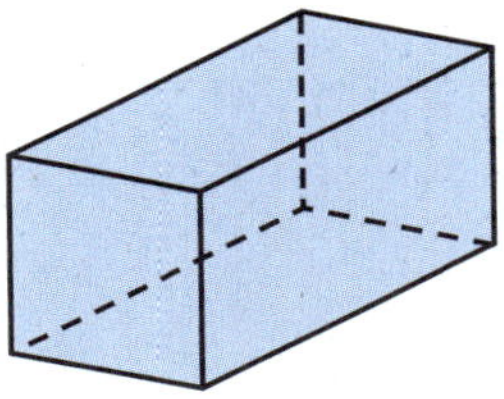

rectangular prism

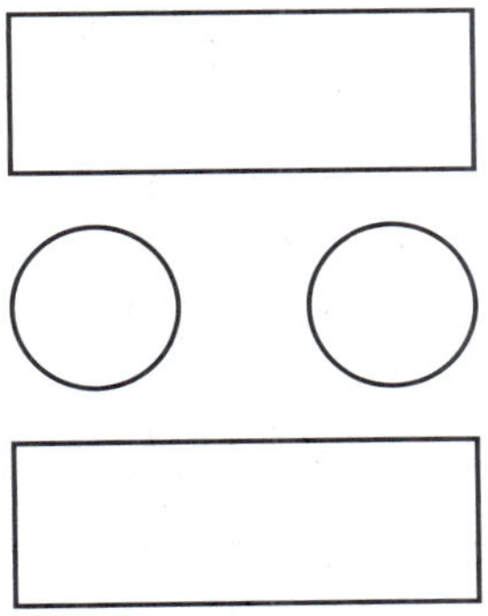

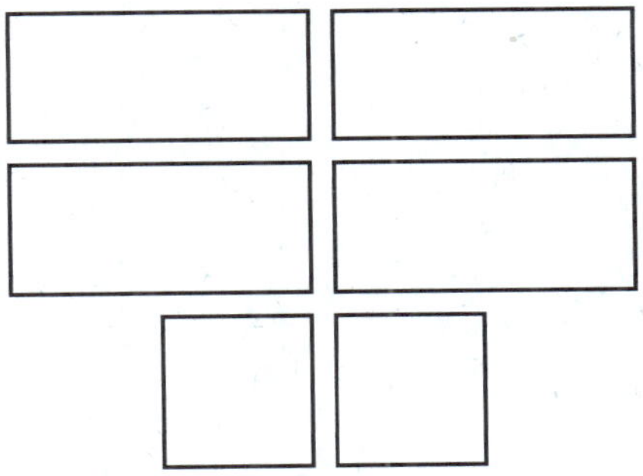

5. Look at the faces of the cube and the faces of the rectangular prism. **Explain** how they are different.

____

____

____

____

____

© Houghton Mifflin Harcourt Publishing Company

PROBLEM SOLVING REAL WORLD

Write Math

6. H.O.T. Use dot paper. Follow these steps to draw a cube.

Step 1 Draw a square. Make each side 4 units long.

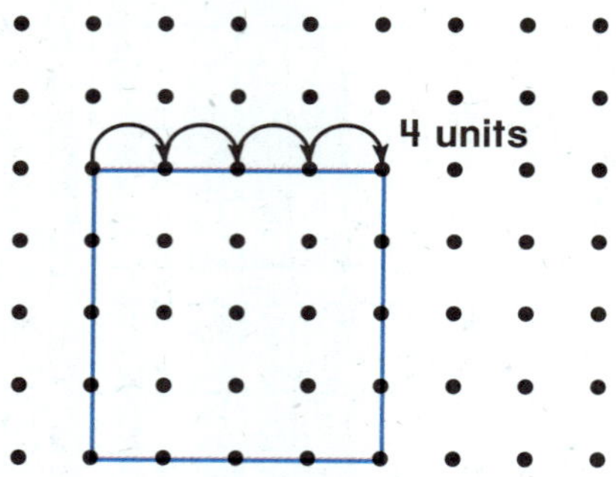

Step 2 Draw edges from 3 vertices, like this.

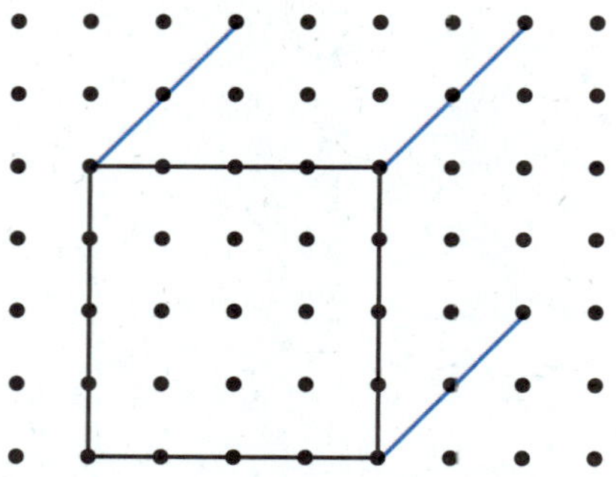

Step 3 Draw 2 more edges.

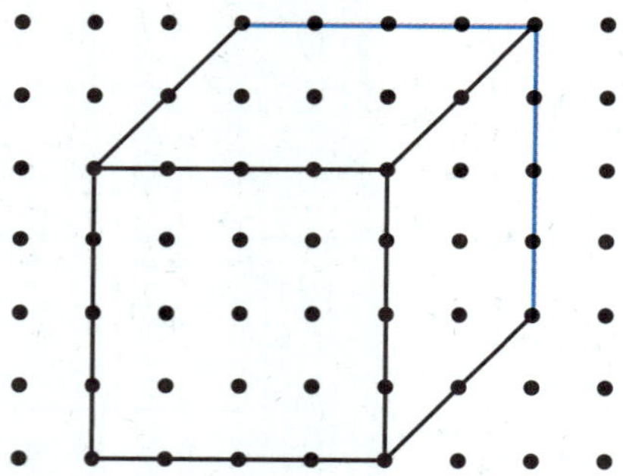

Step 4 Draw 3 dashed edges to show the faces that are not seen.

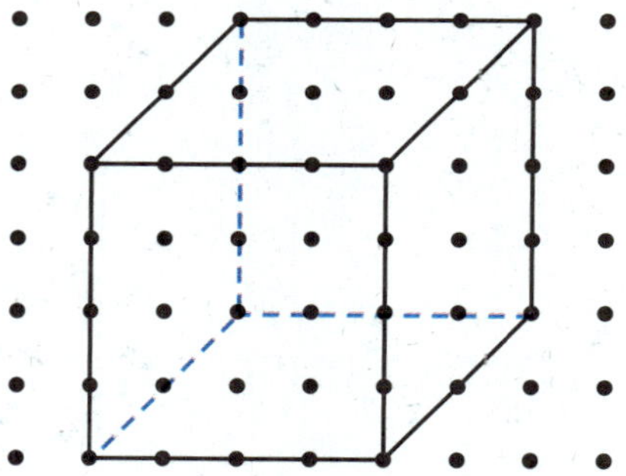

7. **Test Prep** How many faces does a rectangular prism have?

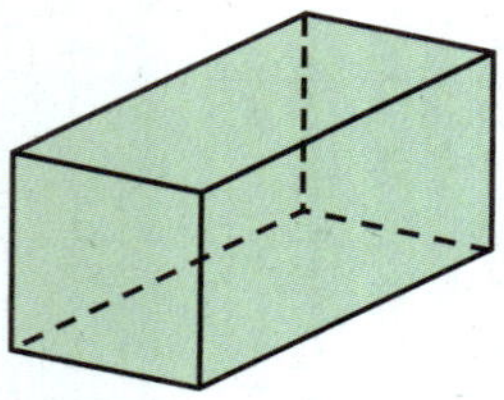

○ 6
○ 8
○ 12
○ 16

TAKE HOME ACTIVITY • Have your child tell you about the faces on a cereal box or another kind of box.

© Houghton Mifflin Harcourt Publishing Company

FOR MORE PRACTICE: Standards Practice Book, pp. P241–P242

Name ______________________________

Two-Dimensional Shapes

Essential Question What shapes can you name just by knowing the number of sides and vertices?

COMMON CORE STANDARD **CC.2.G.1**
Reason with shapes and their attributes.

Listen and Draw

Use a ruler. Draw a shape with 3 straight sides.
Then draw a shape with 4 straight sides.

Math Talk

Describe how your shapes are different from the shapes a classmate drew.

MATHEMATICAL PRACTICES

FOR THE TEACHER • Have children use rulers as straight edges for drawing the sides of shapes. Have children draw a two-dimensional shape with 3 sides and then a two-dimensional shape with 4 sides.

© Houghton Mifflin Harcourt Publishing Company

Model and Draw

You can count **sides** and **vertices** to name two-dimensional shapes. Look at how many sides and vertices each shape has.

triangle

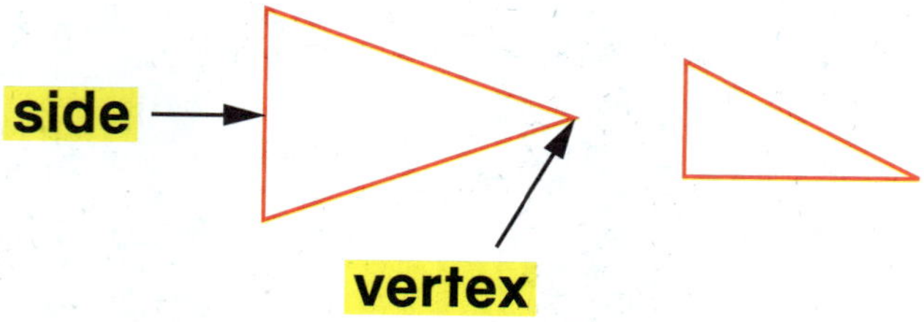

3 sides
3 vertices

quadrilateral	**pentagon**	**hexagon**
		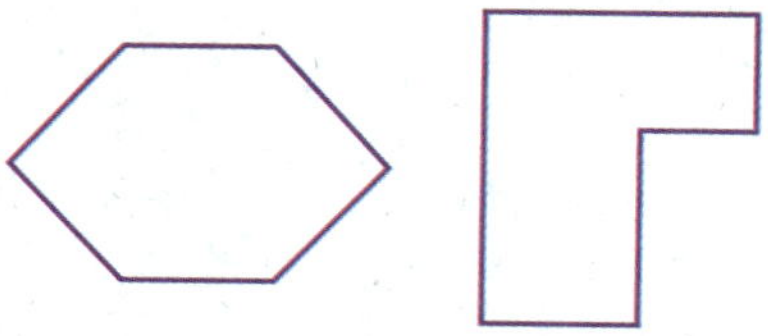
4 sides	____ sides	____ sides
____ vertices	____ vertices	____ vertices

Share and Show

Math Board

Write the number of sides and the number of vertices.

1. triangle

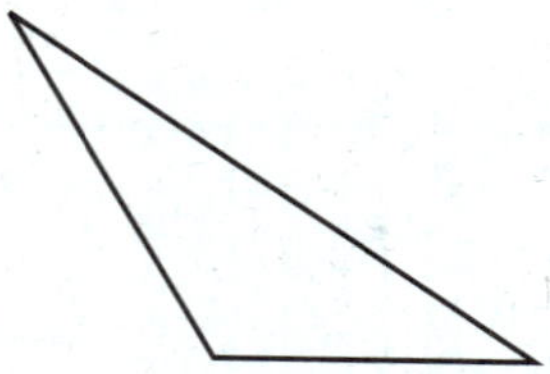

____ sides
____ vertices

2. hexagon

____ sides
____ vertices

3. pentagon

____ sides
____ vertices

© Houghton Mifflin Harcourt Publishing Company

Name ______________________

On Your Own

Write the number of sides and the number of vertices. Then write the name of the shape.

pentagon
triangle
hexagon
quadrilateral

4.

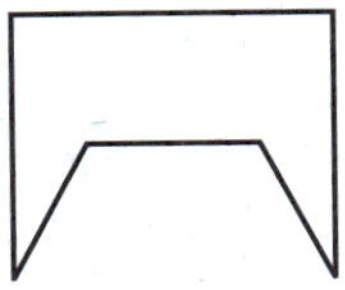

_____ sides
_____ vertices
____

5.

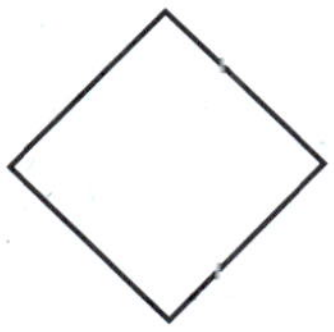

_____ sides
_____ vertices
____

6.

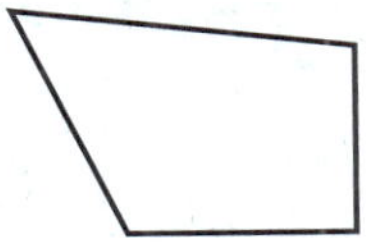

_____ sides
_____ vertices
____

7.

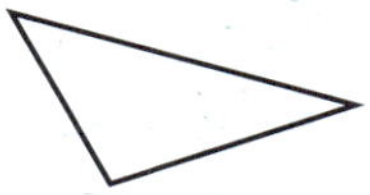

_____ sides
_____ vertices
____

8.

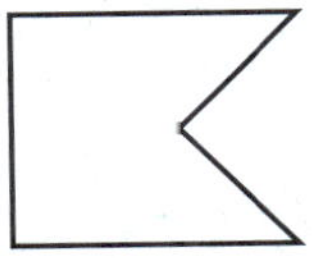

_____ sides
_____ vertices
____

9.

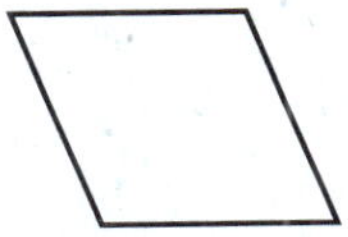

_____ sides
_____ vertices
____

H.O.T. Draw more sides to make the shape.

10. pentagon

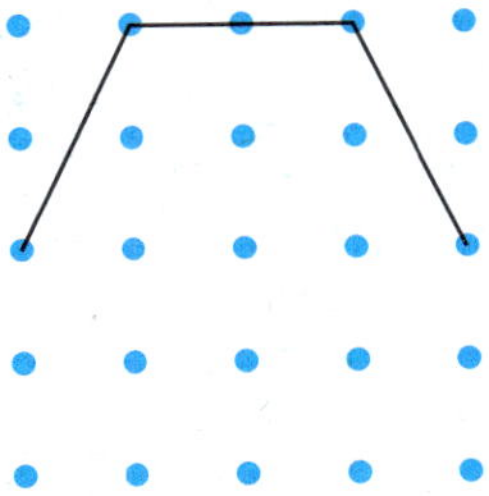

11. quadrilateral

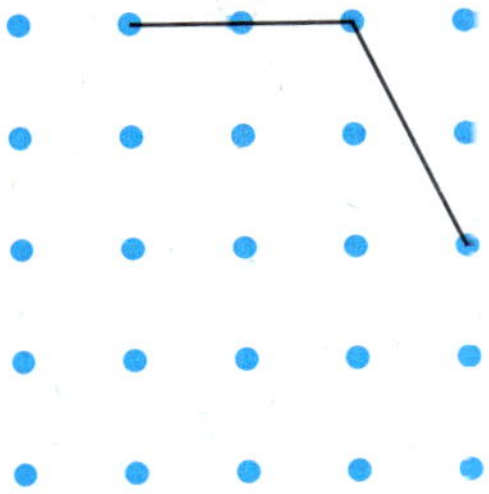

12. hexagon

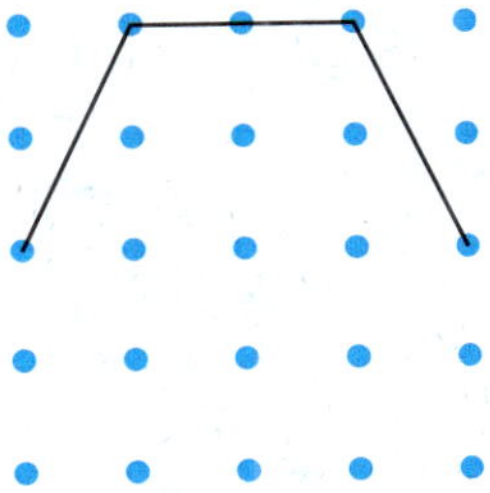

© Houghton Mifflin Harcourt Publishing Company

PROBLEM SOLVING REAL WORLD

Write Math

Solve. Draw or write to explain.

13. Alex is making a hexagon and a pentagon with straws. He uses one straw for each side of each shape. How many straws does he need?

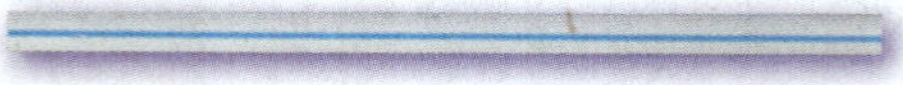

_______ straws

14. Mrs. Johnson buys 2 boxes of crayons. There are 8 crayons in each box. How many crayons are in the two boxes?

_______ crayons

15. H.O.T. Ed draws a shape that has 4 sides. It is not a square. It is not a rectangle. Draw a shape that could be Ed's shape.

16. Test Prep What is the shape of this sign?

- ○ quadrilateral
- ○ hexagon
- ○ pentagon
- ○ triangle

TAKE HOME ACTIVITY • Ask your child to draw a shape that is a quadrilateral.

© Houghton Mifflin Harcourt Publishing Company

FOR MORE PRACTICE:
Standards Practice Book, pp. P243–P244

Name ____________________

Angles in Two-Dimensional Shapes

Essential Question How do you find and count angles in two-dimensional shapes?

COMMON CORE STANDARD CC.2.G.1
Reason with shapes and their attributes.

Listen and Draw

Use a ruler. Draw two different triangles.
Then draw two different rectangles.

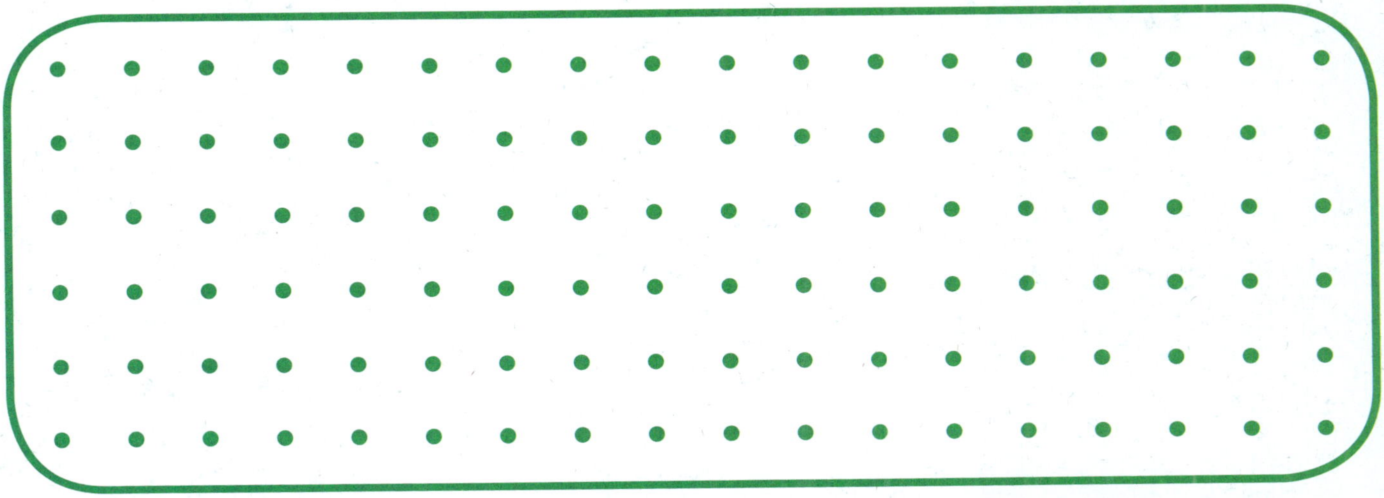

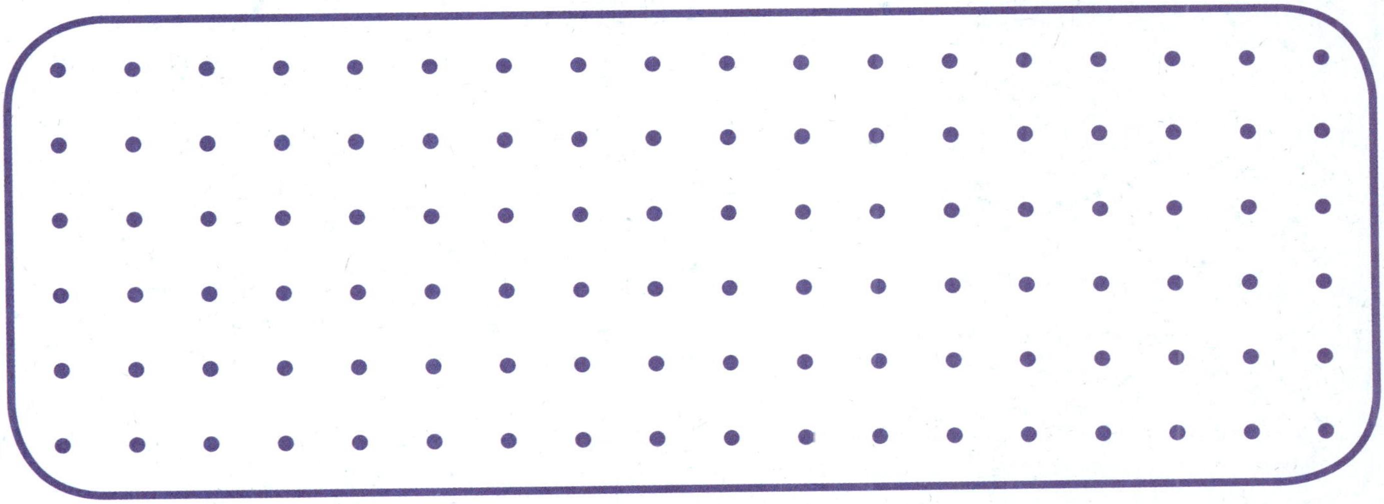

FOR THE TEACHER • Have children use pencils and rulers (or other straight edges) to draw the shapes. Have them draw two different triangles in the green box and two different rectangles in the purple box.

Math Talk

Describe a triangle and a rectangle. Tell about their sides and vertices.

© Houghton Mifflin Harcourt Publishing Company

Model and Draw

When two sides of a shape meet, they form an **angle**.

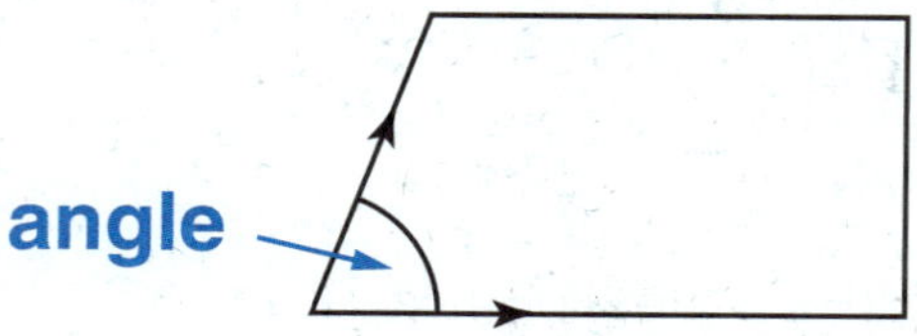

This shape has 3 angles.

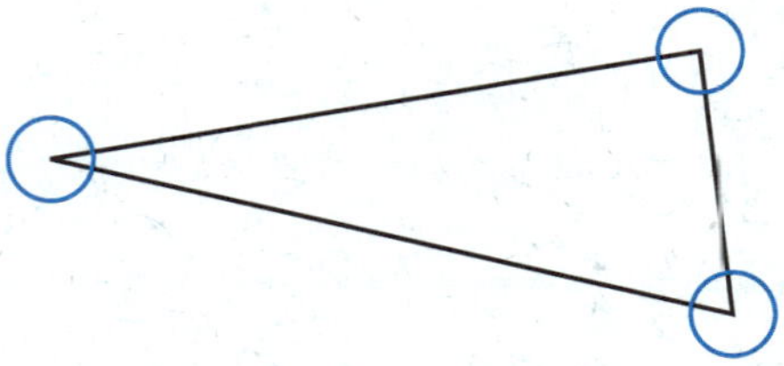

Share and Show

Circle the angles in each shape.
Write how many.

1.

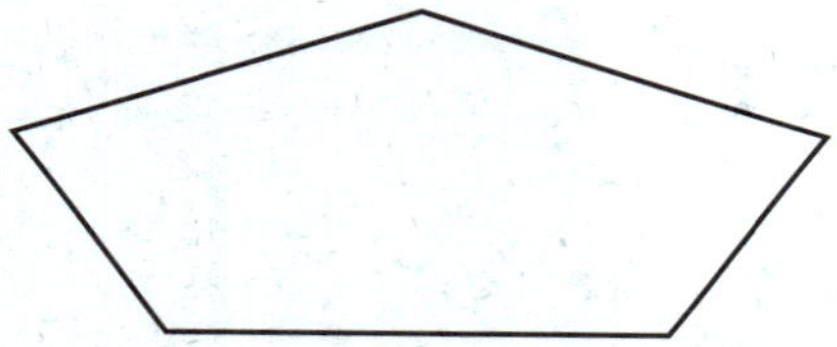

_____ angles

2.

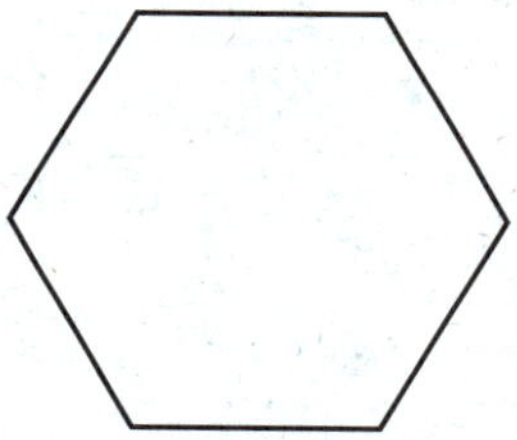

_____ angles

3.

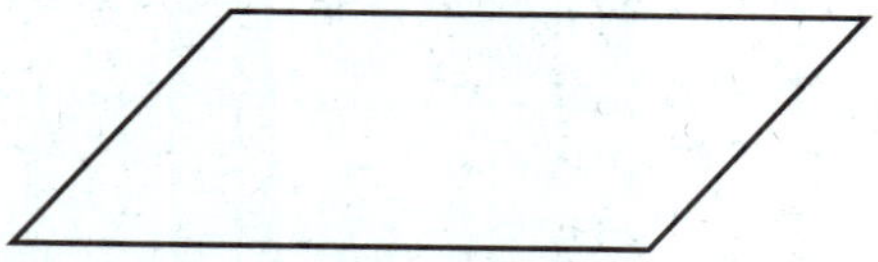

_____ angles

4.

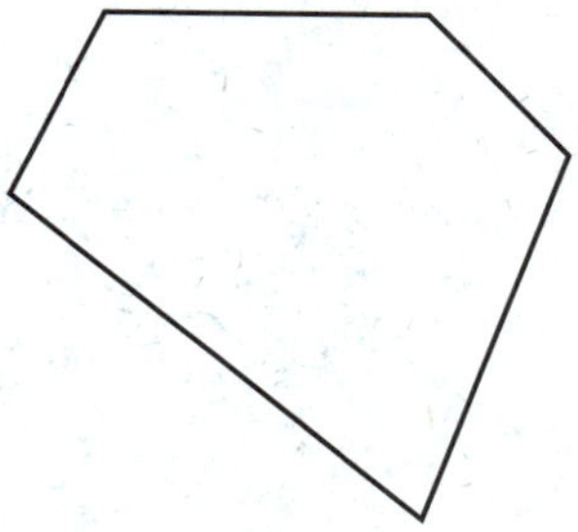

_____ angles

© Houghton Mifflin Harcourt Publishing Company

Name ______________________________

On Your Own

Circle the angles in each shape.
Write how many.

5.

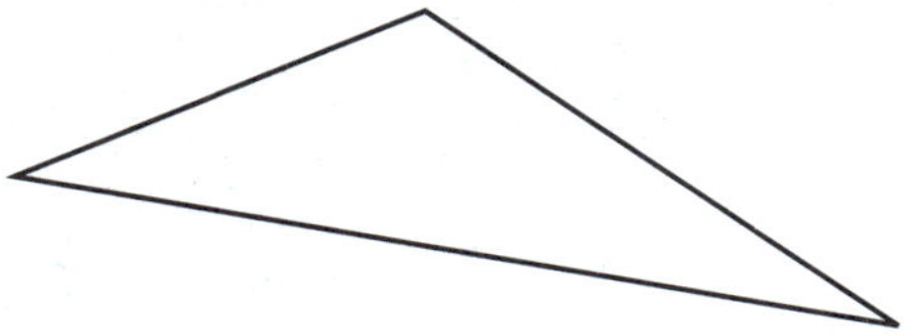

_____ angles

6.

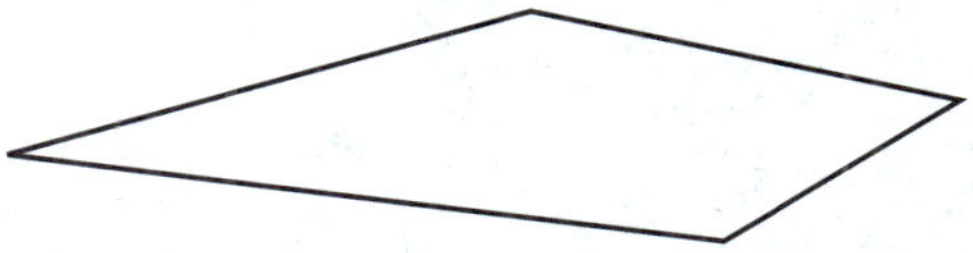

_____ angles

7.

_____ angles

8.

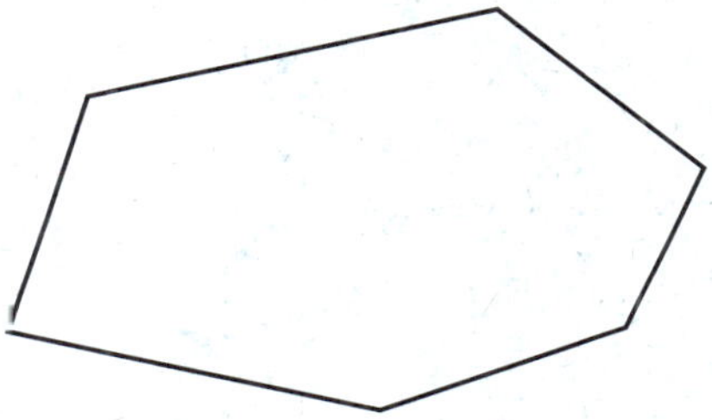

_____ angles

H.O.T. Draw more sides to make the shape.
Write how many angles.

9. pentagon

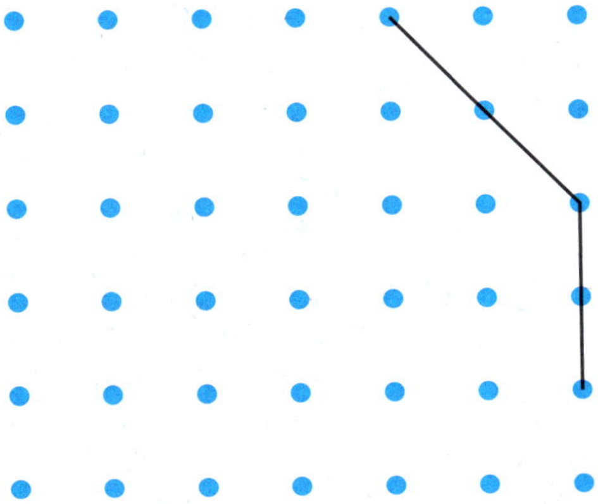

_____ angles

10. quadrilateral

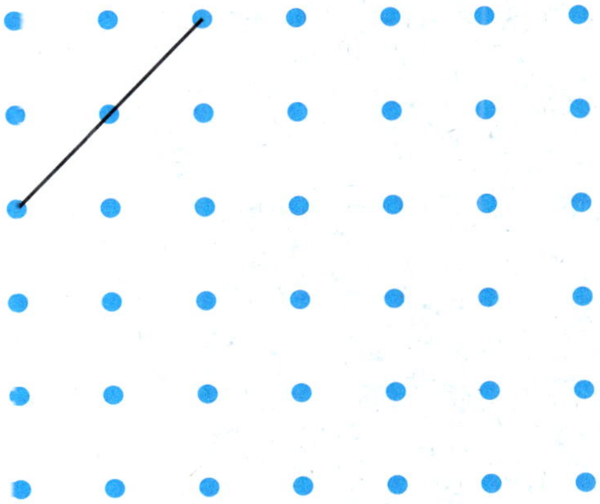

_____ angles

© Houghton Mifflin Harcourt Publishing Company

PROBLEM SOLVING REAL WORLD

Write Math

11. Amy drew 2 two-dimensional shapes that had 7 angles in all. Draw shapes Amy could have drawn.

12. H.O.T. Ben drew 3 two-dimensional shapes that had 11 angles in all. Draw shapes Ben could have drawn.

13. **Test Prep** How many angles does this shape have?

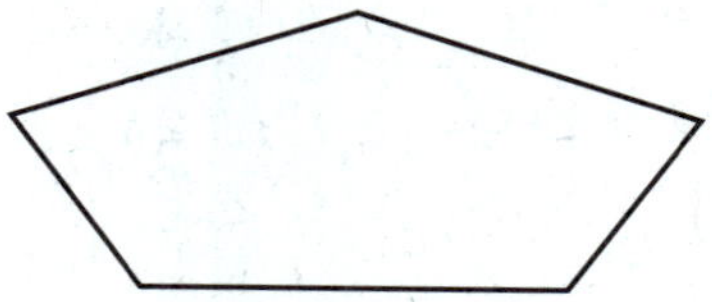

- ○ 6
- ○ 5
- ○ 4
- ○ 3

TAKE HOME ACTIVITY • Ask your child to draw a shape with 4 sides and 4 angles.

FOR MORE PRACTICE:
Standards Practice Book, pp. P245–P246

© Houghton Mifflin Harcourt Publishing Company

Name ____________________

Sort Two-Dimensional Shapes

Essential Question How do you use the number of sides and angles to sort two-dimensional shapes?

COMMON CORE STANDARD **CC.2.G.1**
Reason with shapes and their attributes.

Listen and Draw

Make the shape with pattern blocks.
Draw and color the blocks you used.

Use one block.

Use two blocks.

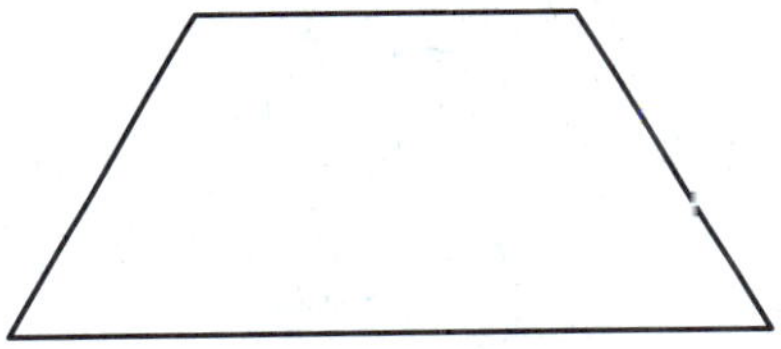

Use three blocks.

FOR THE TEACHER • Tell children that the shape shown three times on the page is a trapezoid. Have children use pattern blocks to make the trapezoid three times: with one pattern block, with two pattern blocks, and then with three pattern blocks.

Math Talk

Describe how you could sort the blocks you used.

MATHEMATICAL PRACTICES

© Houghton Mifflin Harcourt Publishing Company

Model and Draw

Which shapes match the rule?

Shapes with more than 3 sides

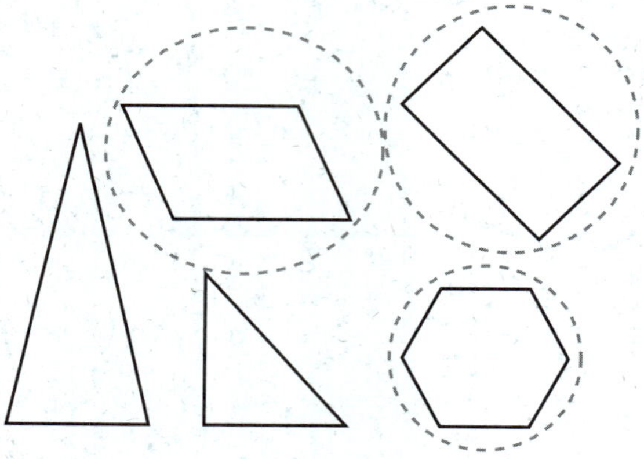

Shapes with fewer than 5 angles

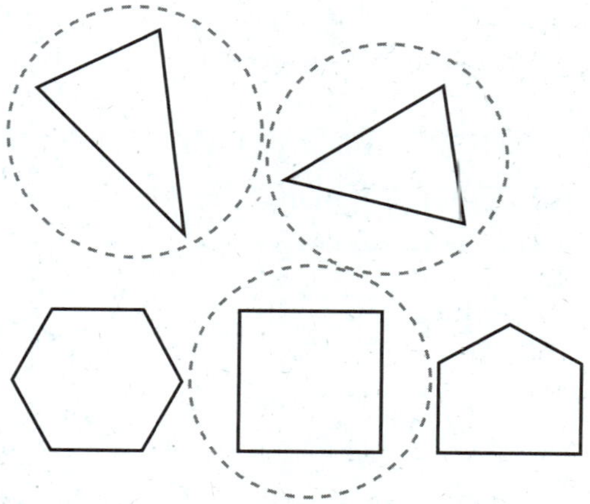

Share and Show

Circle the shapes that match the rule.

1. Shapes with 5 sides

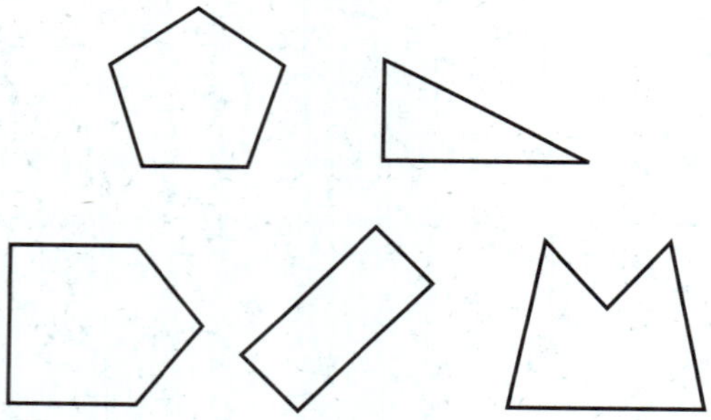

2. Shapes with more than 3 angles

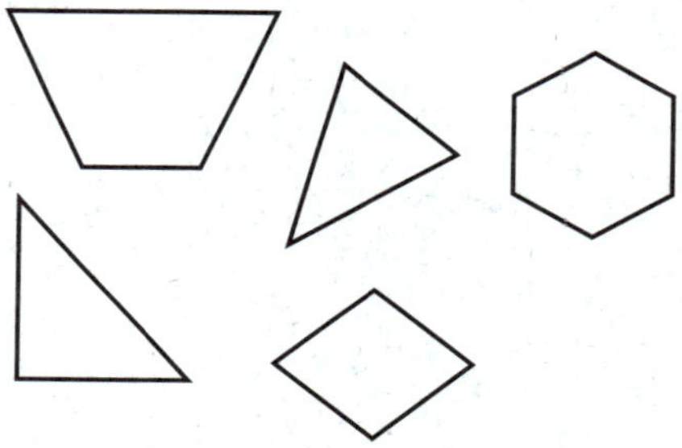

3. Shapes with fewer than 4 angles

4. Shapes with fewer than 5 sides

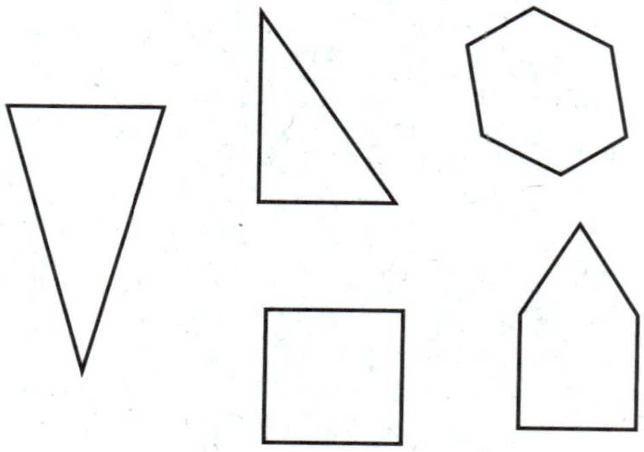

© Houghton Mifflin Harcourt Publishing Company

Name ______________________________

On Your Own

Circle the shapes that match the rule.

5. Shapes with 4 sides

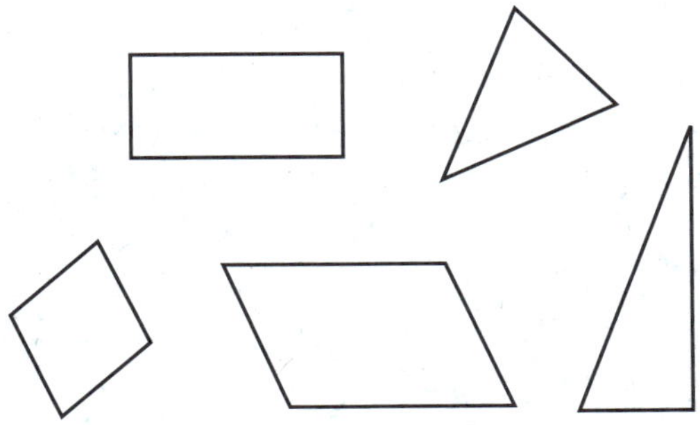

6. Shapes with more than 4 angles

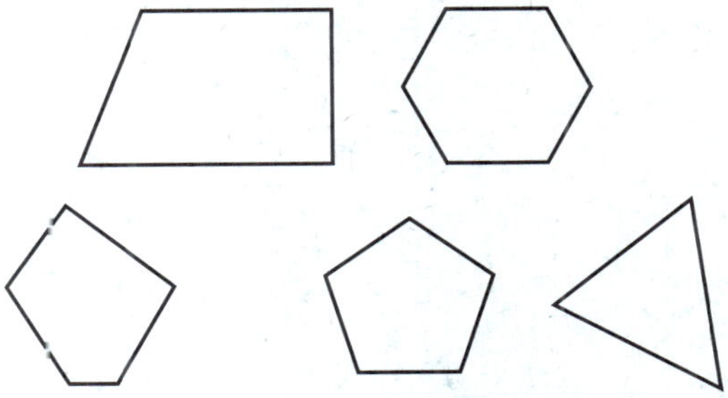

7. Shapes with fewer than 4 angles

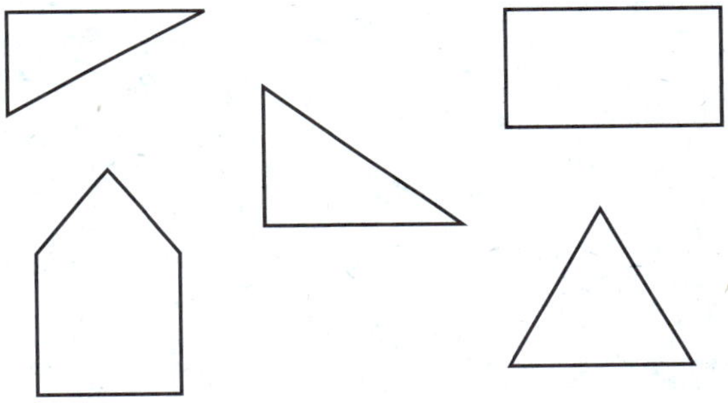

8. Shapes with fewer than 5 sides

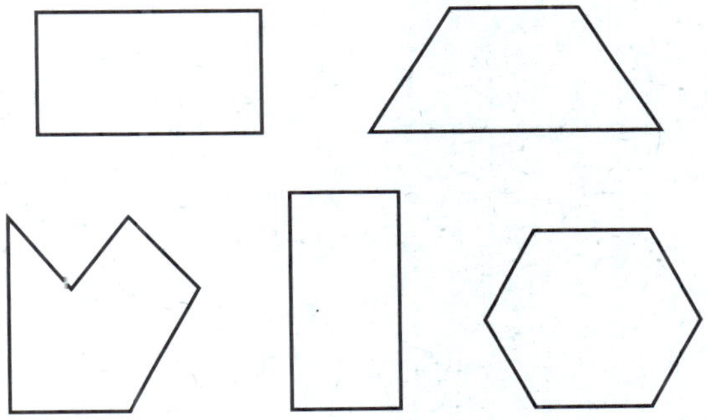

9. H.O.T. Draw three shapes that match the rule. Circle them. Then draw two shapes that do not match the rule.

Shapes with fewer than 5 angles

© Houghton Mifflin Harcourt Publishing Company

PROBLEM SOLVING

Write Math

10. Sort the shapes.

- Use red to color the shapes with more than 4 sides.
- Use blue to color the shapes with fewer than 5 angles.

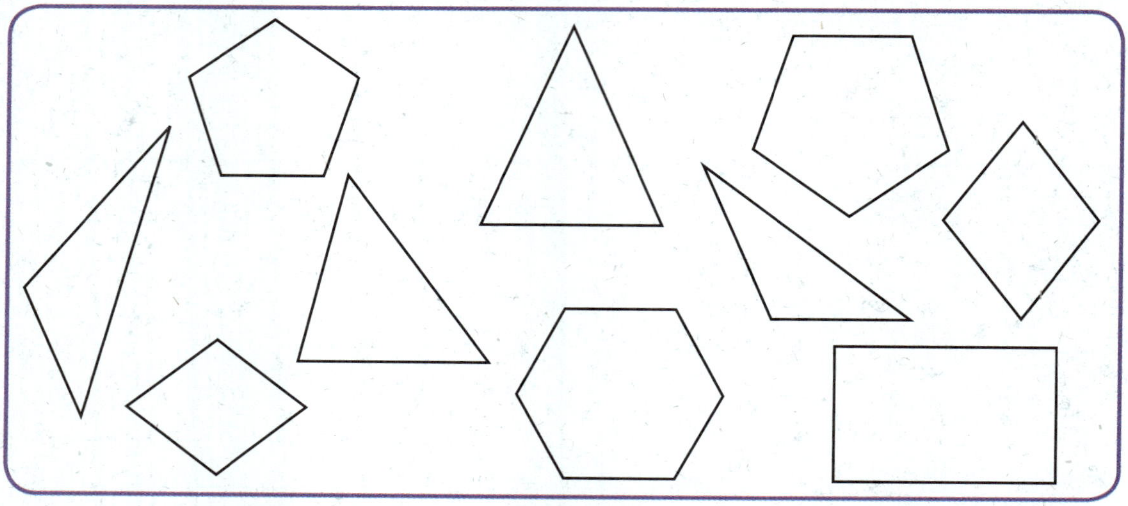

11. H.O.T. Jay plays baseball. He sees that home plate has the shape of a pentagon. How many angles does home plate have?

______ angles

12. Test Prep Which of these shapes has fewer than 4 angles?

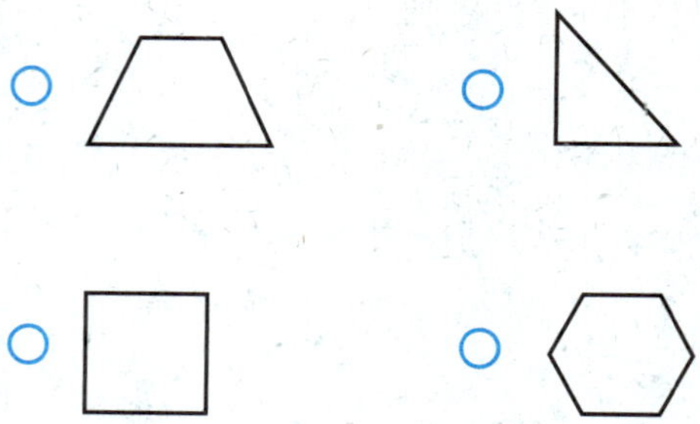

TAKE HOME ACTIVITY • Ask your child to draw some shapes that each have 4 angles.

© Houghton Mifflin Harcourt Publishing Company

FOR MORE PRACTICE:
Standards Practice Book, pp. P247–P248

Name ______________________________

Partition Rectangles

Essential Question How do you find the total number of same-size squares that will cover a rectangle?

HANDS ON
Lesson 11.6

COMMON CORE STANDARD CC.2.G.2
Reason with shapes and their attributes.

Listen and Draw

Put several color tiles together. Trace around the shape to draw a two-dimensional shape.

Math Talk
Is there a different shape that can be made with the same number of tiles? **Explain.**

HOME CONNECTION • After putting together tiles, your child traced around them to draw a two-dimensional shape. This activity is an introduction to partitioning a rectangle into several same-size squares.

© Houghton Mifflin Harcourt Publishing Company

Model and Draw

Trace around color tiles. How many square tiles cover this rectangle?

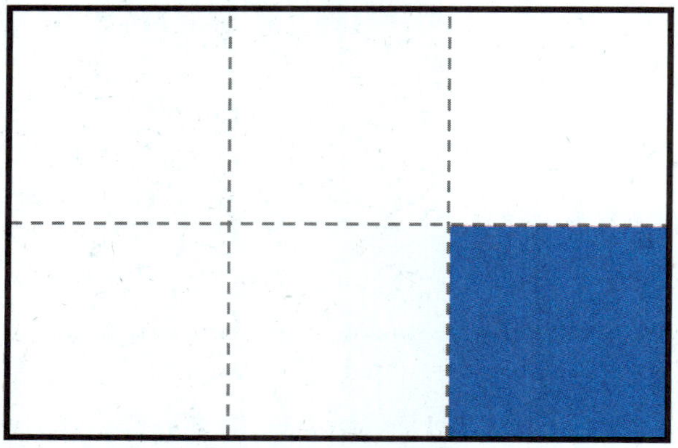

Number of rows: 2

Number of columns: 3

Total: ______ square tiles

Share and Show

Use color tiles to cover the rectangle.
Trace around the square tiles. Write how many.

1.

Number of rows: ______

Number of columns: ______

Total: ______ square tiles

2.

Number of rows: ______

Number of columns: ______

Total: ______ square tiles

© Houghton Mifflin Harcourt Publishing Company

Name ______________________________

On Your Own

Use color tiles to cover the rectangle.
Trace around the square tiles. Write how many.

3. 

Number of rows: ______

Number of columns: ______

Total: ______ square tiles

4. 

Number of rows: ______

Number of columns: ______

Total: ______ square tiles

5. 

Mary started to cover this rectangle with ones blocks. **Explain** how you would estimate the number of ones blocks that would cover the whole rectangle.

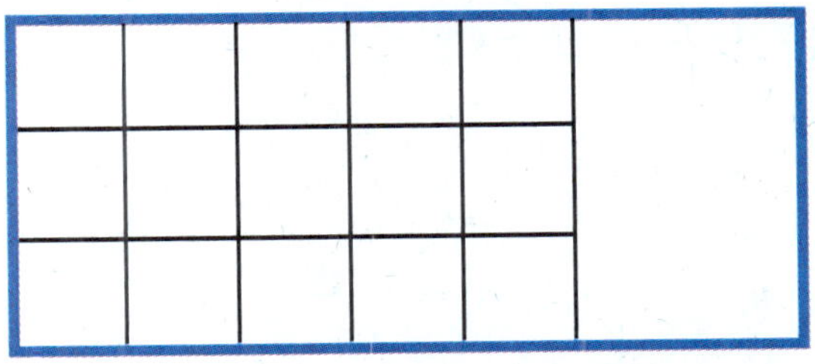

____

____

TAKE HOME ACTIVITY • Have your child describe what he or she did in this lesson.

FOR MORE PRACTICE:
Standards Practice Book, pp. P249–P250

© Houghton Mifflin Harcourt Publishing Company

Name ____________________

Mid-Chapter Checkpoint

Concepts and Skills

Circle the objects that match the shape name. (CC.2.G.1)

1. cylinder				
2. cube				

Write the number of sides and the number of vertices. (CC.2.G.1)

3. quadrilateral

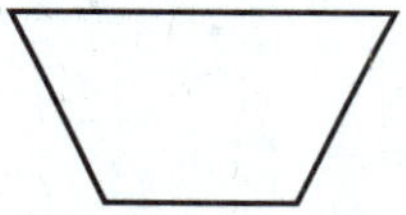

_____ sides

_____ vertices

4. pentagon

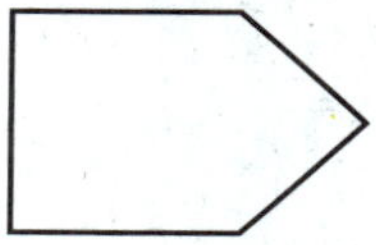

_____ sides

_____ vertices

5. hexagon

_____ sides

_____ vertices

Test Prep

6. Which of these shapes has more than 4 angles? (CC.2.G.1)

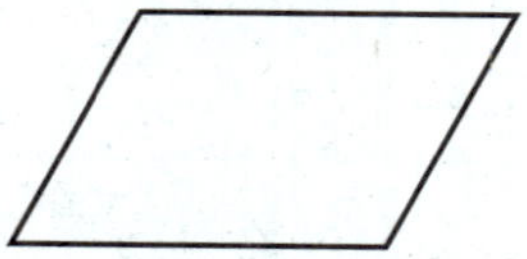

○

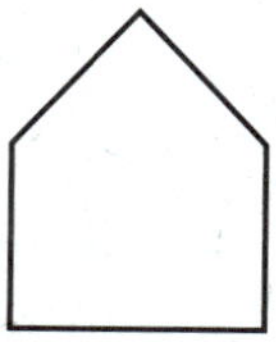

○

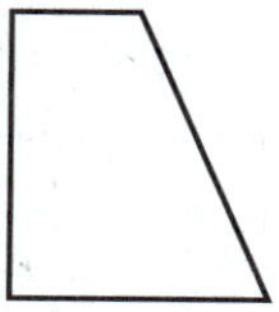

○

○

© Houghton Mifflin Harcourt Publishing Company

Name ______________________________

Equal Parts

Essential Question What are halves, thirds, and fourths of a whole?

COMMON CORE STANDARD CC.2.G.3
Reason with shapes and their attributes.

Listen and Draw

Put pattern blocks together to match the shape of the hexagon. Trace the shape you made.

FOR THE TEACHER • Have children place a yellow hexagon pattern block on the workspace and make the same shape by using any combination of pattern blocks. Discuss how they know if the outline of the blocks they used is the same shape as the yellow hexagon.

Math Talk
Describe how the shapes you used are different from the shapes a classmate used.

MATHEMATICAL PRACTICES

© Houghton Mifflin Harcourt Publishing Company

Model and Draw

The green rectangle is the whole.
It can be divided into equal parts.

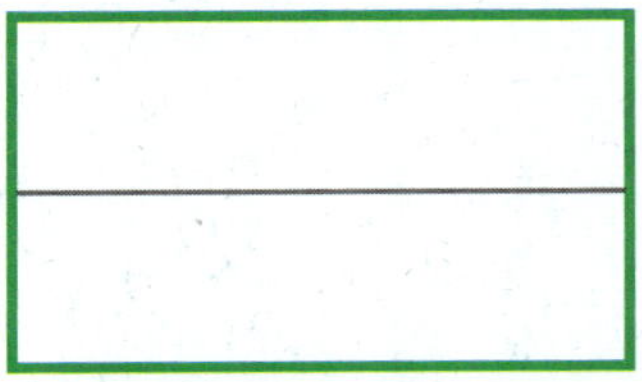

There are 2 **halves**.
Each part is a half.

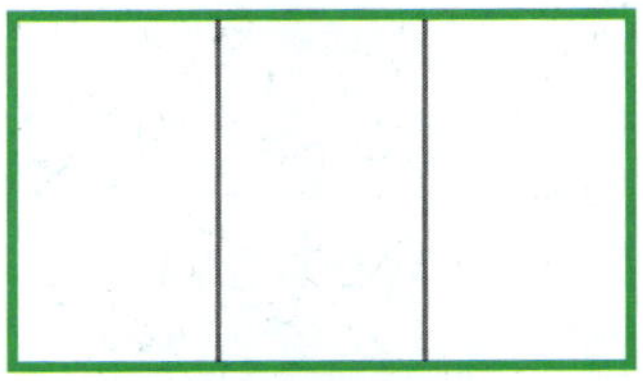

There are 3 **thirds**.
Each part is a third.

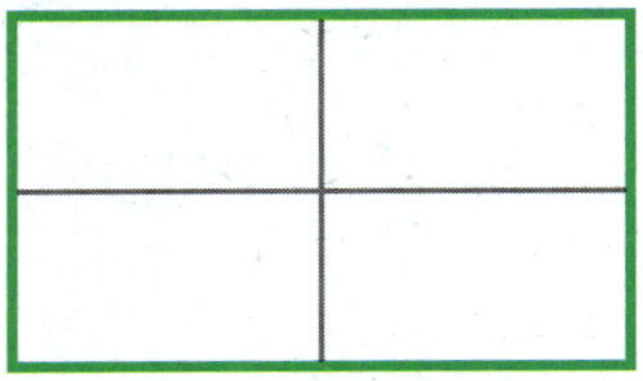

There are 4 **fourths**.
Each part is a fourth.

Share and Show

Math Board

Write how many equal parts there are in the whole.
Write **halves**, **thirds**, or **fourths** to name the equal parts.

1.

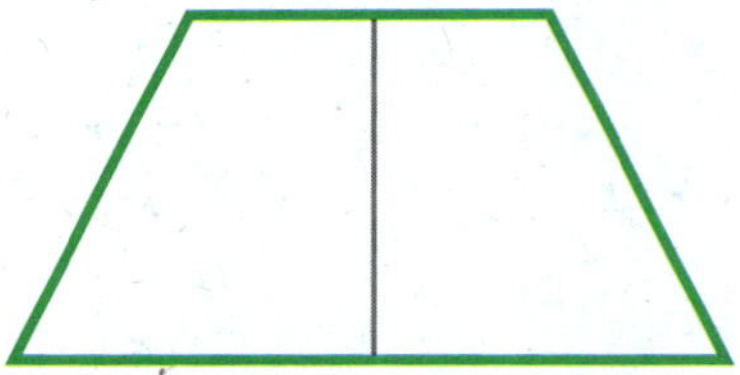

_____ equal parts

____

2.

_____ equal parts

____

3.

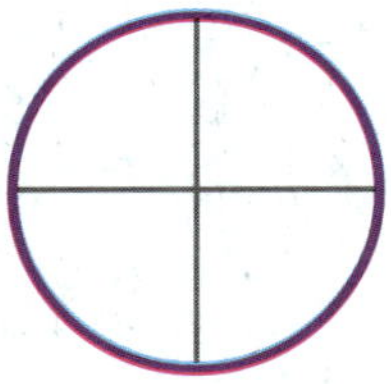

_____ equal parts

____

4.

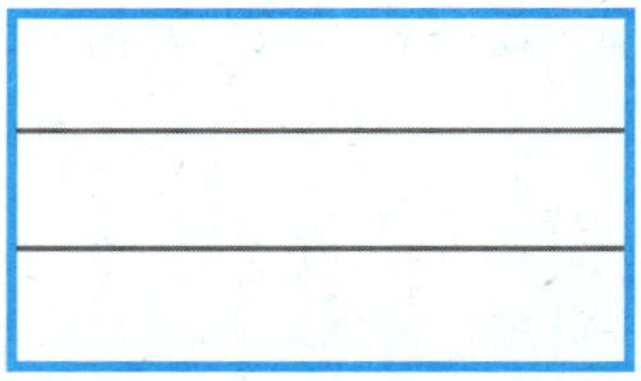

_____ equal parts

____

5.

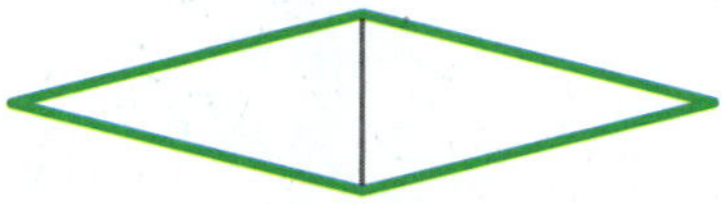

_____ equal parts

____

6.

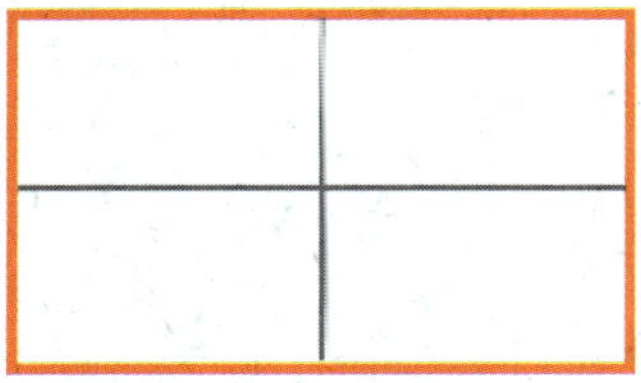

_____ equal parts

____

© Houghton Mifflin Harcourt Publishing Company

Name ______________________________

On Your Own

Write how many equal parts there are in the whole.
Write **halves**, **thirds**, or **fourths** to name the equal parts.

7.
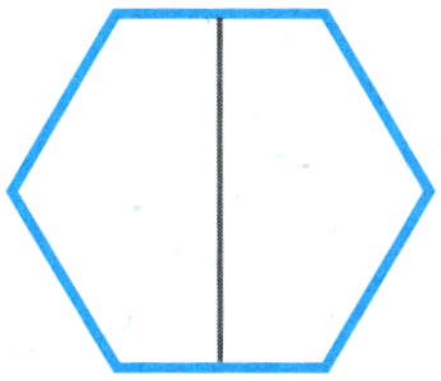

_____ equal parts

____

8.

_____ equal parts

____

9.
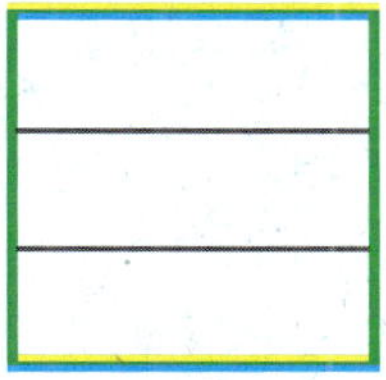

_____ equal parts

____

10.
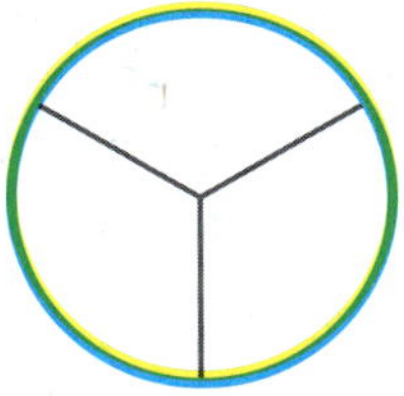

_____ equal parts

____

11.
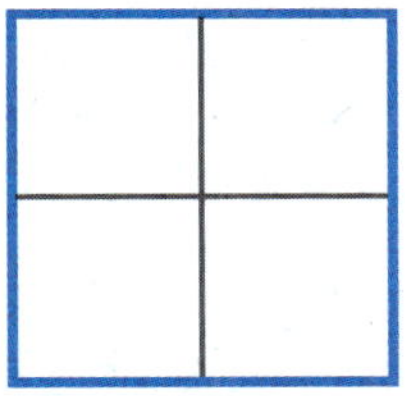

_____ equal parts

____

12.
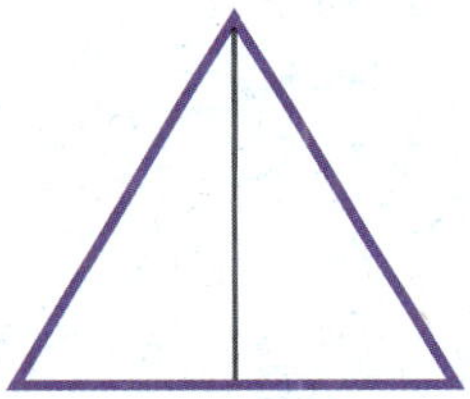

_____ equal parts

____

13.

_____ equal parts

____

14.
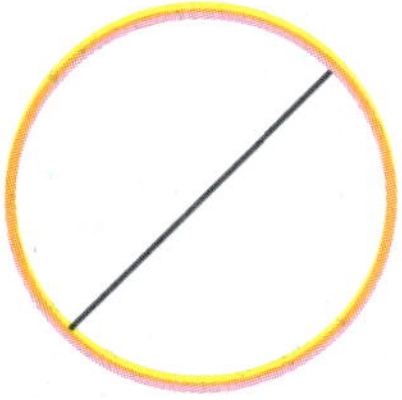

_____ equal parts

____

15.
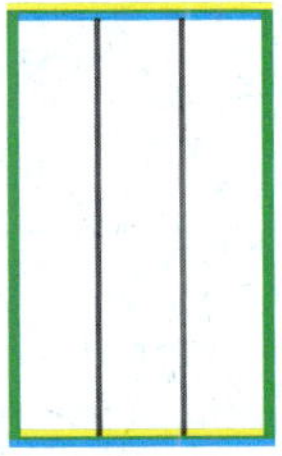

_____ equal parts

____

© Houghton Mifflin Harcourt Publishing Company

PROBLEM SOLVING

Write Math

16. Sort the shapes.

- Draw an X on shapes that do **not** show equal parts.
- Use red to color the shapes that show thirds.
- Use blue to color the shapes that show fourths.

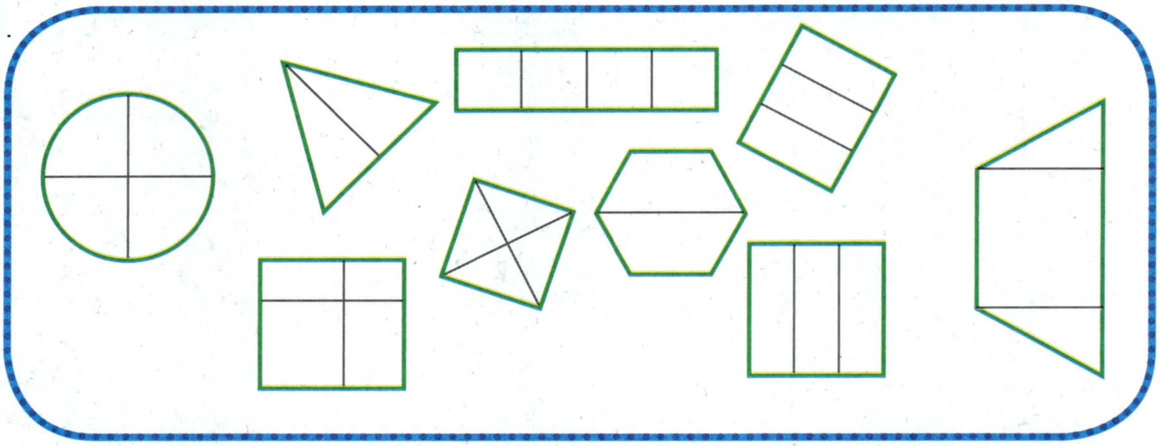

17. H.O.T. Draw to show halves. Explain how you know that the parts are halves.

____

____

18. Test Prep Which shape has parts that are fourths?

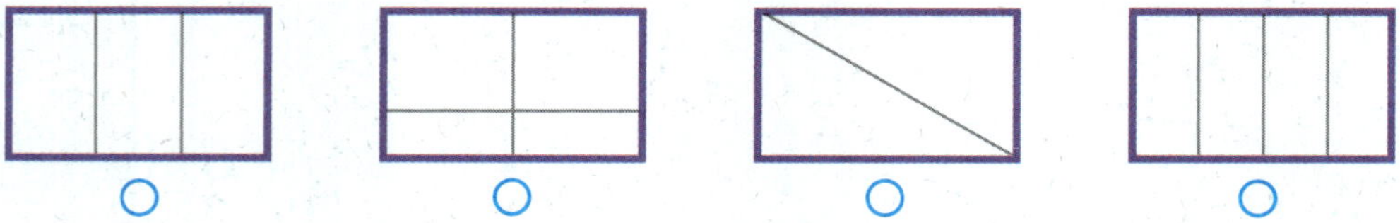

TAKE HOME ACTIVITY • Ask your child to fold one sheet of paper into halves and another sheet of paper into fourths.

FOR MORE PRACTICE:
Standards Practice Book, pp. P251–P252

© Houghton Mifflin Harcourt Publishing Company

Name ______________________________

Show Equal Parts of a Whole

Essential Question How do you know if a shape shows halves, thirds, or fourths?

COMMON CORE STANDARD CC.2.G.3
Reason with shapes and their attributes.

Listen and Draw

Circle the shapes that show equal parts.

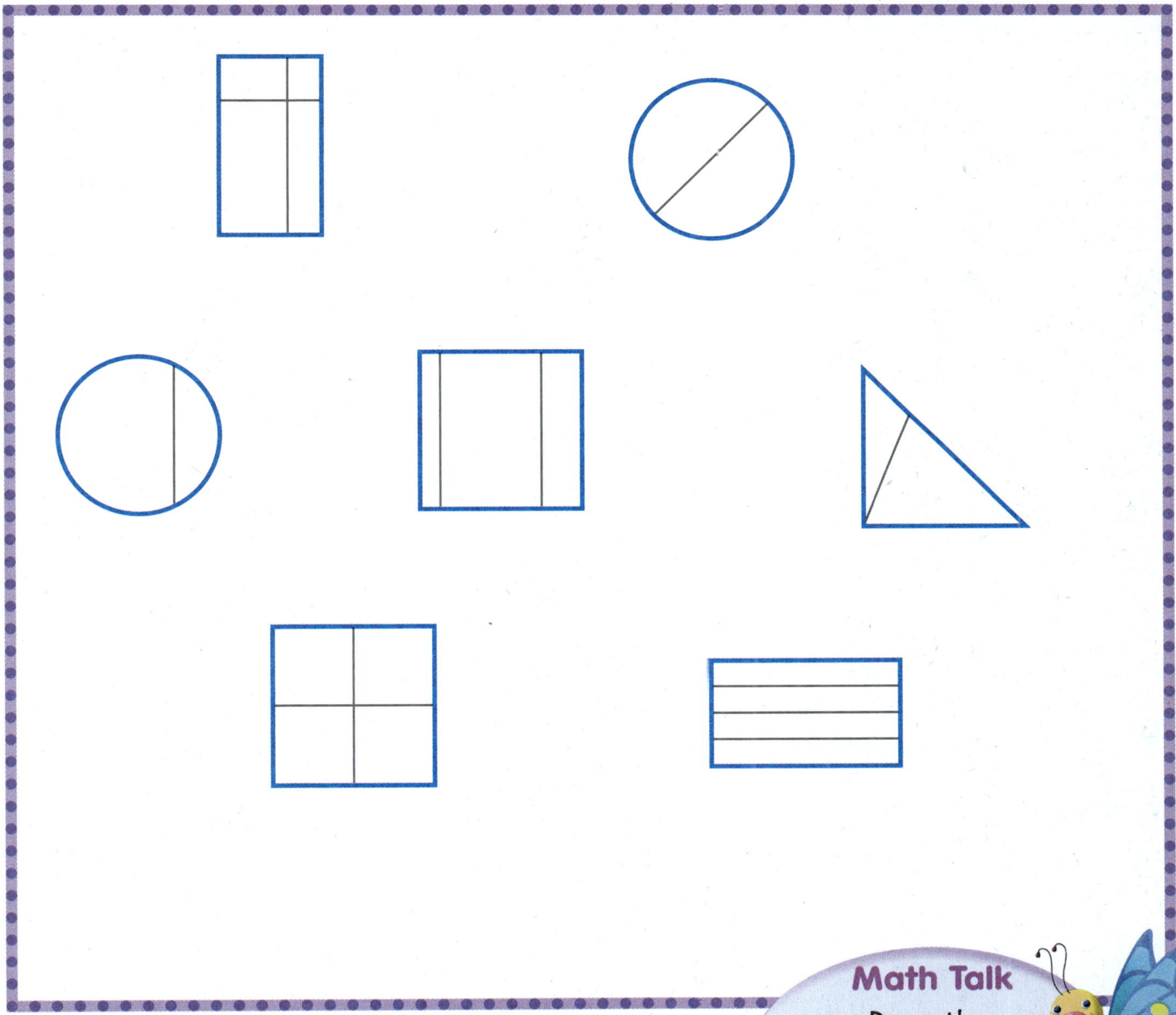

HOME CONNECTION • Your child completed this sorting activity with shapes to review the concept of equal parts.

Math Talk

Does the triangle show halves? **Explain.**

MATHEMATICAL PRACTICES

© Houghton Mifflin Harcourt Publishing Company

Model and Draw

You can draw to show equal parts of a whole.

halves
2 equal parts

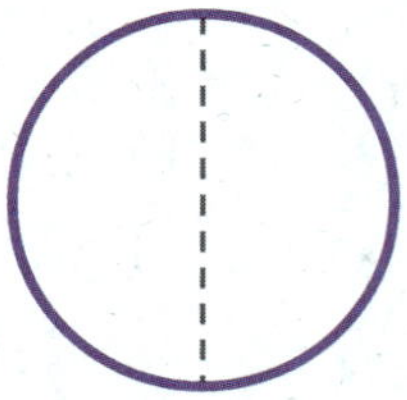

There are 2 halves in a whole.

thirds
3 equal parts

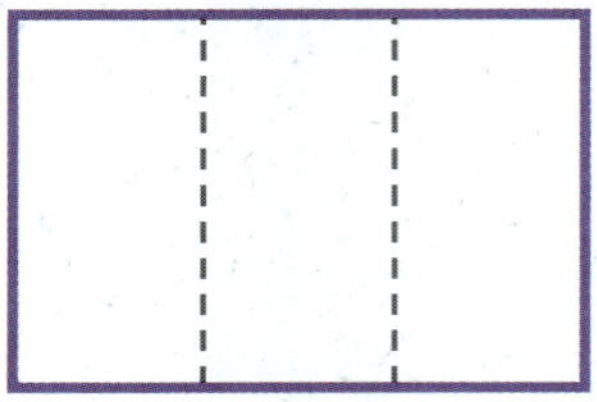

There are 3 thirds in a whole.

fourths
4 equal parts

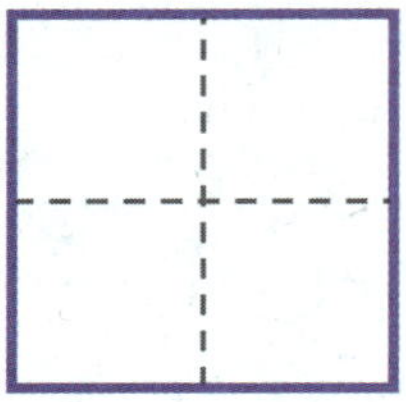

There are 4 fourths in a whole.

Share and Show

Math Board

Draw to show equal parts.

1. thirds

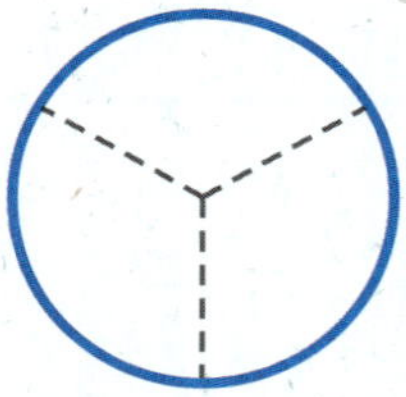

2. halves

3. fourths

4. halves

5. fourths

6. thirds

© Houghton Mifflin Harcourt Publishing Company

Name ______________________

On Your Own

Draw to show equal parts.

7. halves

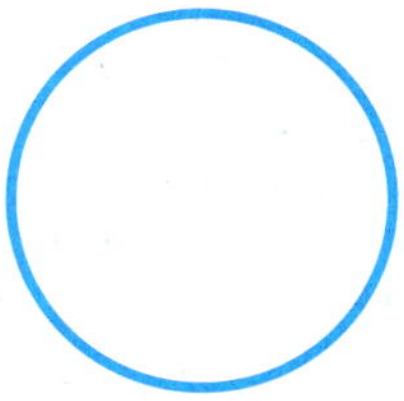

8. fourths

9. thirds

10. thirds

11. halves

12. fourths

13. halves

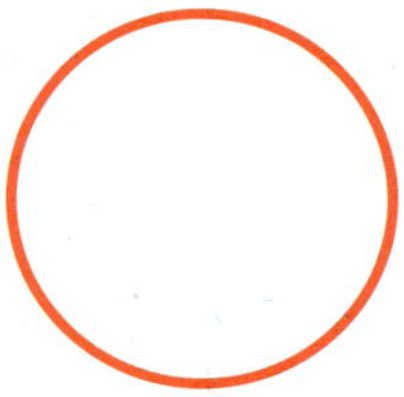

14. thirds

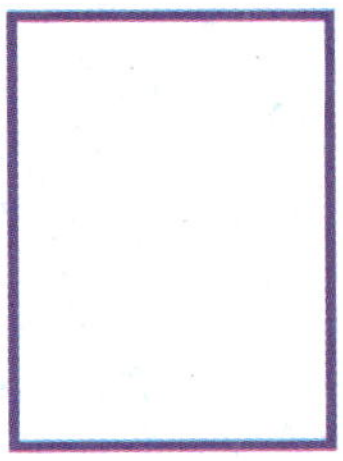

15. fourths

16. Does this shape show thirds? **Explain.**

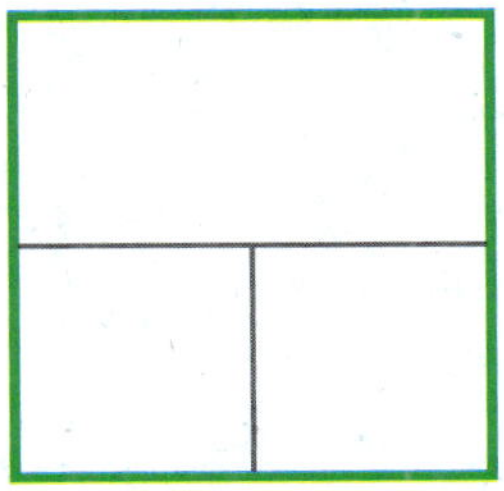

____

____

____

____

© Houghton Mifflin Harcourt Publishing Company

PROBLEM SOLVING REAL WORLD

Write Math

Solve. Write or draw to explain.

17. Mrs. Blackwell has one muffin. She cuts the muffin into halves. How many pieces of muffin does she have?

______ pieces

18. H.O.T. There are two square pizzas. Each pizza is cut into fourths. How many pieces of pizza are there?

______ pieces

19. **Test Prep** A piece of ribbon is cut into thirds. How many pieces of ribbon are there?

- ○ 2
- ○ 3
- ○ 4
- ○ 6

TAKE HOME ACTIVITY • Have your child explain how he or she solved Exercise 18.

© Houghton Mifflin Harcourt Publishing Company

FOR MORE PRACTICE:
Standards Practice Book, pp. P253–P254

Name ______________________________

Describe Equal Parts

COMMON CORE STANDARD CC.2.G.3
Reason with shapes and their attributes.

Essential Question How do you find a half of, a third of, or a fourth of a whole?

Listen and Draw

Find shapes that show fourths and color them green.
Find shapes that show halves and color them red.

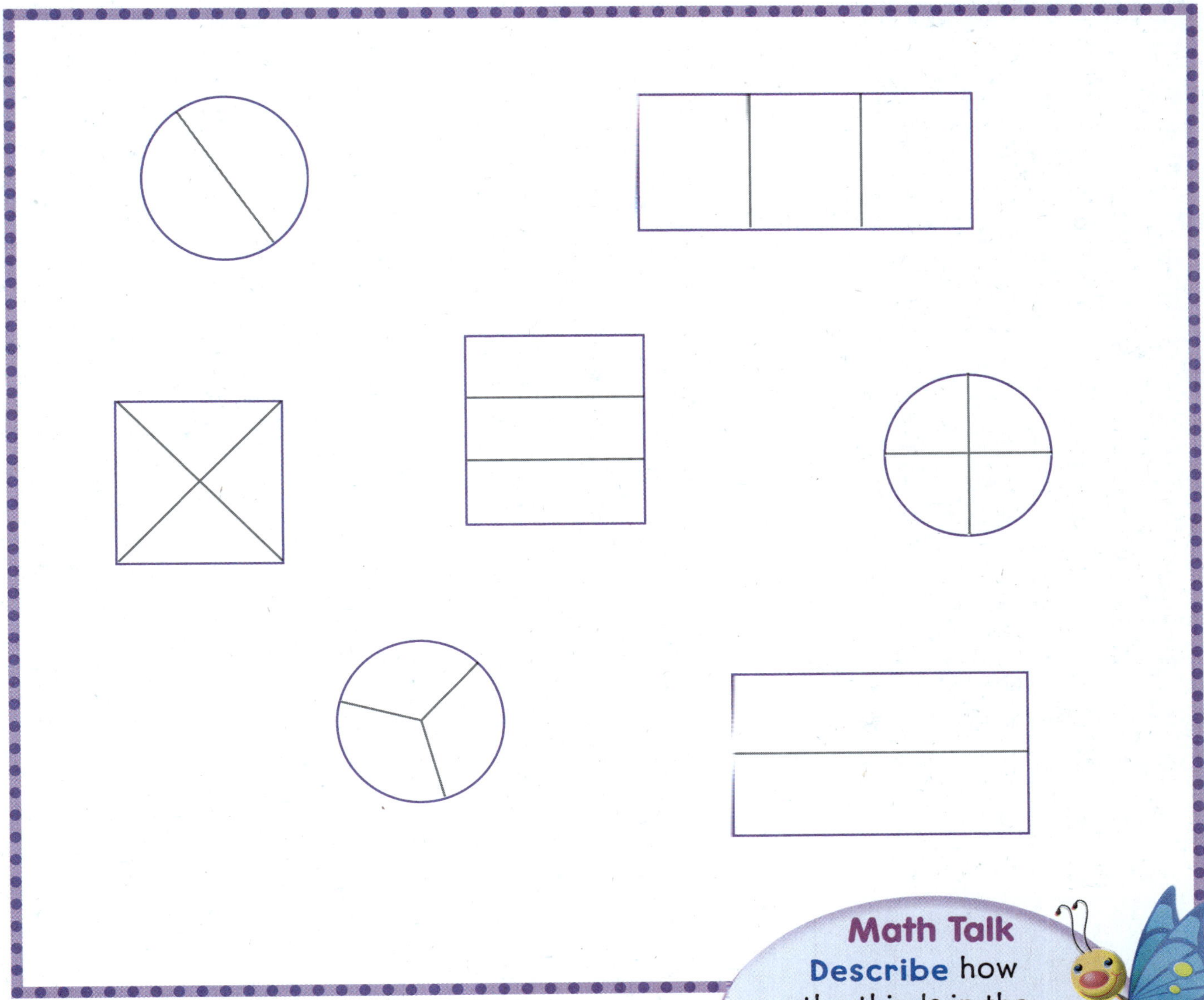

Math Talk
Describe how the thirds in the unshaded shapes compare to each other.

MATHEMATICAL PRACTICES

HOME CONNECTION • Your child identified the number of equal parts in shapes to review describing equal parts of a whole.

© Houghton Mifflin Harcourt Publishing Company

Model and Draw

These are some ways to show and describe an equal part of a whole.

1 of 4 equal parts is called a **quarter of** that shape.

2 equal parts

A **half of** the shape is green.

3 equal parts

A **third of** the shape is green.

4 equal parts

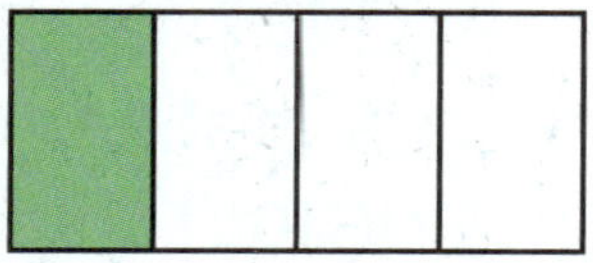

A **fourth of** the shape is green.

Share and Show

Math Board

Draw to show thirds.
Color a third of the shape.

1.

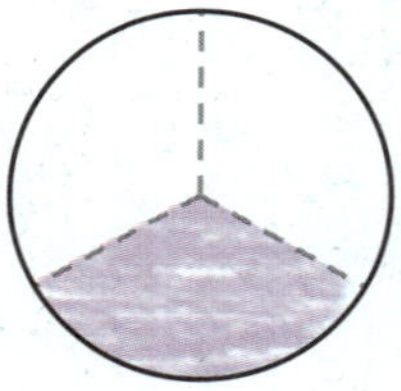

2.

3.

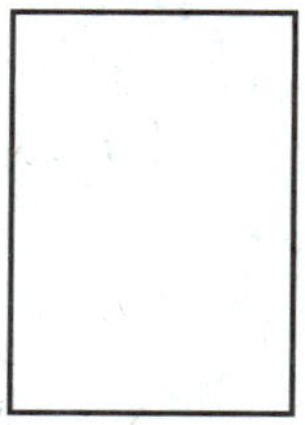

Draw to show fourths.
Color a fourth of the shape.

4.

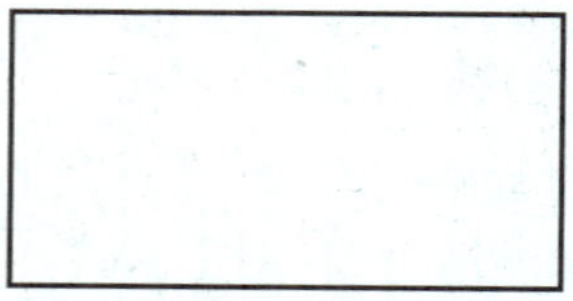

5.

6.

© Houghton Mifflin Harcourt Publishing Company

Name ______________________________

On Your Own

Draw to show halves.
Color a half of the shape.

7.

8.

9.

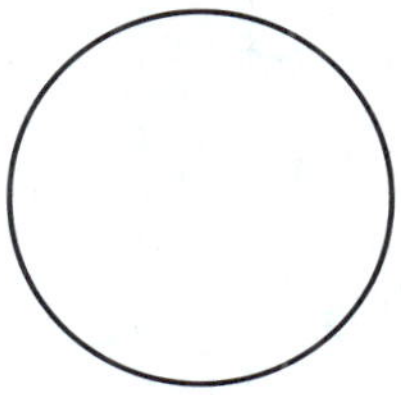

Draw to show thirds.
Color a third of the shape.

10.

11.

12.

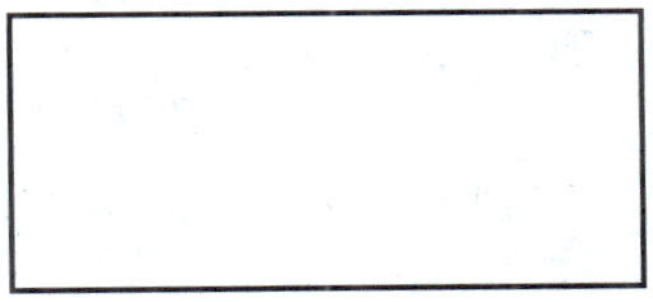

Draw to show fourths.
Color a fourth of the shape.

13.

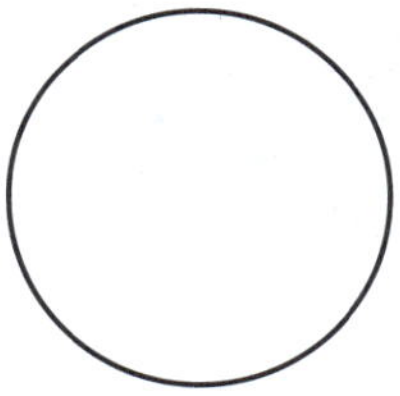

14.

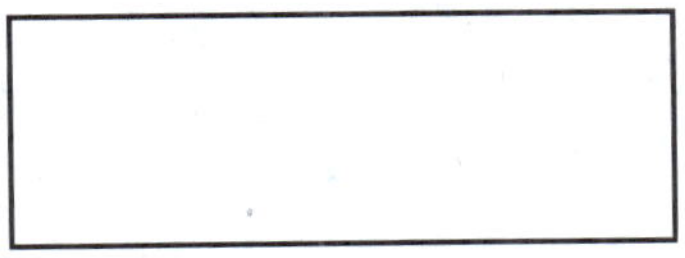

15.

© Houghton Mifflin Harcourt Publishing Company

PROBLEM SOLVING

Write Math

16. Circle all the shapes that have a quarter of the shape shaded.

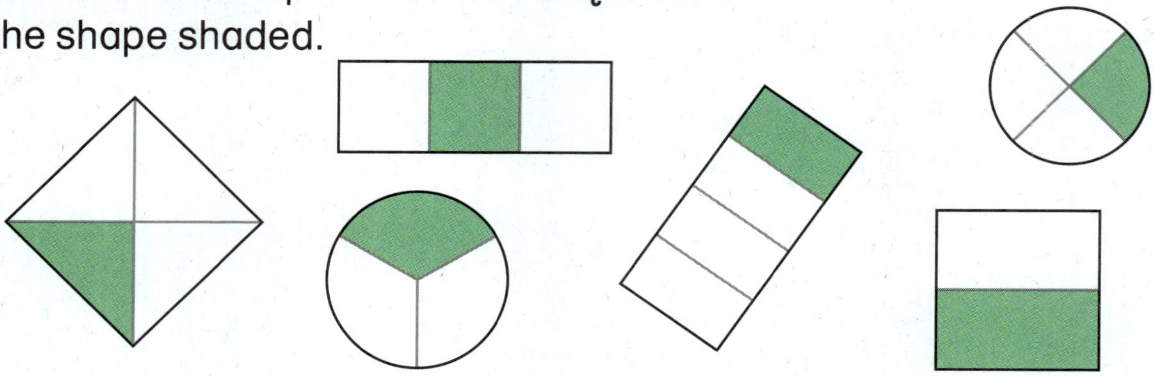

17. H.O.T. Two posters are the same size. A third of one poster is red, and a fourth of the other poster is blue.

Is the red part or the blue part larger? Draw and write to explain.

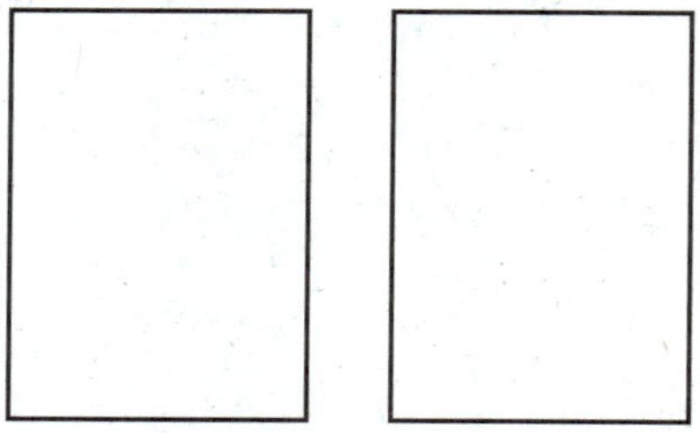

____

____

____

____

18. **Test Prep** Which of these has a third of the shape shaded blue?

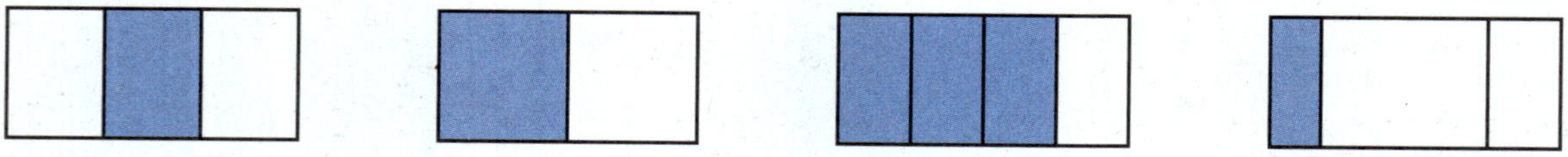

○ ○ ○ ○

TAKE HOME ACTIVITY • Draw a square. Have your child draw to show thirds and color a third of the square.

© Houghton Mifflin Harcourt Publishing Company

FOR MORE PRACTICE: Standards Practice Book, pp. P255–P256

Name ______________________

Problem Solving • Equal Shares

Essential Question How can drawing a diagram help when solving problems about equal shares?

PROBLEM SOLVING
Lesson 11.10

COMMON CORE STANDARD CC.2.G.3
Reason with shapes and their attributes.

There are two sandwiches that are the same size. Each sandwich is divided into fourths, but the sandwiches are cut differently. How might the two sandwiches be cut?

Unlock the Problem REAL WORLD

What do I need to find?

how the sandwiches could be cut

What information do I need to use?

There are _____ sandwiches. Each sandwich is divided into ______________.

Show how to solve the problem.

HOME CONNECTION • Your child drew a diagram to represent and solve a problem about dividing a whole in different ways to show equal shares.

© Houghton Mifflin Harcourt Publishing Company

Try Another Problem

Draw to show your answer.

- What do I need to find?
- What information do I need to use?

1. Roger has two square sheets of paper that are the same size. He wants to cut each sheet into halves. What are two different ways he can cut the sheets of paper?

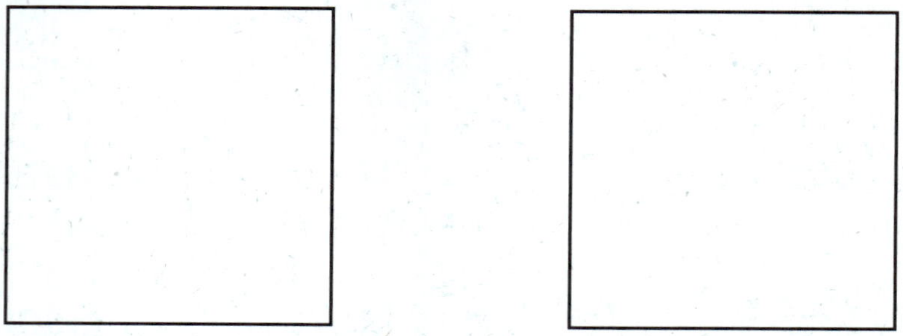

2. Dana has two pieces of cloth that are the same size. She needs to divide each piece into thirds. What are two different ways she can divide the pieces of cloth?

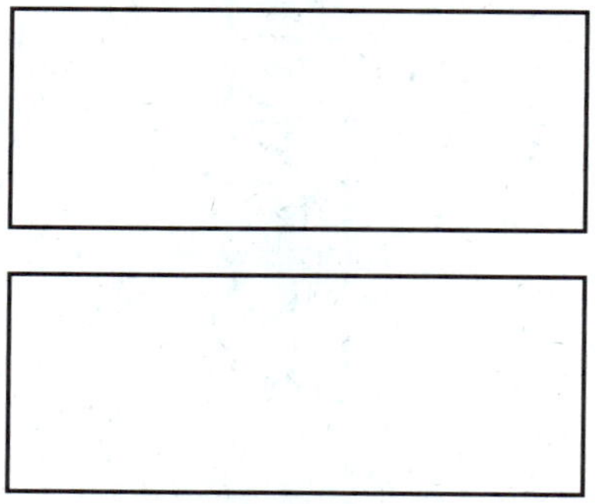

Math Talk

In Problem 2, **explain** how a third of the two pieces of cloth are alike and how they are different.

MATHEMATICAL PRACTICES

© Houghton Mifflin Harcourt Publishing Company

Name ______________________

Share and Show

Math Board

Draw to show your answer.

✓ 3. Brandon has two pieces of toast that are the same size. What are two different ways he can divide the pieces of toast into halves?

✓ 4. Mr. Rivera has two small cakes that are the same size. What are two different ways he can cut the cakes into fourths?

5. Erin has two ribbons that are the same size. What are two different ways she can divide the ribbons into thirds?

© Houghton Mifflin Harcourt Publishing Company

On Your Own

Solve. Write or draw to explain.

Write Math

6. Patty has 75 beads in a box. 28 beads are red and the rest are blue. How many blue beads does Patty have?

_______ blue beads

7. H.O.T. Dave has only quarters and dimes. He has the same number of quarters as dimes. The total value of his coins is 70¢. What coins does Dave have?

_______ quarters

_______ dimes

8. **Test Prep** Emma cuts a piece of paper into fourths like this.

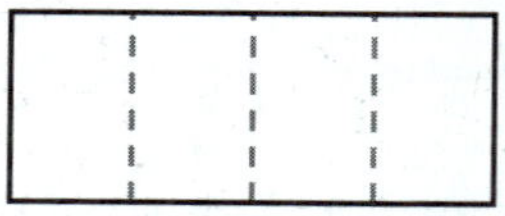

Which of the following shows another way to cut the paper into fourths?

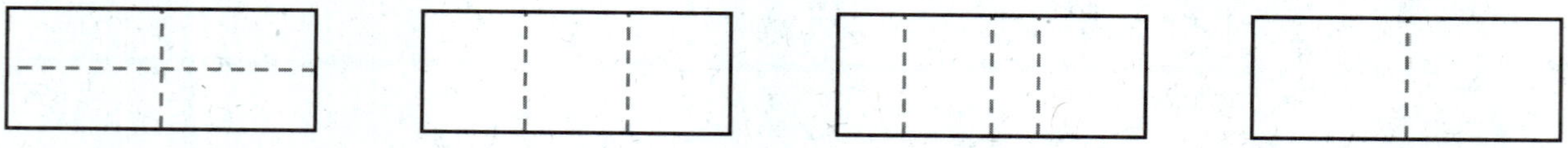

○ ○ ○ ○

TAKE HOME ACTIVITY • Ask your child to draw two rectangles and show two different ways to divide them into fourths.

© Houghton Mifflin Harcourt Publishing Company

FOR MORE PRACTICE: Standards Practice Book, pp. P257–P258

Name ______________________

Chapter 11 Review/Test

Vocabulary

Use a word in the box to complete each sentence.

third of
fourth of
sphere
pentagon

1. A basketball has the shape of a ______________. (p. 510)

2. A ______________ has 5 sides and 5 angles. (p. 518)

3. One of three equal parts of a shape is a ______________ the shape. (p. 542)

Concepts and Skills

Circle the shapes that match the rule. (CC.2.G.1)

4. Shapes with more than 3 angles

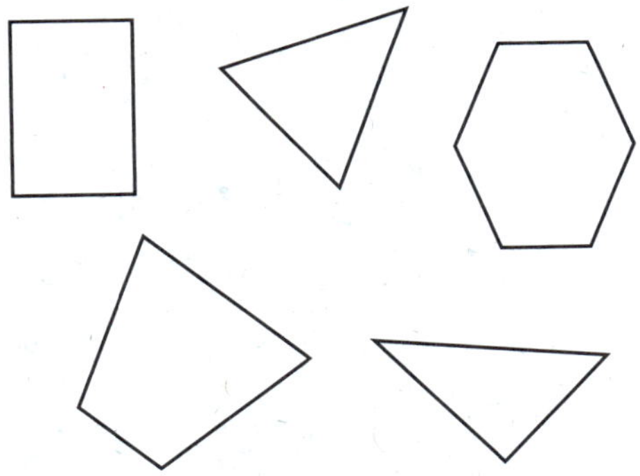

5. Shapes with fewer than 5 sides

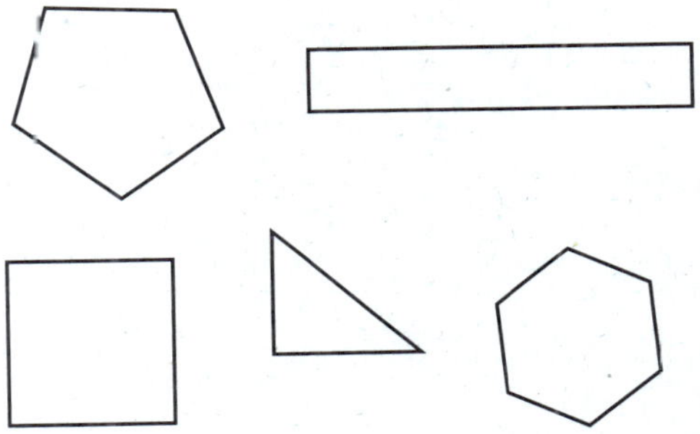

Draw to show equal parts. (CC.2.G.3)

6. thirds

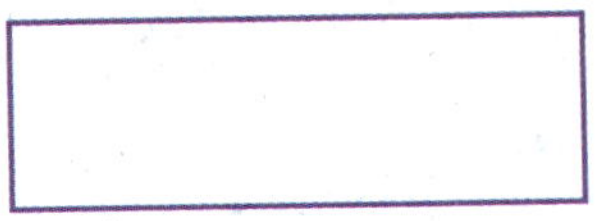

7. halves

8. fourths

© Houghton Mifflin Harcourt Publishing Company

Fill in the bubble for the correct answer choice.

TEST PREP

9. Which of these shapes is a cube? (CC.2.G.1)

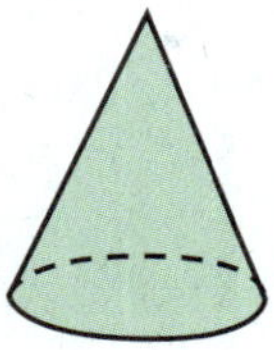 ○
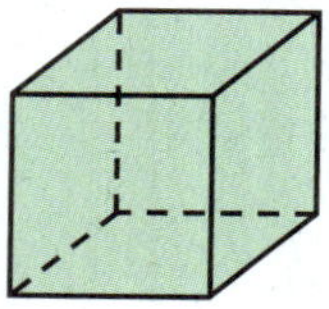 ○
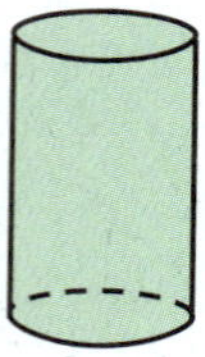 ○
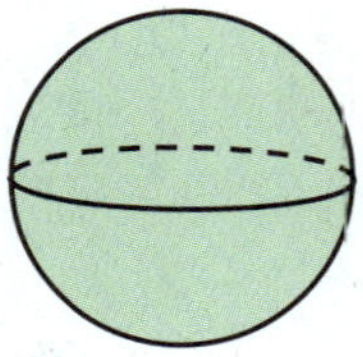 ○

10. Which of these shapes has 5 angles? (CC.2.G.1)

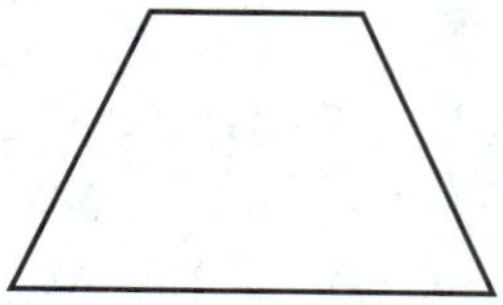 ○
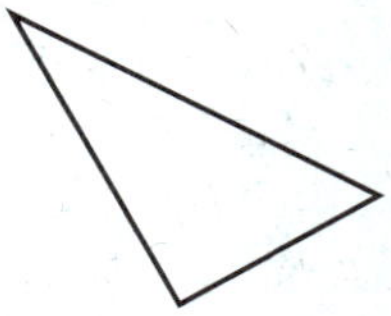 ○
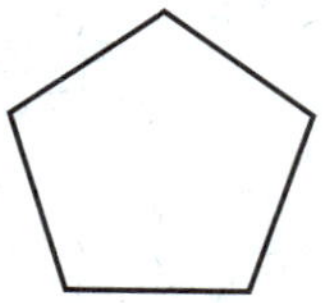 ○
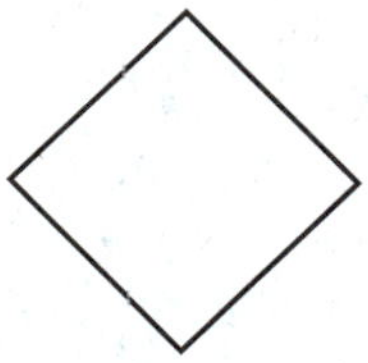 ○

11. Max used square color tiles to cover this rectangle. How many square color tiles did he use to cover the rectangle? (CC.2.G.2)

- ○ 2
- ○ 4
- ○ 6
- ○ 8

© Houghton Mifflin Harcourt Publishing Company

Name ____________________

TEST PREP

Fill in the bubble for the correct answer choice.

12. How many faces does a cube have? (CC.2.G.1)

○ 2
○ 4
○ 6
○ 8

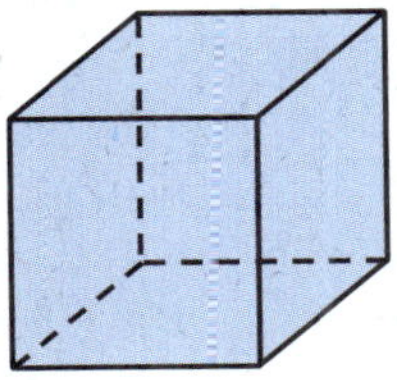

13. James drew a shape that has 4 sides and 4 angles. What is this shape called? (CC.2.G.1)

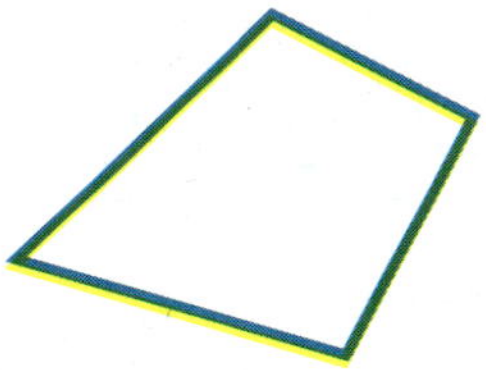

○ triangle
○ quadrilateral
○ hexagon
○ pentagon

14. There is one pizza. If the pizza is cut into fourths, how many pieces of pizza will there be? (CC.2.G.3)

○ 2
○ 3
○ 4
○ 5

© Houghton Mifflin Harcourt Publishing Company

Constructed Response

15. Reggie makes a pentagon and a quadrilateral with toothpicks. He uses one toothpick for each side of a shape. How many toothpicks does he use?

Draw or write to explain your answer. (CC.2.G.1)

_______ toothpicks

Performance Task (CC.2.G.3)

16. Keira has two poster boards that are the same size. She wants to divide each poster board into fourths. What are two different ways that she can divide the poster boards into fourths?

Suppose Keira also has a banner that she wants to divide into thirds. Describe what she should do.

____

____

____

© Houghton Mifflin Harcourt Publishing Company

Picture Glossary

addend **sumando**

5 + 8 = 13

↖ ↗

addends

bar graph **gráfica de barras**

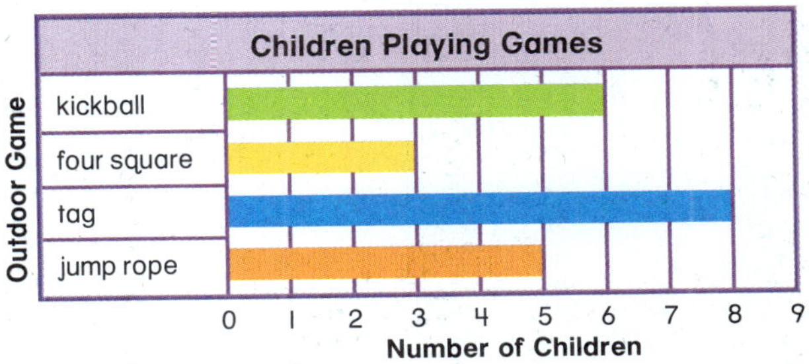

A.M. **a.m.**

Times after midnight and before noon are written with A.M.

11:00 A.M. is in the morning.

cent sign **signo de centavo**

53¢

↑

cent sign

angle **ángulo**

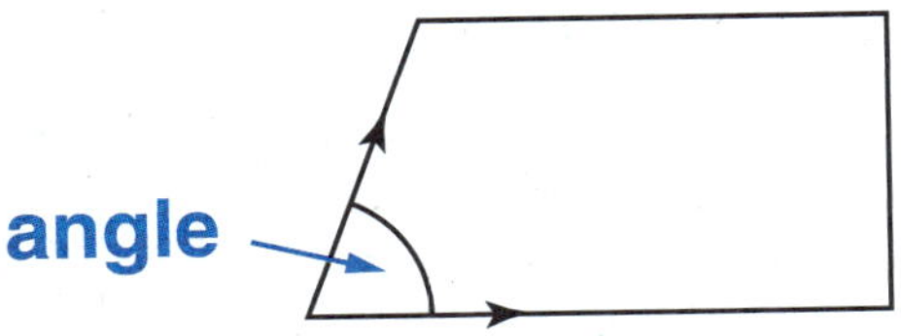

centimeter **centímetro**

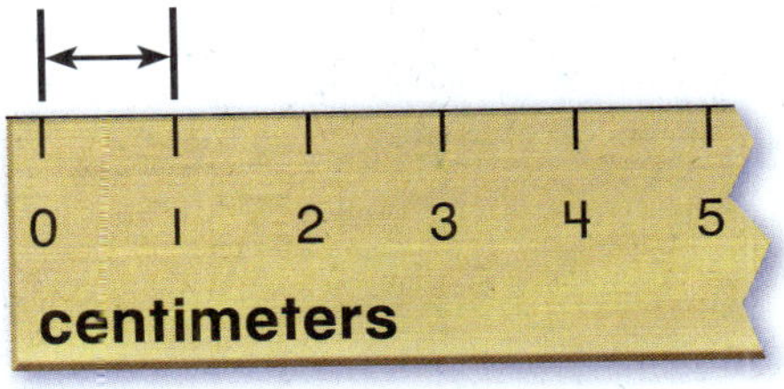

© Houghton Mifflin Harcourt Publishing Company

compare **comparar**

Use these symbols when you **compare**: $>$, $<$, $=$.

$241 > 234$

$123 < 128$

$247 = 247$

cone **cono**

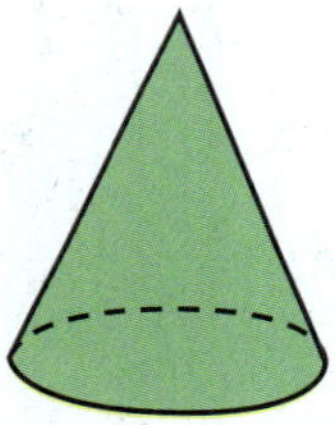

cube **cubo**

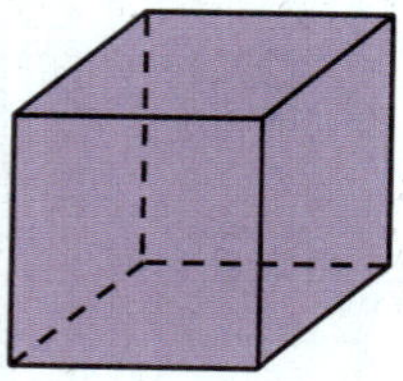

cylinder **cilindro**

data **datos**

Favorite Lunch	
Lunch	**Tally**
pizza	𝍷𝍷𝍷𝍷
sandwich	𝍸 𝍷
salad	𝍷𝍷𝍷
pasta	𝍸

The information in this chart is called **data**.

decimal point **punto decimal**

$1.00
↑
decimal point

© Houghton Mifflin Harcourt Publishing Company

difference **diferencia**

9 − 2 = 7

↑ difference

dollar **dólar**

One **dollar** is worth 100 cents.

digit **dígito**

0, 1, 2, 3, 4, 5, 6, 7, 8, and 9 are **digits**.

dollar sign **signo de dólar**

$1.00

↑ **dollar sign**

dime **moneda de 10¢**

A **dime** has a value of 10 cents.

edge **arista**

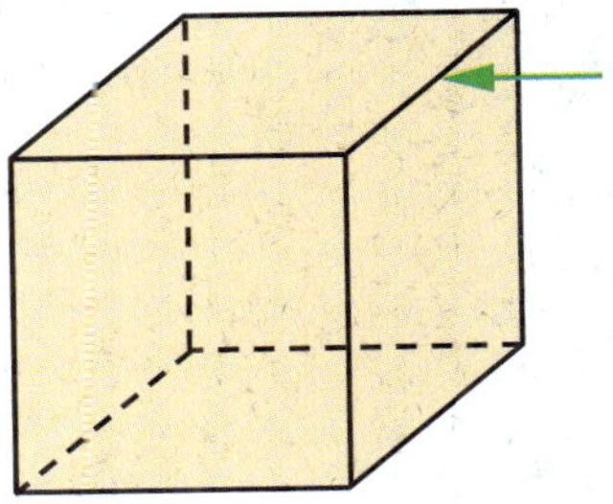

An **edge** is formed where two faces of a three-dimensional shape meet.

© Houghton Mifflin Harcourt Publishing Company

even par

2, 4, 6, 8, 10, . . .

even numbers

face cara

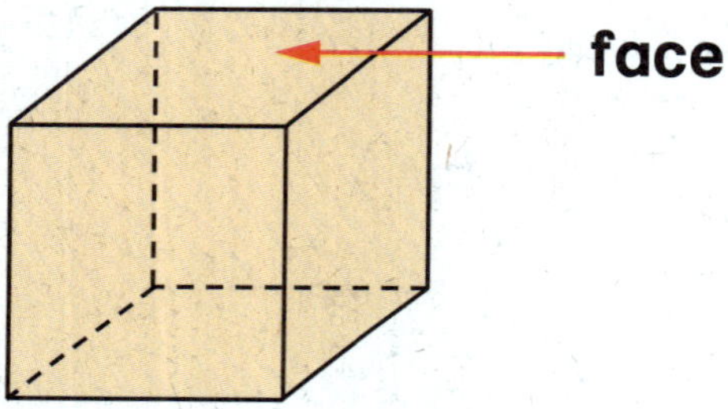

Each flat surface of this cube is a **face**.

foot pie

1 **foot** is the same length as 12 inches.

fourth of cuarto de

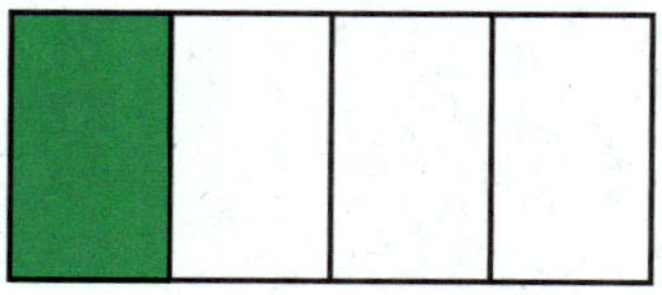

A **fourth of** the shape is green.

fourths cuartos

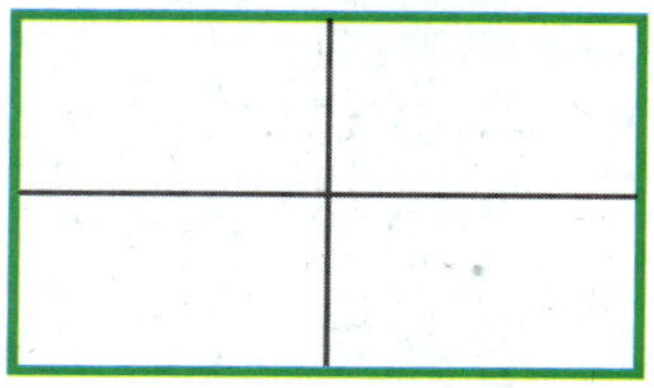

This shape has 4 equal parts. These equal parts are called **fourths**.

half of mitad de

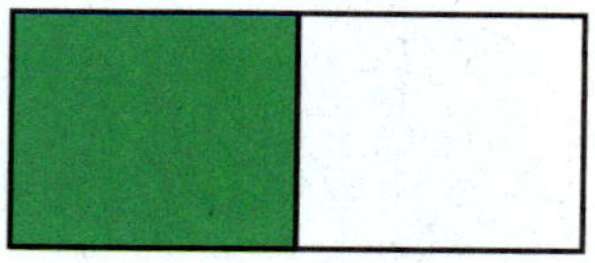

A **half of** the shape is green.

© Houghton Mifflin Harcourt Publishing Company

halves mitades

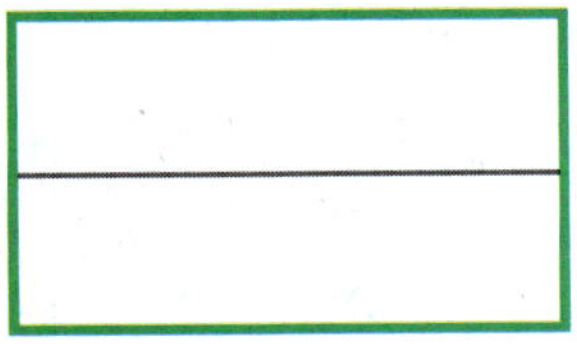

This shape has 2 equal parts. These equal parts are called **halves**.

hexagon hexágono

A two-dimensional shape with 6 sides is a **hexagon**.

hundred centena

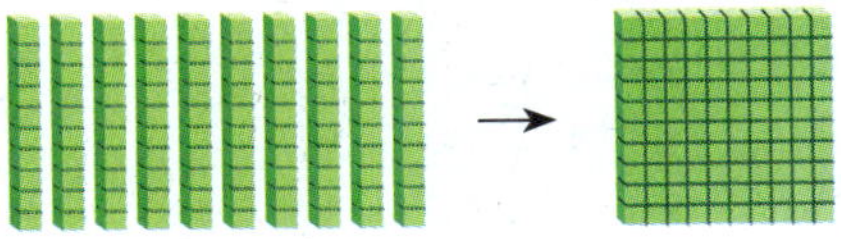

There are 10 tens in 1 **hundred**.

inch pulgada

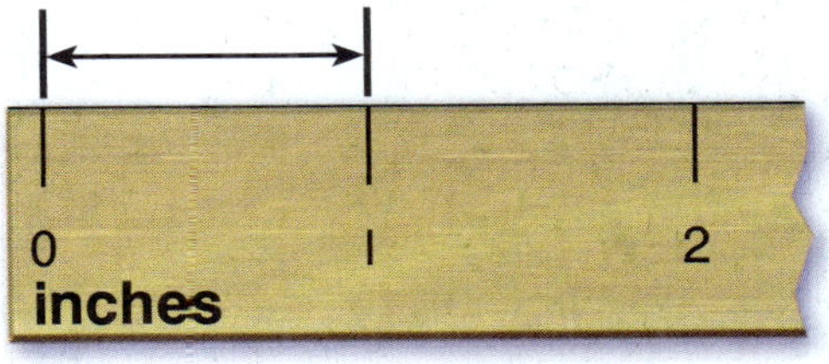

is equal to (=) es igual a

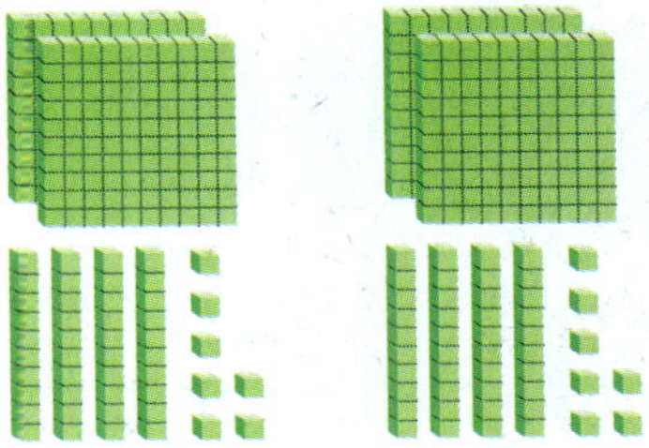

247 **is equal to** 247.
247 = 247

is greater than (>) es mayor que

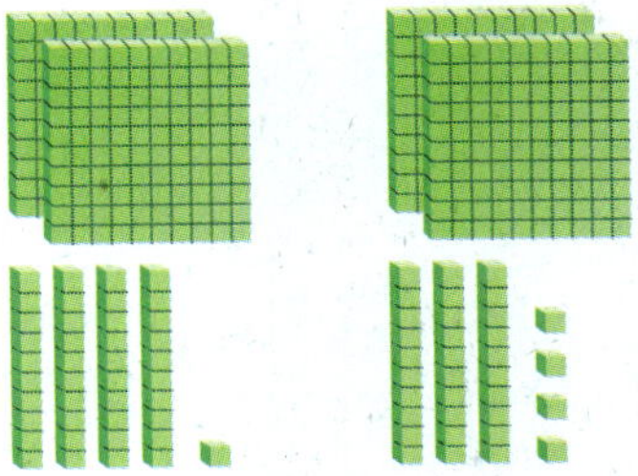

241 **is greater than** 234.
241 > 234

© Houghton Mifflin Harcourt Publishing Company

is less than (<) **es menor que**

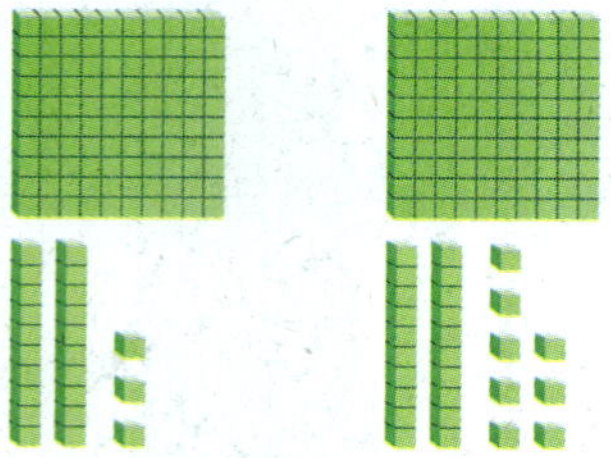

123 **is less than** 128.

$123 < 128$

line plot **diagrama de puntos**

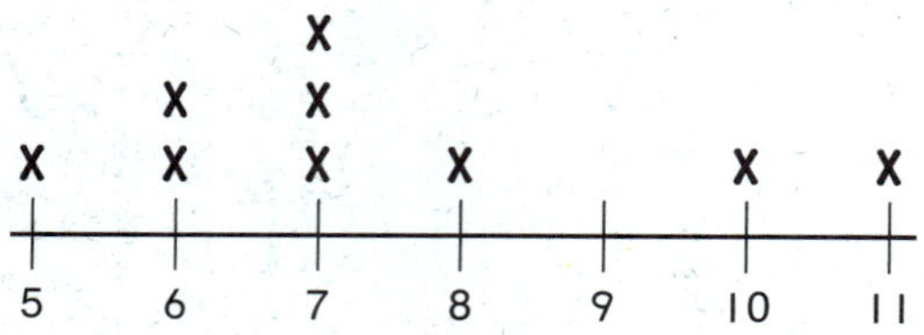

Lengths of Paintbrushes in Inches

measuring tape **cinta métrica**

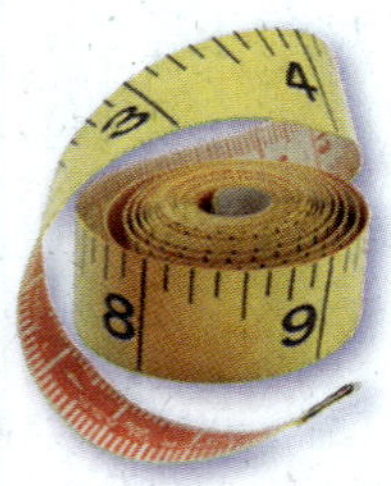

meter **metro**

1 **meter** is the same length as 100 centimeters.

midnight **medianoche**

Midnight is 12:00 at night.

minute **minuto**

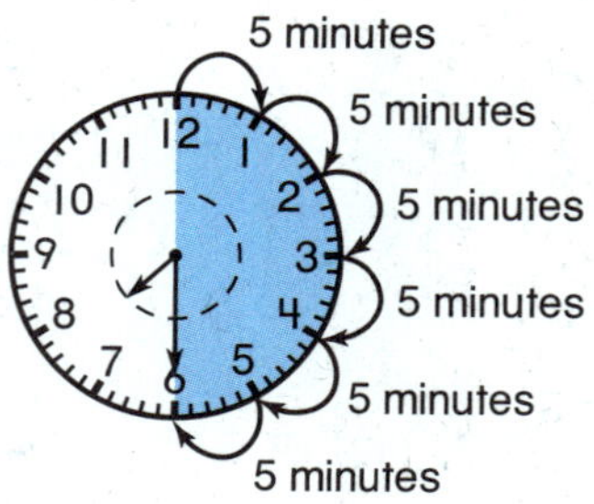

There are 30 **minutes** in a half hour.

© Houghton Mifflin Harcourt Publishing Company

nickel moneda de 5¢

A **nickel** has a value of 5 cents.

noon mediodía

Noon is 12:00 in the daytime.

odd impar

1, 3, 5, 7, 9, 11, . . .

odd numbers

penny moneda de 1¢

A **penny** has a value of 1 cent.

pentagon pentágono

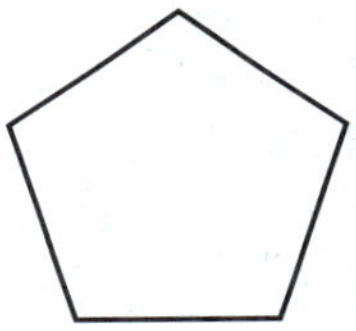

A two-dimensional shape with 5 sides is a **pentagon**.

picture graph gráfica con dibujos

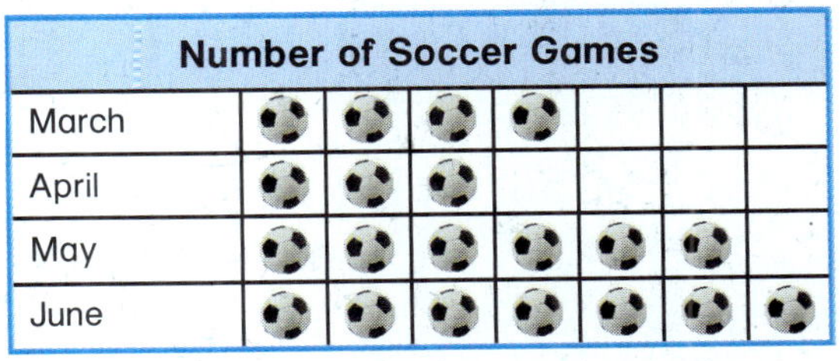

Key: Each ⚽ stands for 1 game.

© Houghton Mifflin Harcourt Publishing Company

P.M. **p.m.**

Times after noon and before midnight are written with **P.M.**
11:00 P.M. is in the evening.

quadrilateral **cuadrilátero**

A two-dimensional shape with 4 sides is a **quadrilateral**.

quarter **moneda de 25¢**

A **quarter** has a value of 25 cents.

quarter of **cuarta parte de**

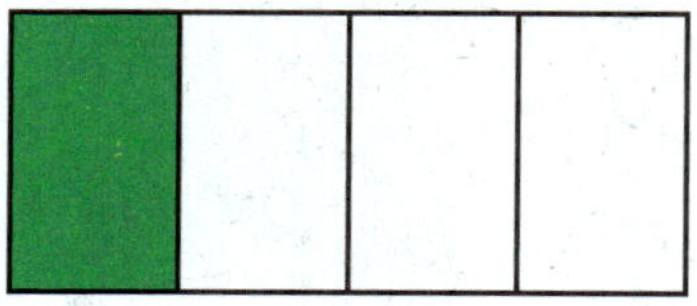

A **quarter of** the shape is green.

quarter past **y cuarto**

15 minutes after 8
quarter past 8

rectangular prism **prisma rectangular**

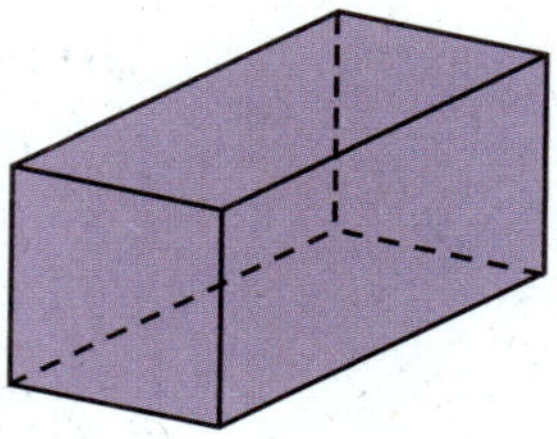

© Houghton Mifflin Harcourt Publishing Company

regroup **reagrupar**

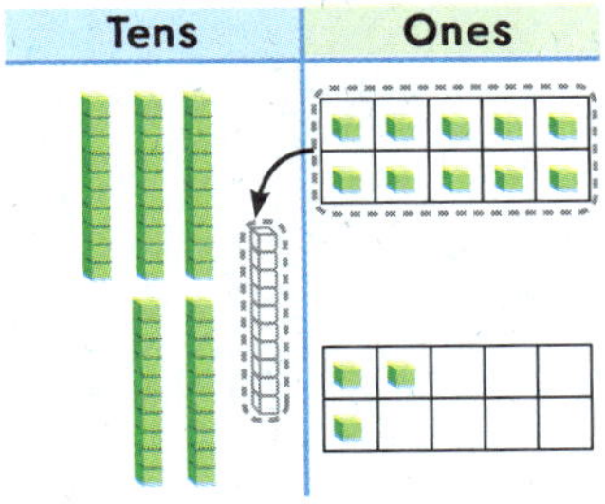

You can trade 10 ones for 1 ten to **regroup**.

sum **suma o total**

$9 + 6 = 15$

sum

side **lado**

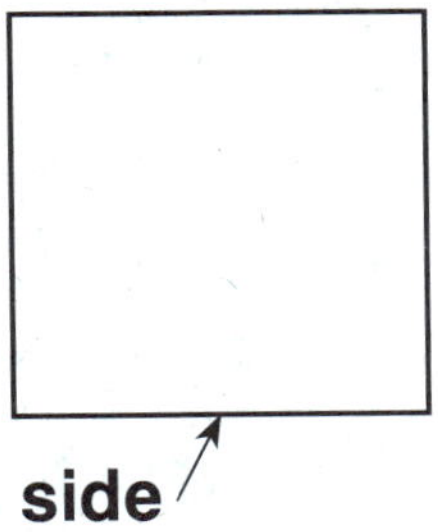

This shape has 4 **sides**.

survey **encuesta**

Favorite Lunch	
Lunch	**Tally**
pizza	||||
sandwich	~~||||~~ |
salad	|||
pasta	~~||||~~

A **survey** is a collection of data from answers to a question.

sphere **esfera**

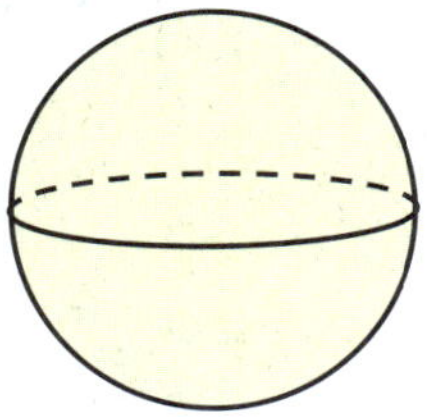

third of **un tercio de**

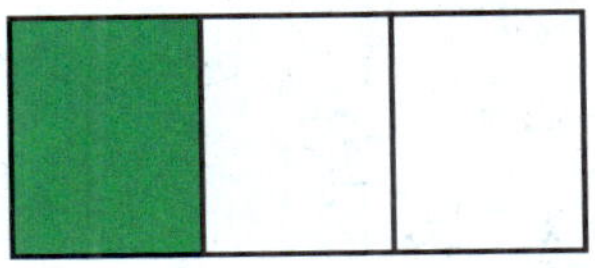

A **third of** the shape is green.

© Houghton Mifflin Harcourt Publishing Company

thirds tercios

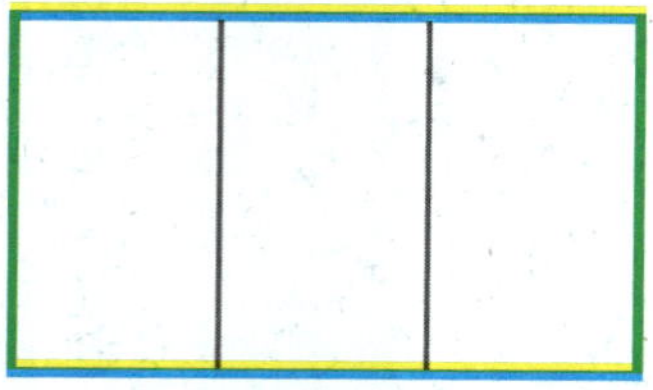

This shape has 3 equal parts. These equal parts are called **thirds**.

thousand millar

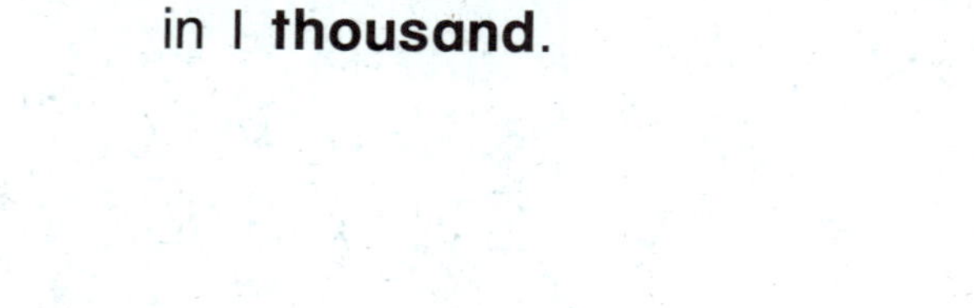

There are 10 hundreds in 1 **thousand**.

vertex/vertices vértice/vértices

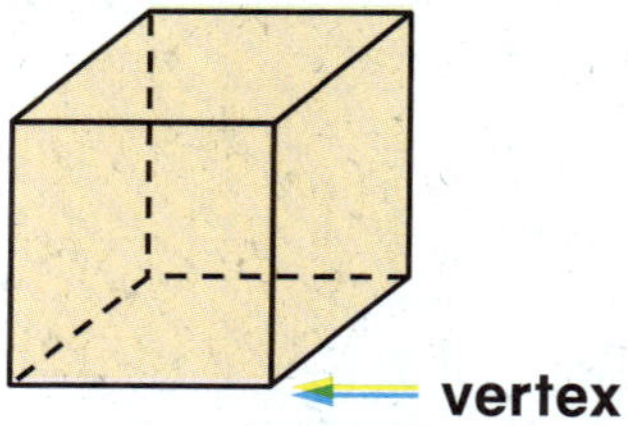

A corner point of a three-dimensional shape is a **vertex**.

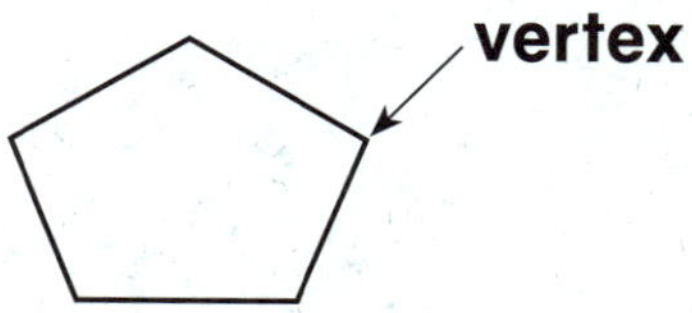

This shape has 5 **vertices**.

yardstick regla de 1 yarda

A **yardstick** is a measuring tool that shows 3 feet.

© Houghton Mifflin Harcourt Publishing Company

Photo Credits

KEY: (t) top, (b) bottom, (l) left, (r) right, (c) center, (bg) background, (fg) foreground, (i) inset

Cover: (bg) Peter Beck/Corbis; (bg) Glowimages/Corbis; (bg) Oxford Scientific/Photollibrary; (bg) Don Hammond/Design Pics/Corbis; (bg) GK Hart/Vikki Hart/Getty Images; (fg) Frank Krahmer/Getty Images; (fg) Ian O'Leary/Getty Images.

Copyright Page: (bg) Purestock/Getty Images; (tl) Danita Delimont/Alamy Images; (br) Don Hammond/Design Pics/Corbis.

Author Page: (br) altrendo nature/Getty Images; (bg) Purestock/Getty Images; (br) Daniel J. Cox/Getty Images.

Table of Contents: v (r) FoodPix/Getty Images; vi (bg) PhotoDisc/Getty Images; (fg) Martin Strmiska/Alamy; vii (l) Joe Belanger/Alamy; (bg) Edith Held/Corbis; viii (fg) Roy Morsch/CORBIS; ix (bg) Craig Aurness/CORBIS; x (bg) Greg Vaughn/Alamy; xi (bg) Organics image library/Alamy; xii (bg) Frank Whitney/Getty Images.

Critical Area: 9 (bg) FoodPix/Getty Images; 20 (tl) PhotoDisc/Getty Images; 53 (bg) Uyen Le/Getty Images; 64 (b) Corbis; (t) Kirsty Pargeter/Alamy; 66 (cr) C Squared Studios/PhotoDisc/Getty Images; 72 (b) Corel Stock Photo Library; 80 (br) Getty Images.

Critical Area: 99 (tl) Getty Images; 100 (tl) Digital Vision/Getty Images; 109 (bg) David Tipling/Getty Images; 110 (c) Eric Nathan/Alamy Images; 111 (tc) Nigel J Dennis/NHPA; 112 (tc) Danita Delimont/Alamy; 113 (c) Juniors Bildarchiv/F307/Alamy; 114 490-F, AlaskaStock; 115 (c) Stan Osolinski/PhotoLibrary/Getty Images; (r) Danita Delimont/Alamy; (l) Eric Nathan/Alamy Images; 116 (t) Stan Osolinski/PhotoLibrary/Getty Images; 117 (bg) Martin Strmiska/Alamy; 118 (tcl) PhotoAlto/Getty Images; 124 (c) PhotoDisc/Getty Images; (bc) Image Club Graphics/Eyewire/Getty Images; 128 (t) PhotoDisc/Getty Images; 132 (b) Getty Images; 136 (b) Artville/Getty Images; 140 (b) (c) PhotoDisc/Getty Images; 148 (b) Comstock/Getty Images; 150 (b) Artville/Getty Images; 151 (cl) Getty Images; 152 (t) PhotoDisc/Getty Images; 154 (bcl) Artville/Getty Images; 155 (bc) Juniors Bildarchiv/Alamy; (b) PhotoDisc/Getty Images; 156 (b) Stockbyte/Getty Images; 159 (c) Getty Images; 160 (b) Judith Collins/Alamy; 164 (c) (bc) PhotoDisc/Getty Images; (t) Getty Images; 167 (cl) PhotoDisc/Getty Images; (cr) Artville/Getty Images; (br) Royalty-Free/Alamy; 169 (bg) Edith Held/Corbis; 176 (t) PhotoDisc/Getty Images; (tc) Digital Vision/Alamy; 180 (b) Digital Vision/Alamy; (c) PhotoDisc/Getty Images; 188 (b) Ingram; 207 (t) (c) PhotoDisc/Getty Images; 210 (cl) PhotoDisc/Getty Images; 211 (tl) (bl) PhotoDisc/Getty Images; (cl) Bobbi Tull/PhotoDisc/Getty Images; 212 (tr) PhotoDisc/Getty Images; 220 (t) Brand X Pictures/Getty Images; 222 (t) Brand X Pictures/Getty Images; 223 Judith Collins/Alamy; 225 (bg) Bob Jensen/Alamy; 236 (br) Comstock/Getty Images; 240 (c) Corbis; 260 (t) imagebroker/Alamy; 263 (t) (c) PhotoDisc/Getty Images; 264 (c) PhotoDisc/Getty Images; 266 (tr) Charles Smith/Corbis; (cl) Corel Stock Photo Library; 267 (bl) GK Hart/Vikki Hart/PhotoDisc/Getty Images; (t) Corbis; 272 (br) Siede Preis/PhotoDisc/Getty Images; (c) PhotoDisc/Getty Images; 274 (cr) Vernon Leach/Alamy; 275 (l) Comstock/Getty Images; (r) PhotoDisc/Getty Images; 277 (bg) Roy Morsch/CORBIS; 284 (c) Artville/Getty Images; 300 (b) Siede Preis/PhotoDisc/Getty Images; 303 (b) Brand X Pictures/Getty Images; 304 (b) PhotoDisc/Getty Images; 308 (tl) PhotoDisc/Getty Images; 316 (br) Tetra Images/Alamy; 320 (l) (r) PhotoDisc/Getty Images; 322 (l) Ingram; (r) Alan and Sandy Carey/PhotoDisc/Getty Images; 323 (c) PhotoDisc/Getty Images; 326 Eric Nathan/Alamy Images; 333 (bg) Allen Wallace/Getty Images; 364 (c) Judith Collins/Alamy; (t) Kirsty Pargeter/Alamy.

Critical Area: 378 (tl) Getty Images; (cr) PhotoDisc/Getty Images; (bl) Getty Images/Stockdisc; (br) PhotoDisc/Getty Images; 379 (tr) Randy Faris/Corbis; (bl) Bananastock/Jupiterimages/Getty Images; (br) Jupiterimages/Getty Images; 385 (bg) Greg Vaughn/Alamy; 410 (bc) PhotoDisc/Getty Images; 415 (tc) MAPS.com/CORBIS; (bc) PhotoDisc/Getty Images; 418 (tr) PhotoDisc/Getty Images; 419 (bc) D. Hurst/Alamy; 426 (t) Ingram; 429 (bg) Frank Whitney/Getty Images; 430 (c) Stockbyte Silver/Alamy; 440 (bc) Flat Earth Royalty Free Photograph/Fotosearch; 452 (tr) Robert McGouey/Alamy; 454 (t) PhotoDisc/Getty Images; 455 (bc) WidStock/Alamy; 456 (b) Comstock/Getty Images; 466 Artville/Getty Images; 474 (tr) PhotoDisc/Getty Images; 476 (c) Getty Images.

Critical Area: 502 (tr) PhotoDisc/Getty Images; 505 (bg) Barbara Leslie/Getty Images; 506 (tcl) PhotoDisc/Getty Images; (br) Artville/Getty Images; (tcr) Corbis; 510 (c) Corbis; (bcr) Mettafoto/Alamy; 511 (tc) David J. Green/Alamy; (bc) Getty Images; 520 (b) Stockbyte/Getty Images; 532 (tcr) David J. Green/Alamy; (bcl) PhotoDisc/Getty Images; 540 (t) D. Hurst/Alamy; 551 (b) C Squared Studios/PhotoDisc/Getty Images.

All other photos Houghton Mifflin Harcourt libraries and photographers; Guy Jarvis, Weronica Ankarorn, Eric Camden, Don Couch, Doug Dukane, Ken Kinzie, April Riehm, and Steve Williams.

© Houghton Mifflin Harcourt Publishing Company